AF521964

THIS MEANS NOTHING

LE BIJOUTIER

pH powerHouse Books
Brooklyn, NY

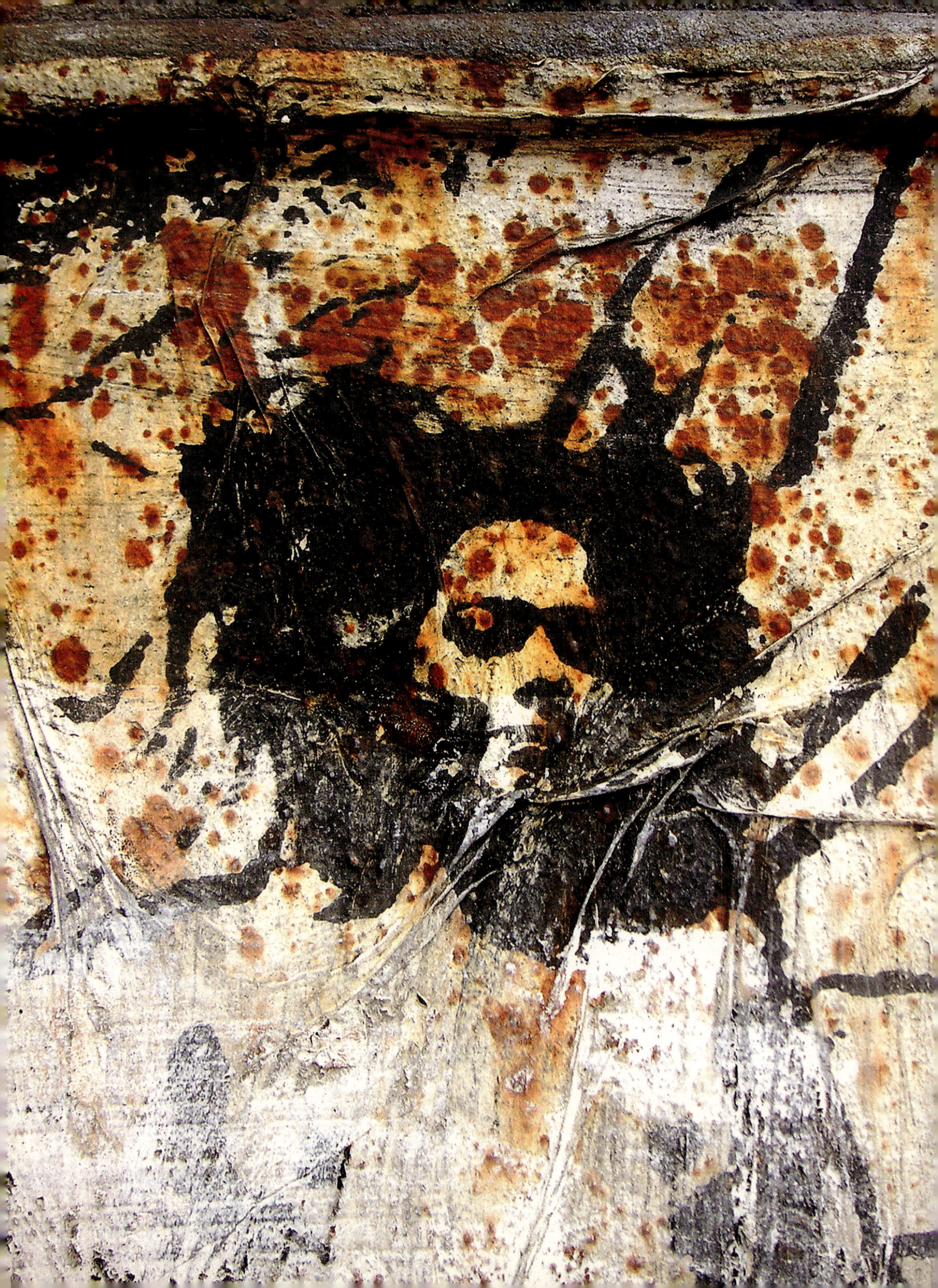

I've been roaming around New York City for years—all five boroughs, visiting every year on the dot. I was lucky enough to witness some of the last spray-painted subway cars whipping through town like moving canvases, proudly displaying the styles and signatures through which their authors scored fame. But in April of 2005, I returned to NYC after several years of missing my annual trip. The shock was immediate. The whole city was painted, etched, labeled, and studded with various subspecies of graffiti.

Signs, stickers, chalk drawings, paintings, tags, stencils, posters, and other markings had been plastered all over the city—to phone booths, doors, fences, walls, sidewalks, rooftops, street signs, traffic lights, trash cans, utility poles.... It seemed like no surface had escaped this new form of urban expression, or the ingenuity of its creators. Their invasion of New York (and other cities) had transformed the streets.

It was about a decade ago that things on the streets started to change; graffiti is no longer the *only* illegal, subversive, and self-identifying medium of urban graphic expression. Street activism and modern street art have moved up the ladder of urban culture, staking their places in NYC's collection of trademarks and landmarks. Though these artists have been operating under the same code of rules and specifications that evolved in the graff world, the current war on the streets is being fought with different weapons.

Let me make myself clear; I have no intention whatsoever of downplaying the impact that contemporary graffiti has had and continues to have on our urban landscapes. In fact, I think of these newer street expressions as evolutions or mutations of traditional graffiti. It's true that most of these new artists don't have a background in graffiti—or even hip-hop culture—but they are its rightful heirs. And while they do sometimes use aerosol spray paint as a medium, the real mark of their graff influence is in the simple truth of their behavior and their attitude as artists: creating and exposing artwork in defiance of the laws, at their own risk.

Like graffiti, modern street art also has boundary-crossing, even international influences. For over 30 years, NYC has been the home and the catalyst for hip-hop culture, and therefore graff culture. So I think of it as the barometer for any movement within urban culture, including the practices of street art, which tend to follow the rule of "More. Bigger. Better." With that in mind, I covered the downtown area and all five boroughs—and sure enough, they all boasted artwork that had evolved according to their own proud specificities.

I noticed that after a certain period of exposure, much of the artwork changed as time itself became an artist, adding its own expression through rust, fading, discoloration, peeling, and tears. There were also countless new artists constantly emerging onto the scene, working in waves and often employing a signature logo, message, shape, or color—just as their graff forefathers had done a generation or so before.

In the midst of my wanderings over the last two years—and the subconscious foundation of what would become *This Means Nothing*—I came across the two key shots featured on the front and back covers. I found myself researching during my walks around town: reading live captions of the events on the street scene, taking in thousands of messages, questioning everything I saw, and at times, putting myself in danger as well—all out of love of photography and of the discovery of these archives of urban expression. When the "THIS MEANS NOTHING" sticker showed up, I nearly gave it all up myself. But I kept on, because I was addicted. (I knew that a long time ago.)

One year later, in October of 2006, I shot the "THIS CHANGES EVERYTHING" sticker, which has made its way to the book's back cover. It appeared to me when I was on my way to the powerHouse Arena, with well over 50 photographs I'd chosen for the *No Sleep 'Til Brooklyn* exhibit. I knew then that my addiction had not been in vain. And this time, the shot truly "changed everything."

Everywhere I go, I let my eyes guide my path through the urban maze. Left, right, back, forward—and then stepping back again so I don't miss a thing. I get the vibe of every new place by looking at its walls, trying to read its untold stories. Here is what New York City has given me to see.

LE BUOUTIER

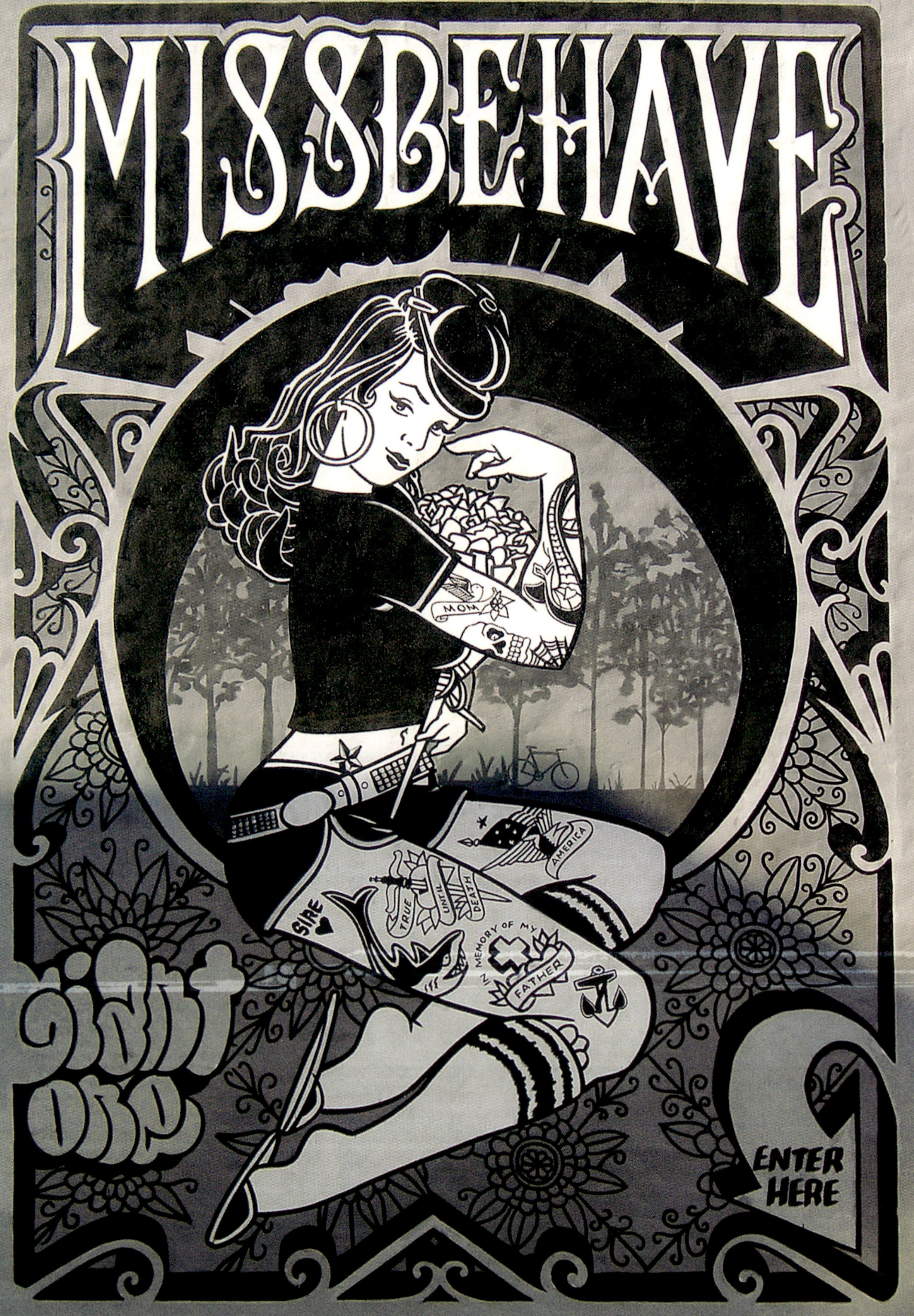

MISSBEHAVE
MOM
AMERICA
SIRE
TRUE UNTIL DEATH
IN MEMORY OF MY FATHER
ENTER HERE
"I JUST TO MYSELF
WHAT PEOPLE THINK
ABOUT ME IS WHATEVER"

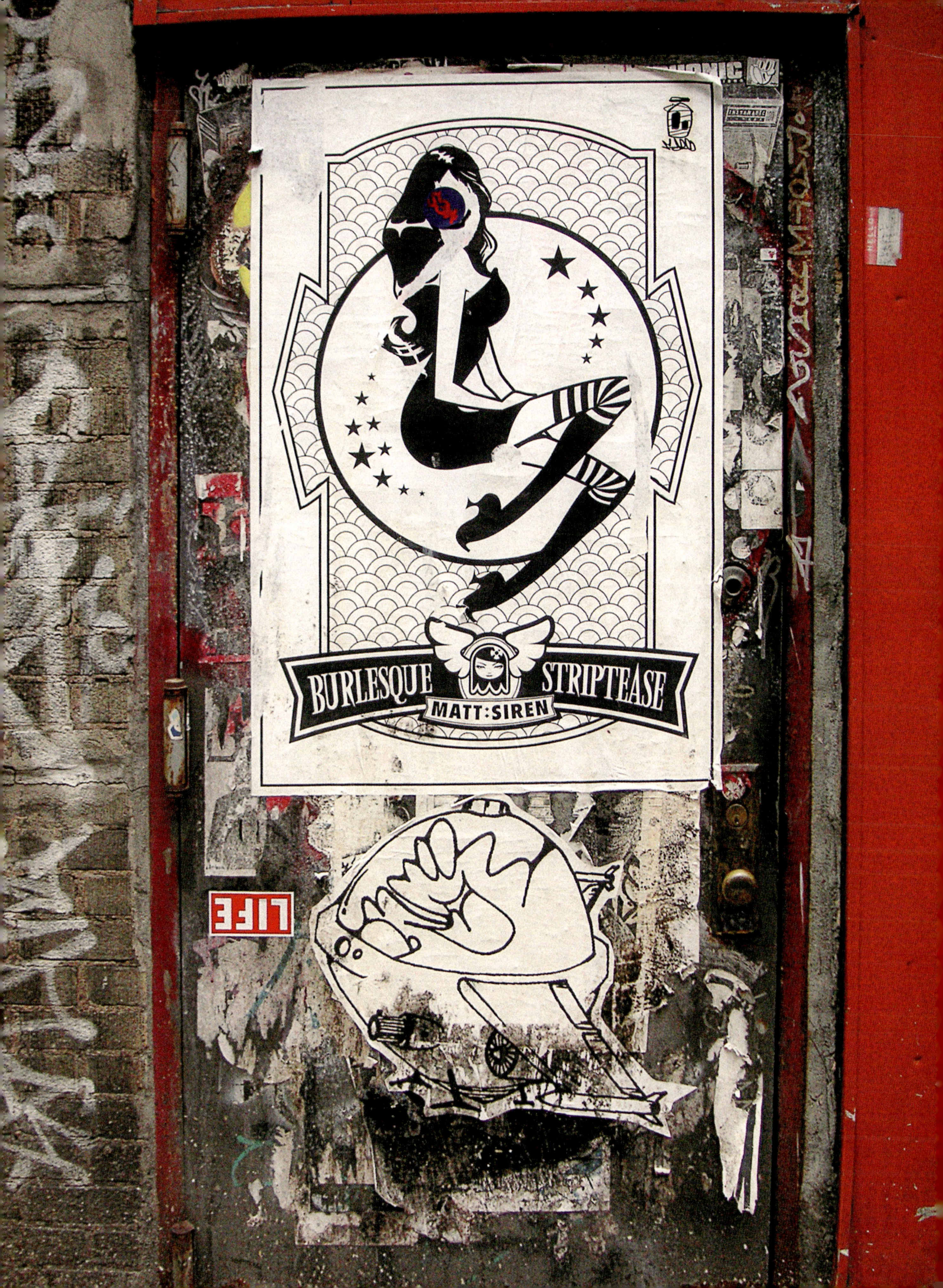
BURLESQUE
STRIPTEASE
MATT:SIREN
LIFE

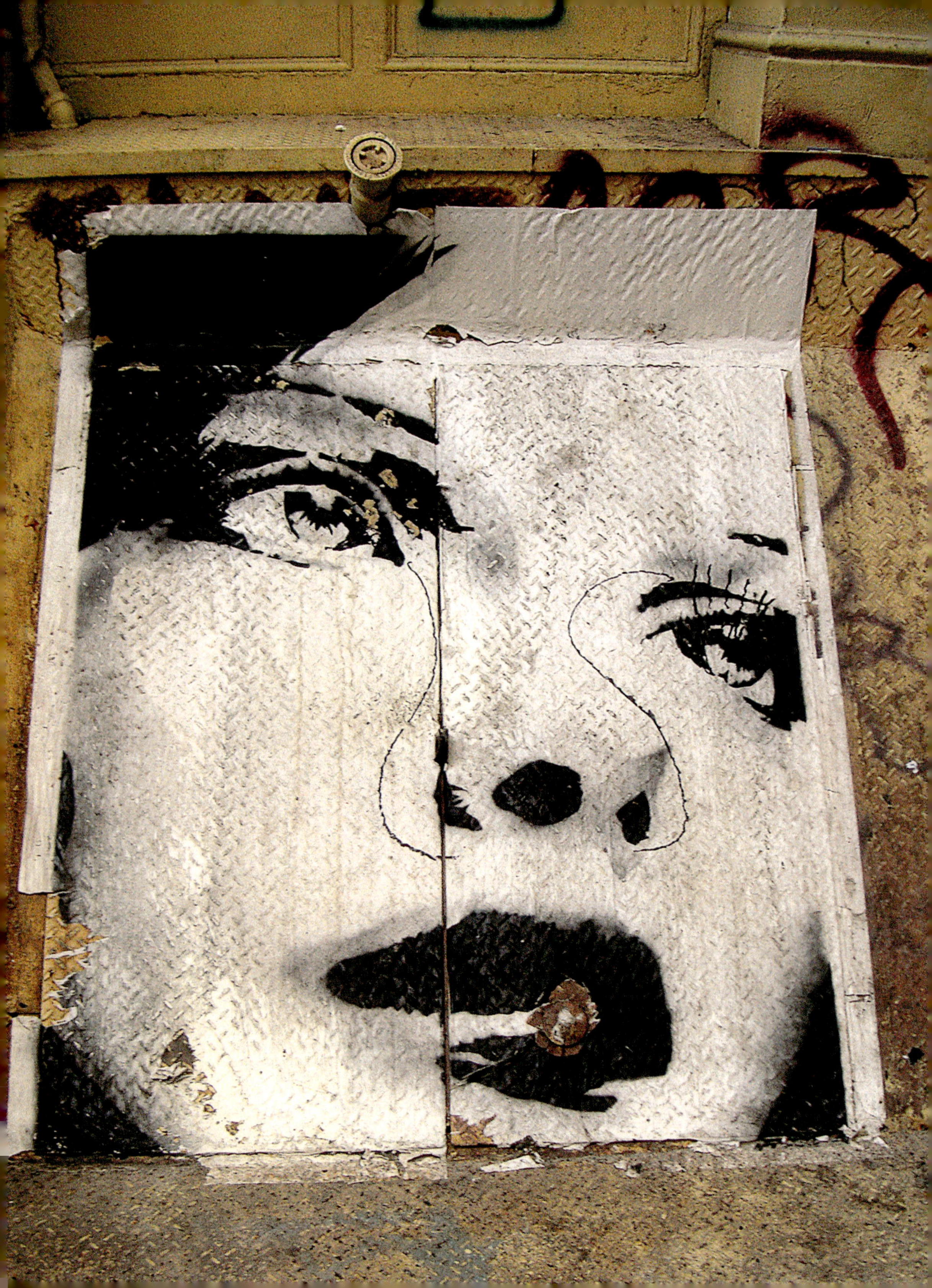

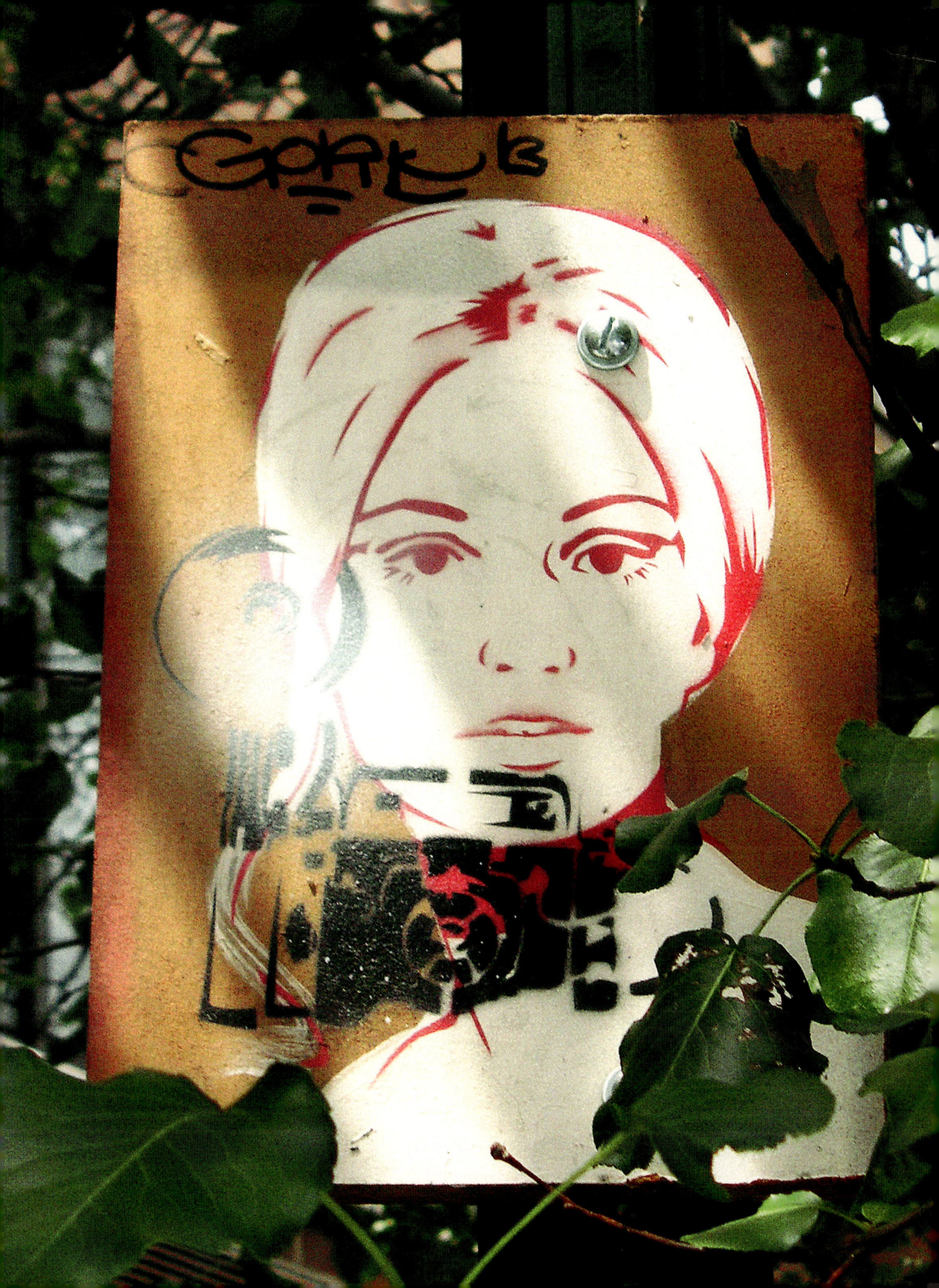

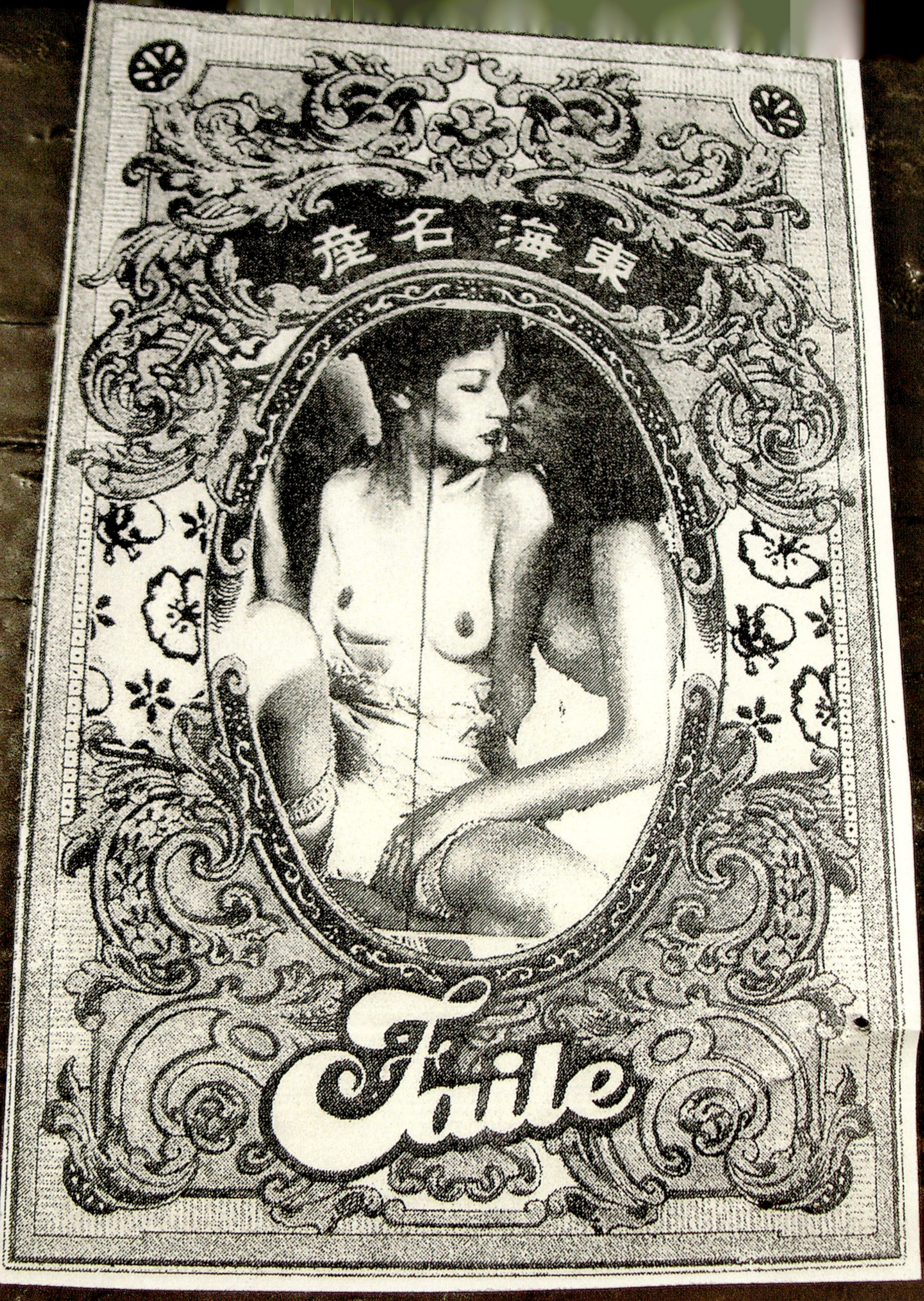
東海名產
Faile

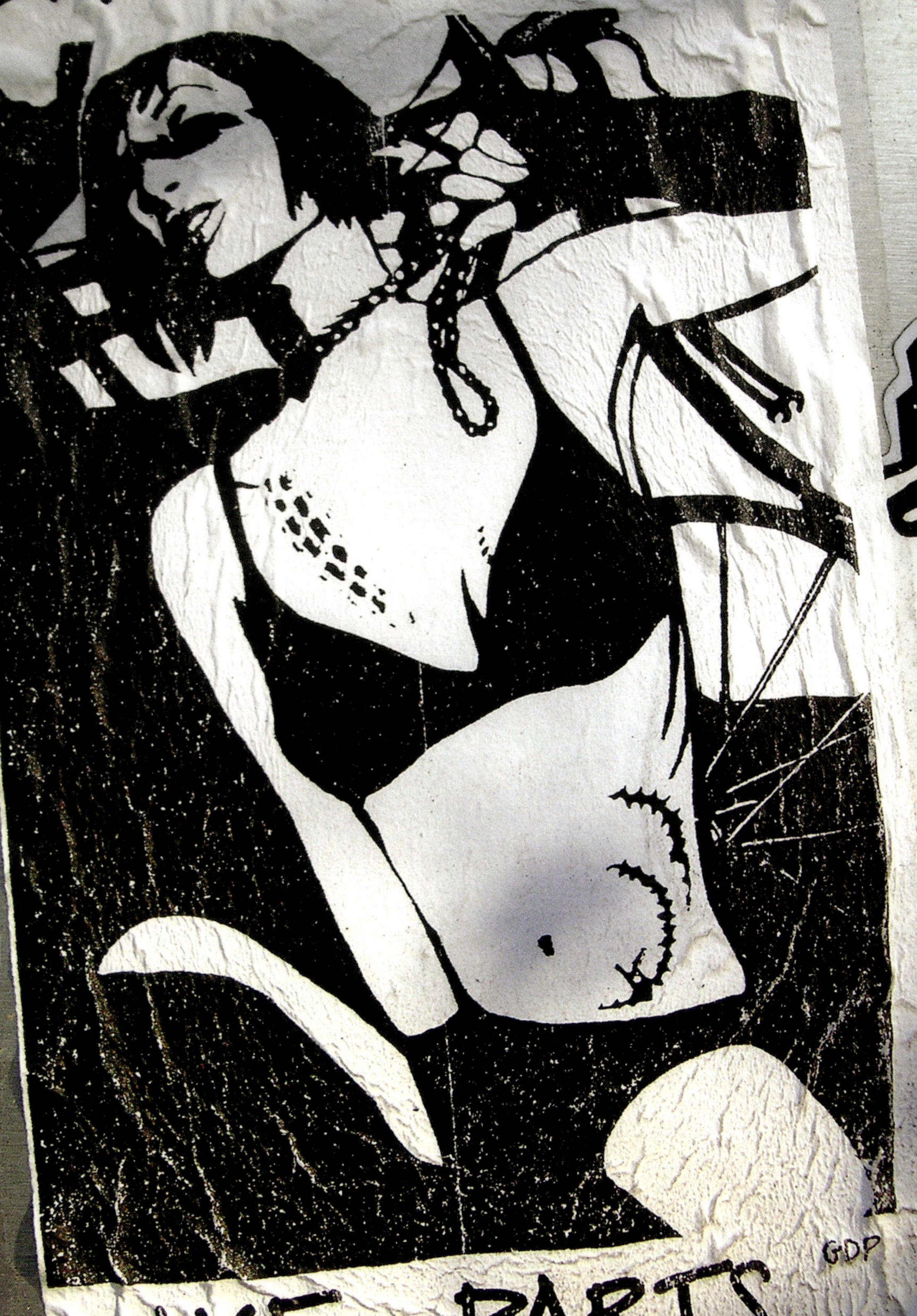
BEAT ME WITH
BIKE PARTS
GDP

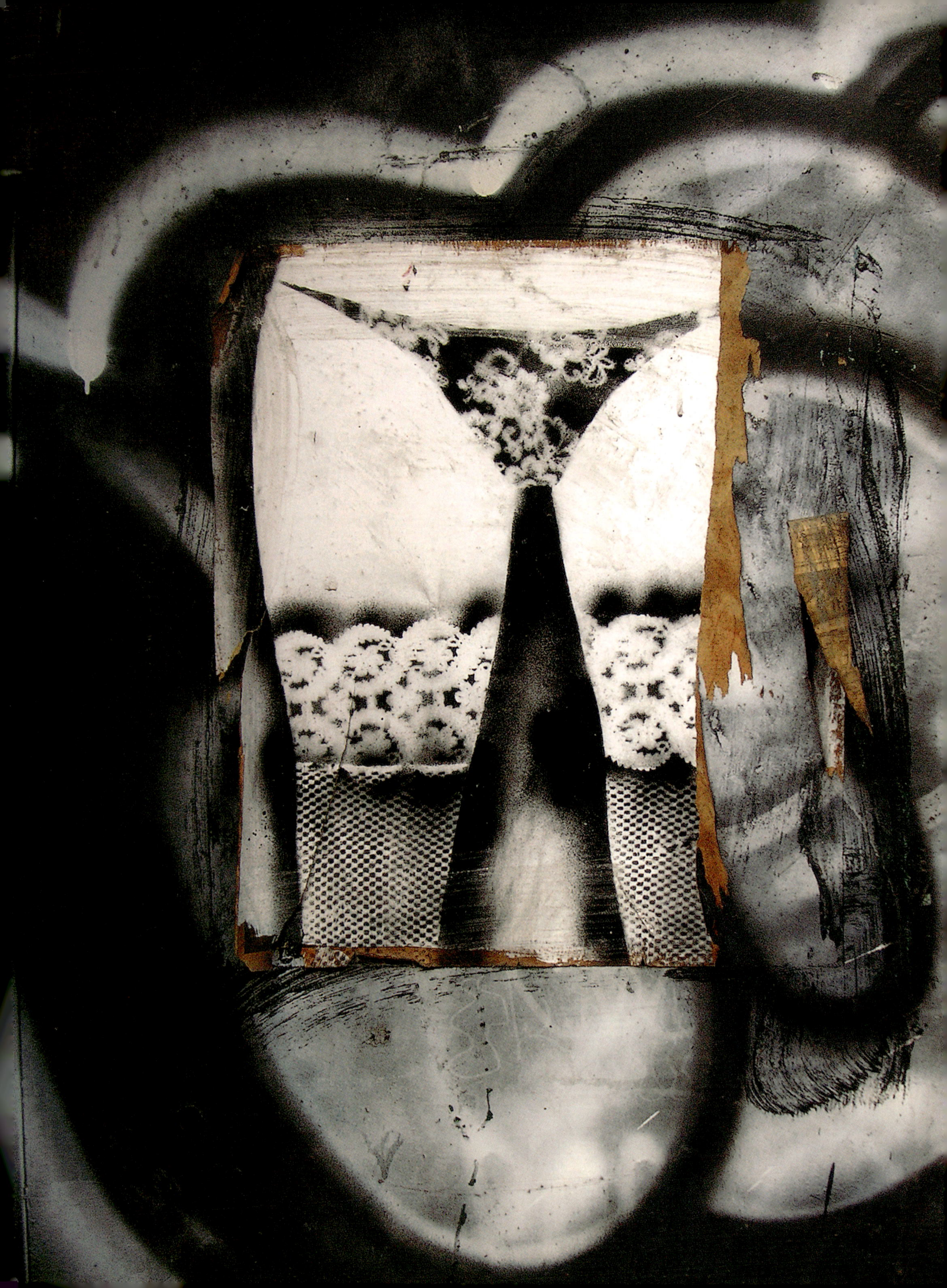

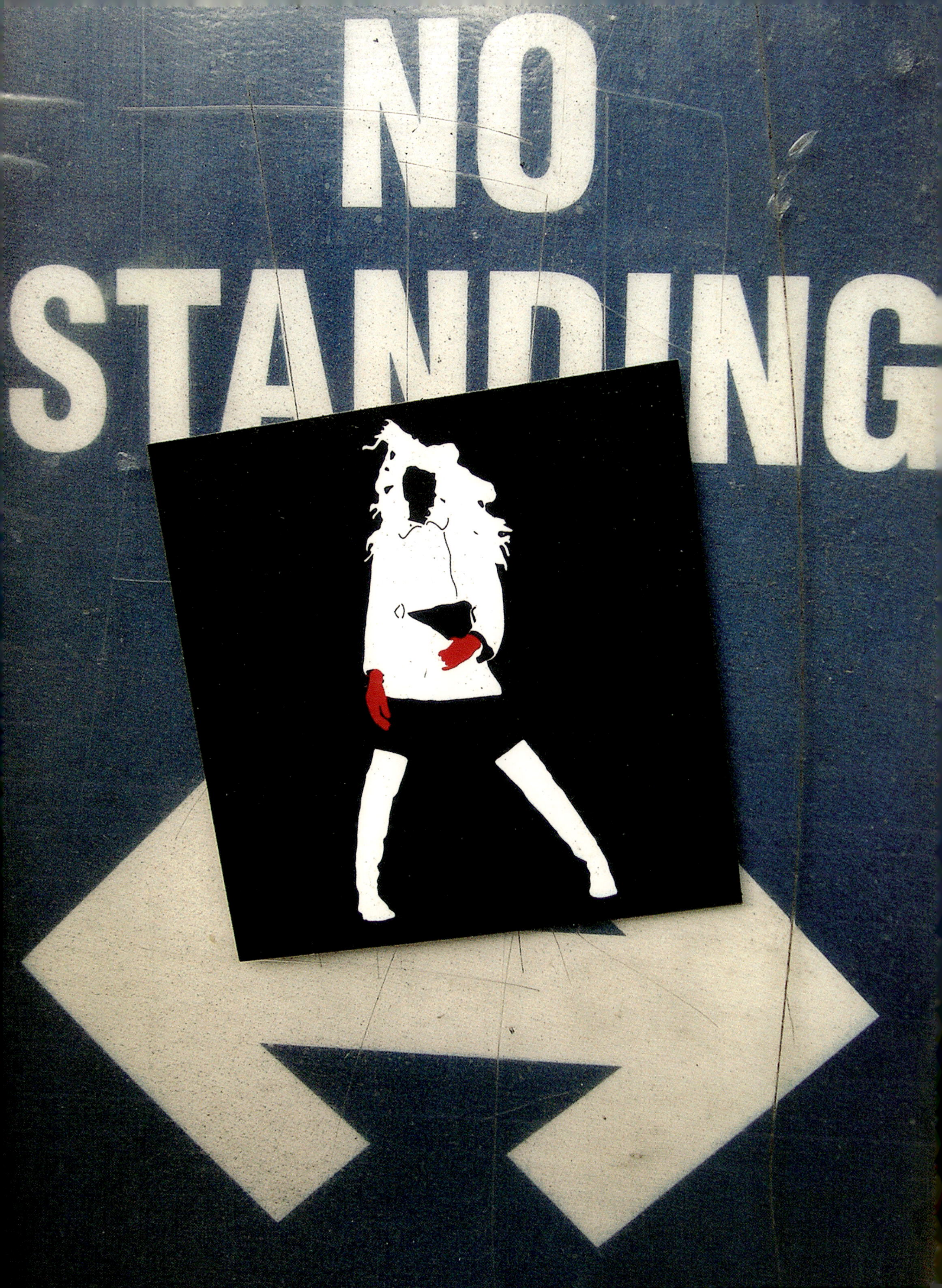
NO
STANDING

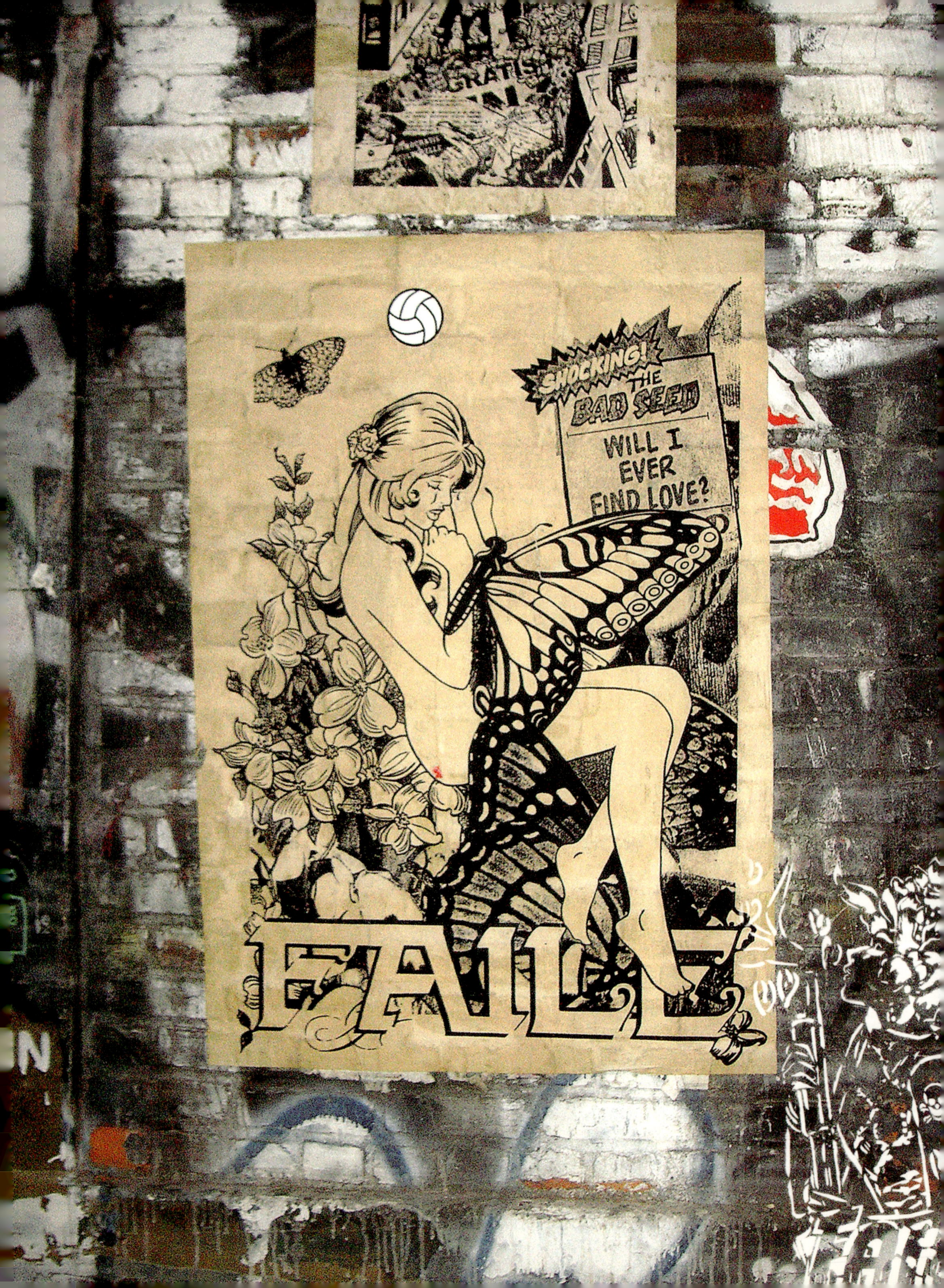
GRATIS
SHOCKING!
THE BAD SEED
WILL I EVER FIND LOVE?
FAILE

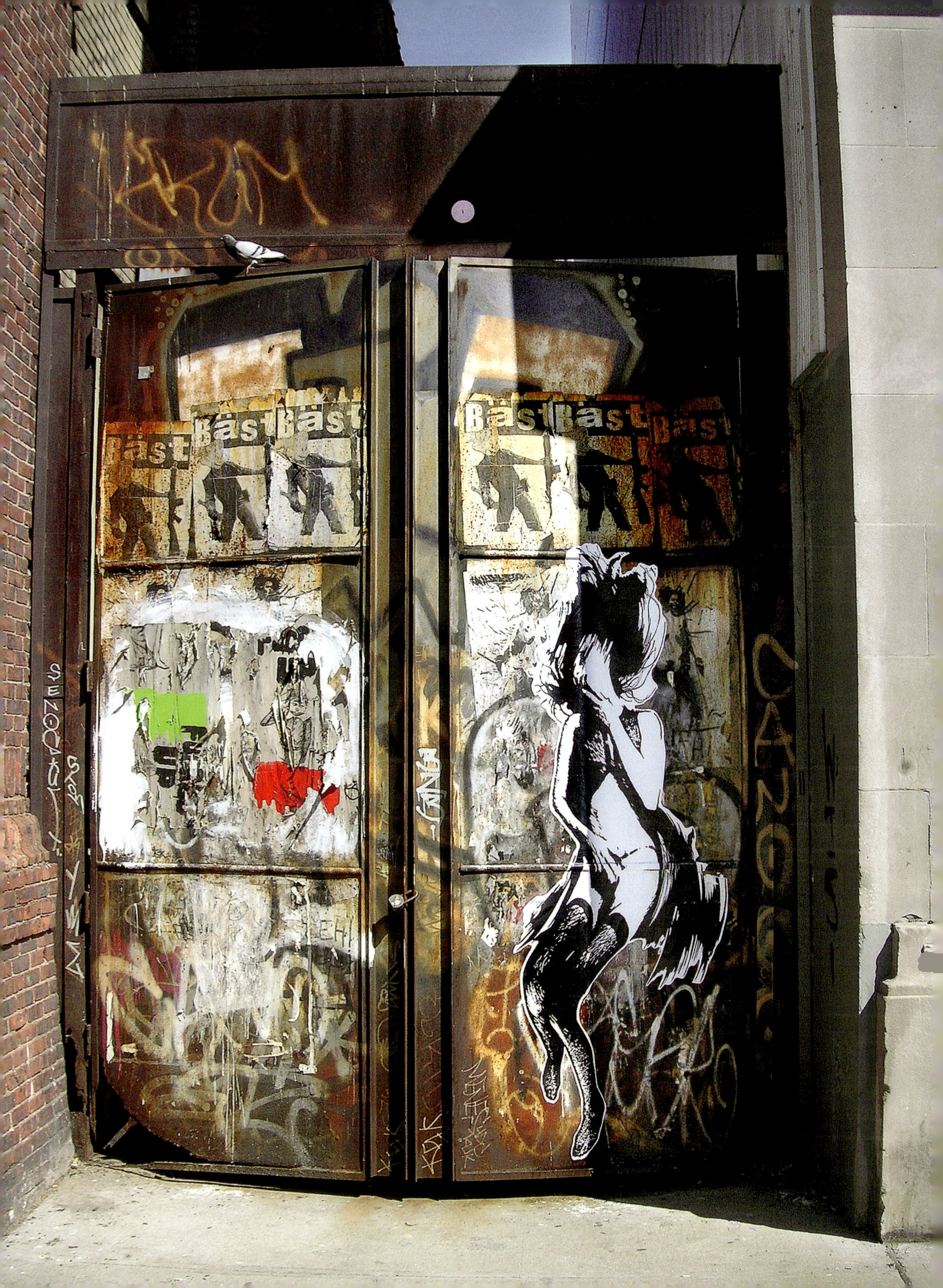
Bäst Bäst Bäst
Bäst Bäst Bäst

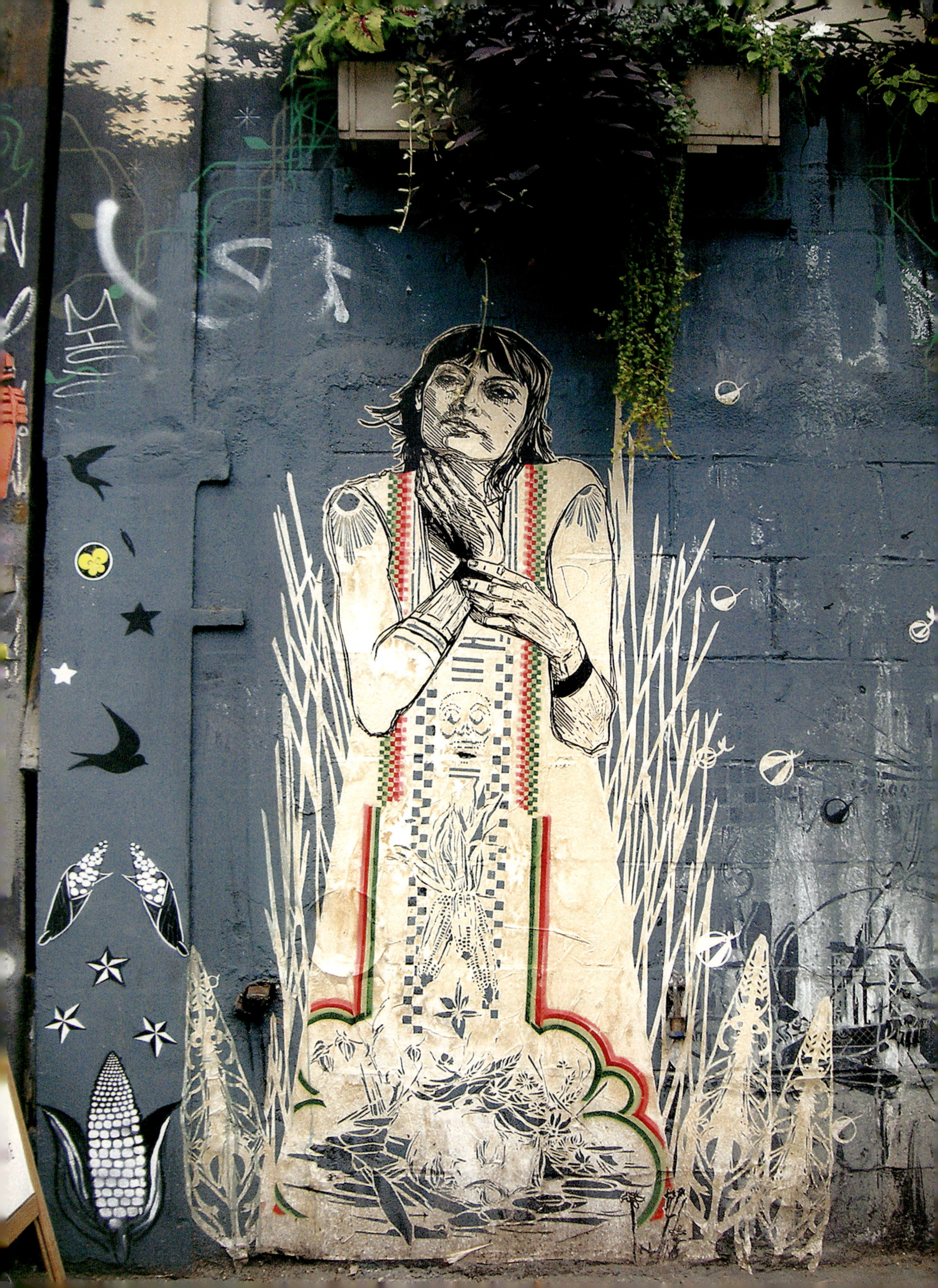

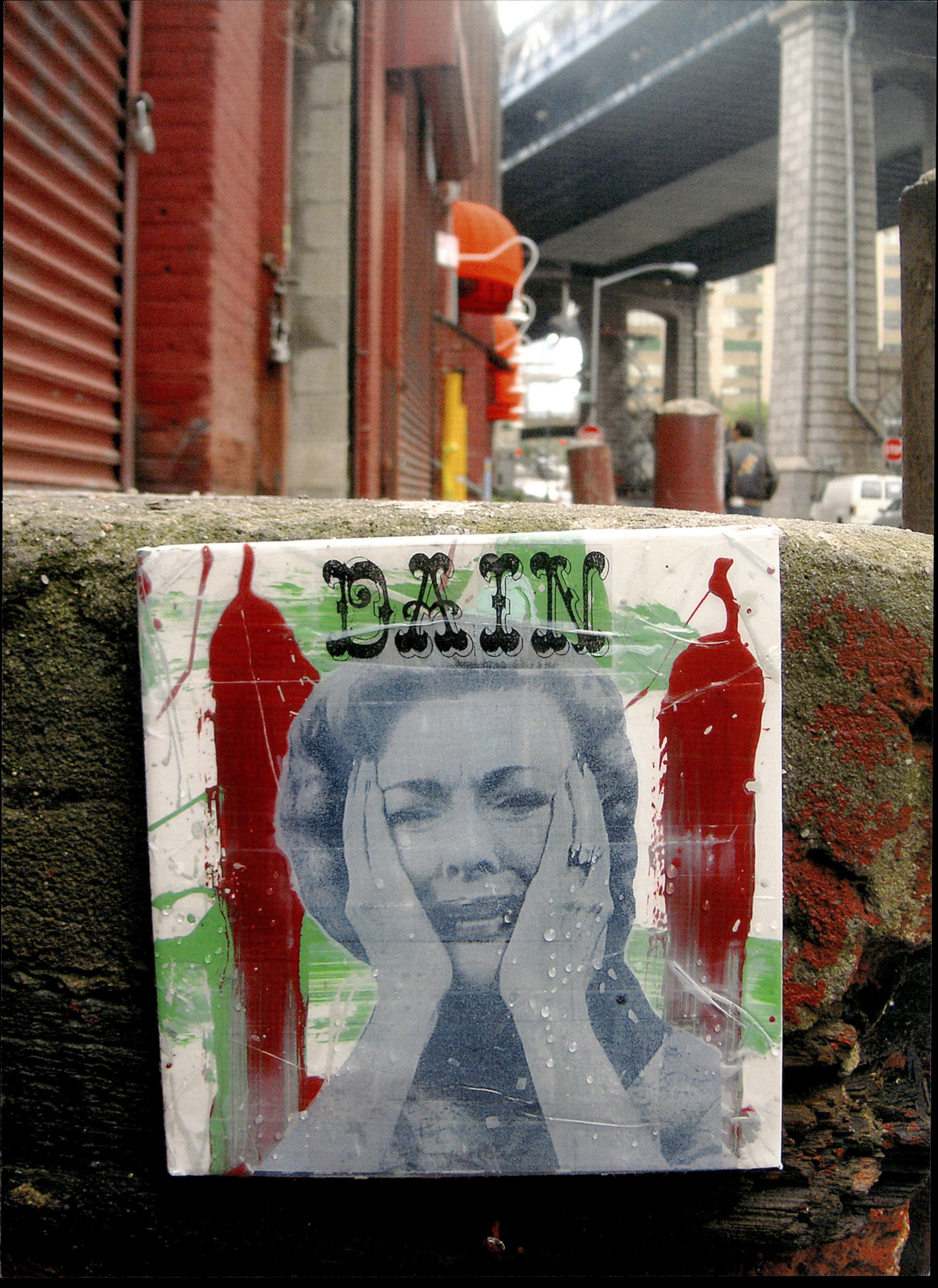
DAIN

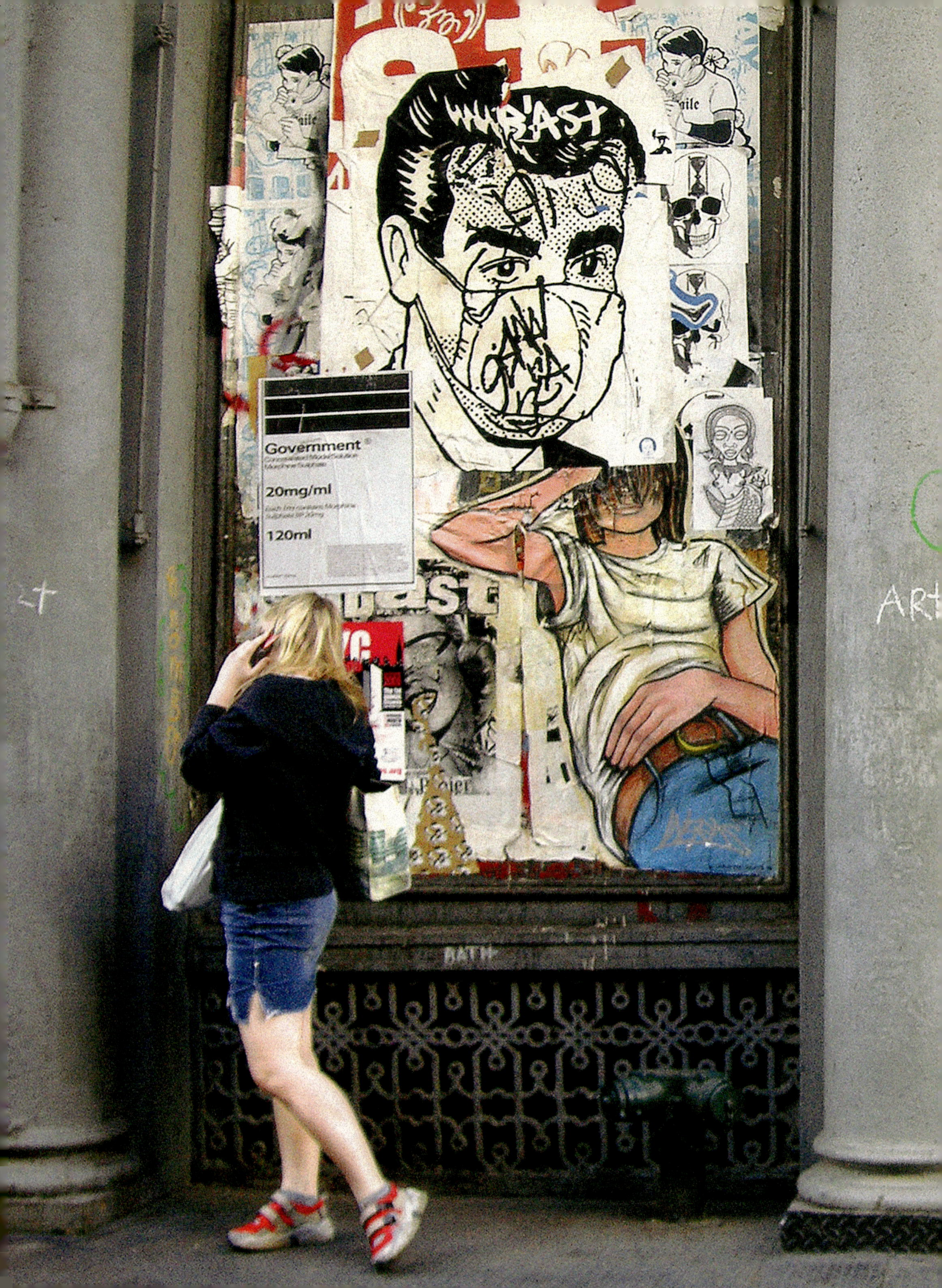
Government
20mg/ml
120ml

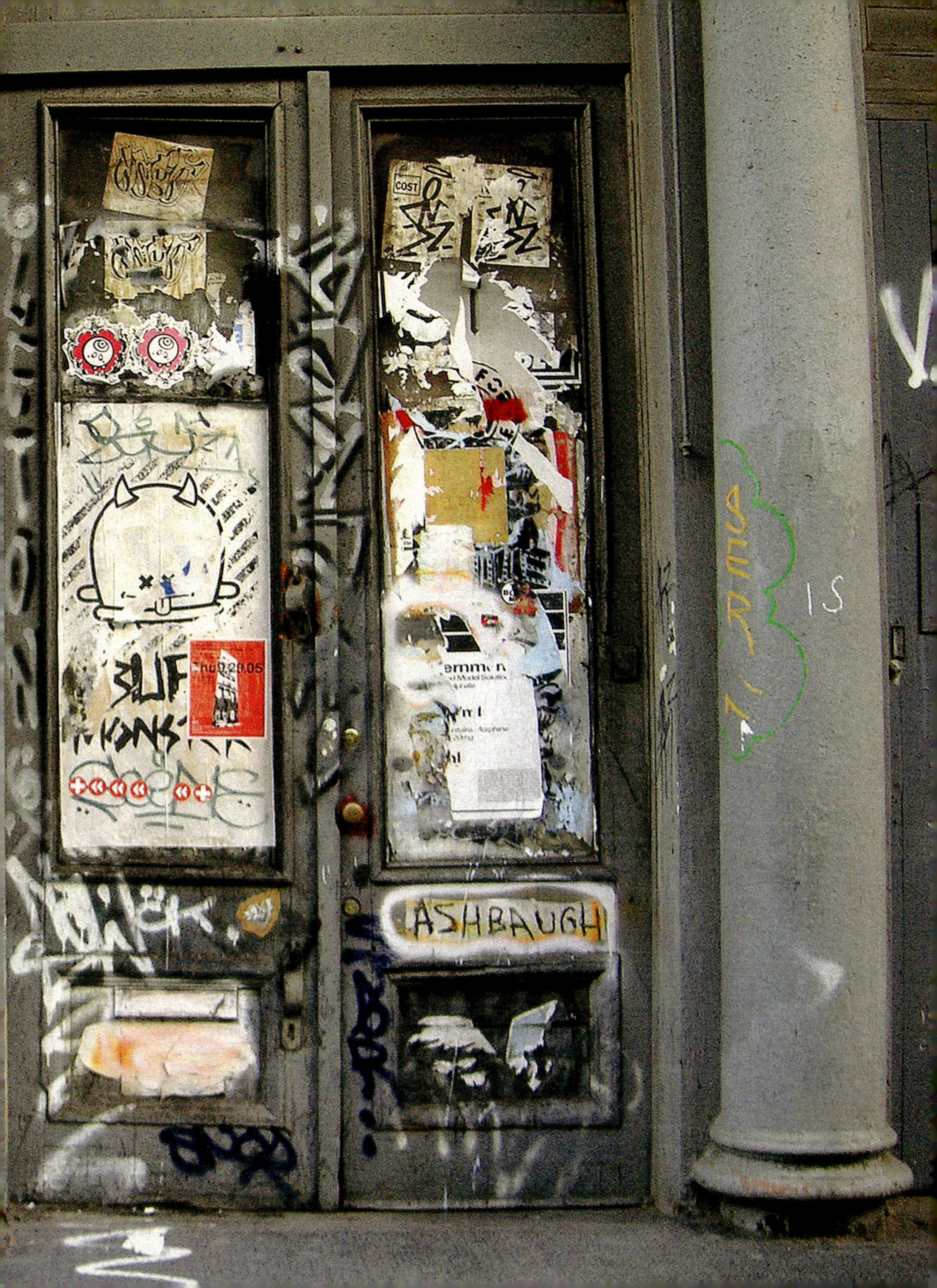
COST
ASHBAUGH
IS

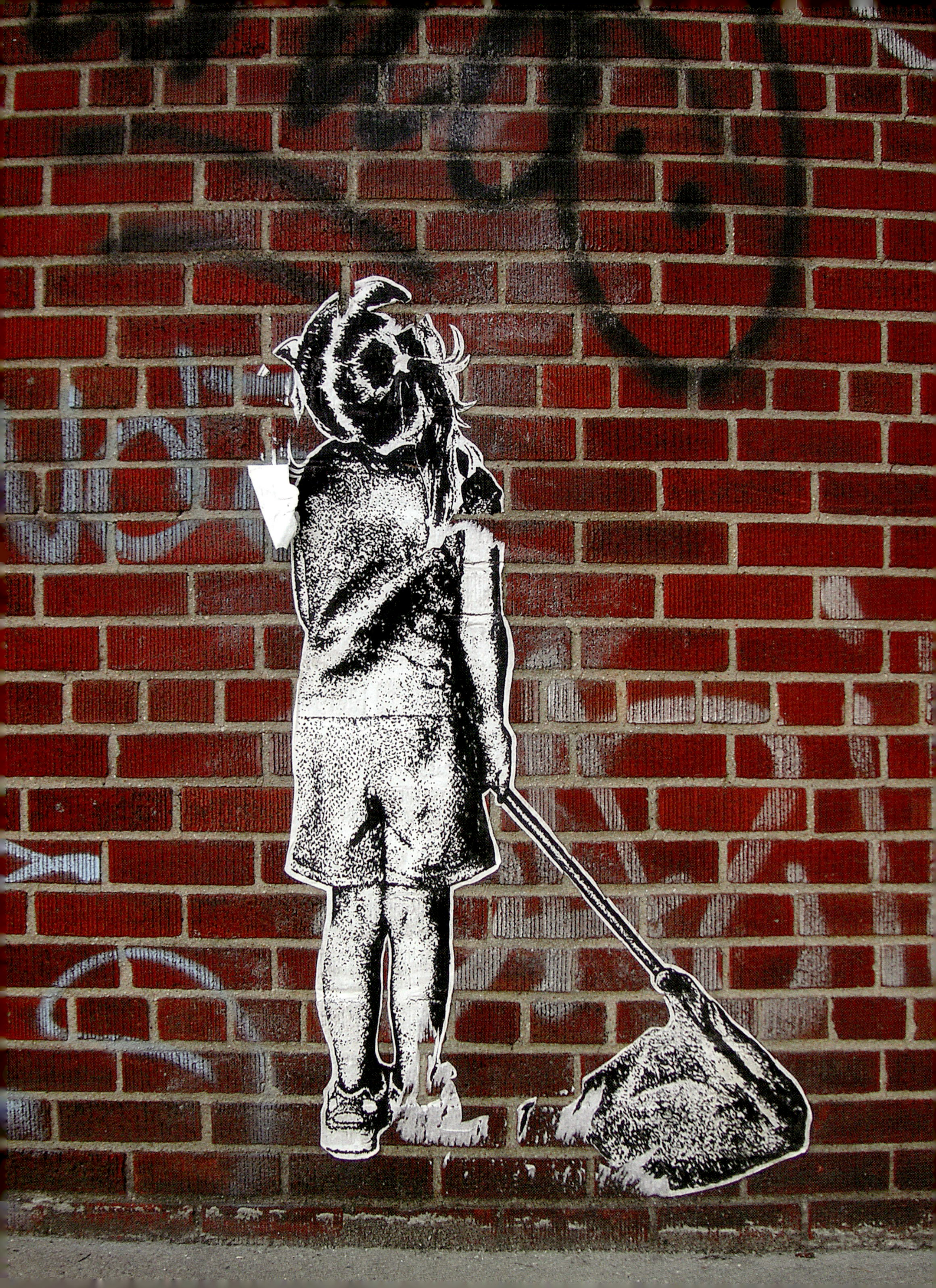

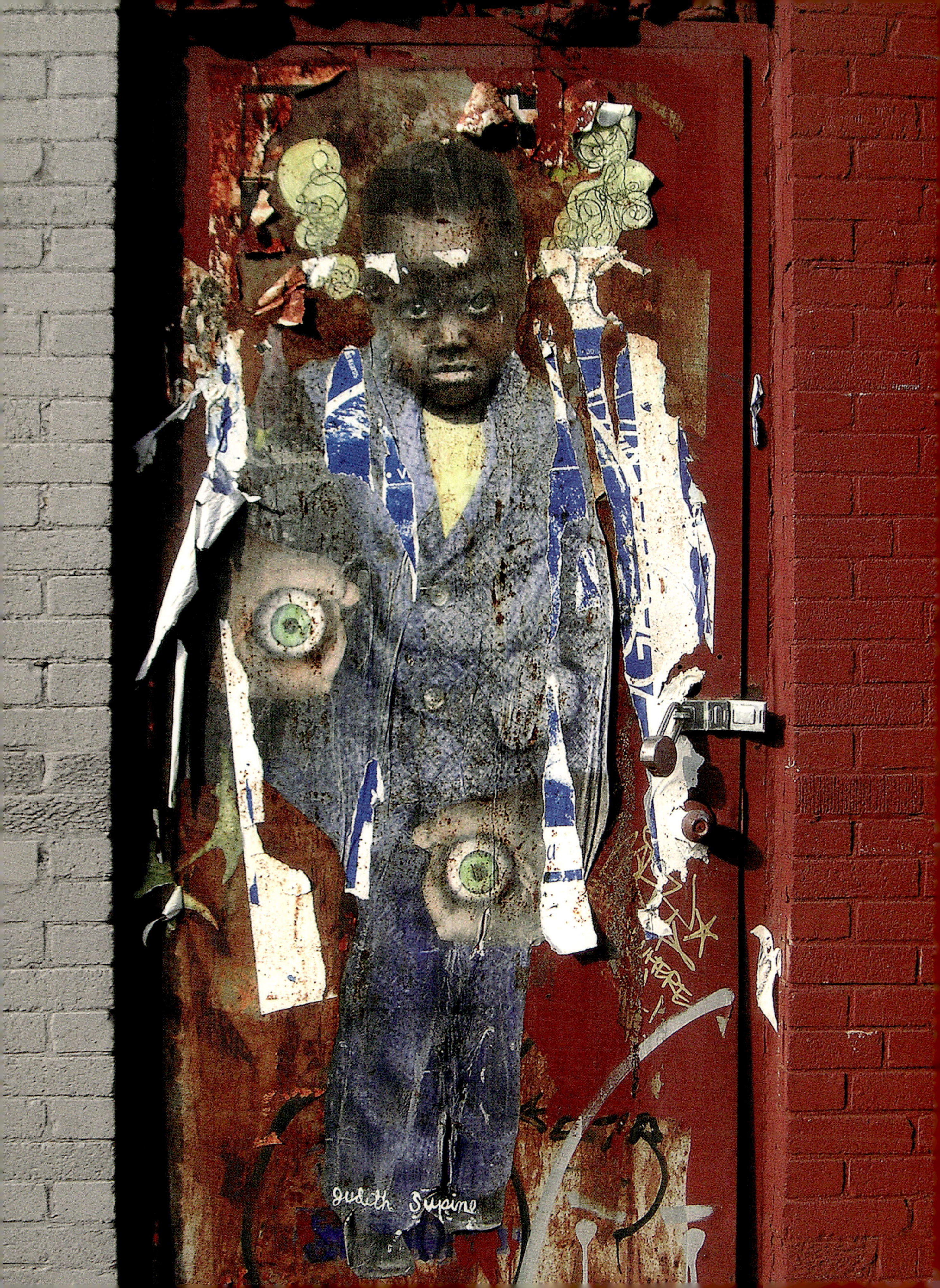
Judith Supine

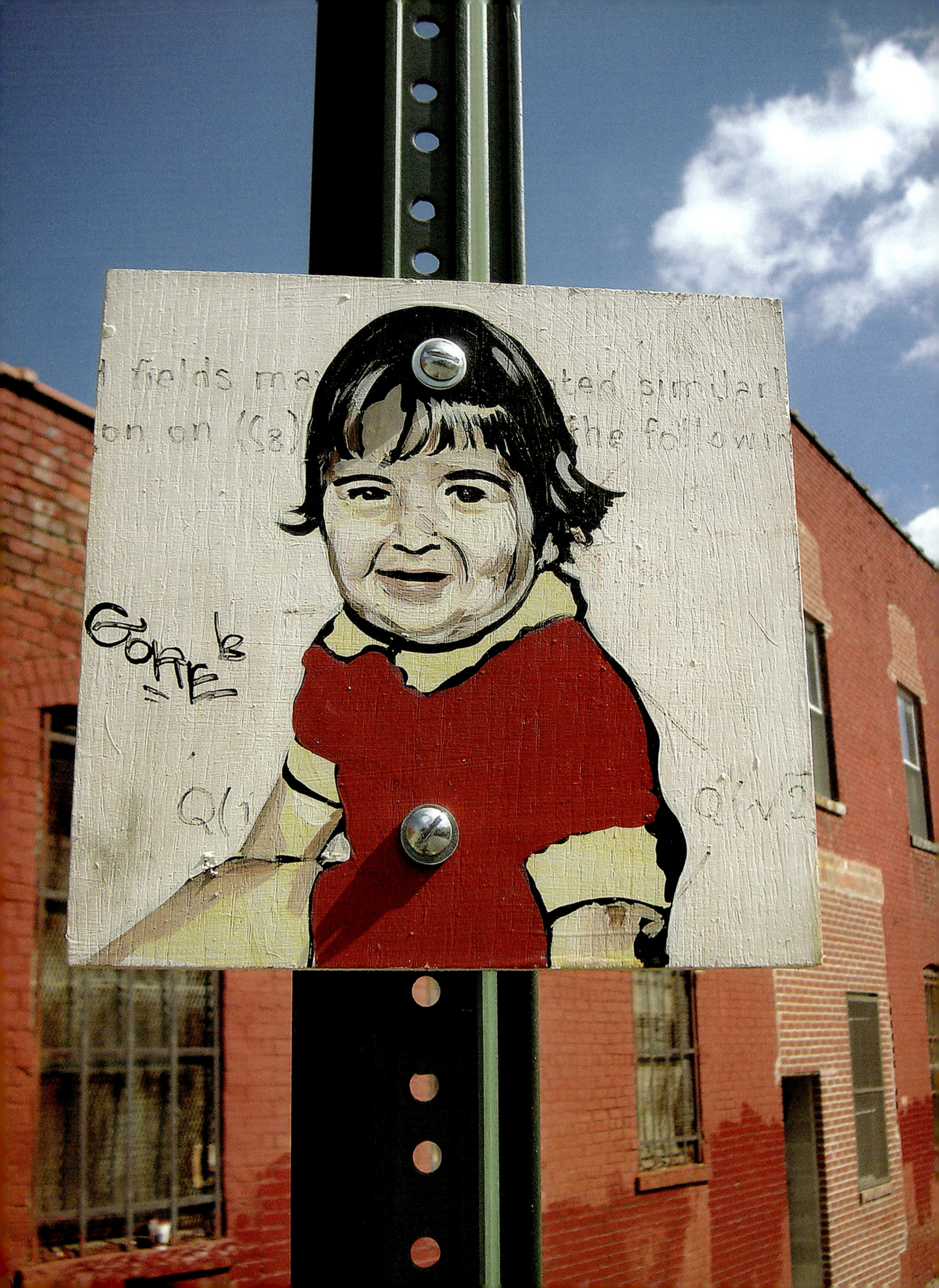

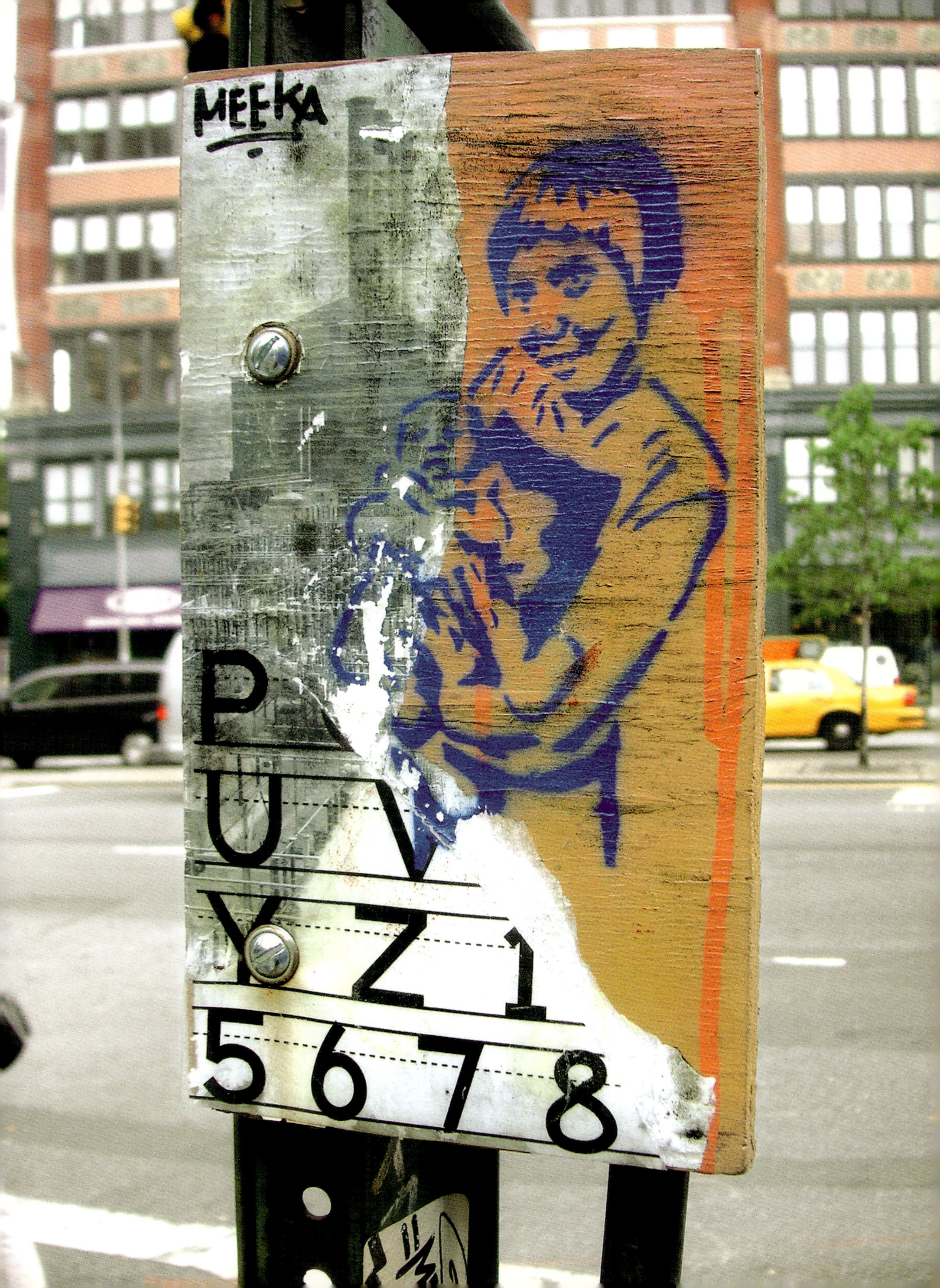
MEEKA
P U V
Y Z 1
5 6 7 8

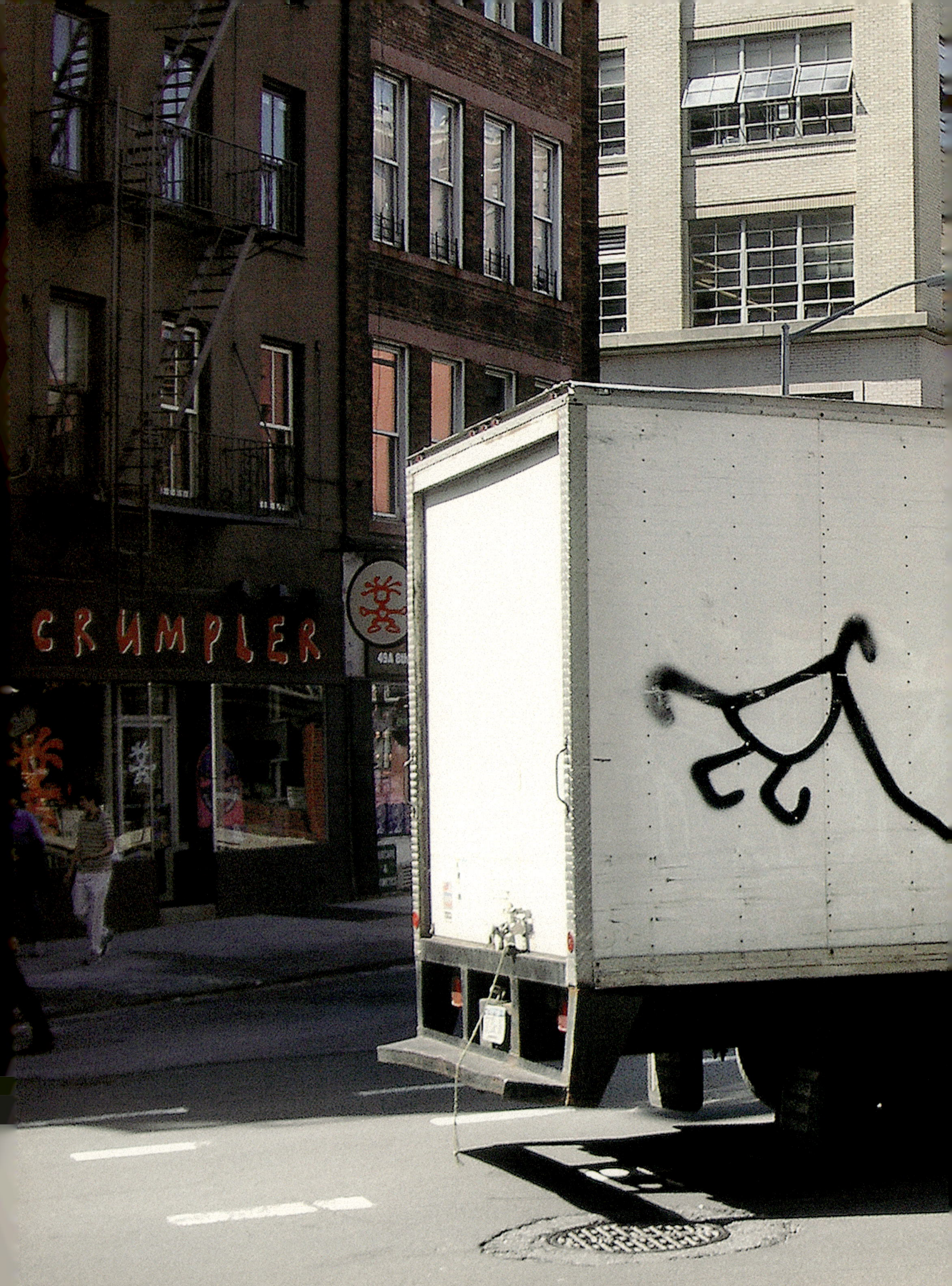
CRUMPLER

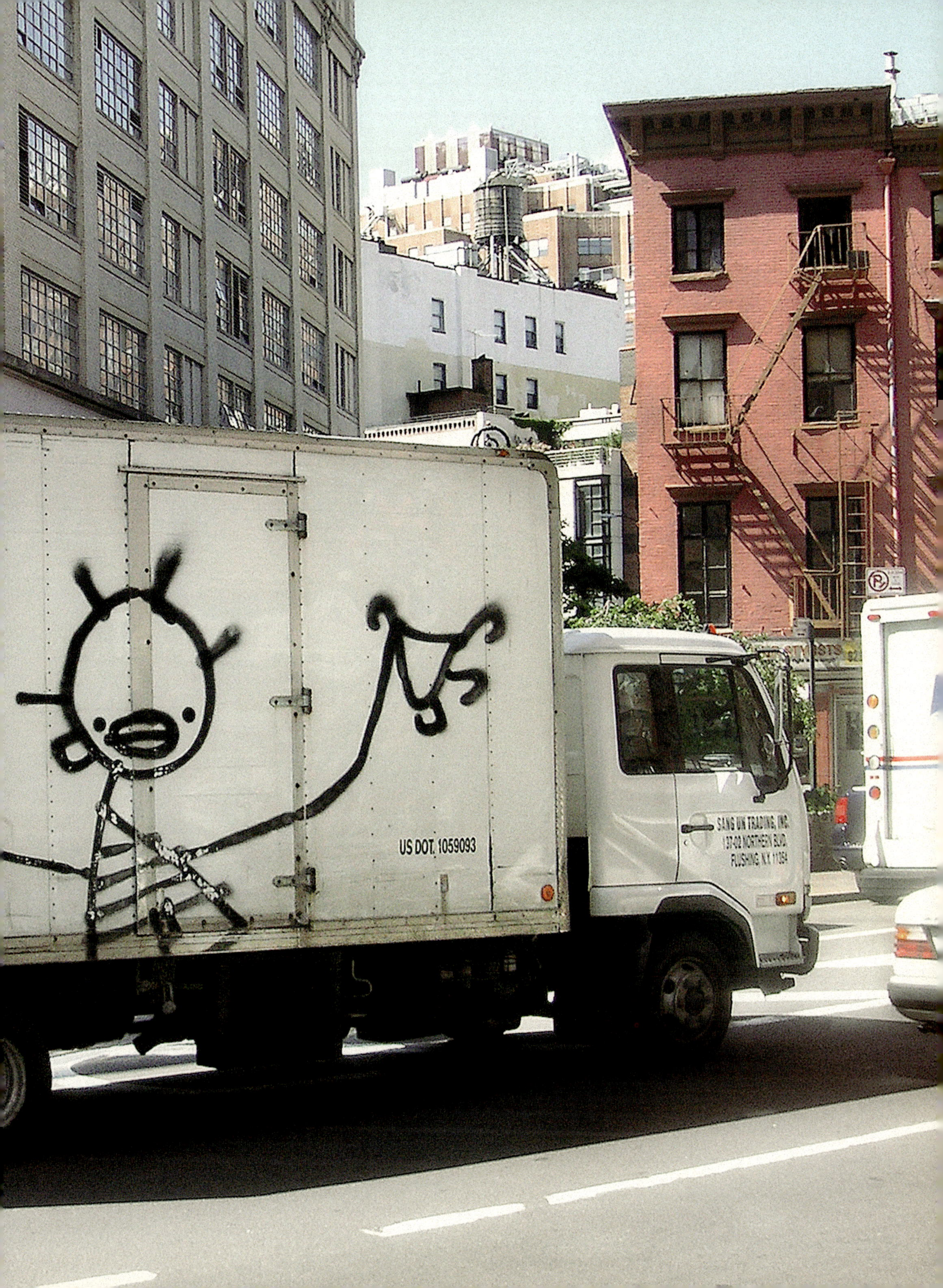
US DOT 1059093

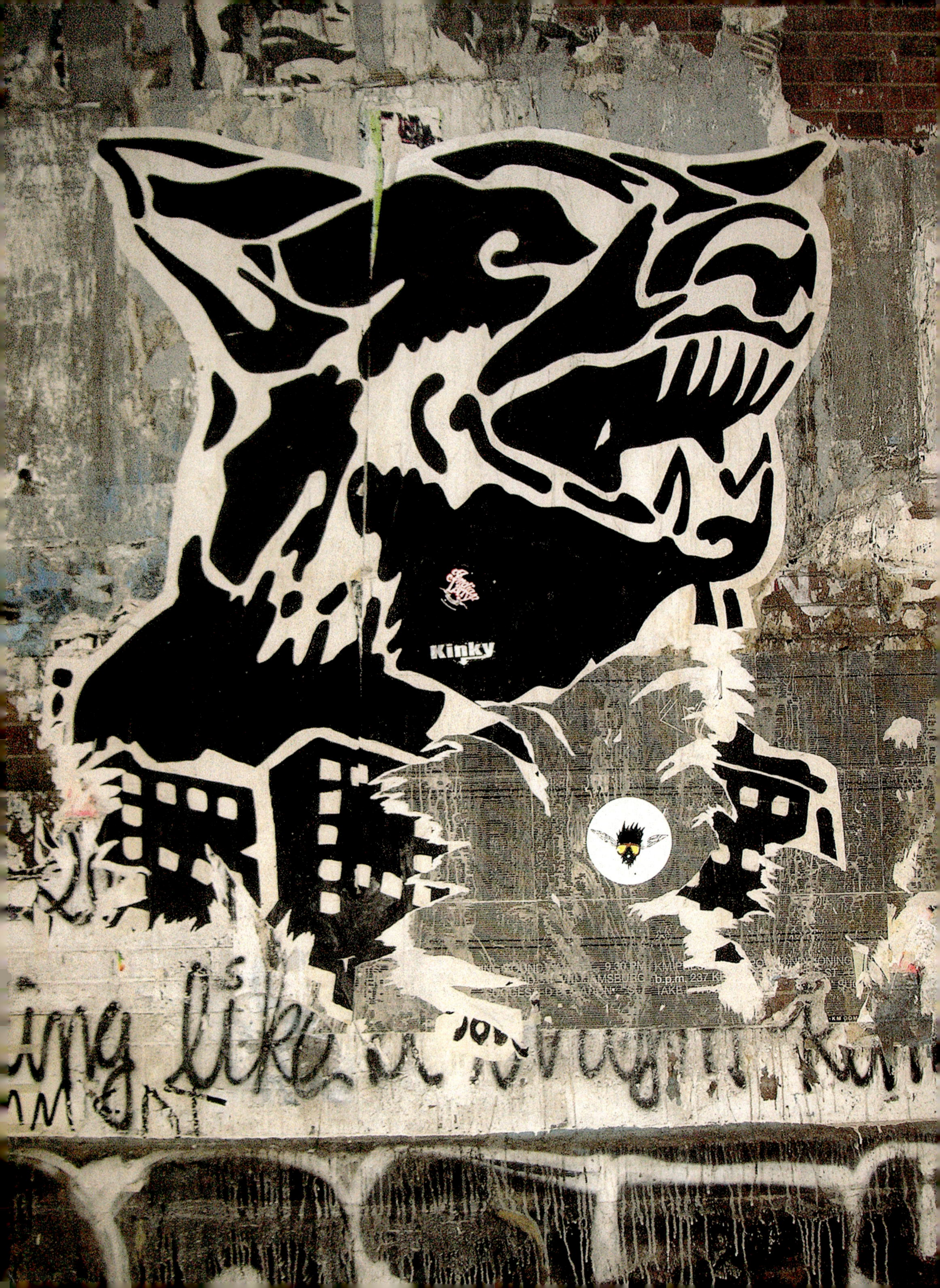
Kinky

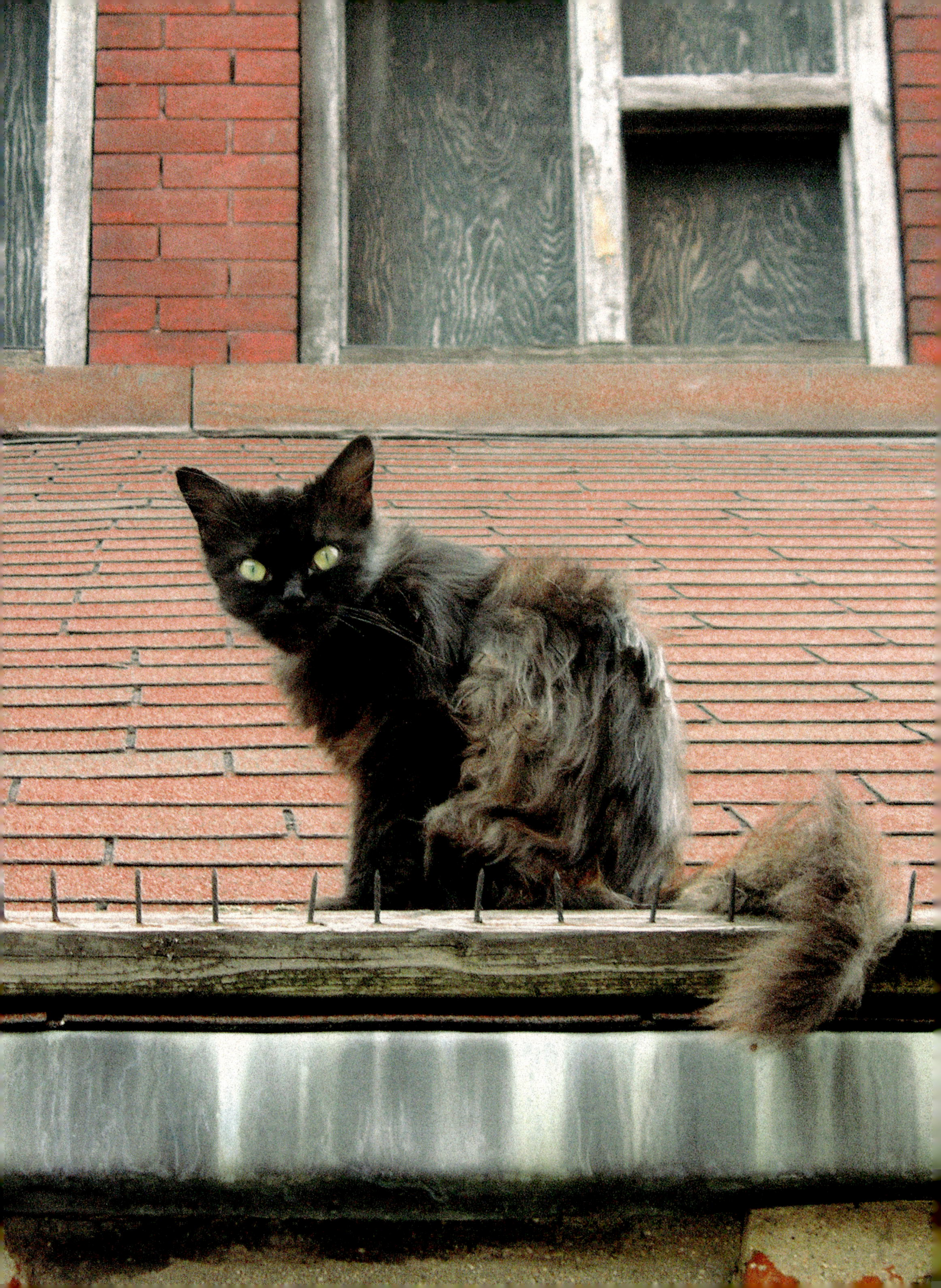

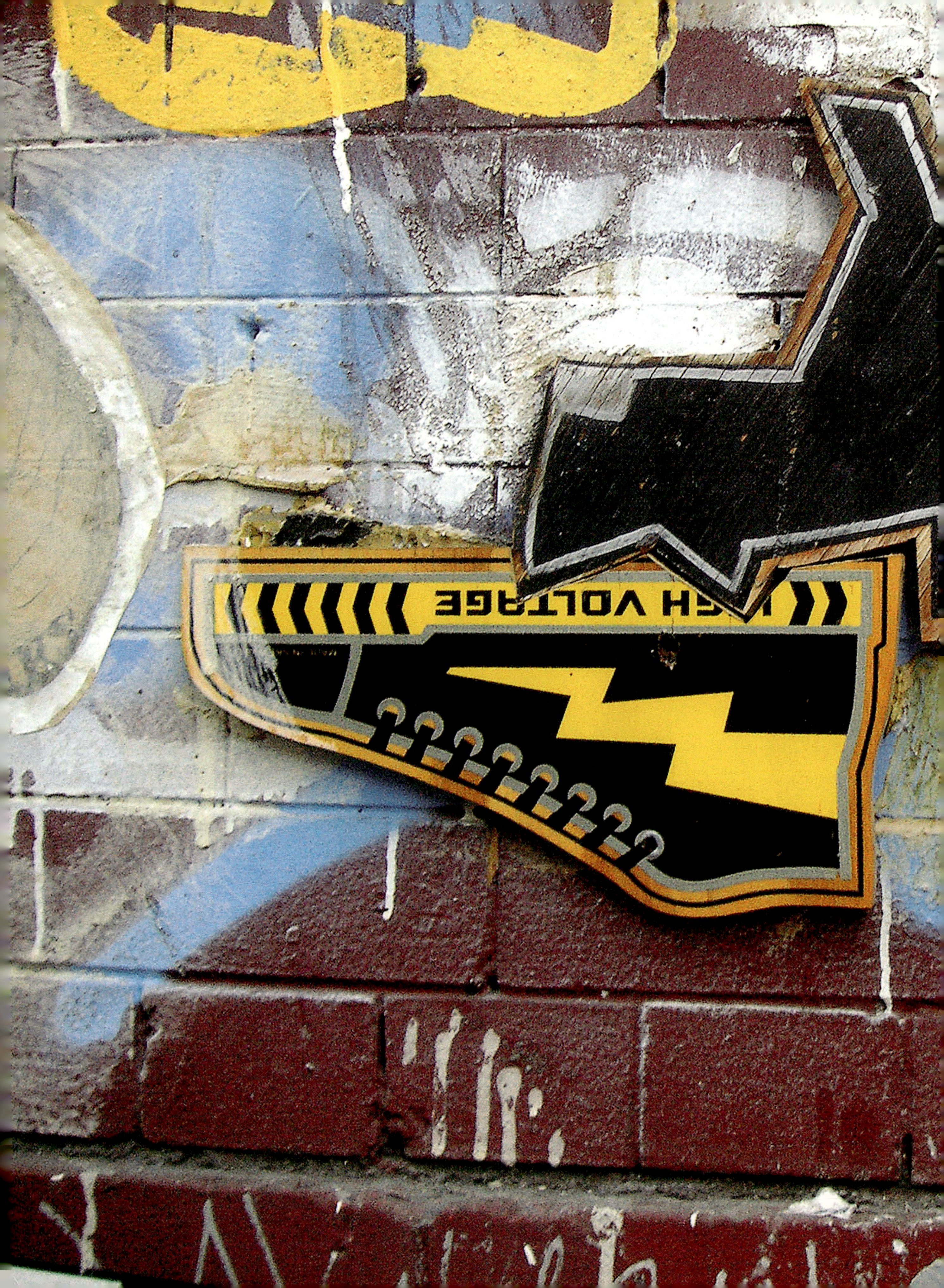
VOLTAGE

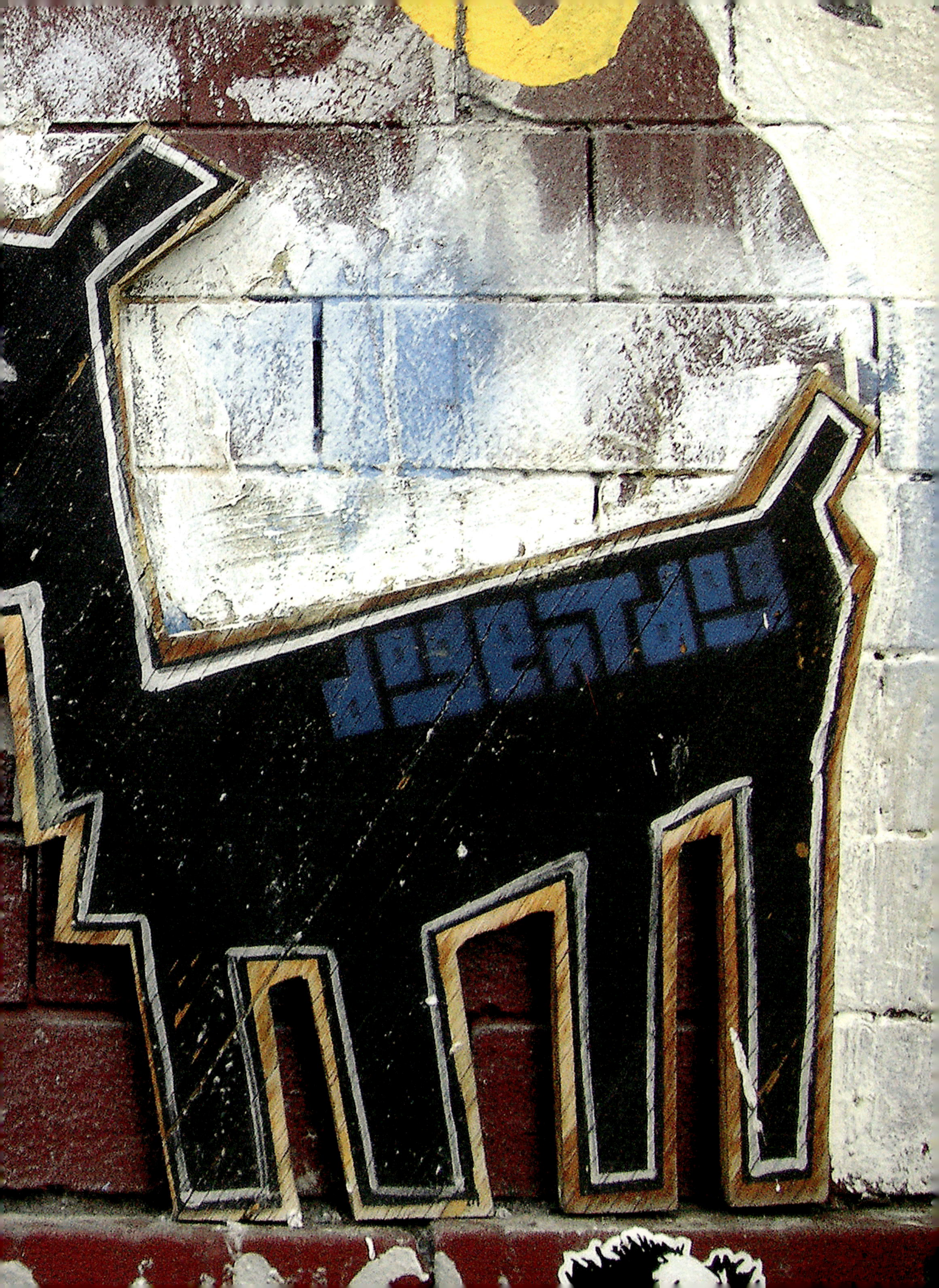

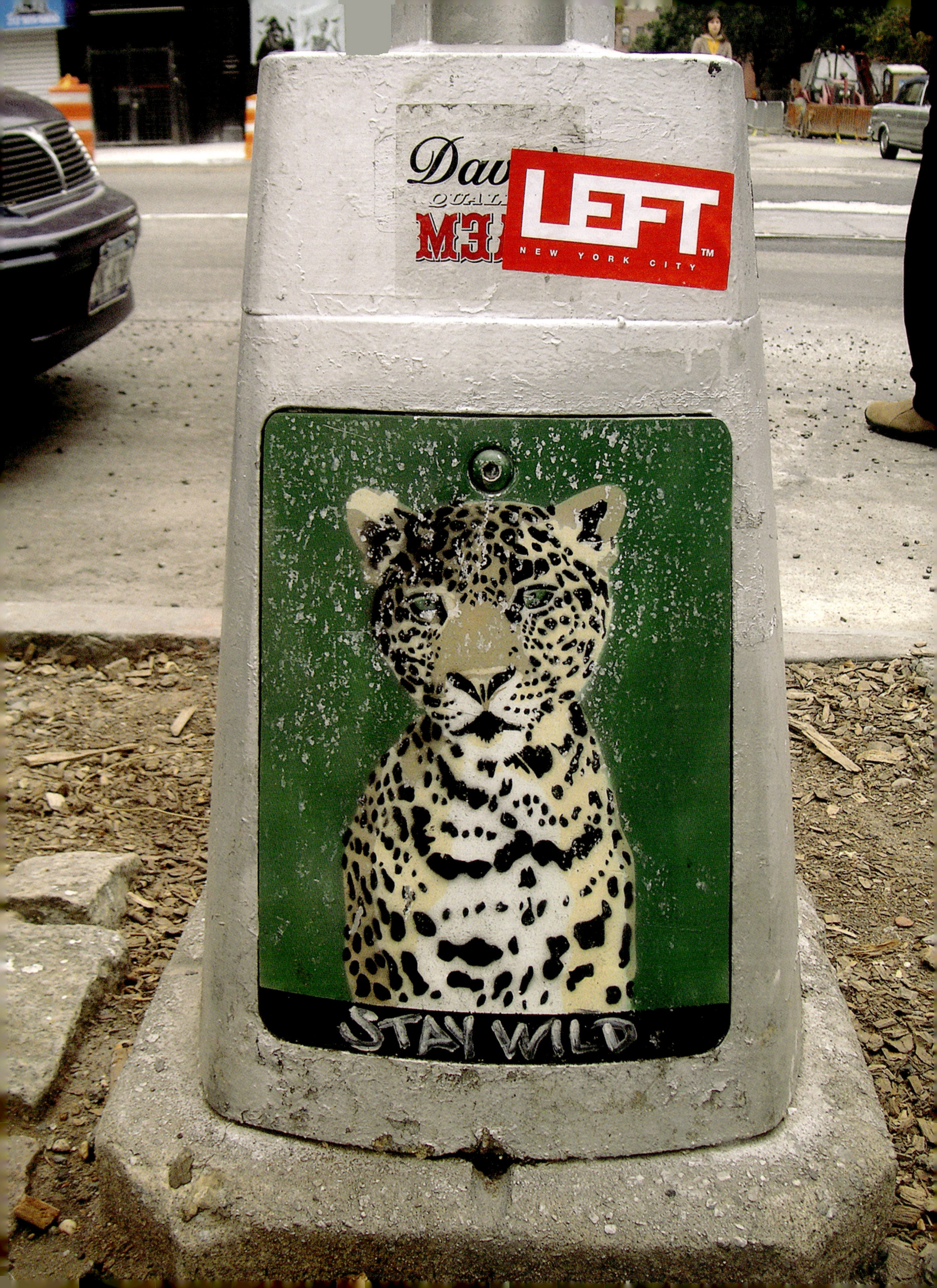
LEFT
NEW YORK CITY
STAY WILD

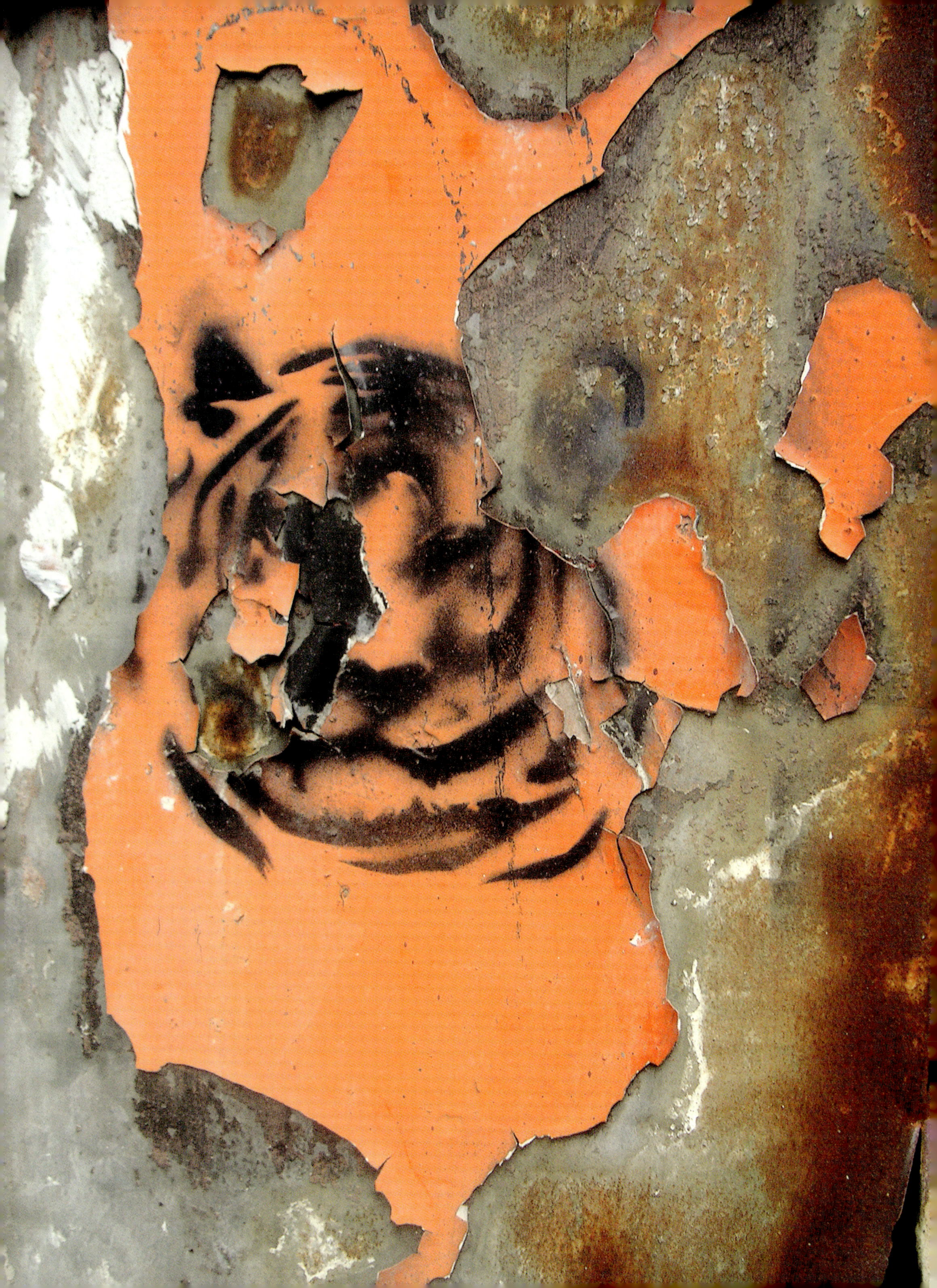

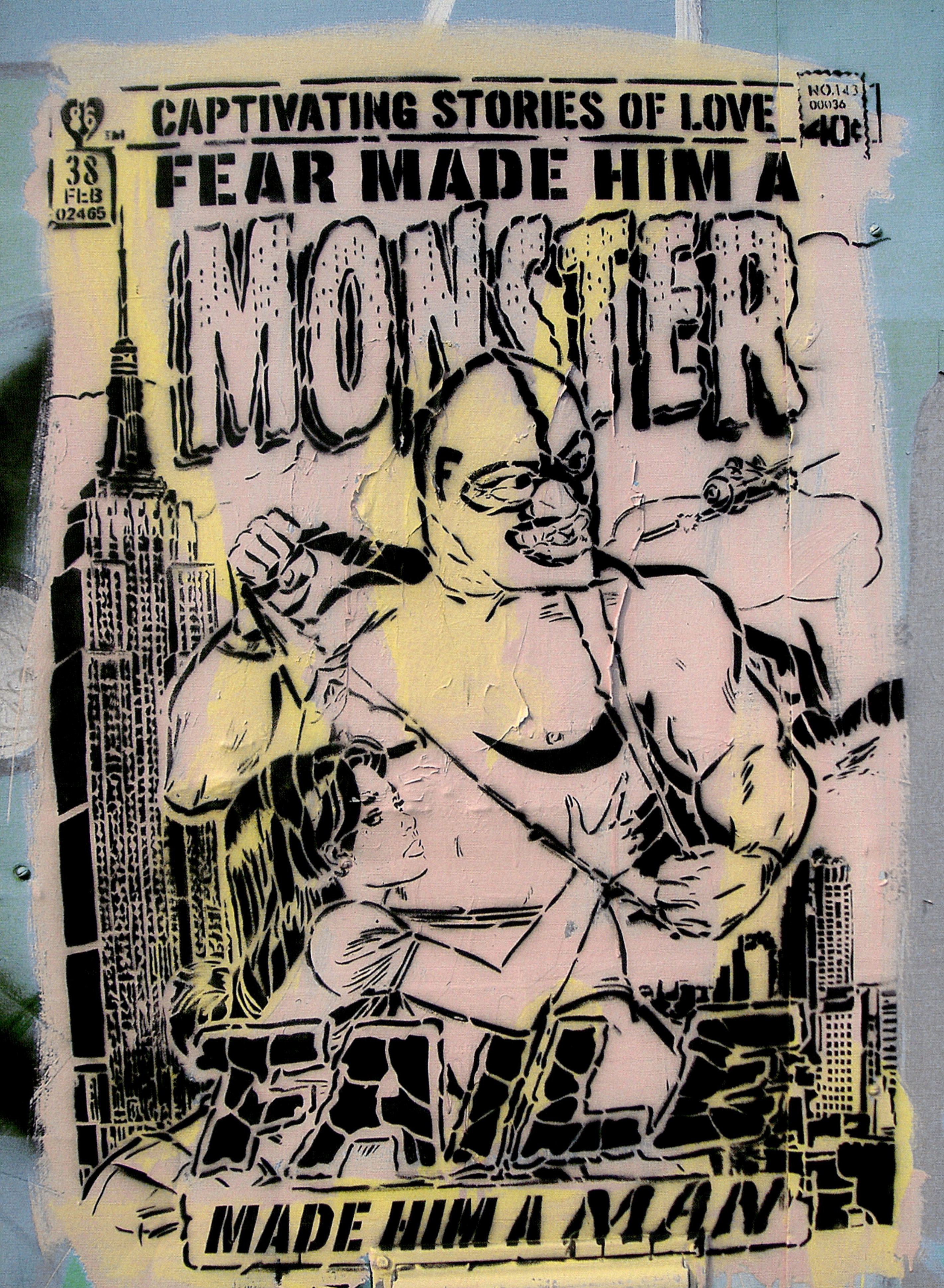

CAPTIVATING STORIES OF LOVE
38
FEB
02465
NO.143
00036
40¢
FEAR MADE HIM A
MONSTER
FAILE
MADE HIM A MAN

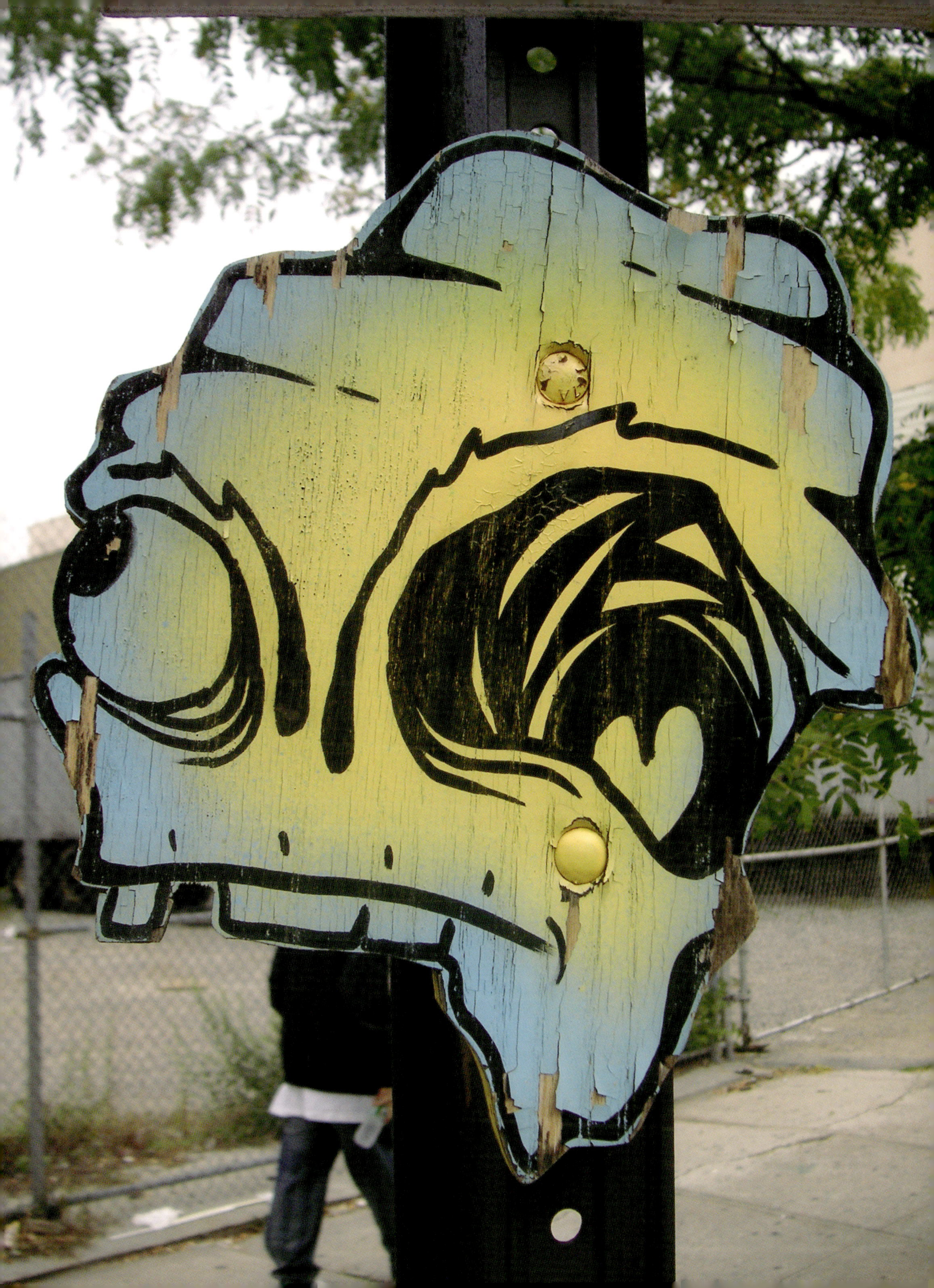

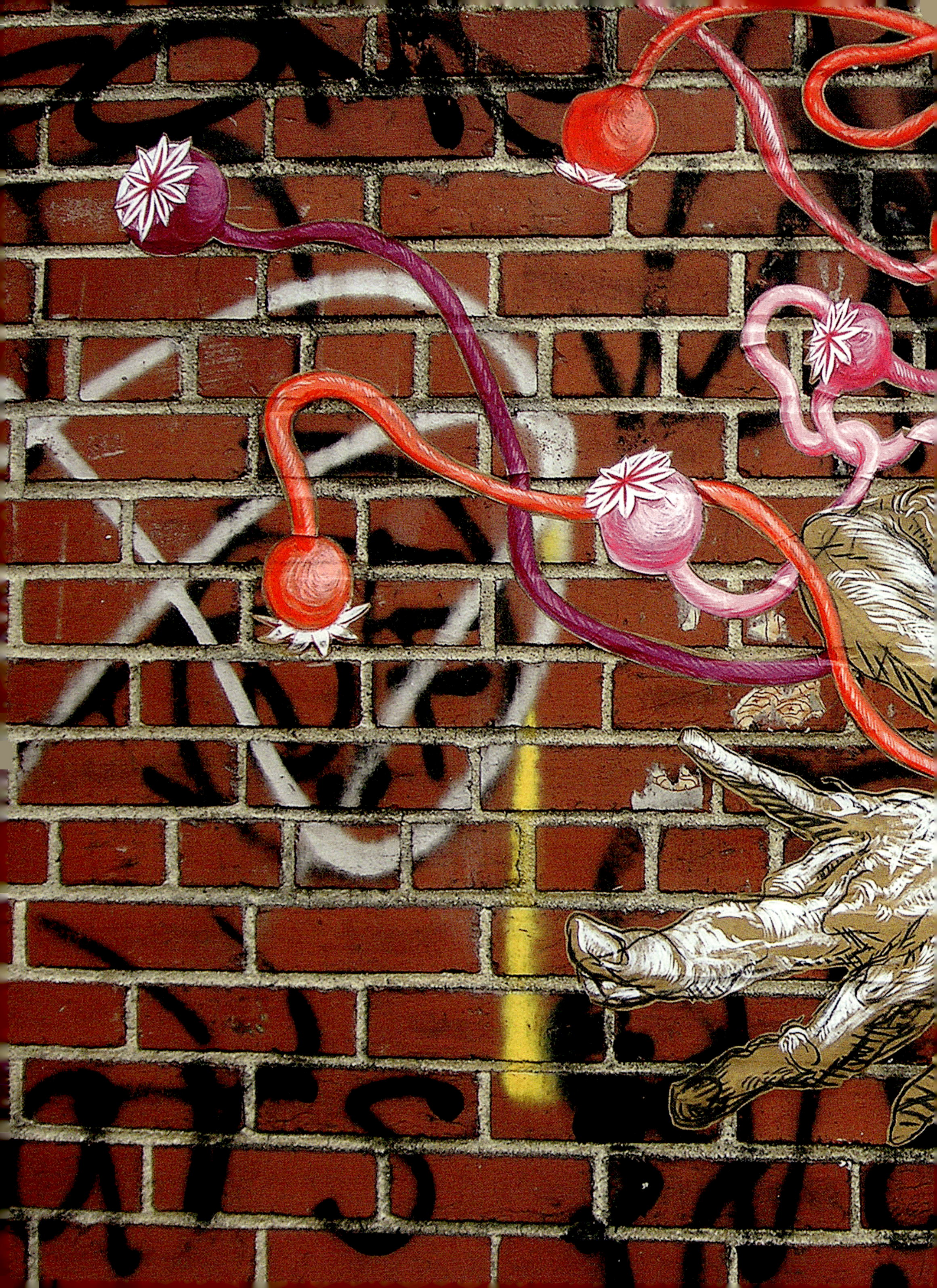

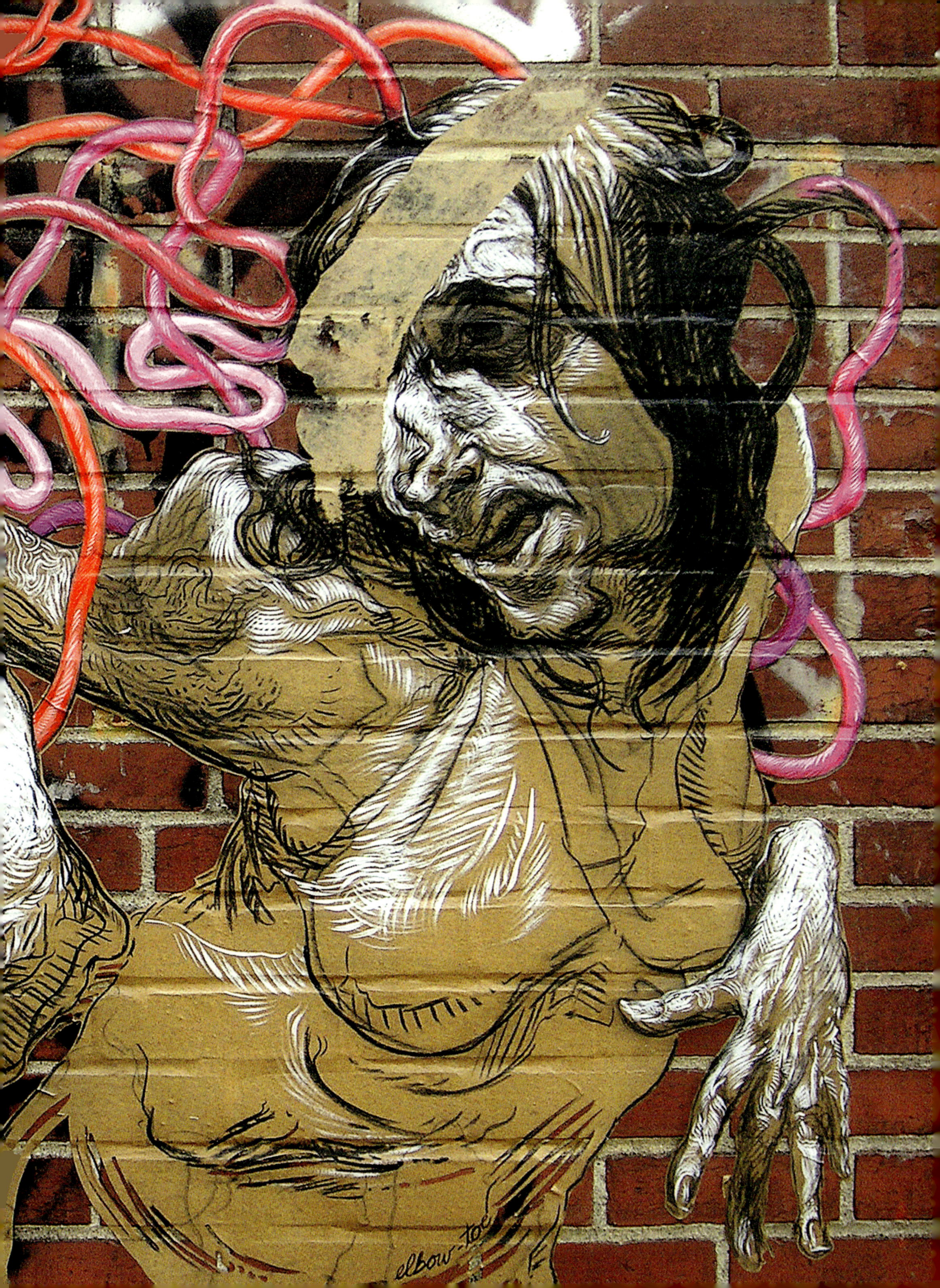
elbow-toe

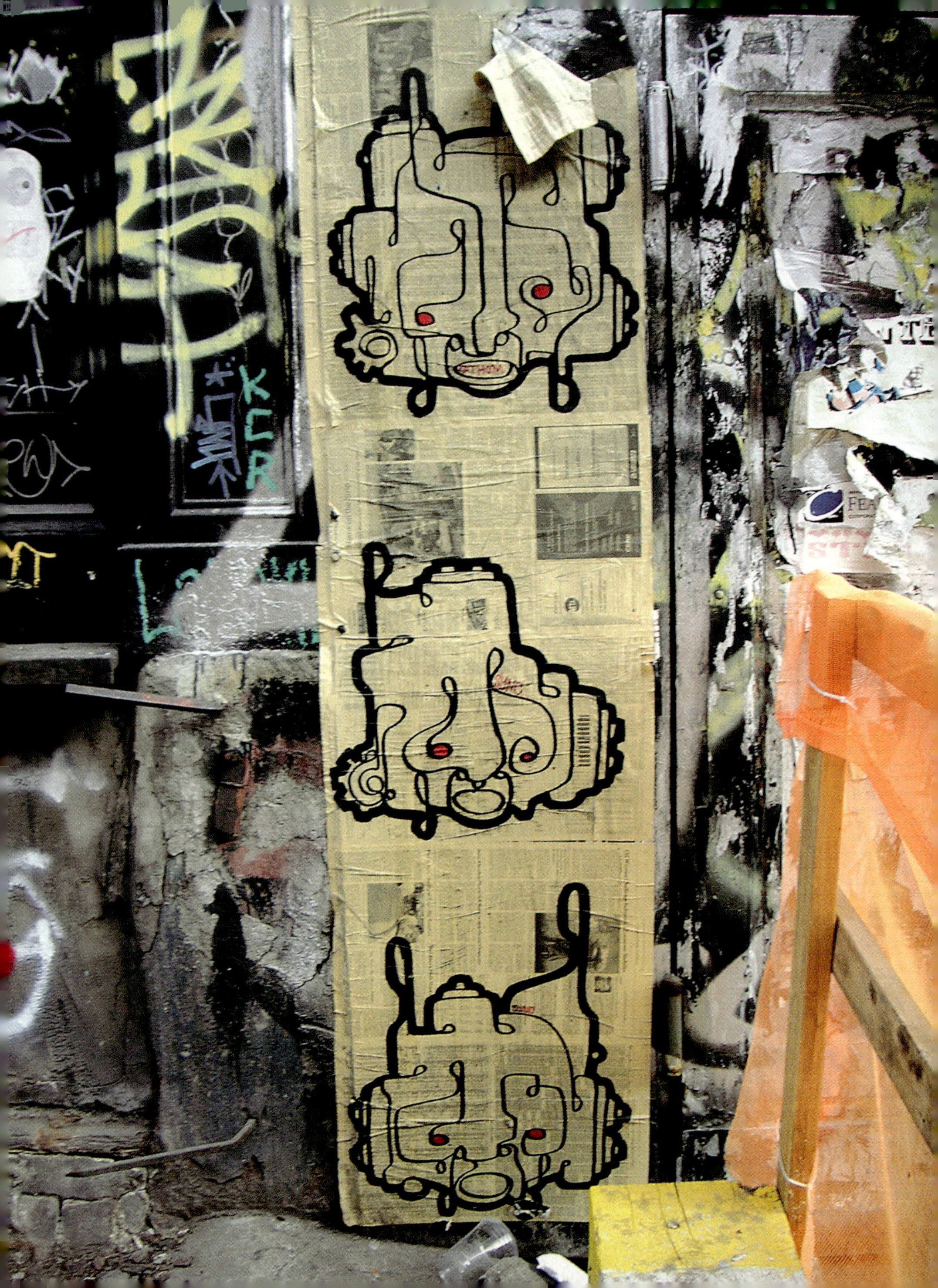

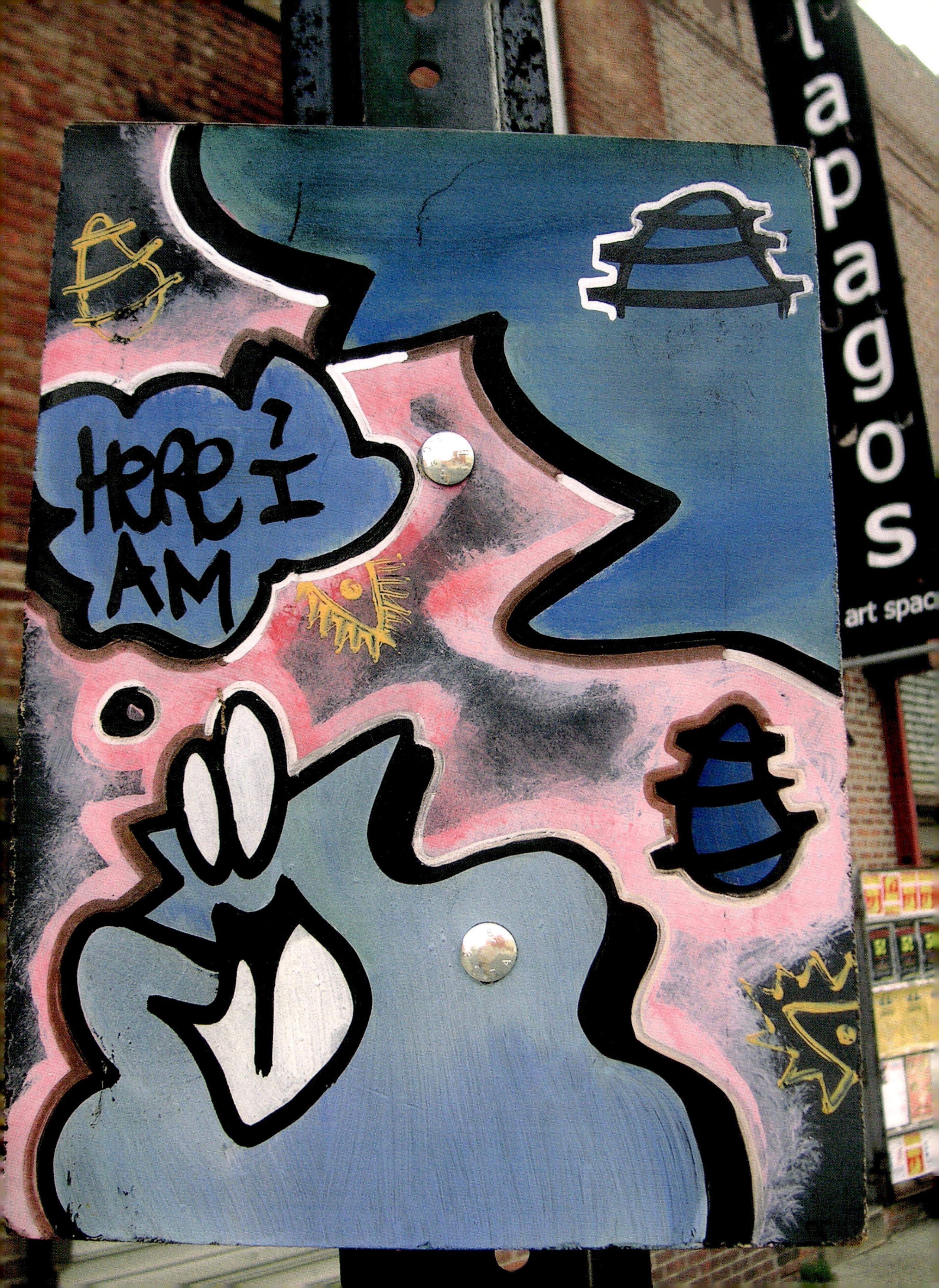
HERE I AM
lapagos
art spac

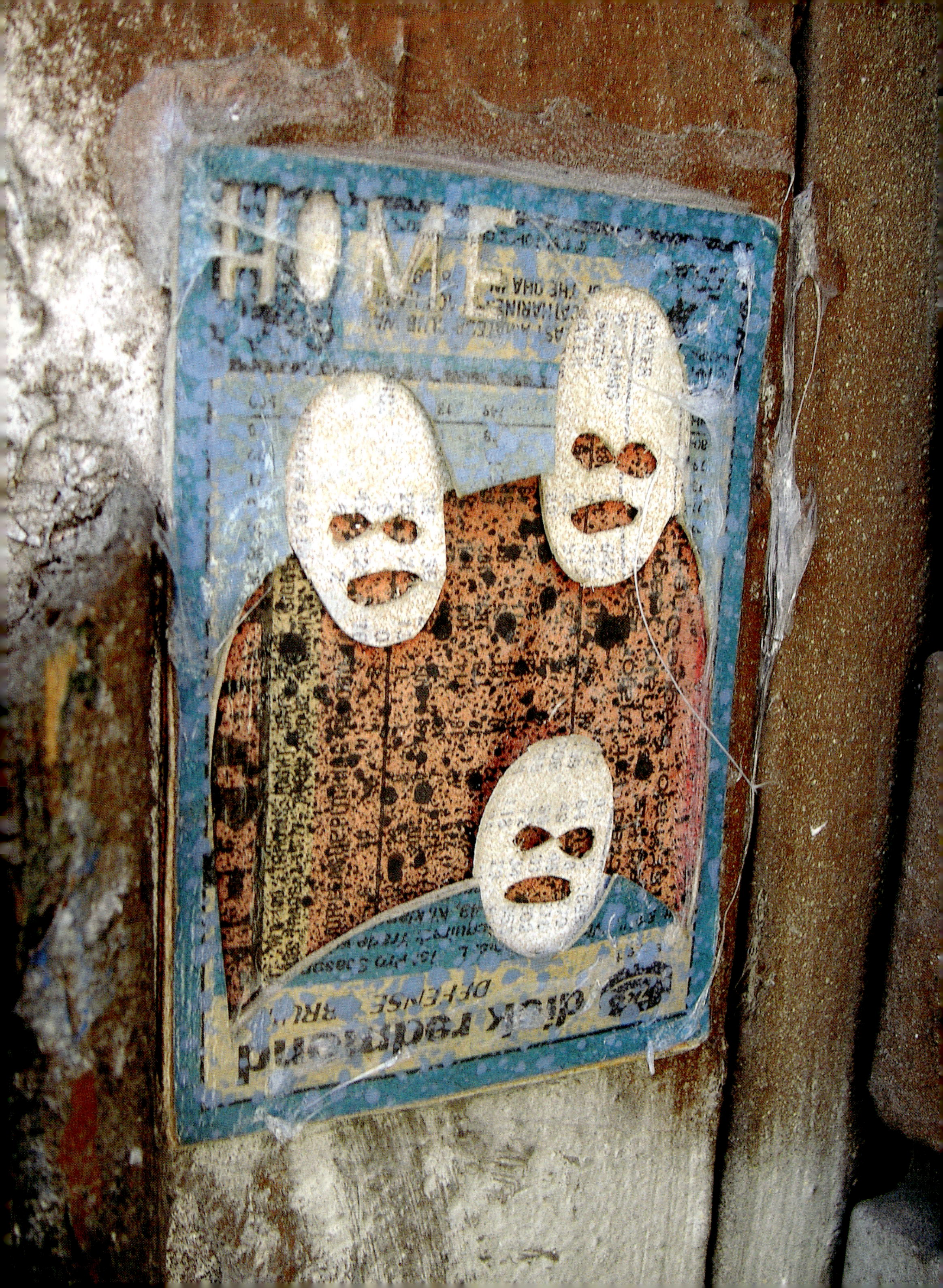
HOME

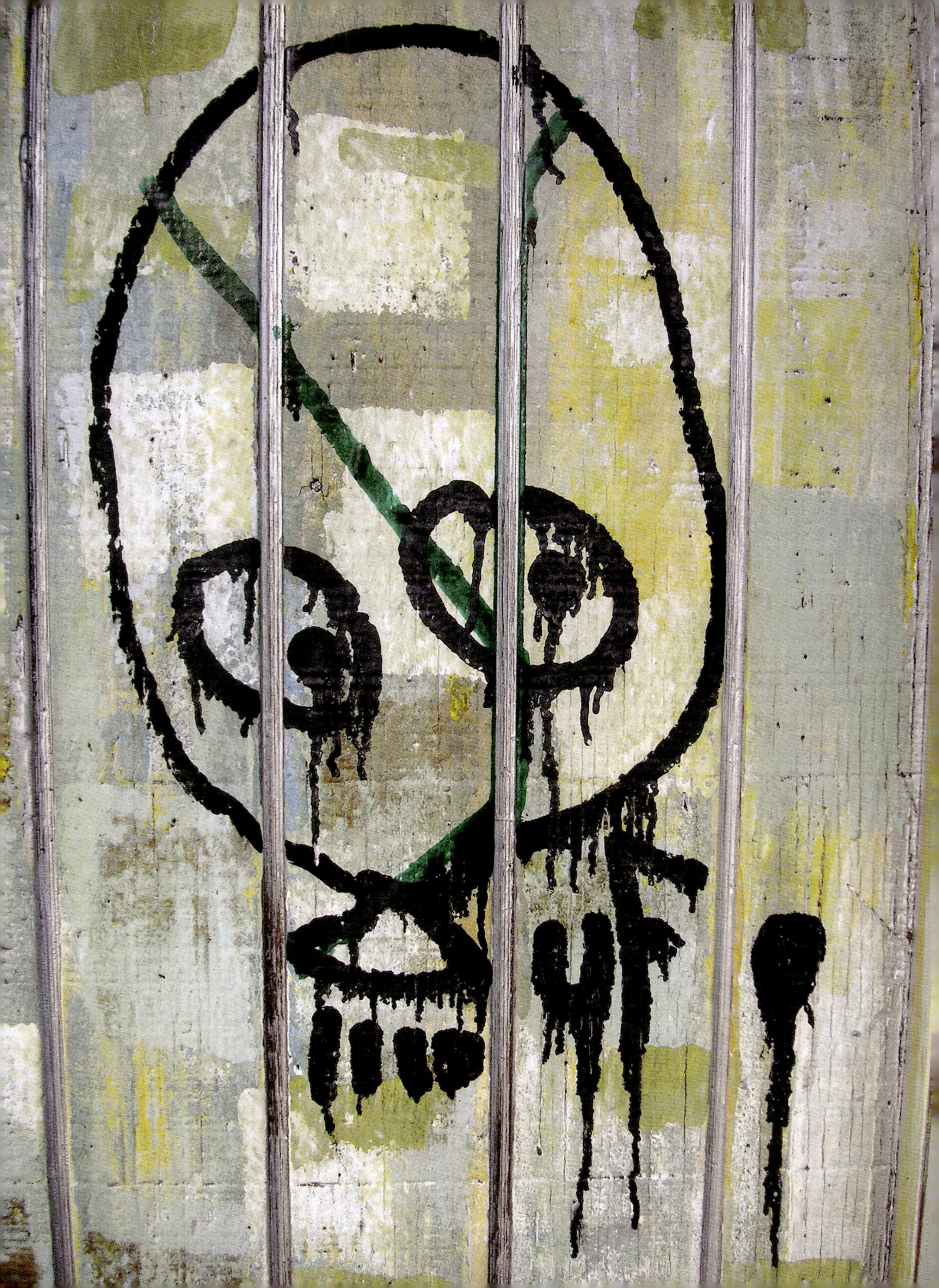

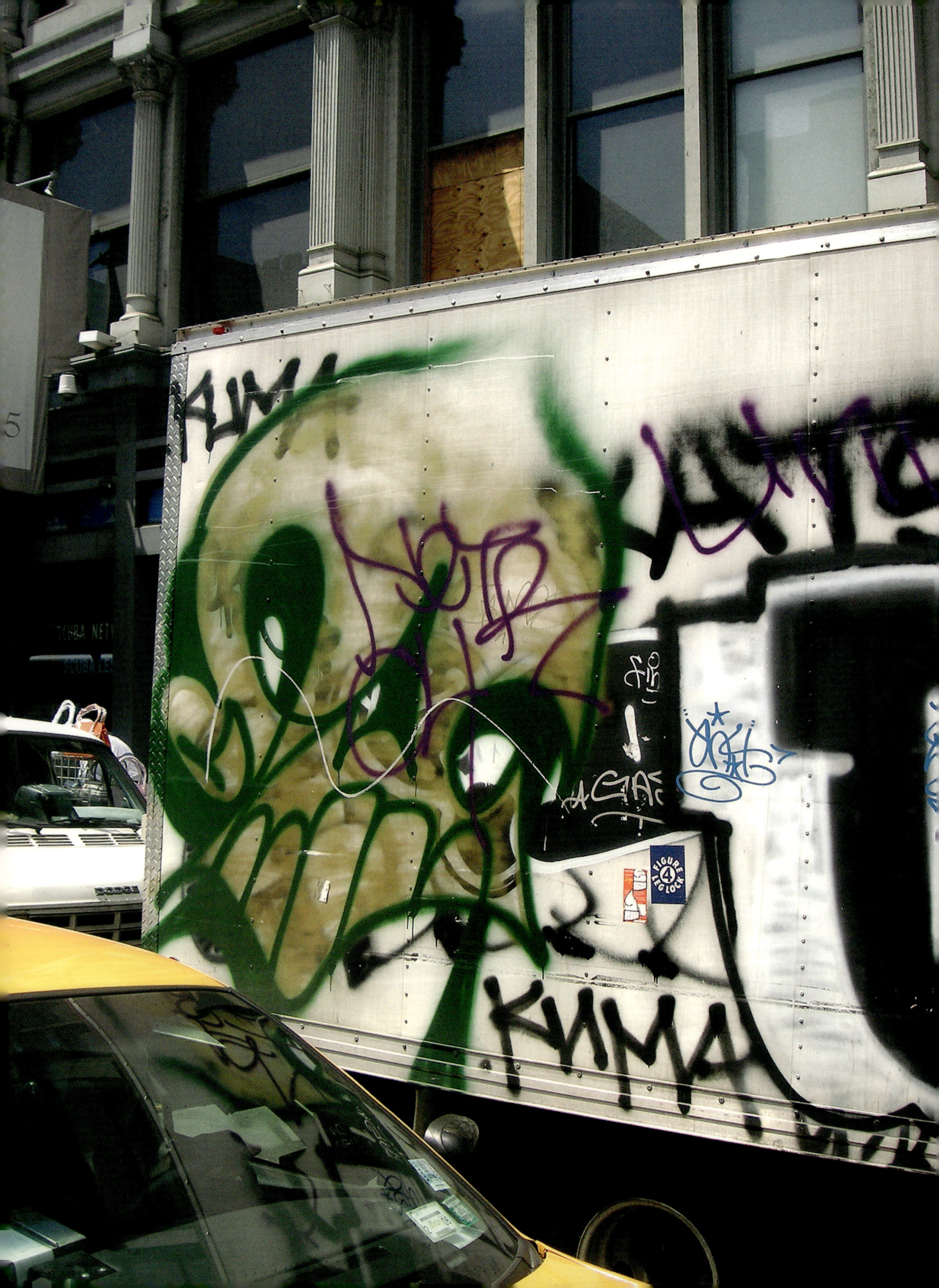
KUMA
FIGURE 4 LEG LOCK
KUMA

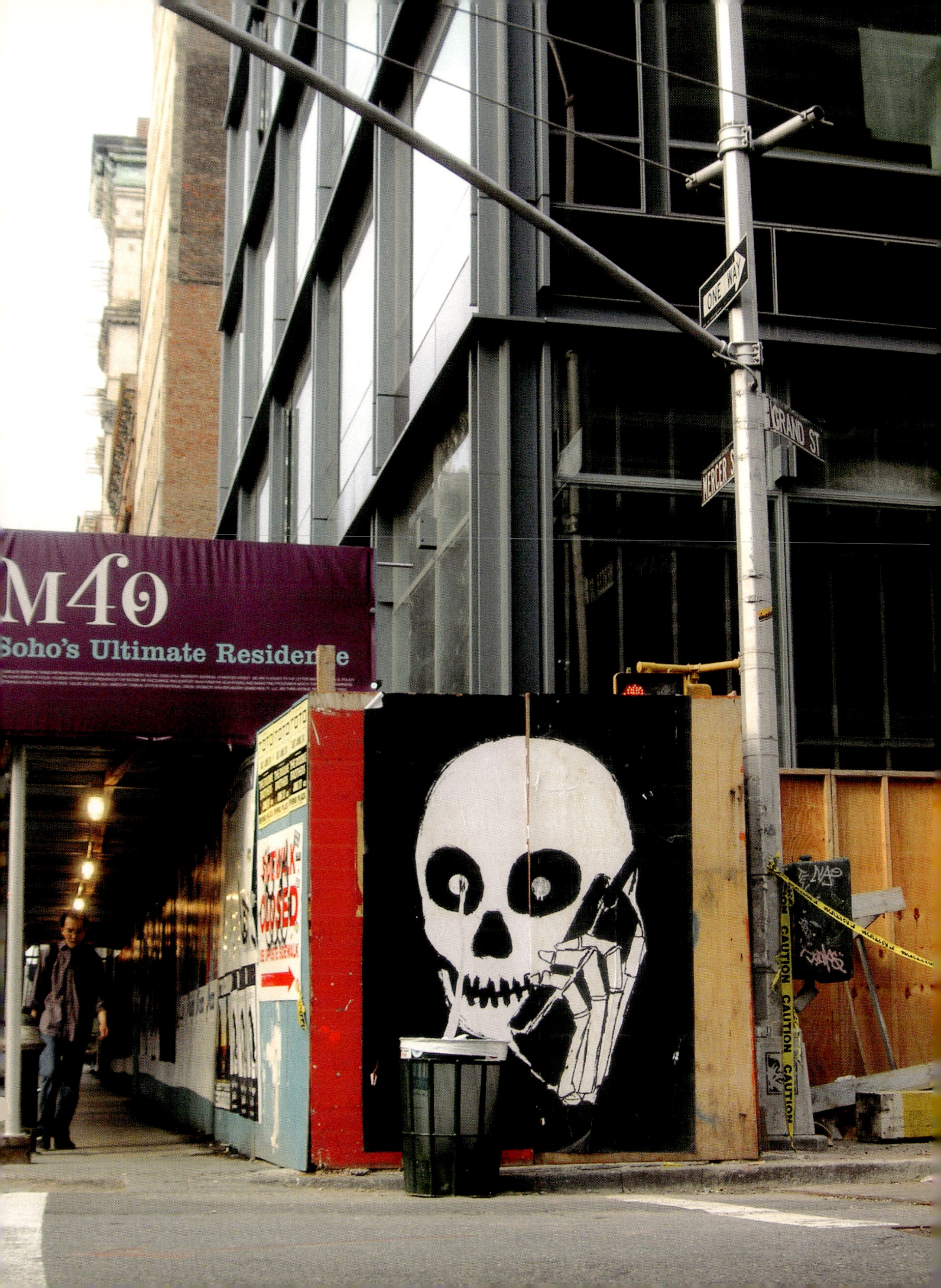
M40
Soho's Ultimate Residen e
ONE WAY
GRAND ST
MERCER S
SIDEWALK
CLOSED
CAUTION

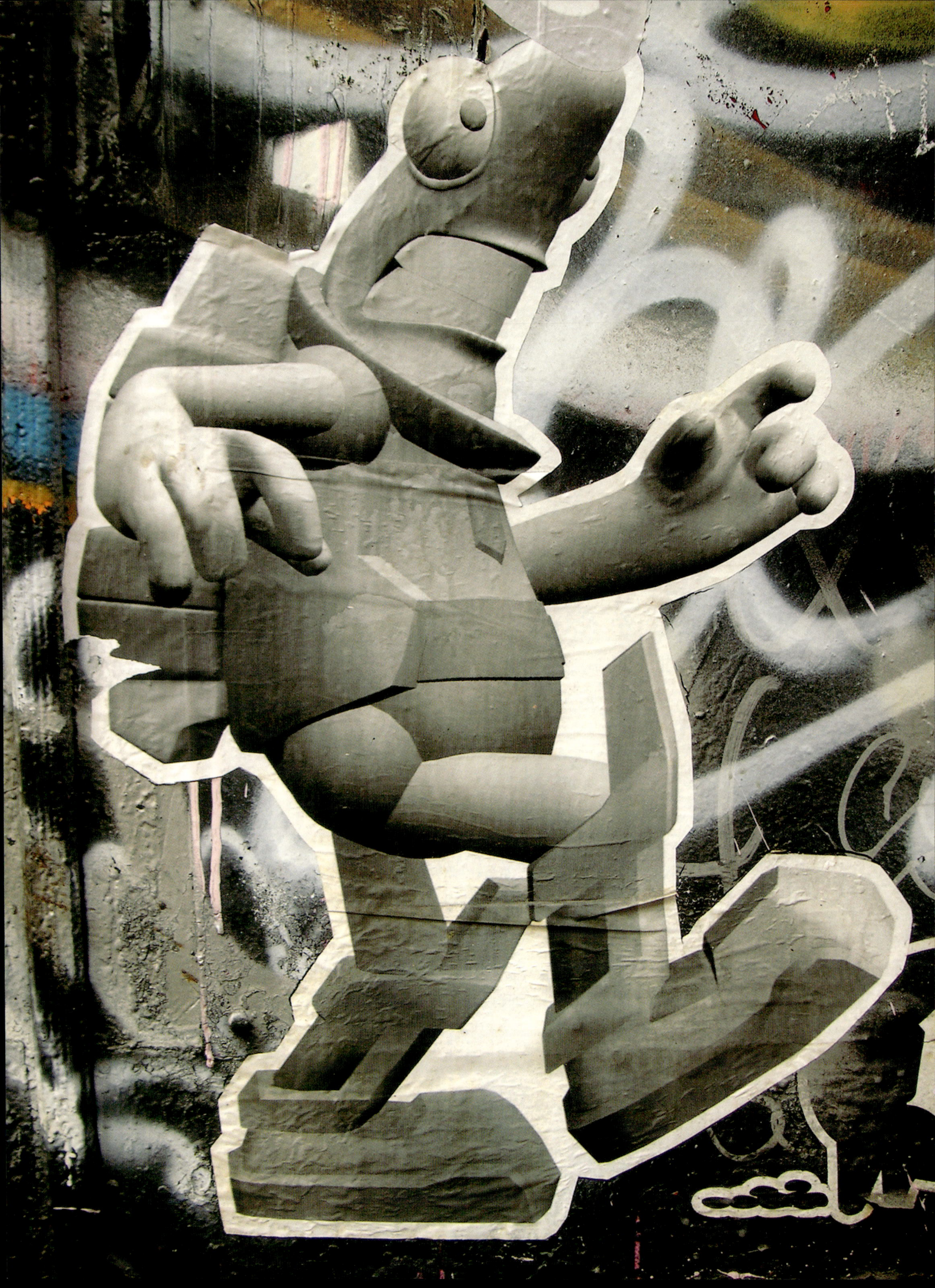

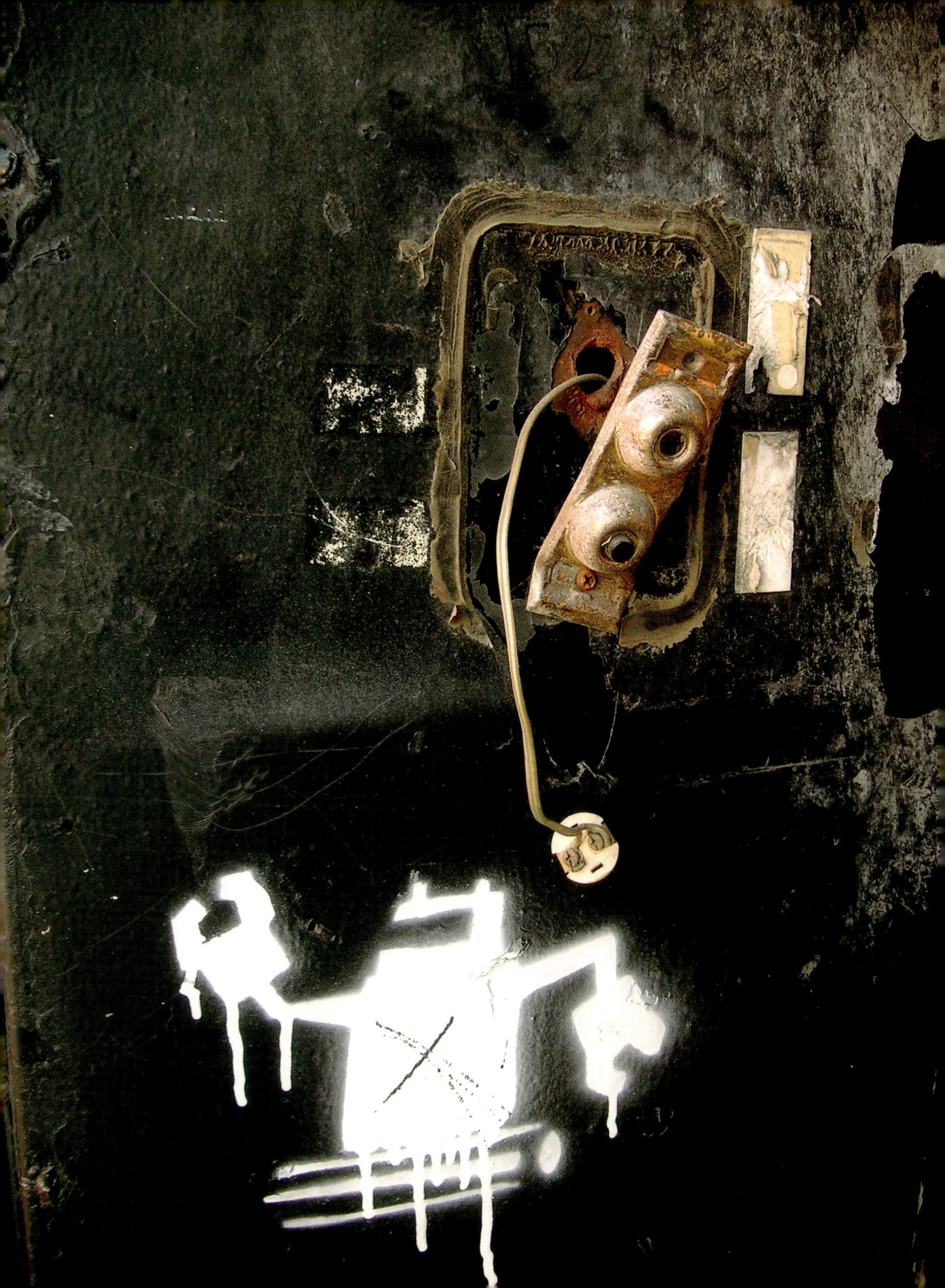

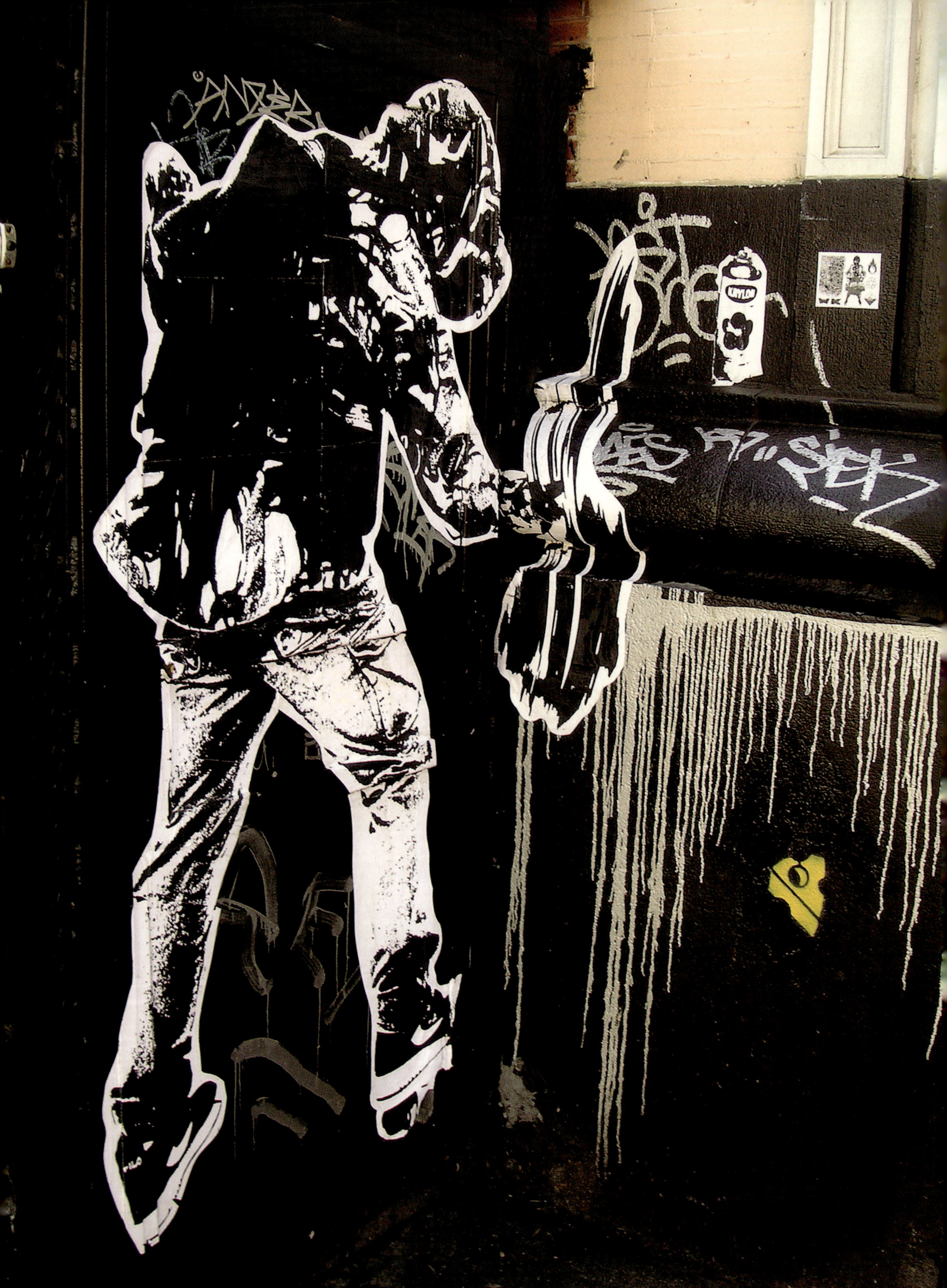

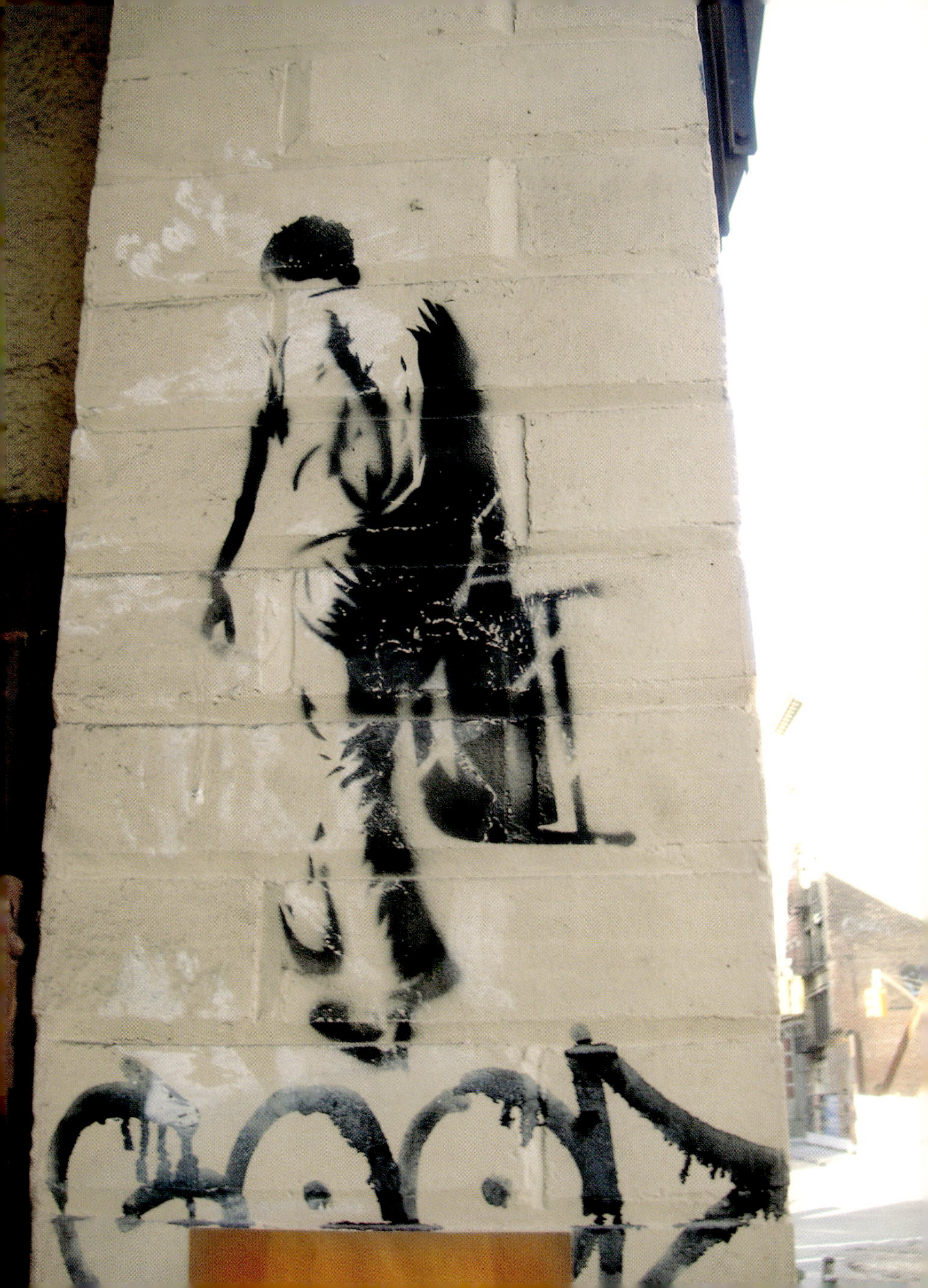

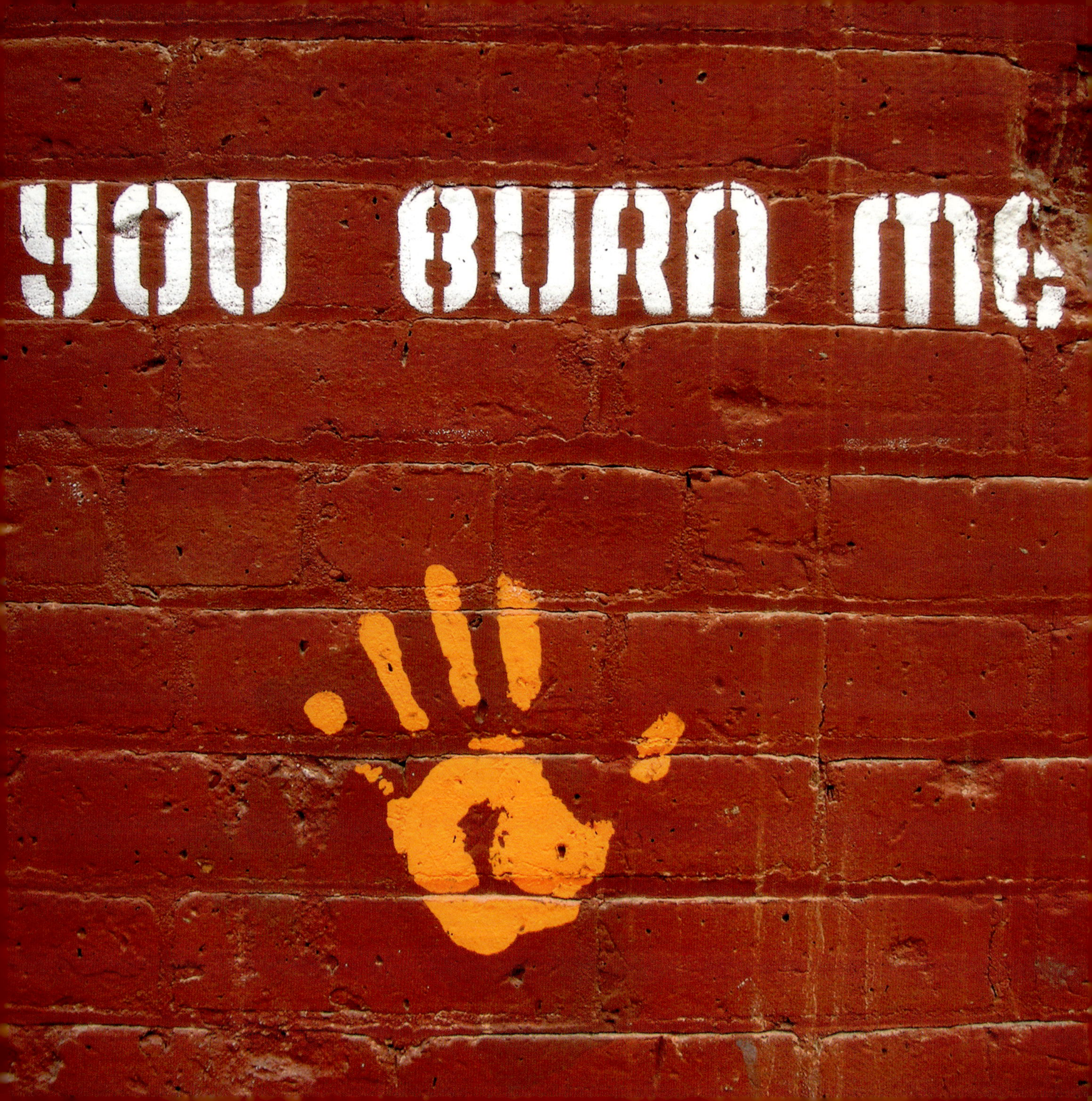
YOU BURN ME

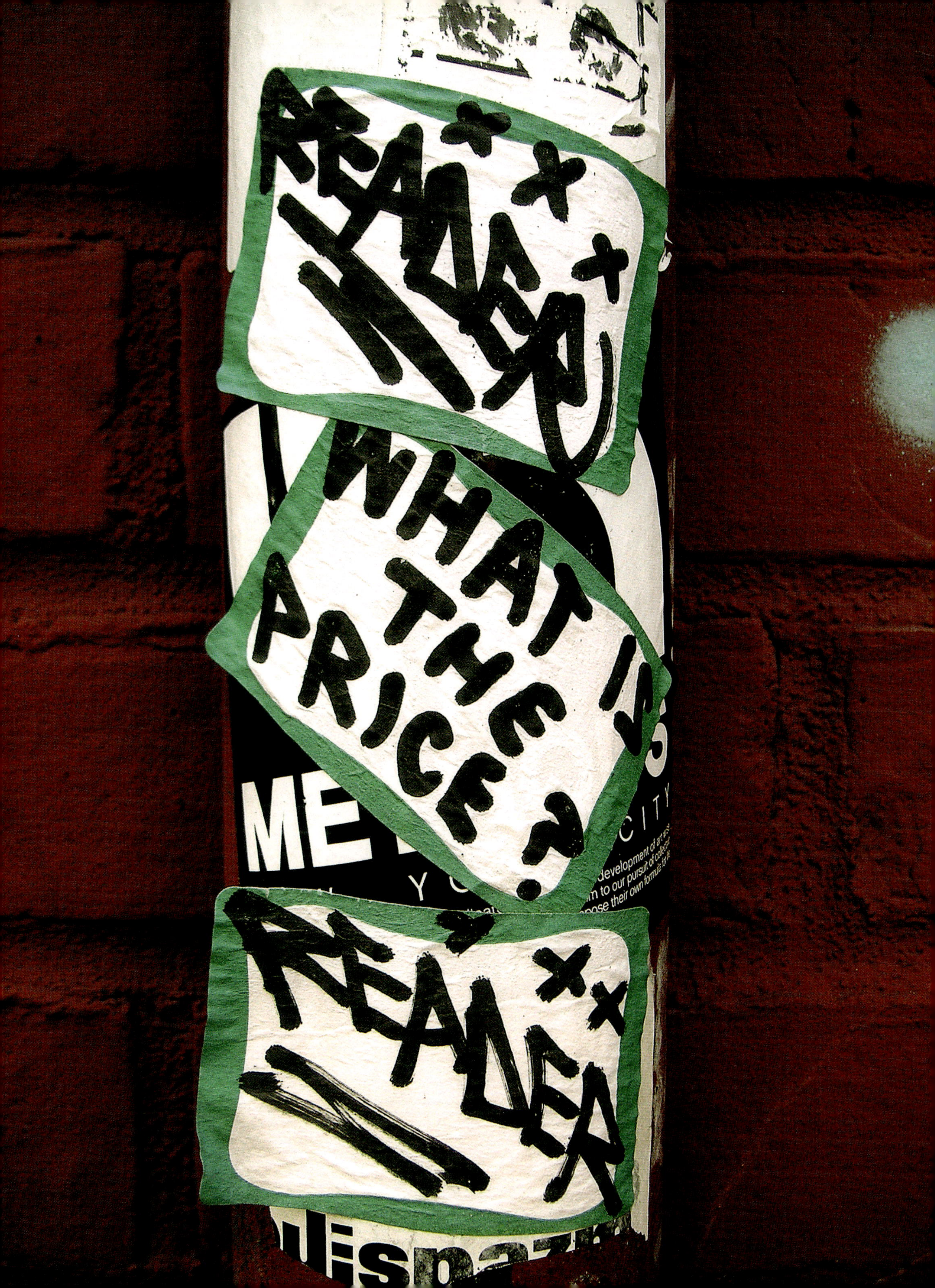
READER
WHAT IS THE PRICE?
READER

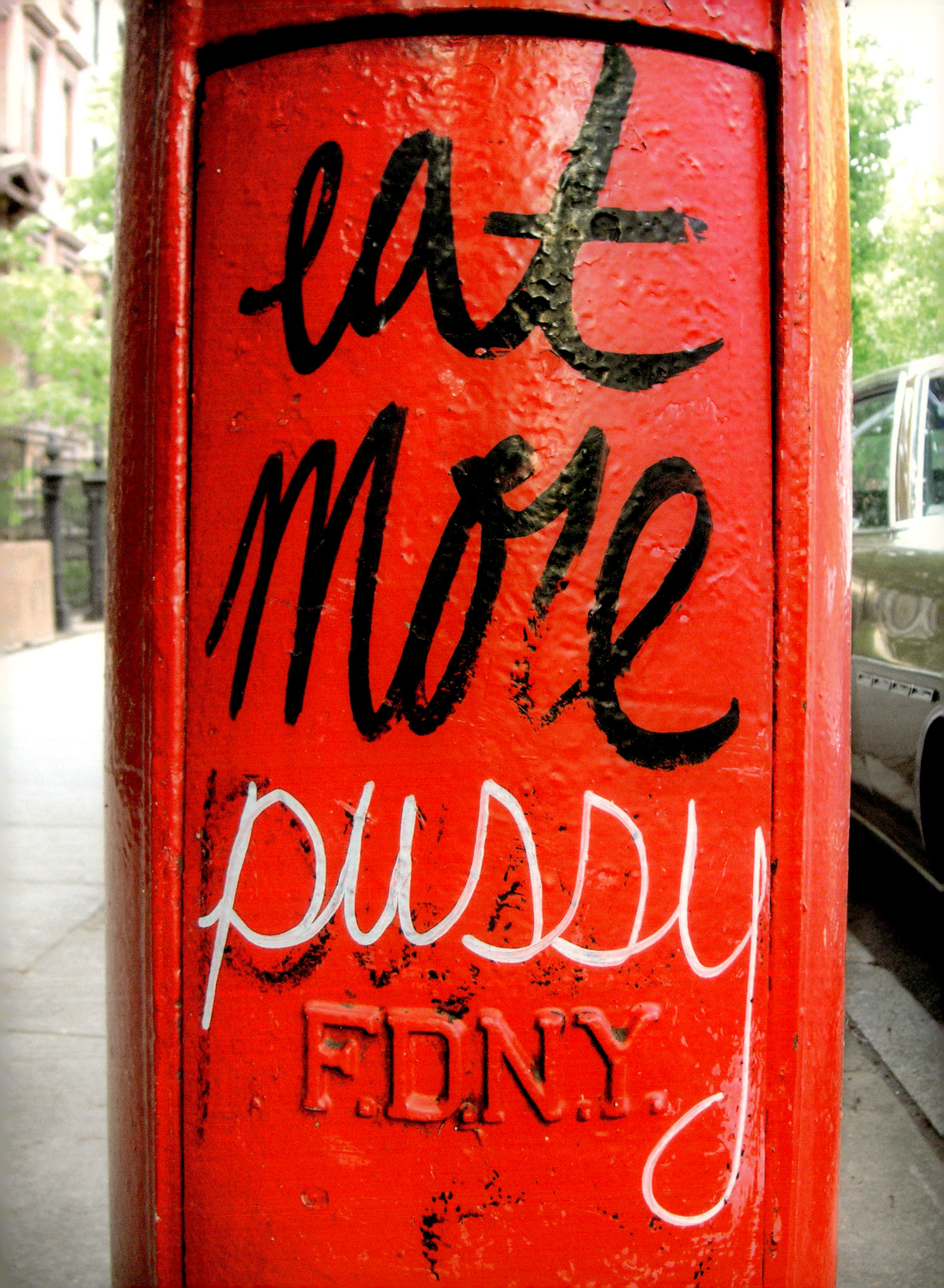
eat
more
pussy
F.D.N.Y.

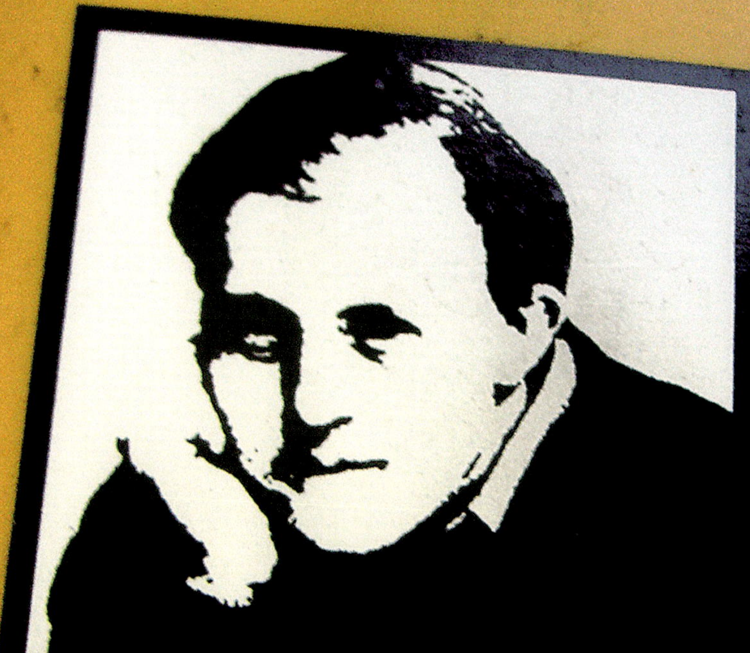
eating is
serious

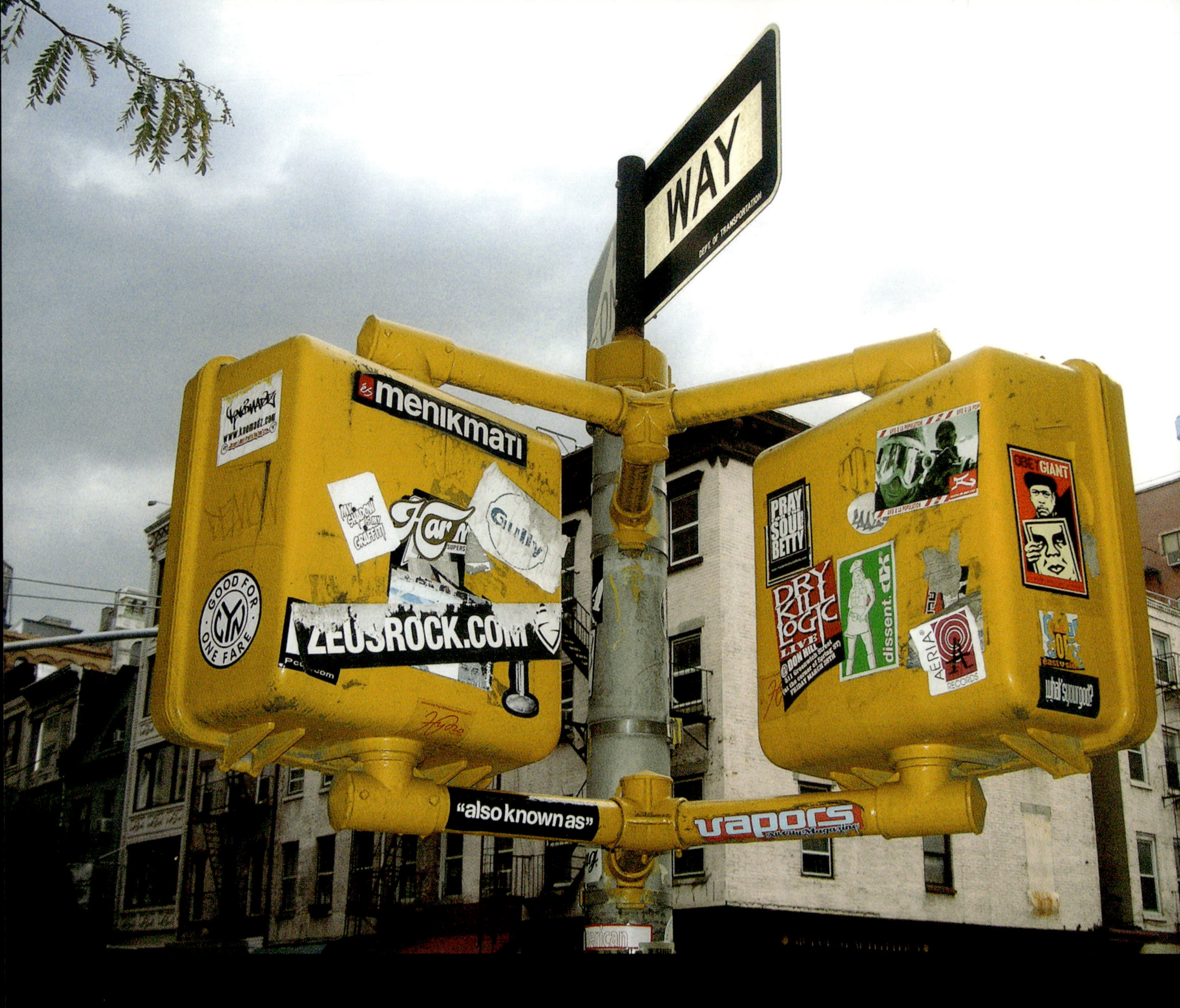
WAY
DEPT. OF TRANSPORTATION
menikmati
www.knomadz.com
ZEUSROCK.COM
GOOD FOR ONE FARE
CYN
PRAY FOR SOUL BETTY
DRY KILL LOGIC
LIVE
@ DON HILL
dissent.
OBEY GIANT
AERIA RECORDS
what'supgod?
"also known as"
vapors

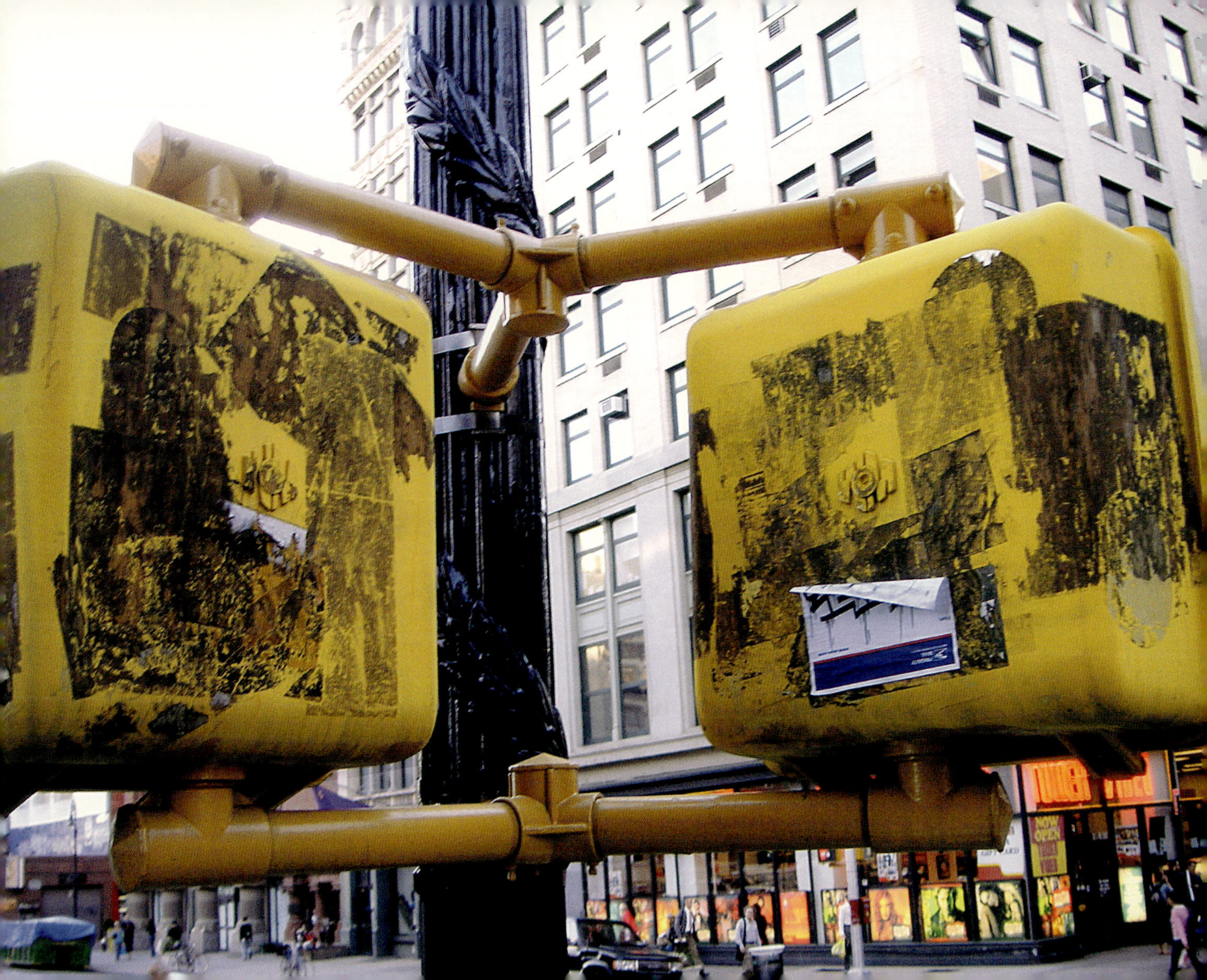

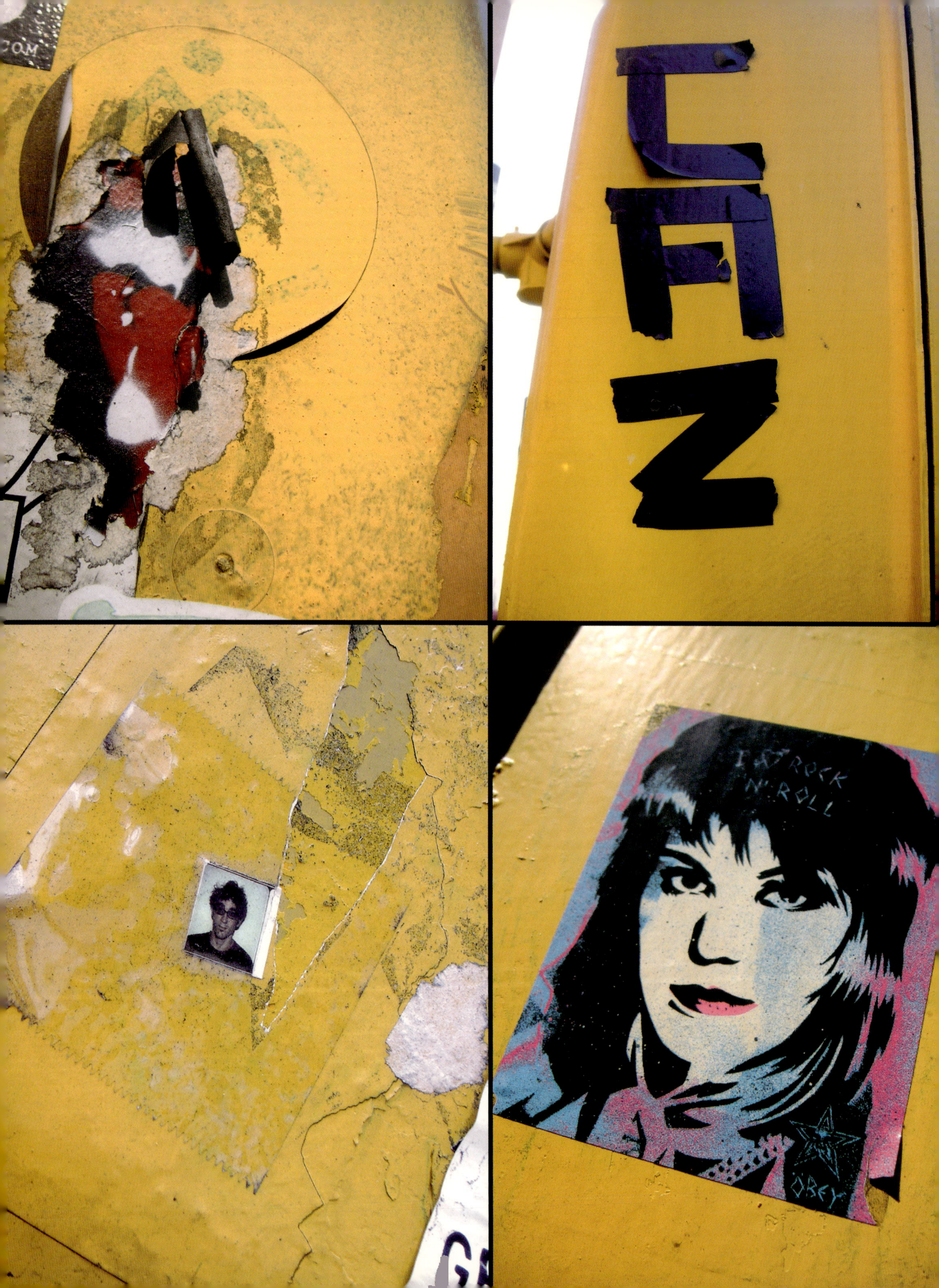
COM
CAZ
ROCK N' ROLL
OBEY

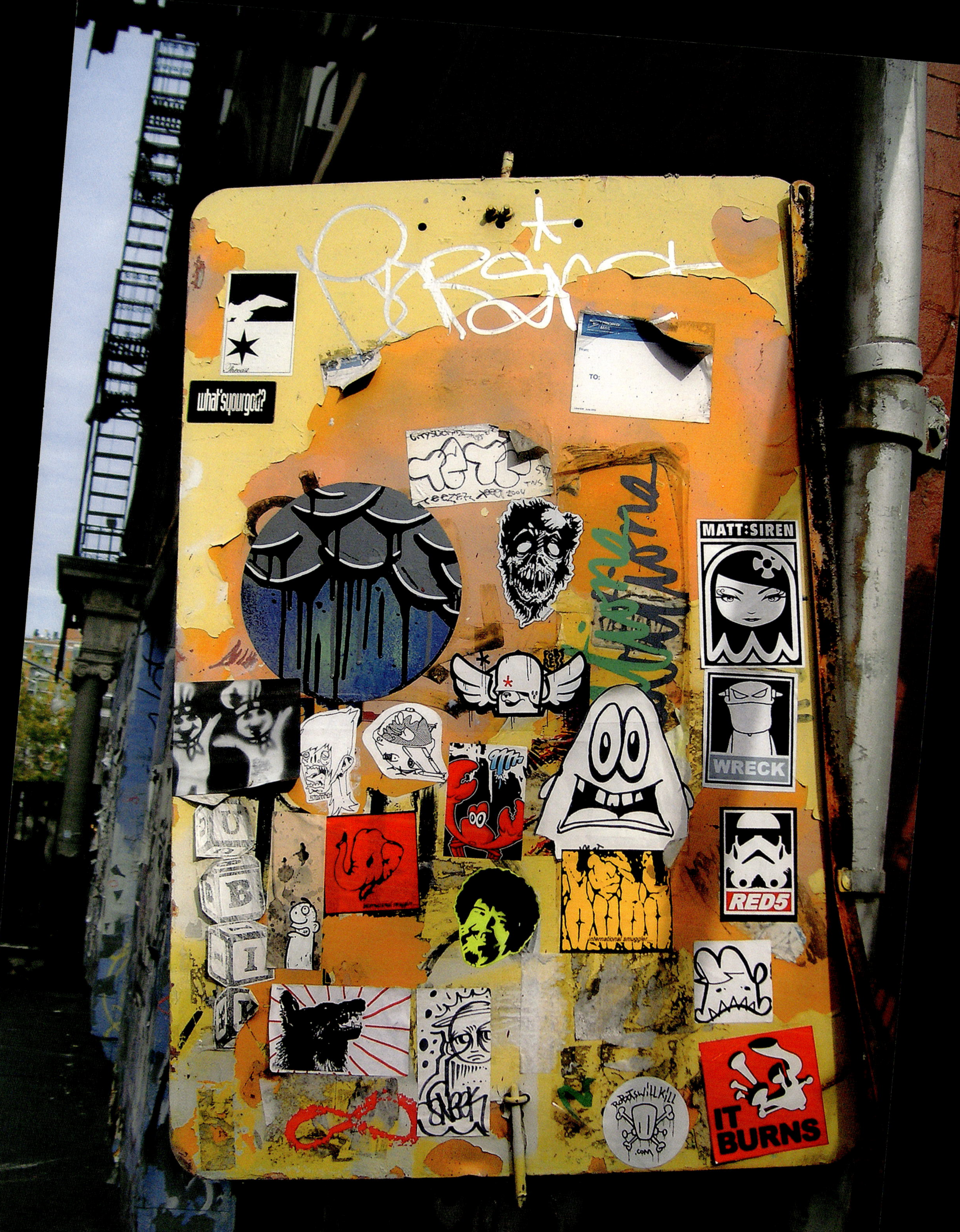
what'syourgod?
TO:
MATT:SIREN
WRECK
RED5
IT BURNS

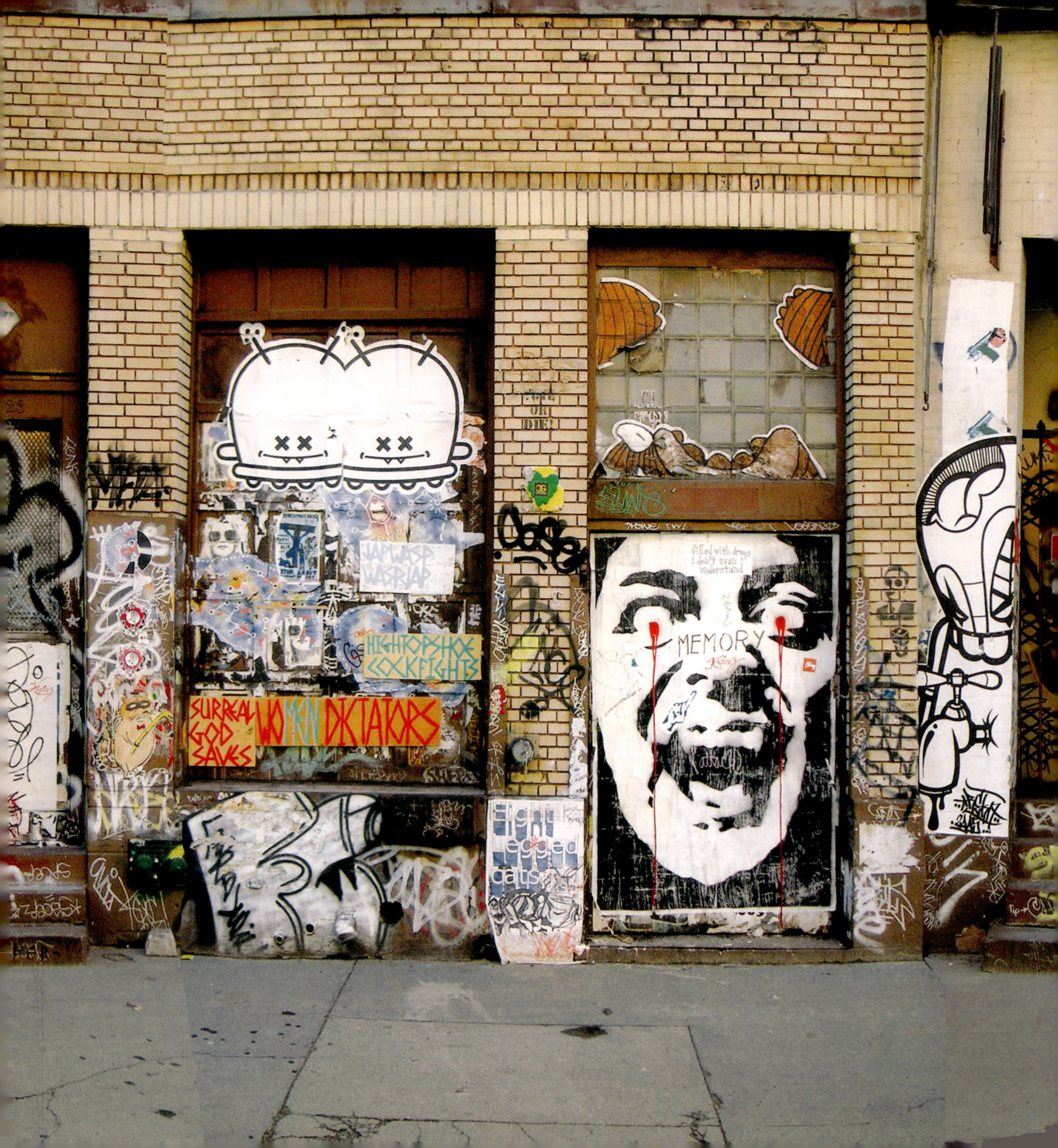
JAPWASP
WASPJAP
HIGHTOPSHOE
COCKFIGHTS
SURREAL
GOD
SAVES
WOMEN DICTATORS
filled with drugs
I don't even
understand
MEMORY
Eight
Legged
cats

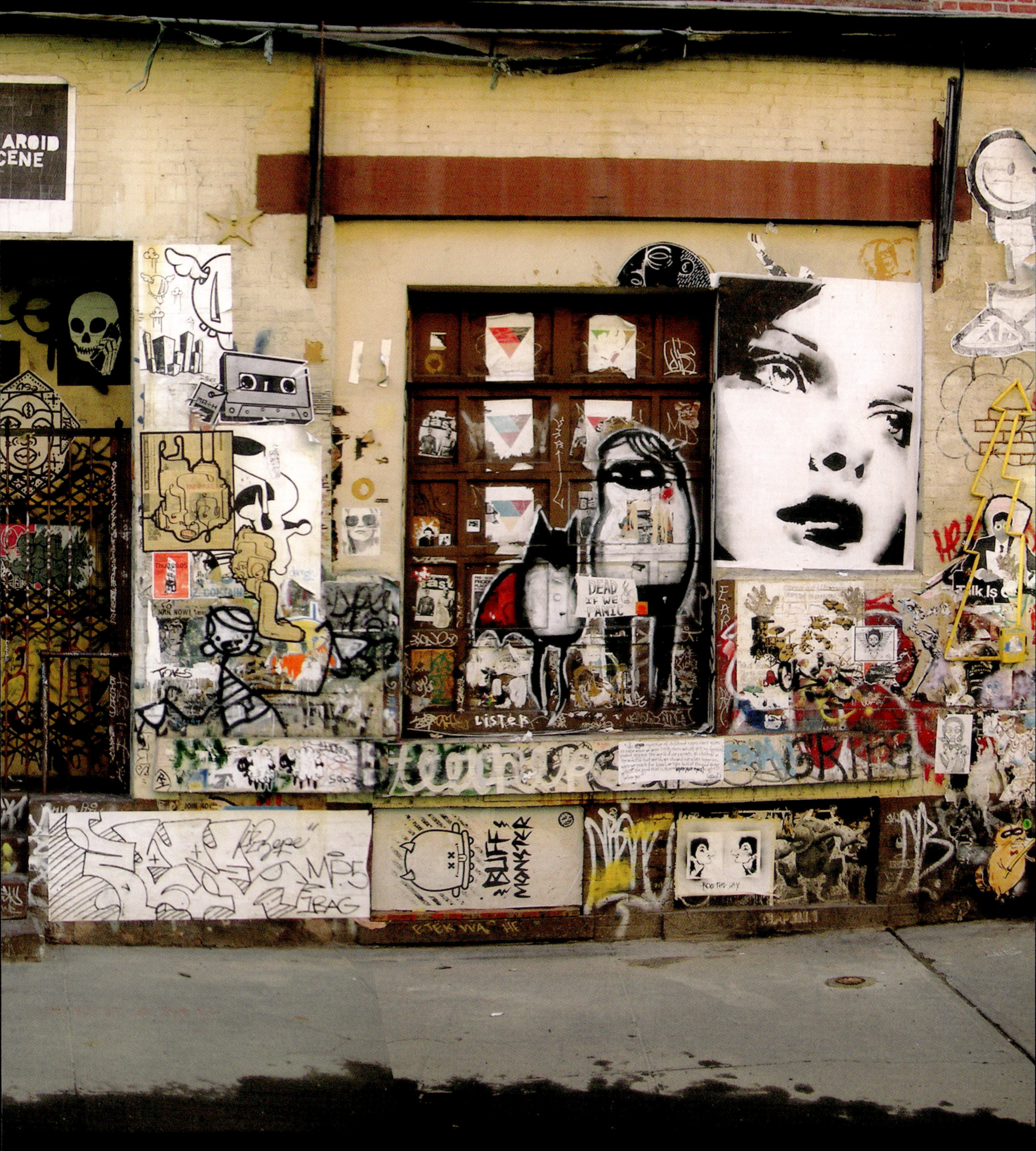
AROID
CENE
DEAD
IF WE
PANIC
LISTER
BUFF MONSTER
Talk Is

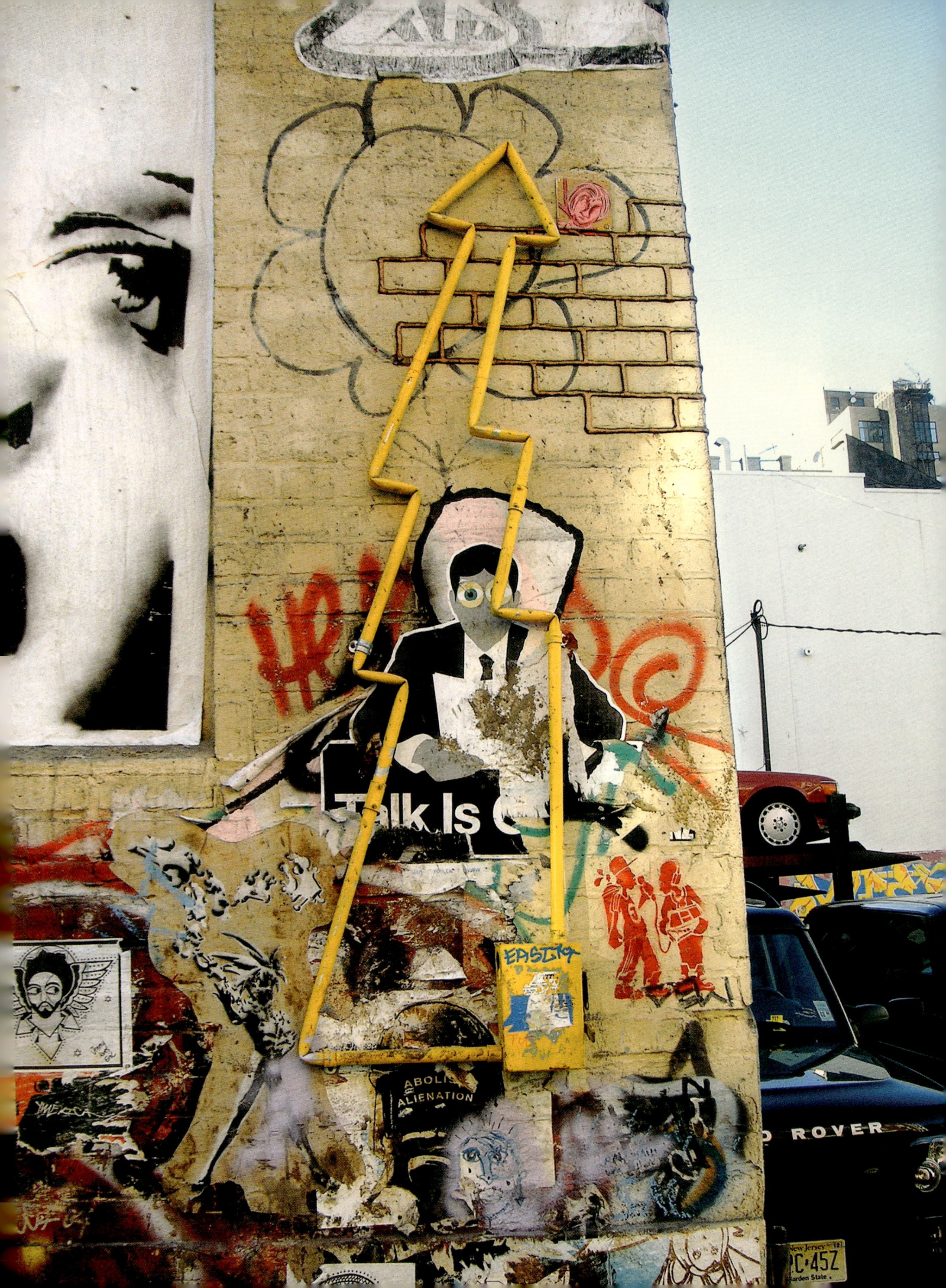
Talk Is C
ABOLISH
ALIENATION
ROVER

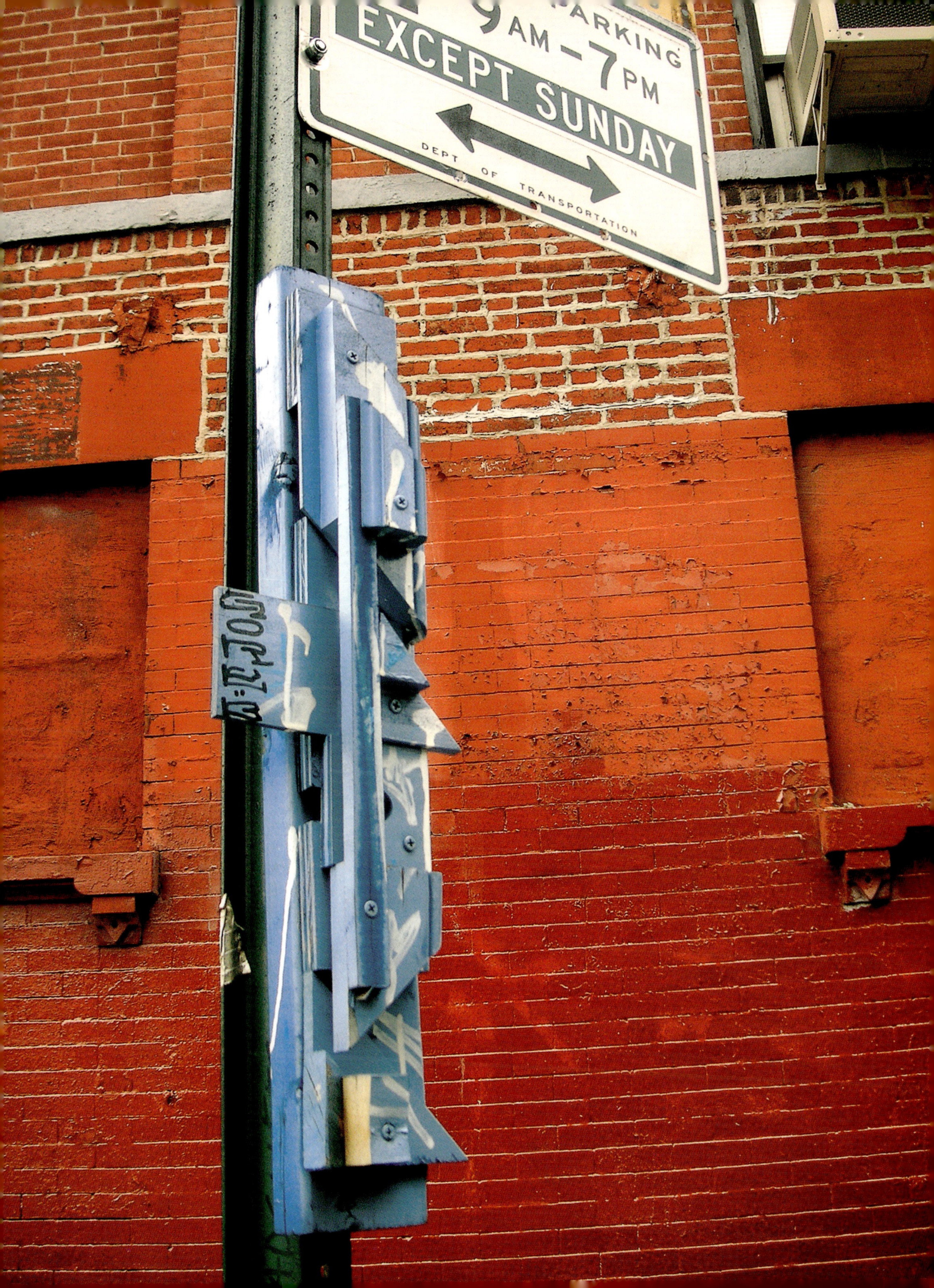
9AM–7PM
EXCEPT SUNDAY
DEPT OF TRANSPORTATION

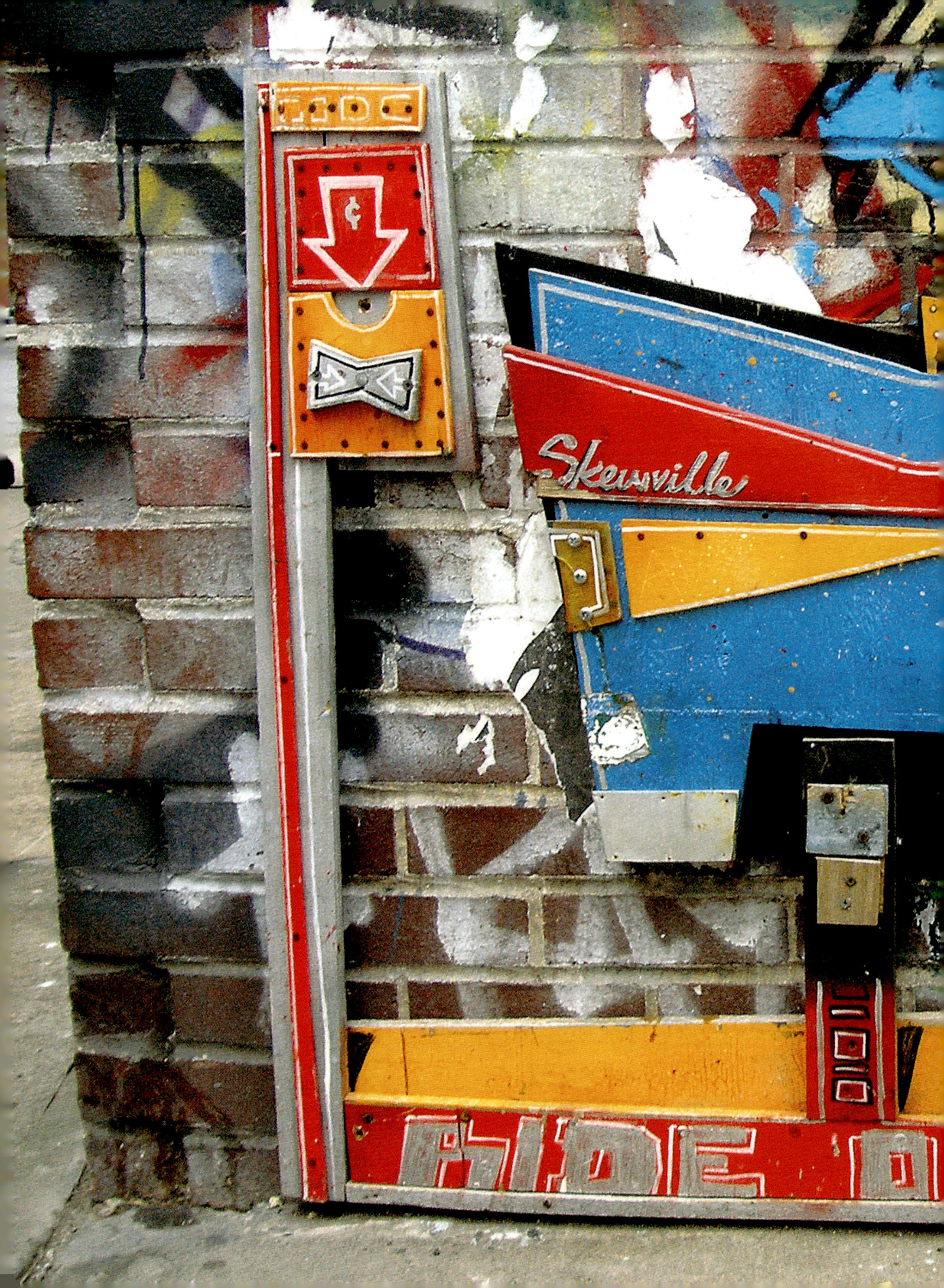
Skewville

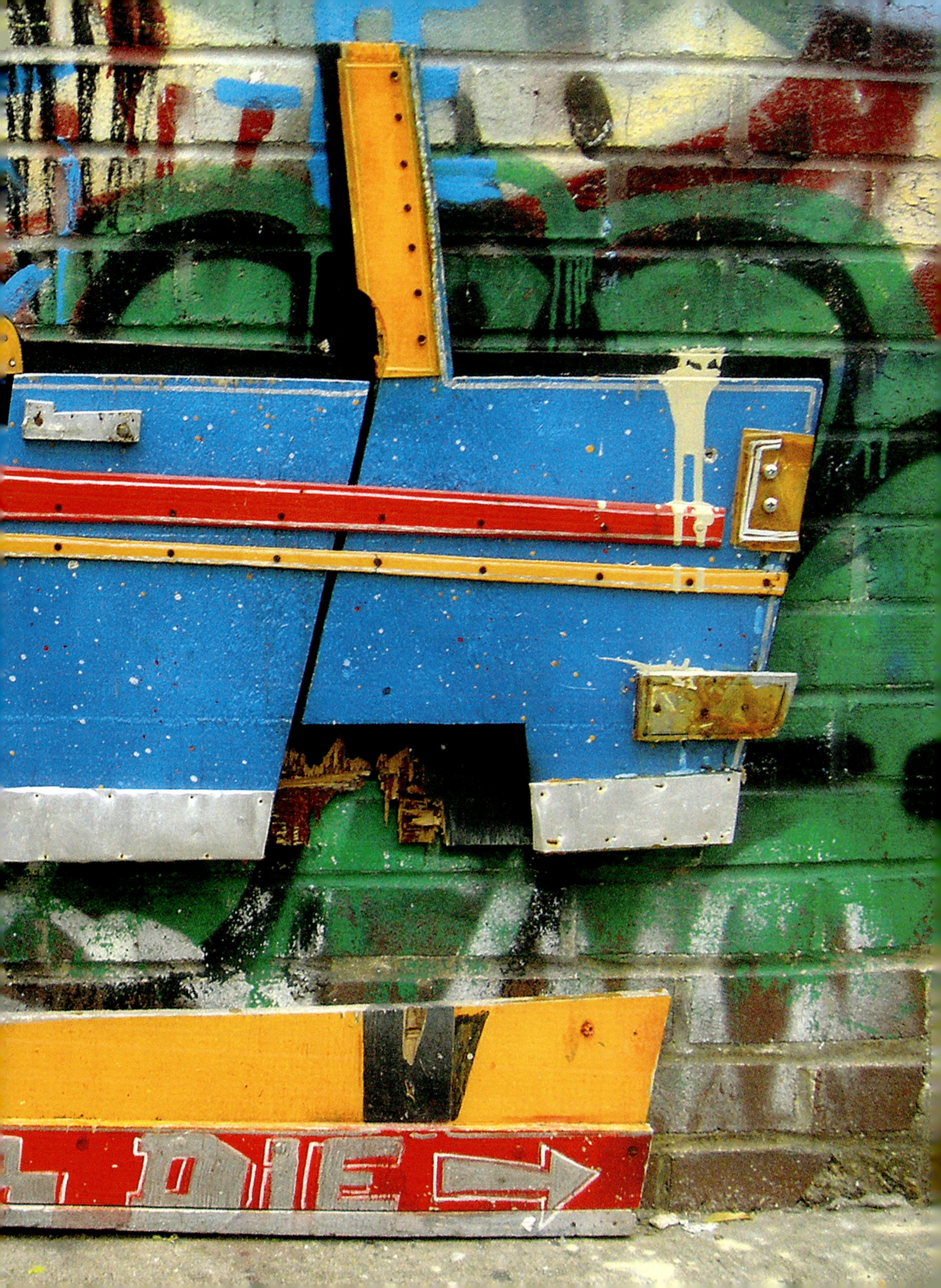

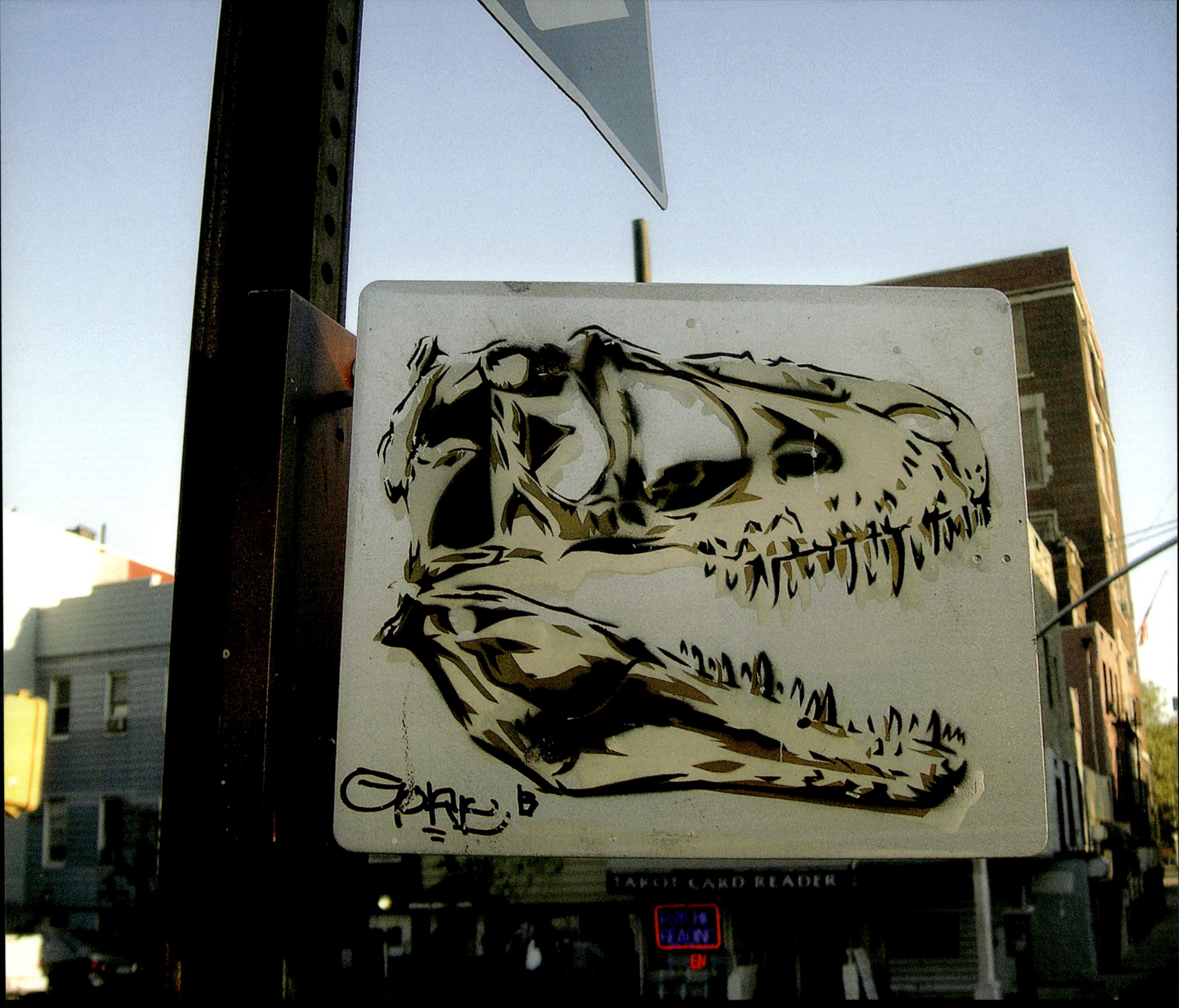
TAROT CARD READER

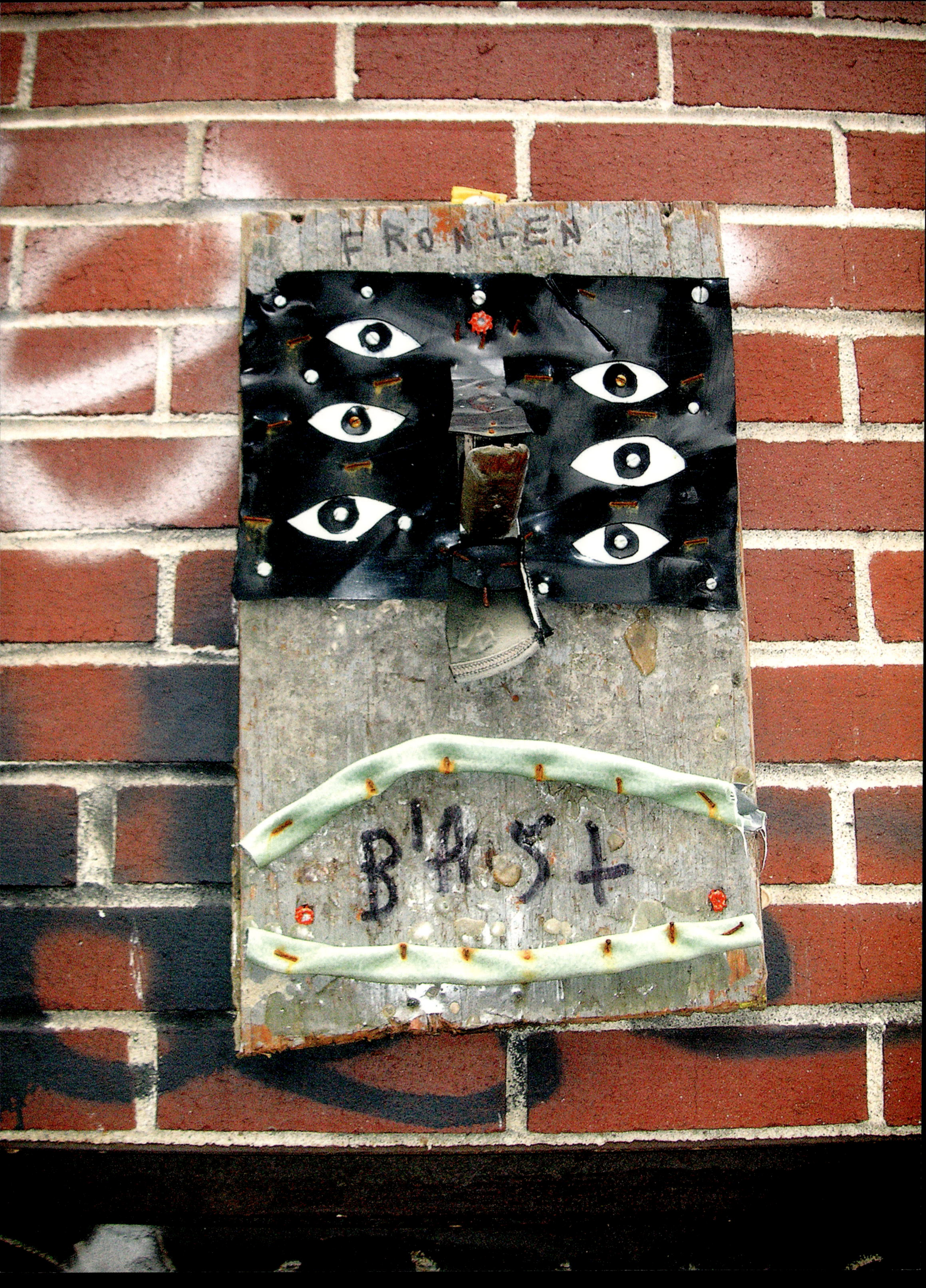
FRONTEN
B'AST

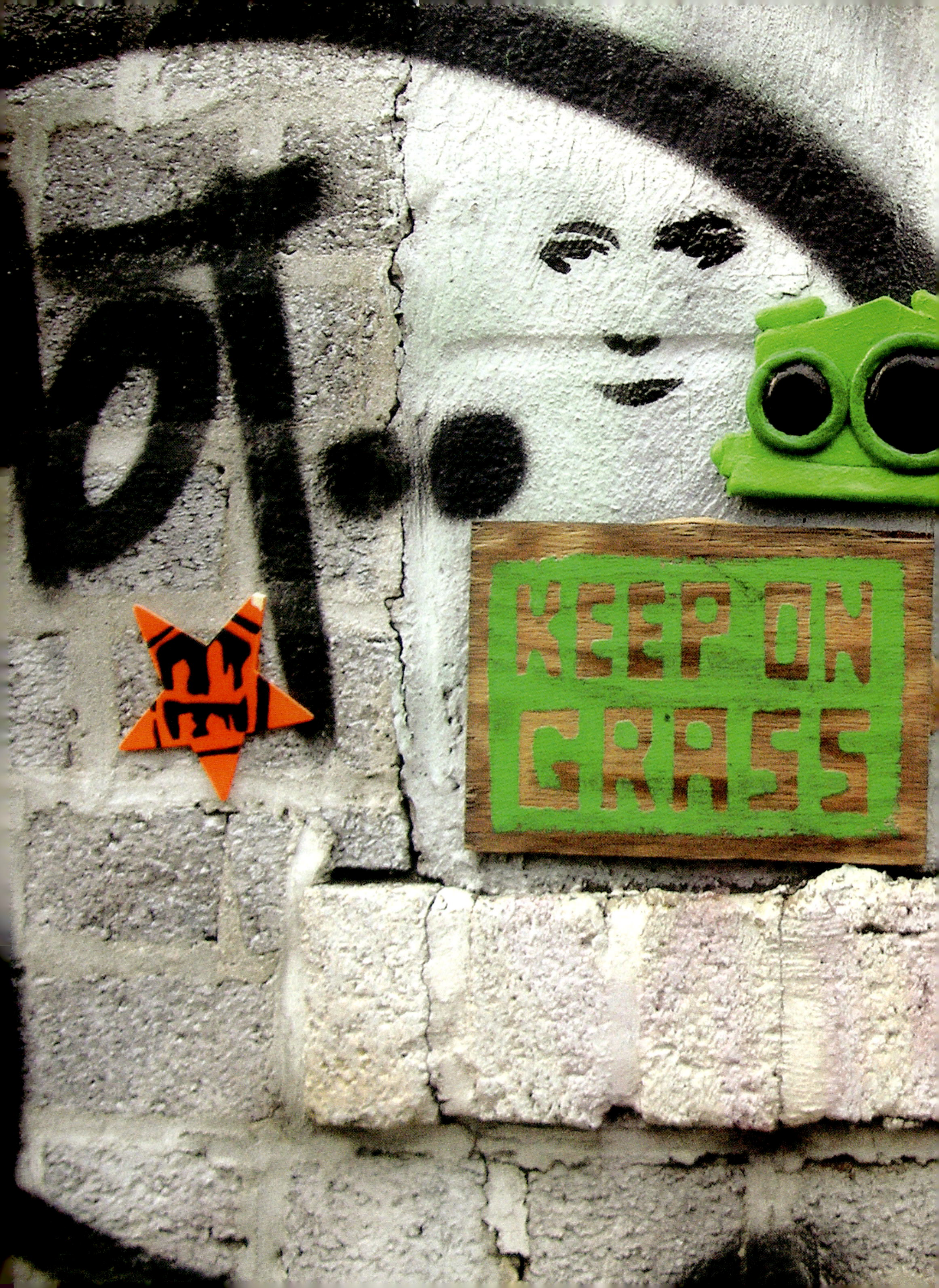

KEEP ON
GRASS

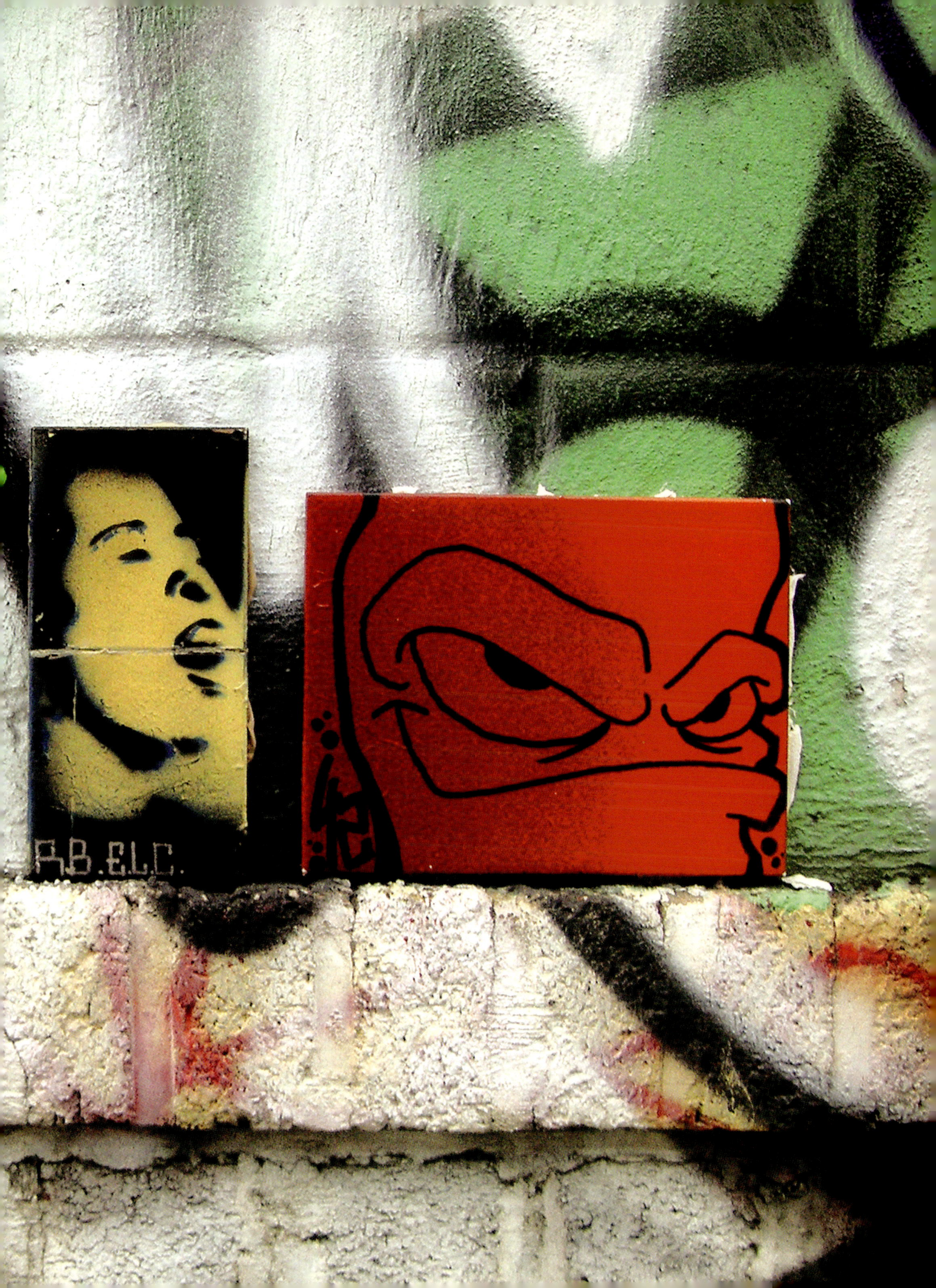
R.B.E.L.C.

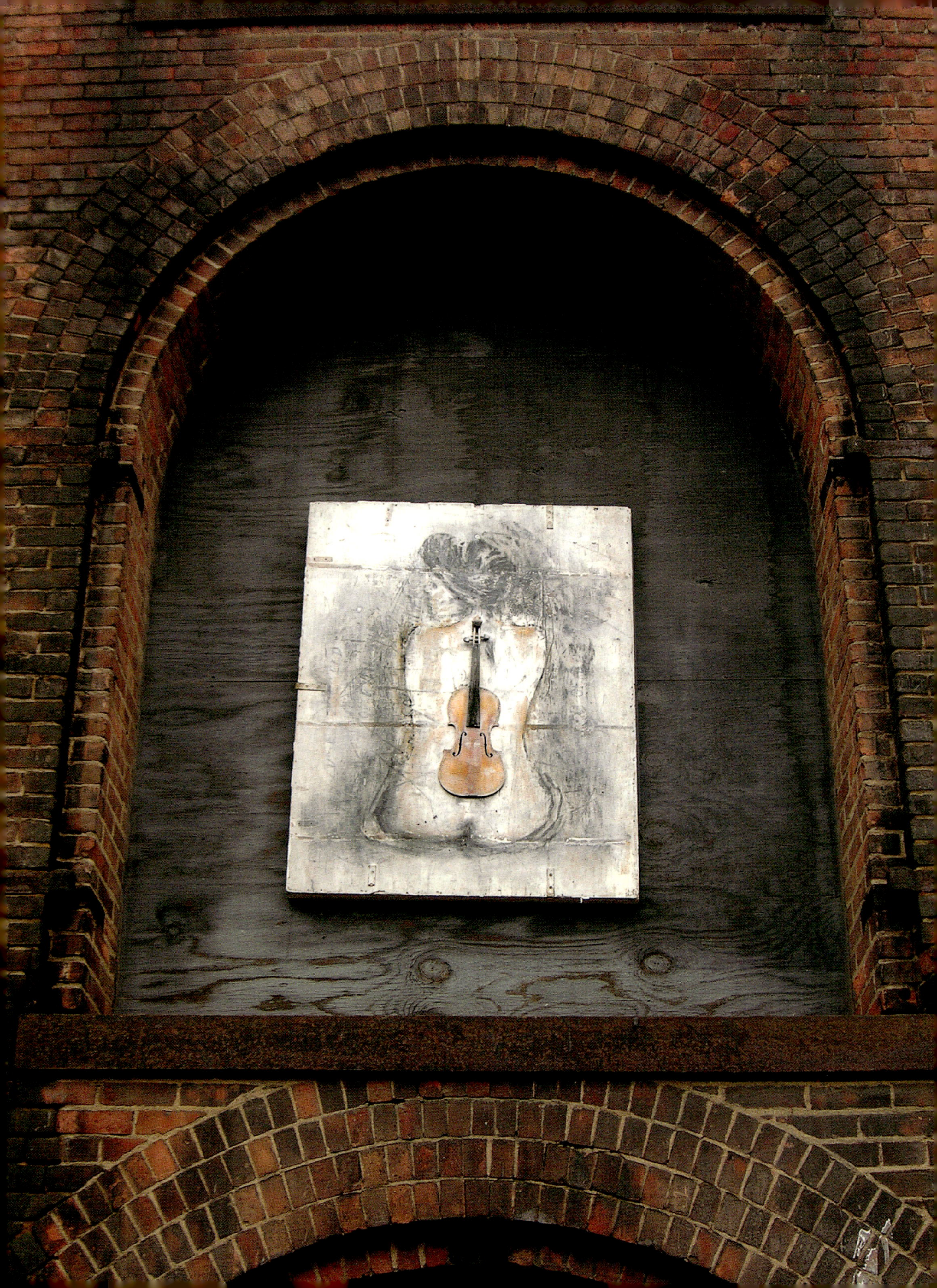

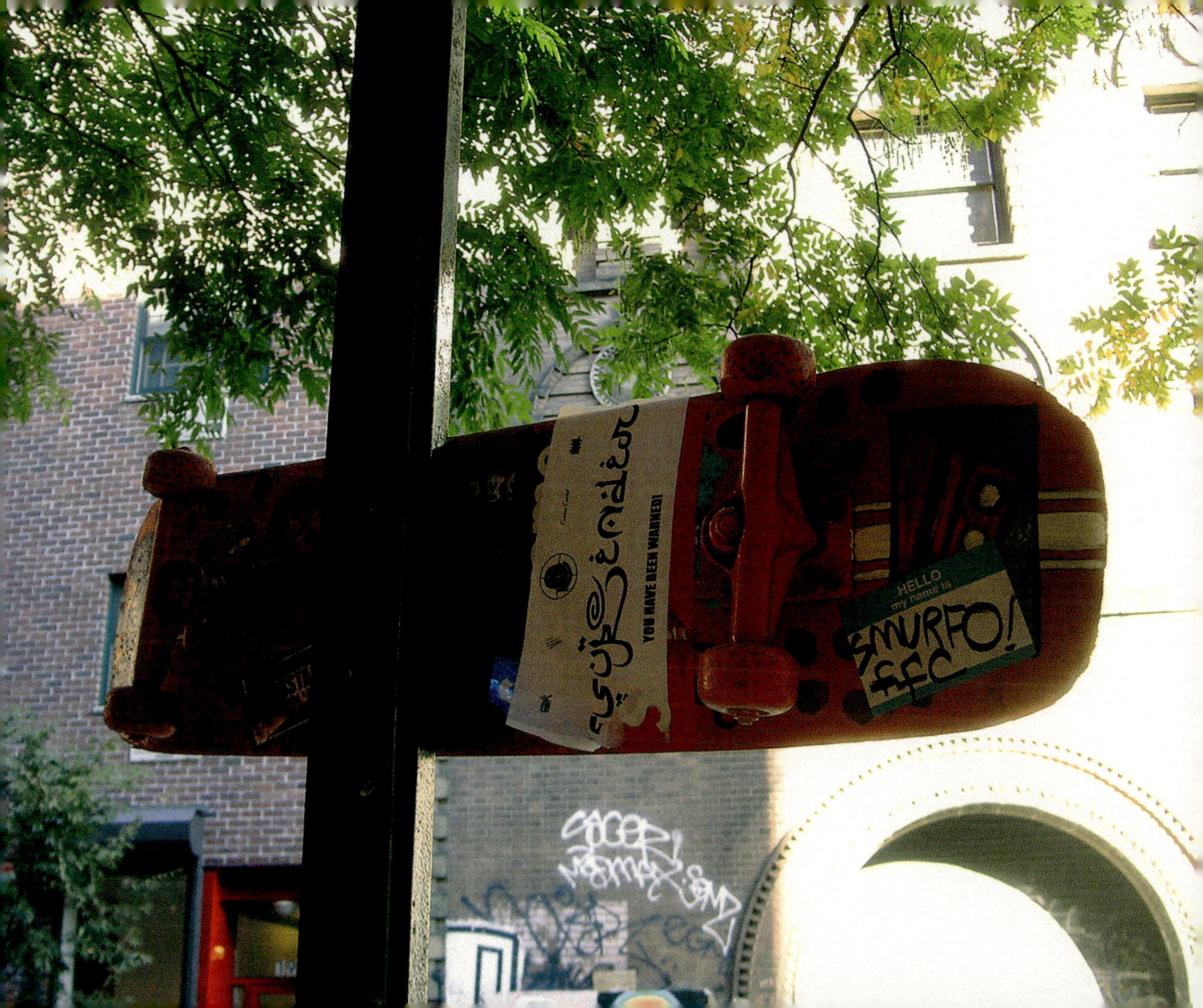
YOU HAVE BEEN WARNED!
HELLO
my name is
SMURFO!
FFC

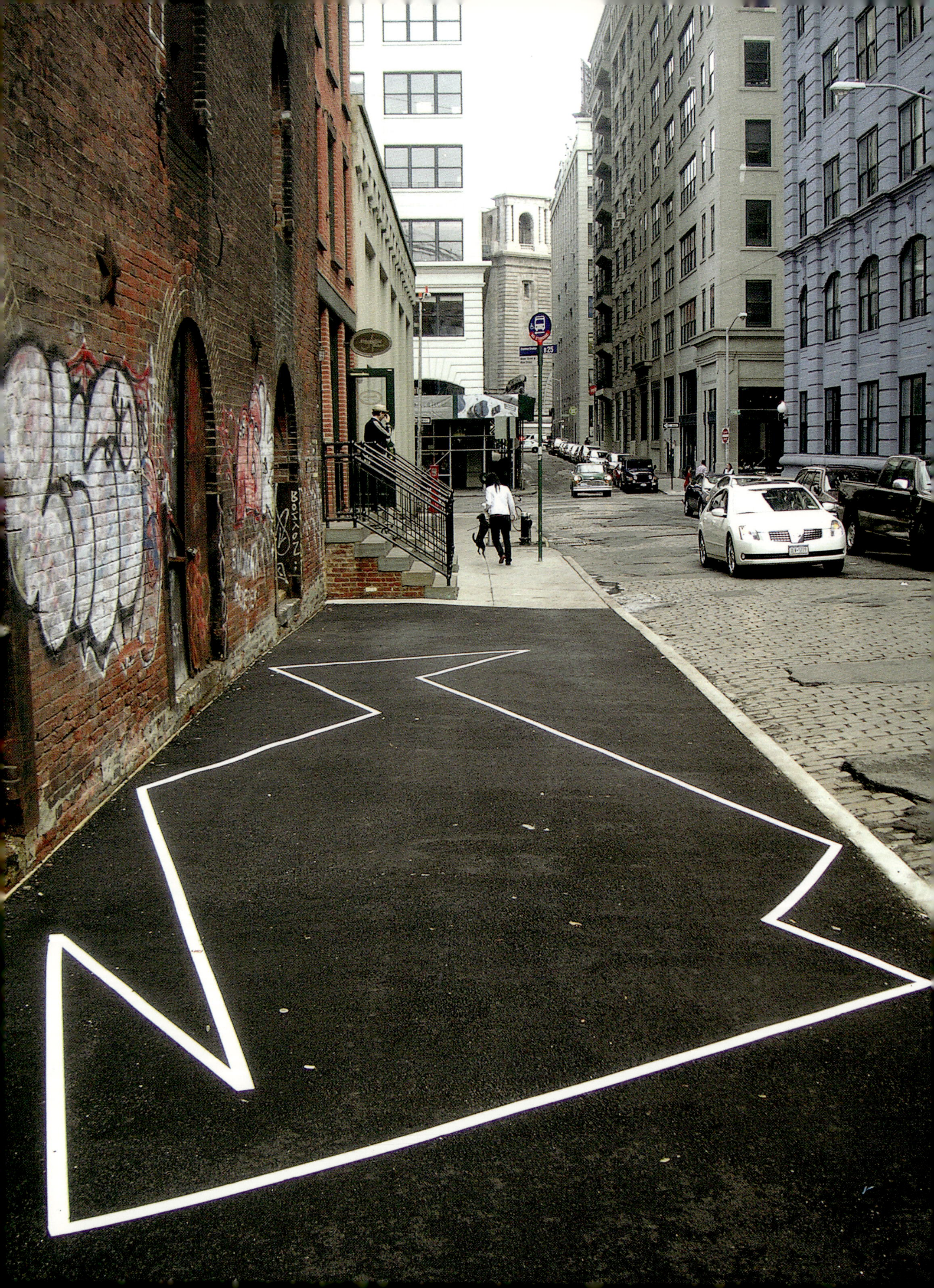

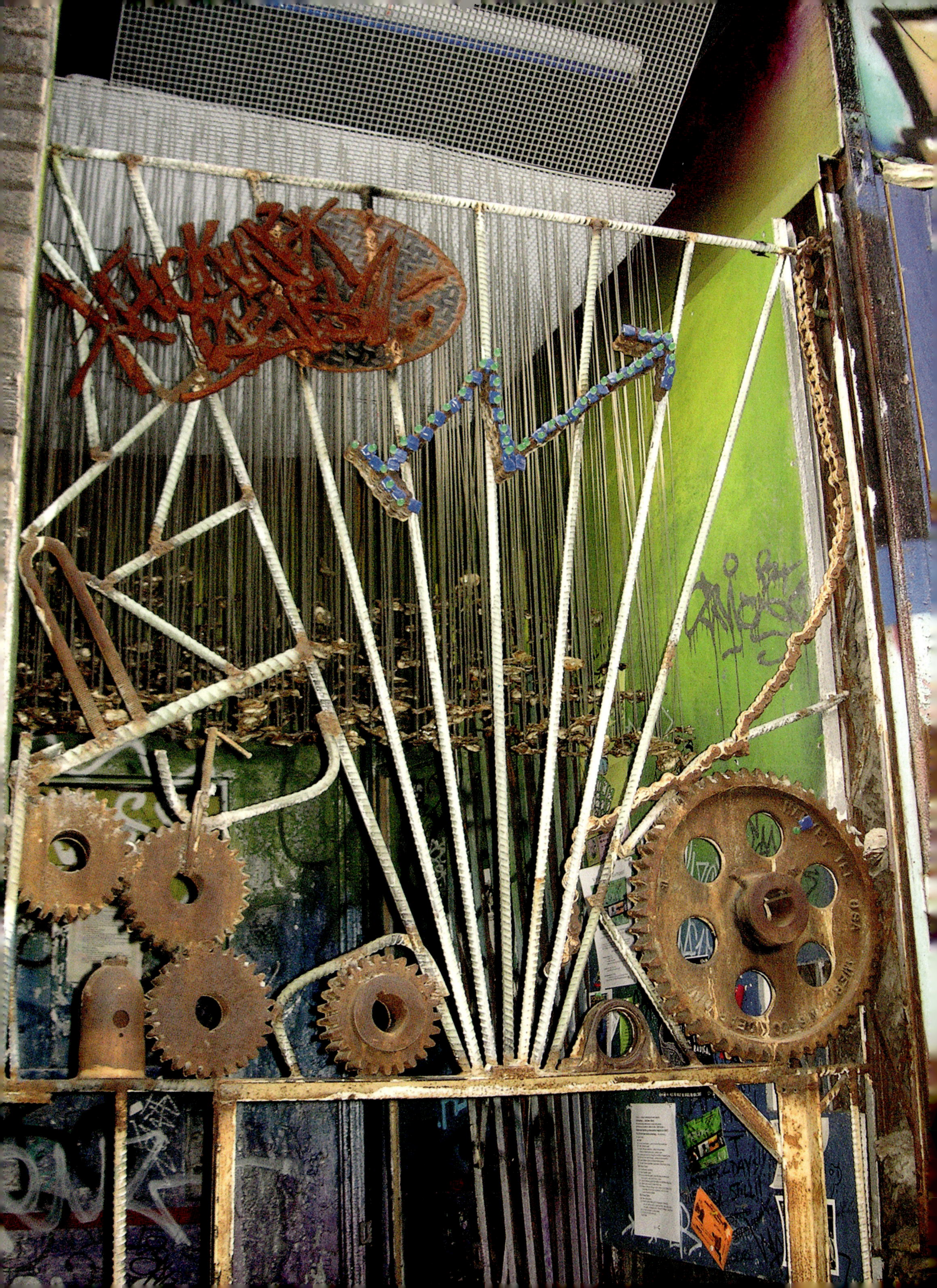

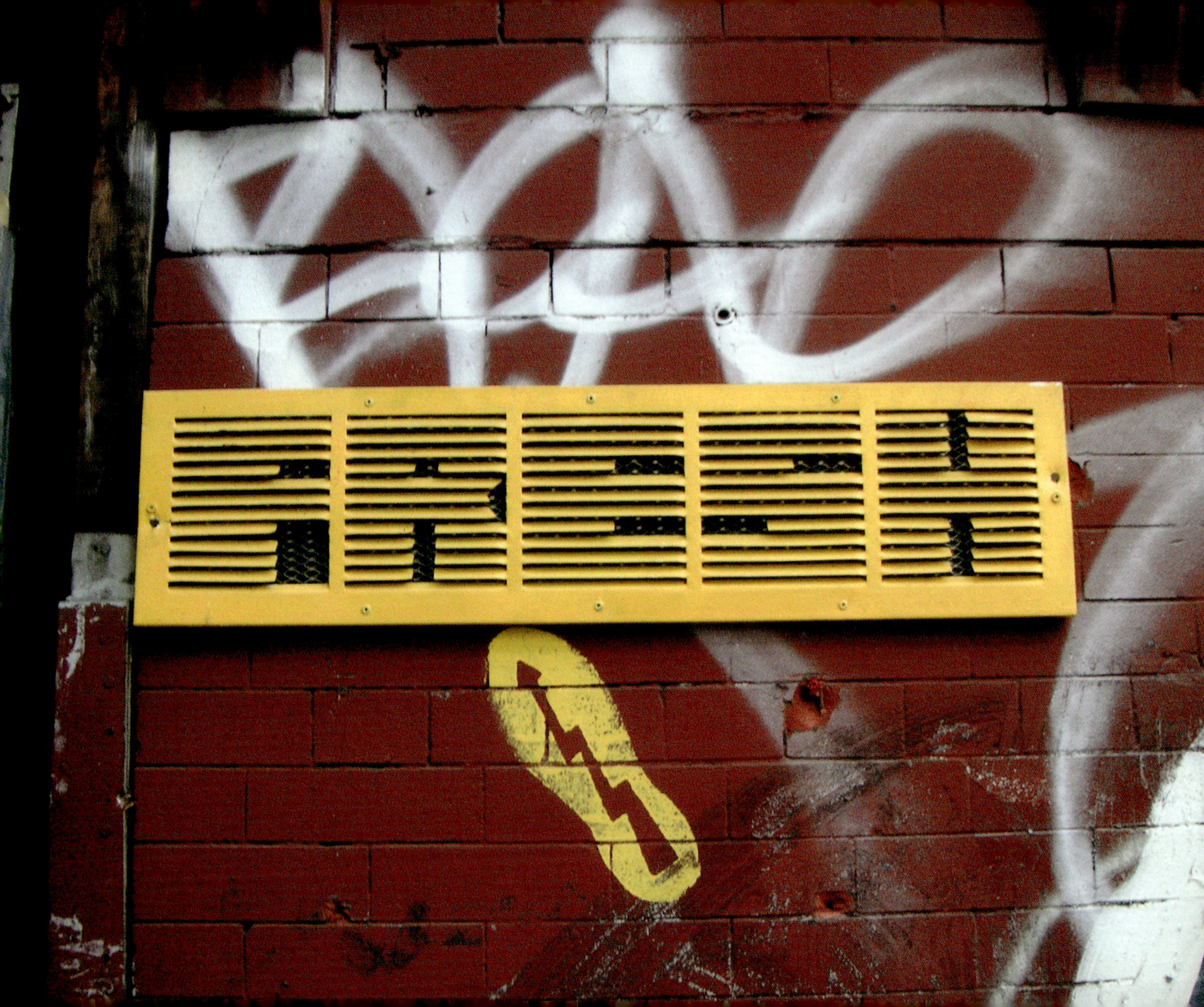

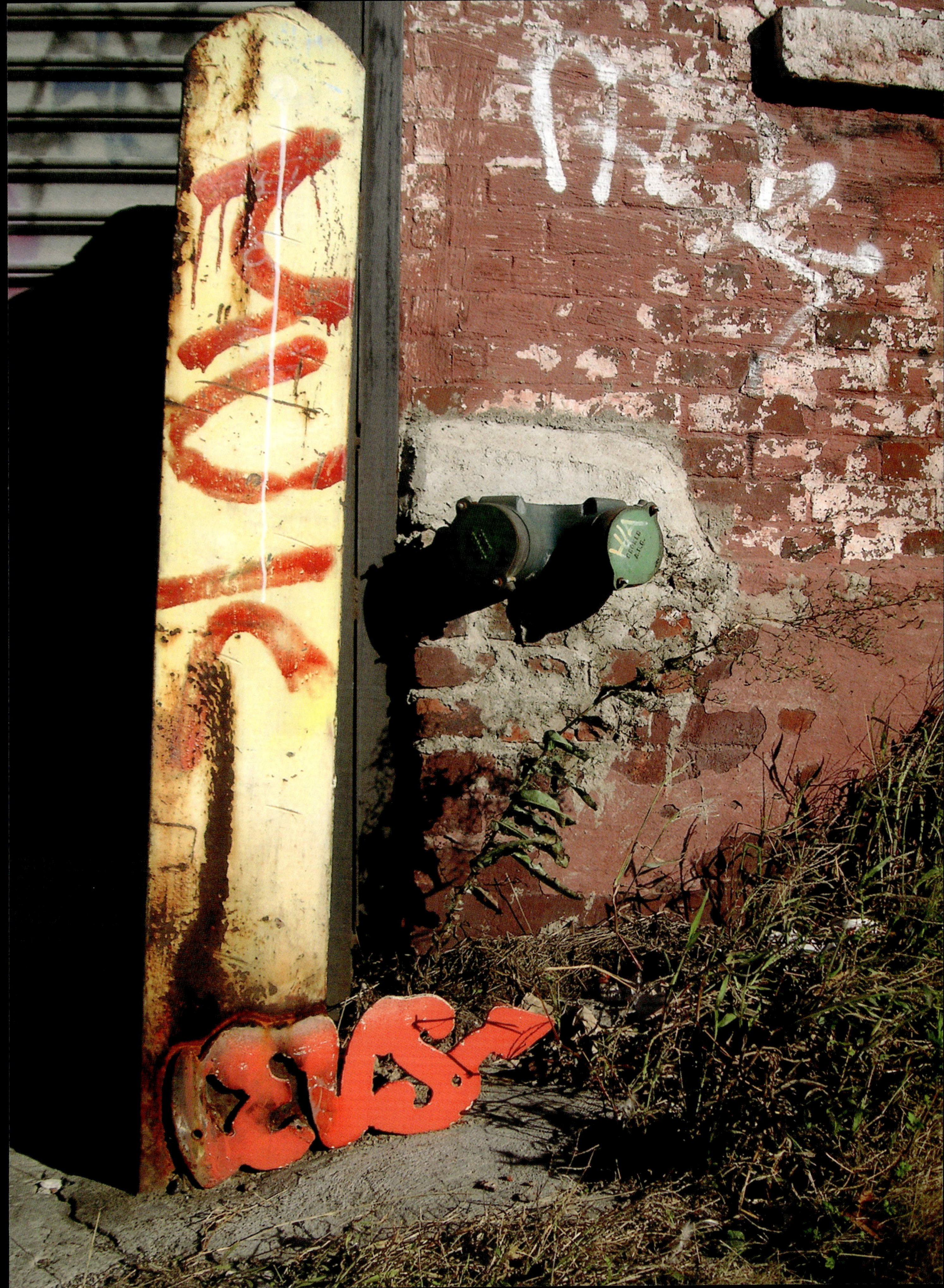

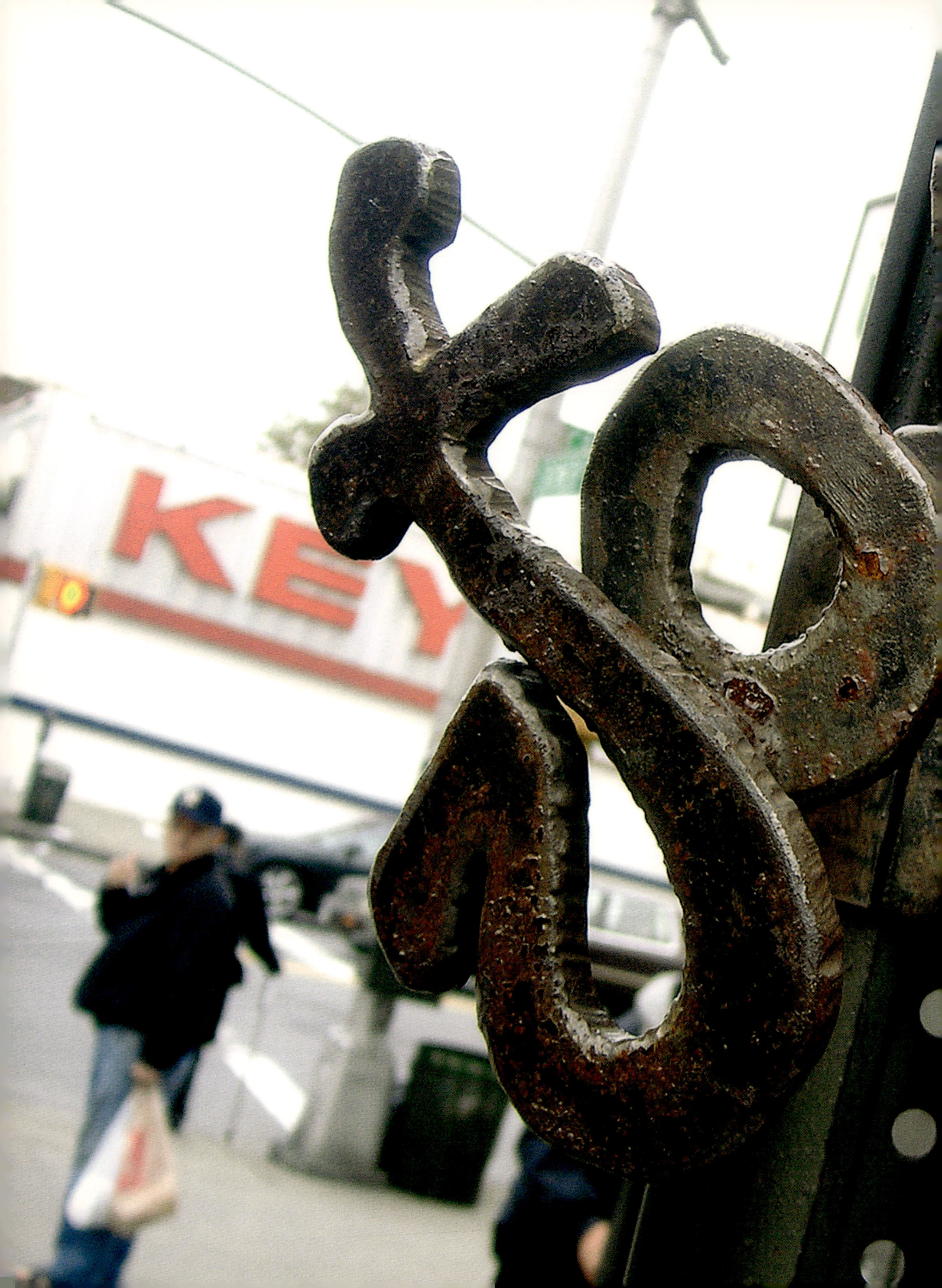
KEY

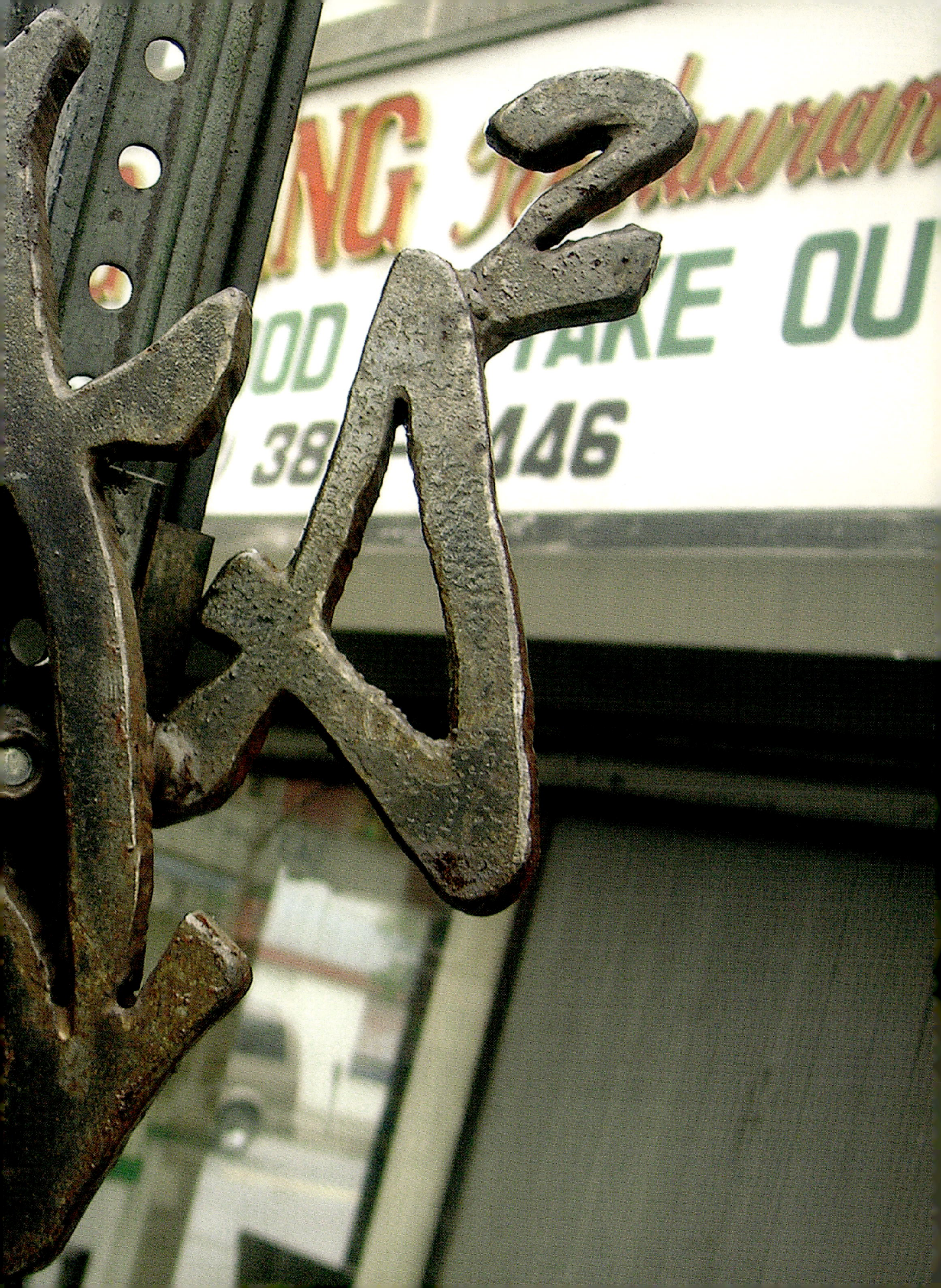
NG
OOD
AKE OU
38
446

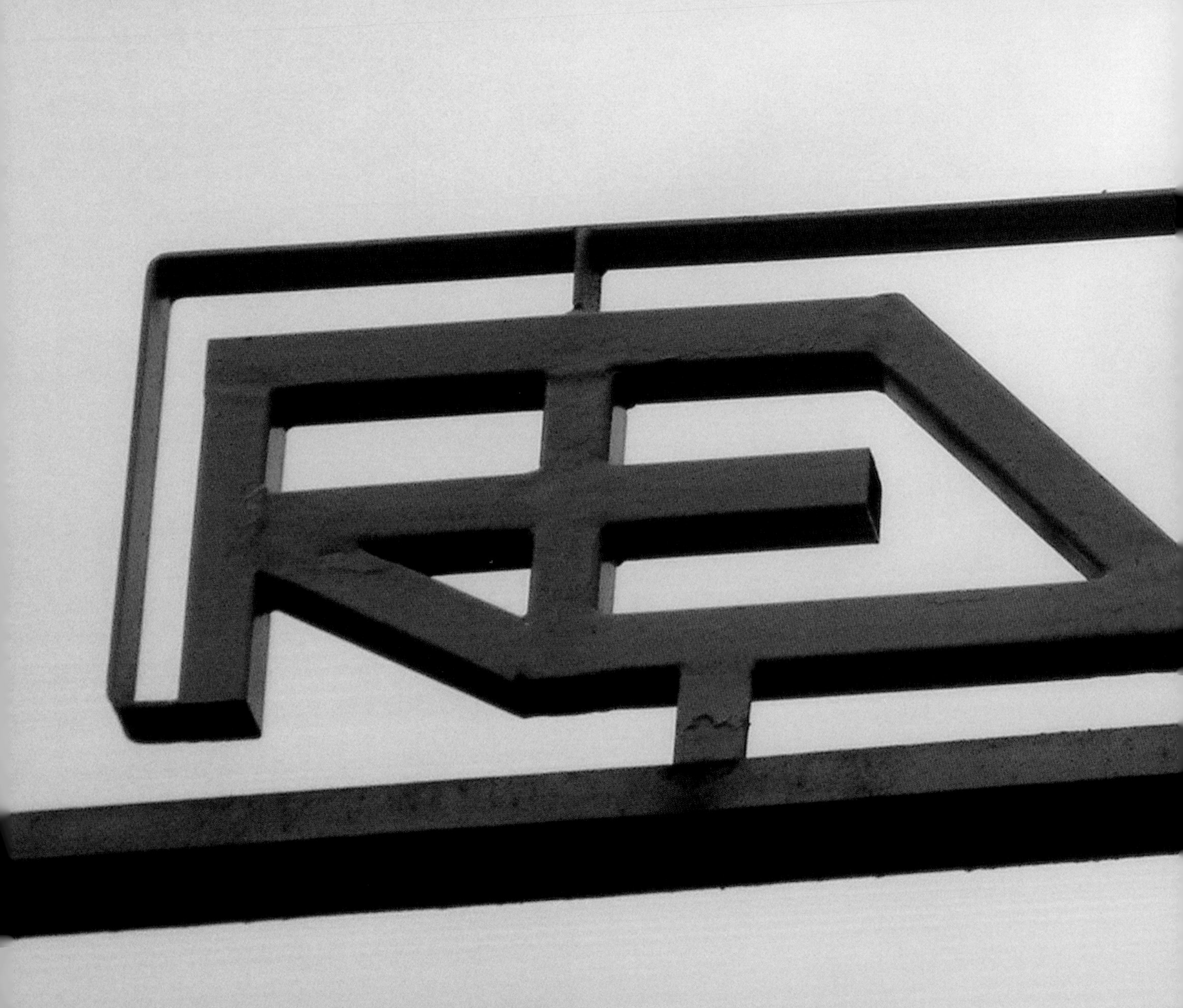

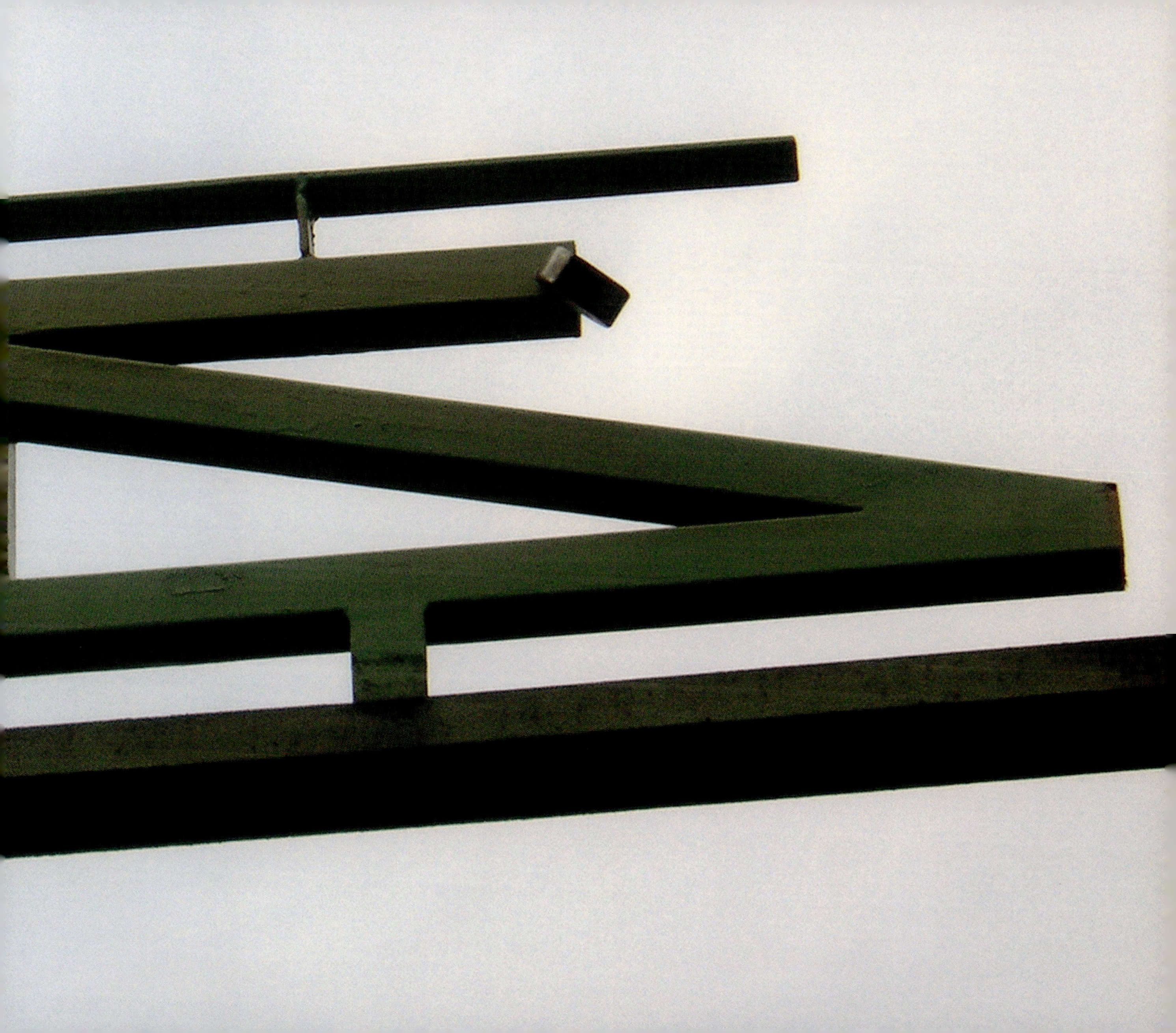

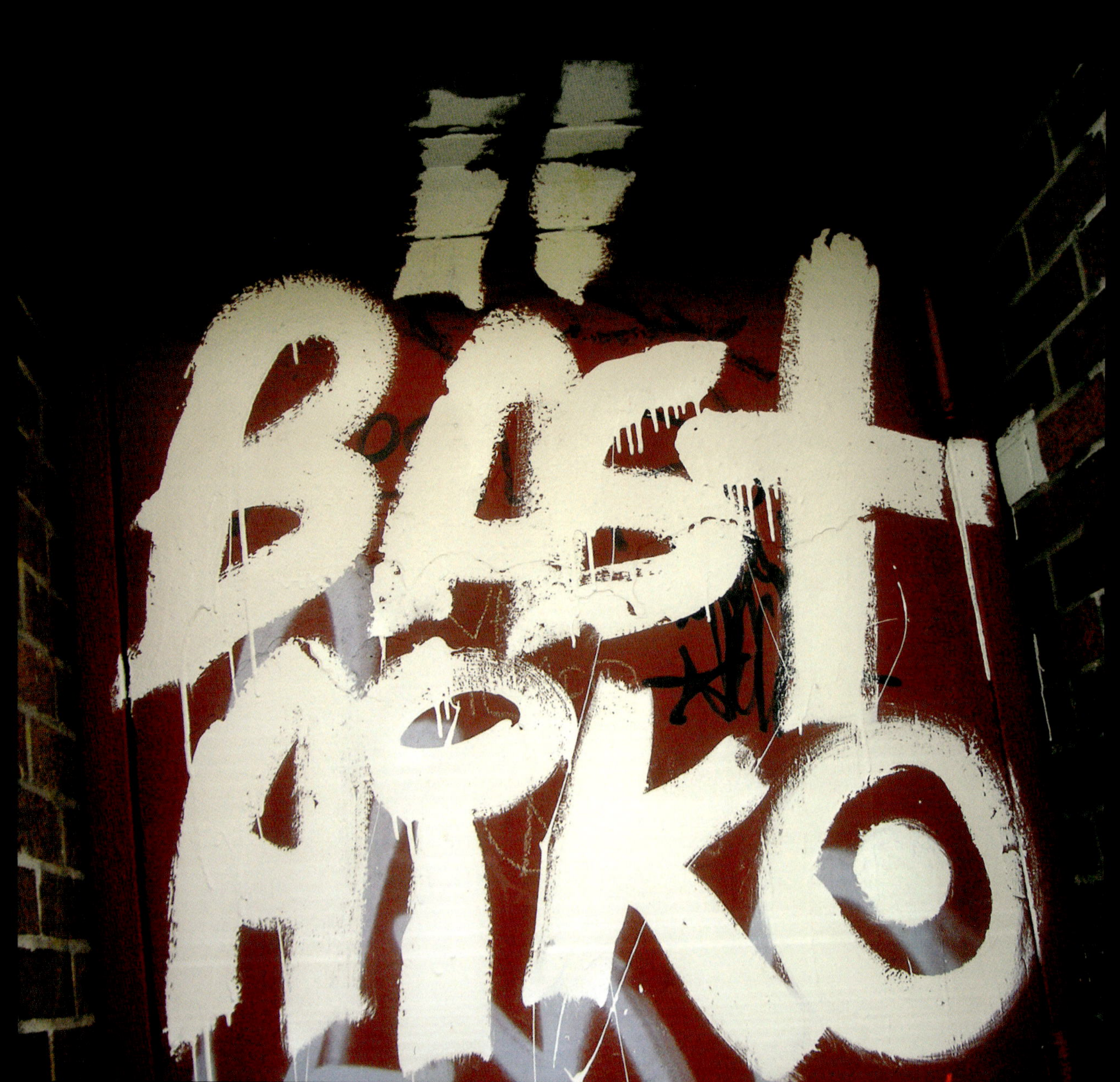
BAST
AIKO

BLAH BLAH
BLAH BLAH
BLAH BLAH
BLAH BLAH
BLAH
BLAH BLAH
BLAH

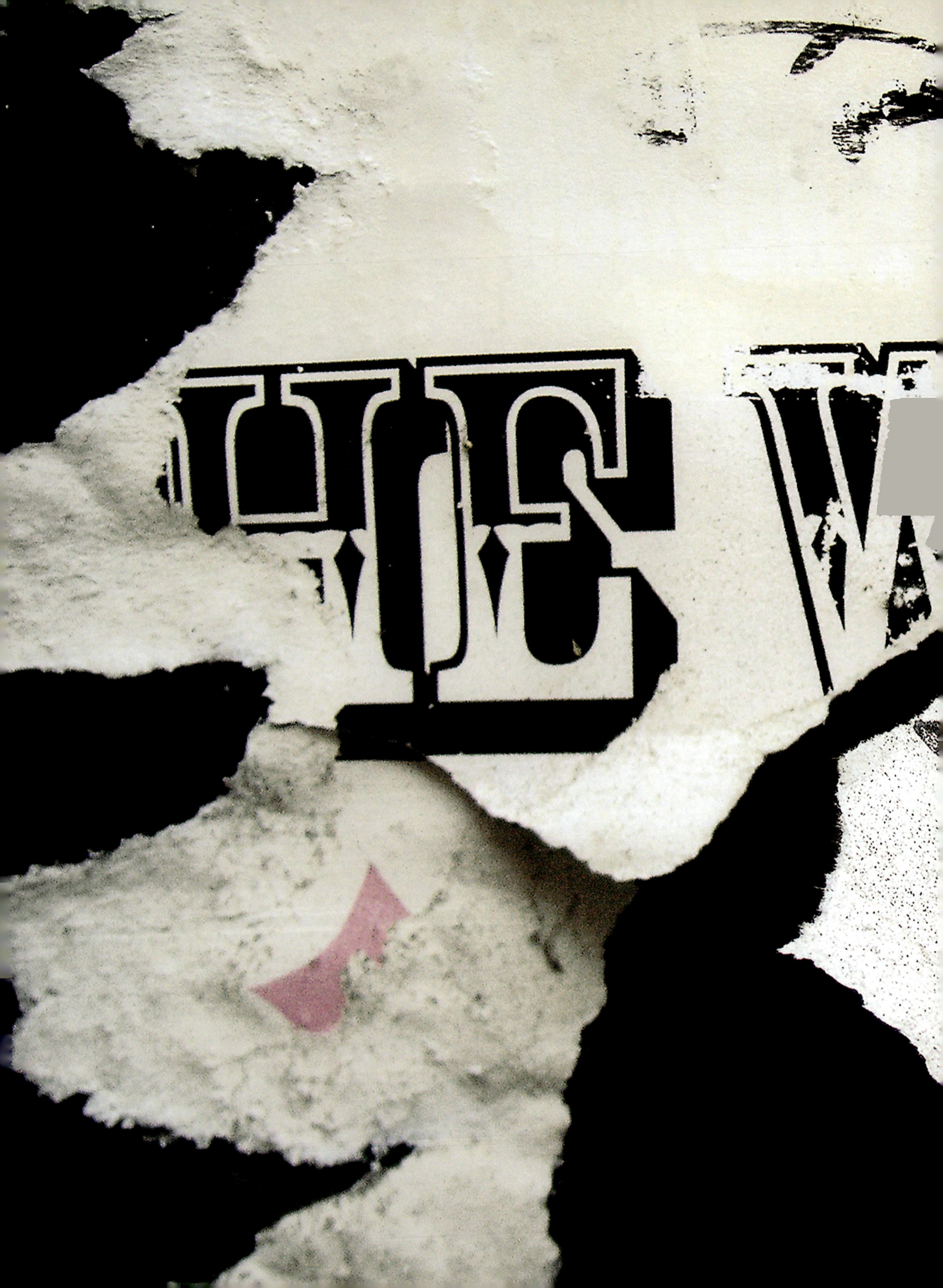

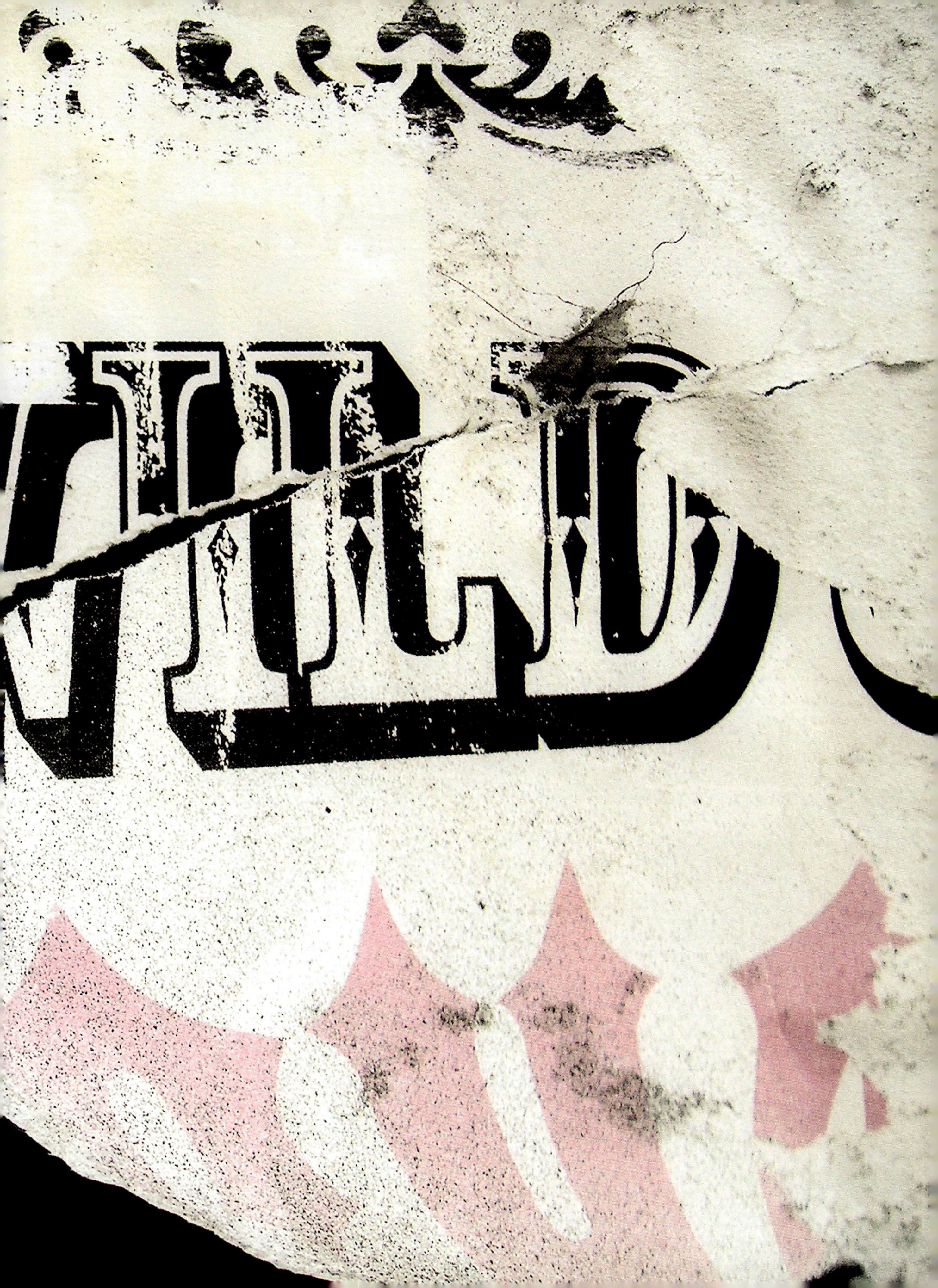

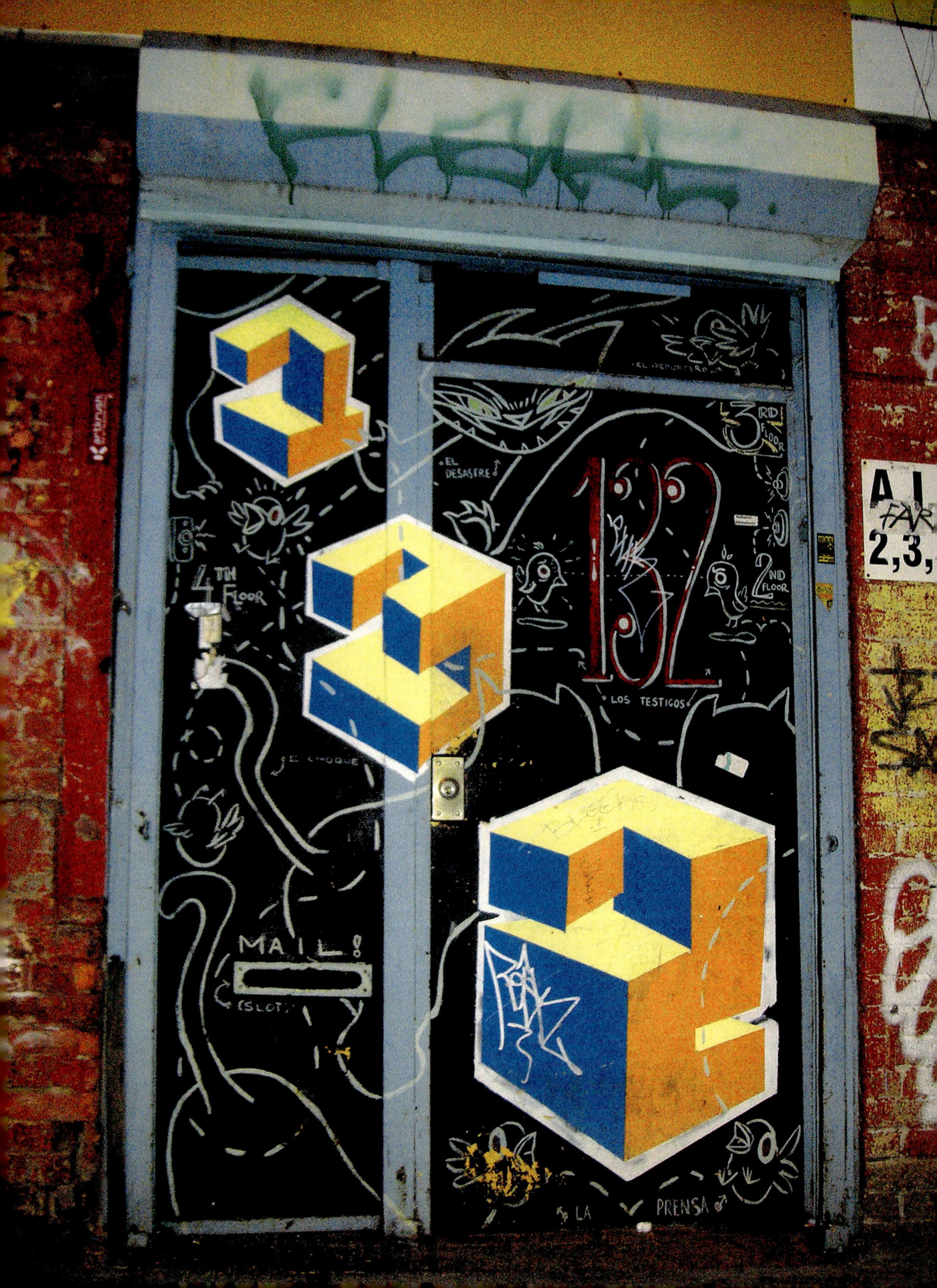

EL REPORTERO
3RD FLOOR
EL DESASTRE
132
4TH FLOOR
2ND FLOOR
LOS TESTIGOS
MAIL!
(SLOT)
LA PRENSA
2,3,

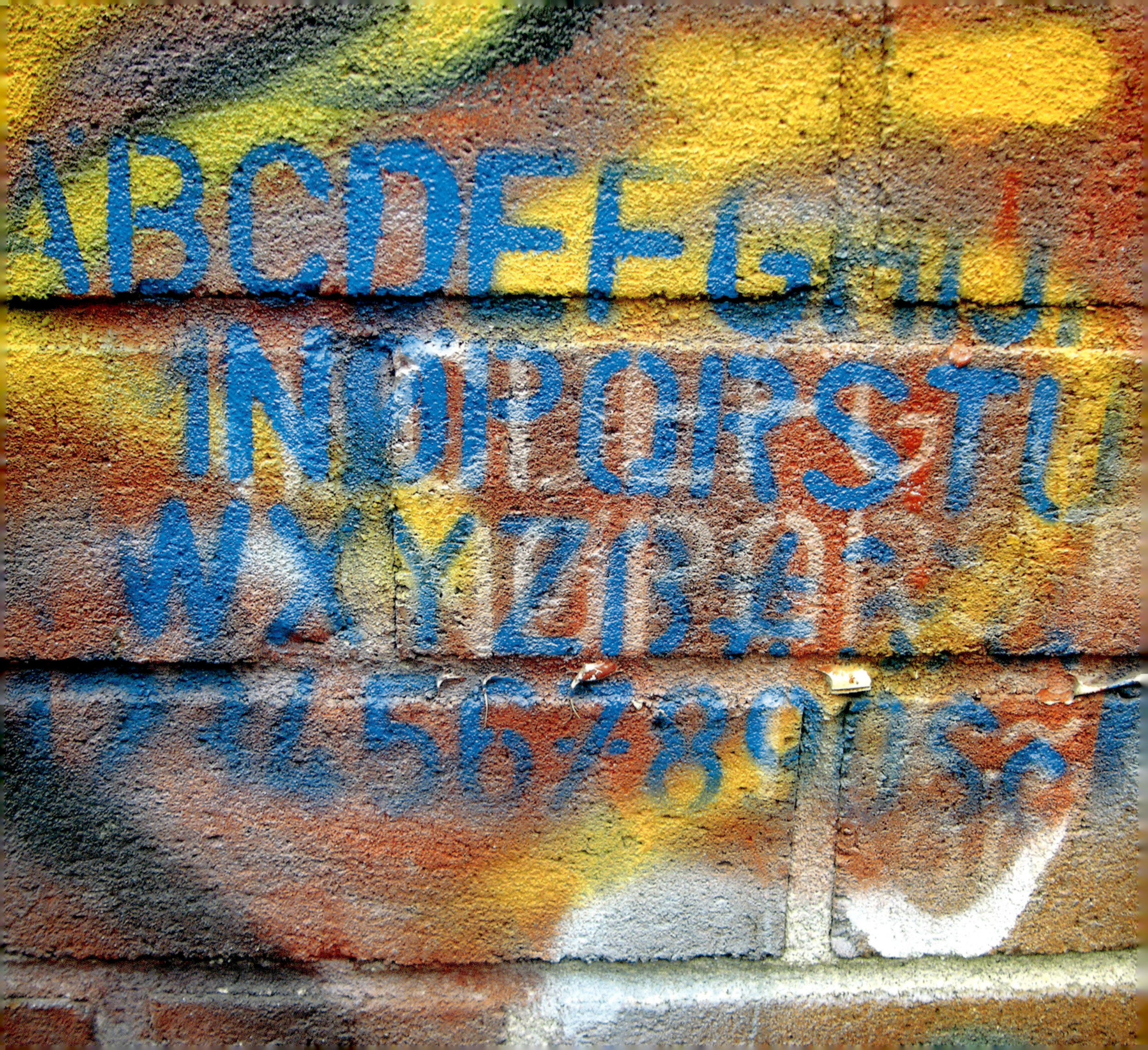

BCDEFG
NOPQRSTU
WXYZ
56789

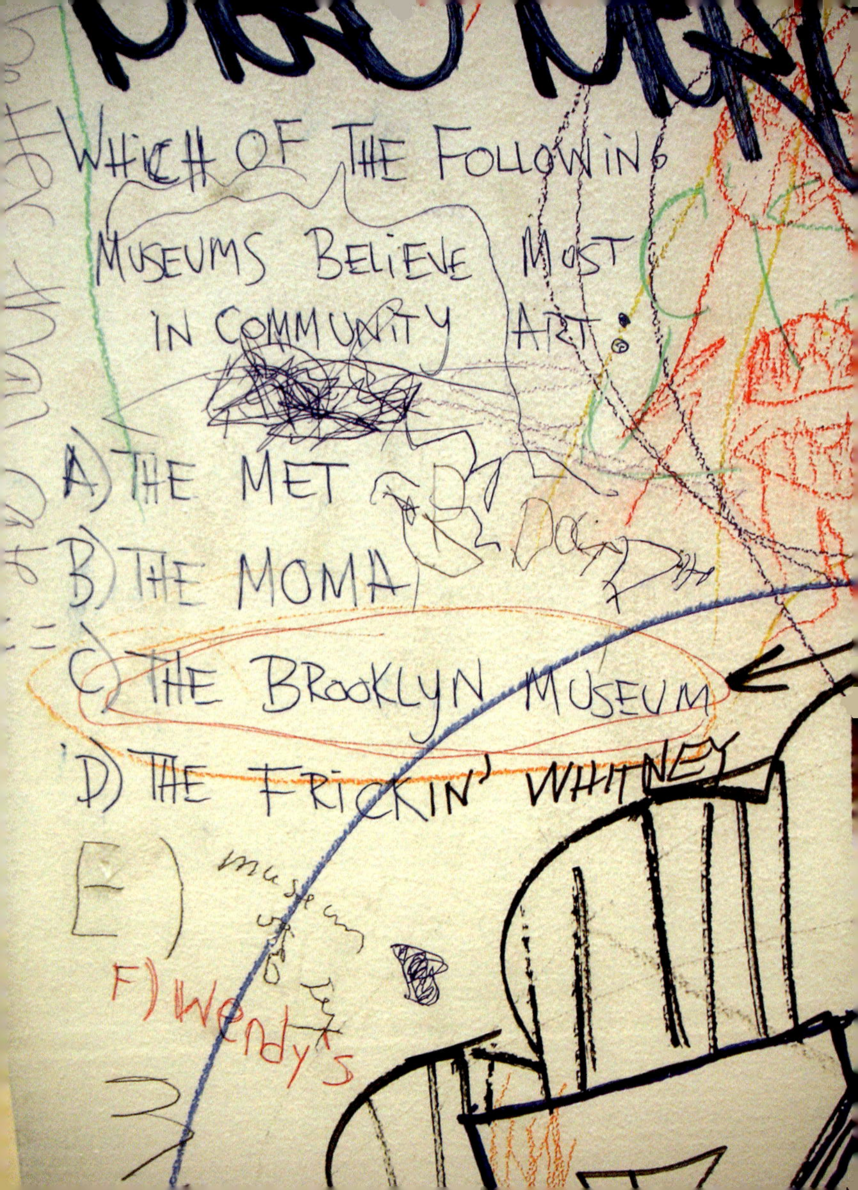
WHICH OF THE FOLLOWING
MUSEUMS BELIEVE MOST
IN COMMUNITY ART?
A) THE MET
B) THE MOMA
C) THE BROOKLYN MUSEUM
D) THE FRICKIN' WHITNEY
E)
F) Wendy's

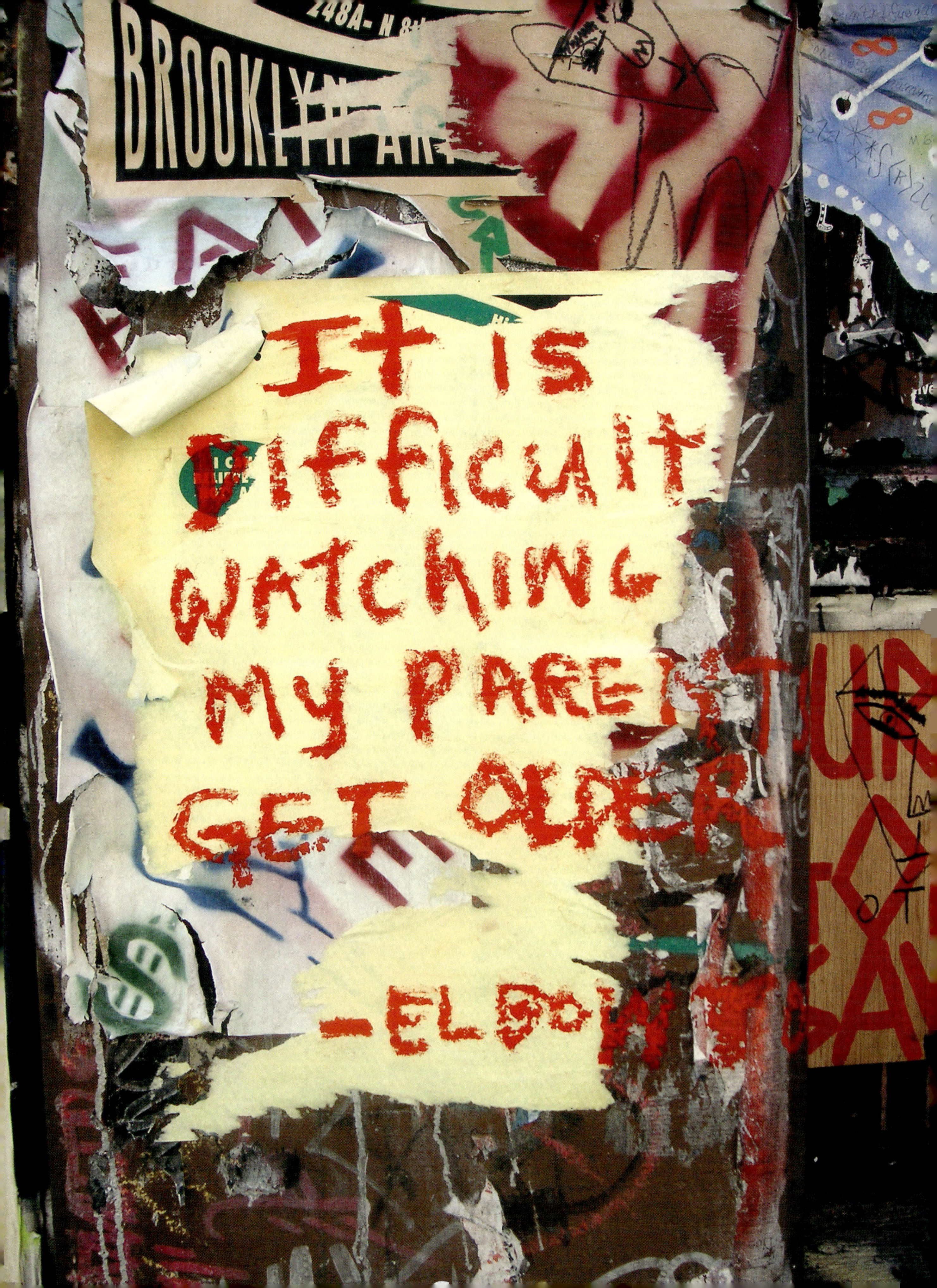
BROOKLYN
It is
Difficult
watching
My PARE
GET OLDER
-ELBOW

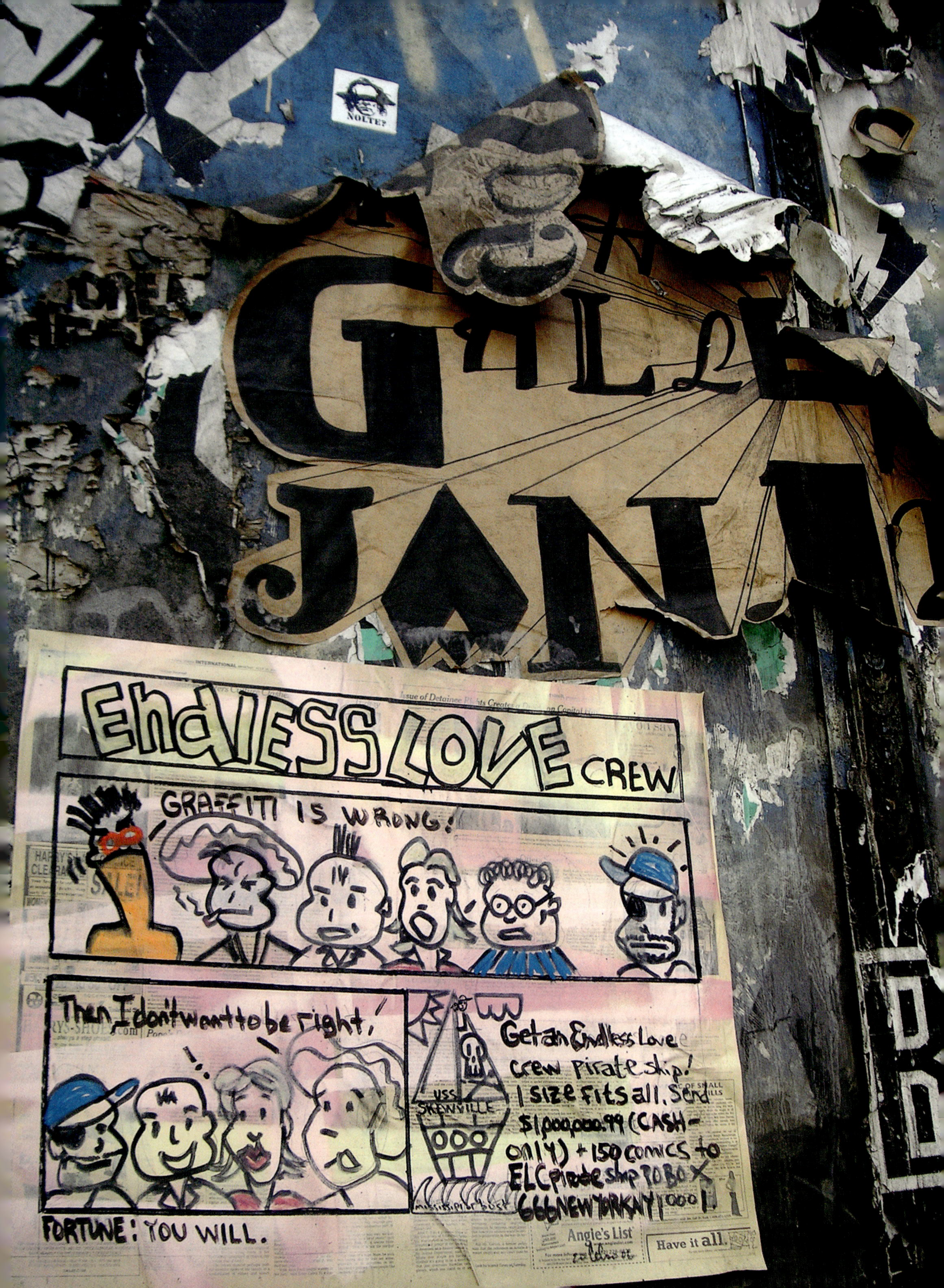
NOLTE?
EndlESS LOVE CREW
GRAFFITI IS WRONG!
Then, I don't want to be right,
Get an Endless Love crew pirate ship! 1 size fits all. Send $1,000,000.99 (CASH-ONLY) + 150 comics to ELC pirate ship PO BOX 666 NEW YORK NY 10001
USS SKEWVILLE
FORTUNE: YOU WILL.
Angie's List
Have it all.

"the repetition of childhood experience gives
s pause. when we were little, there was as yet no agonized
protest against the world of our parents. as children in
the midst of that world, we showed ourselves superior—
when we reach for banal, we take hold of the good along
with it—the good that is there **(open your eyes)** right
before you."

(attack)

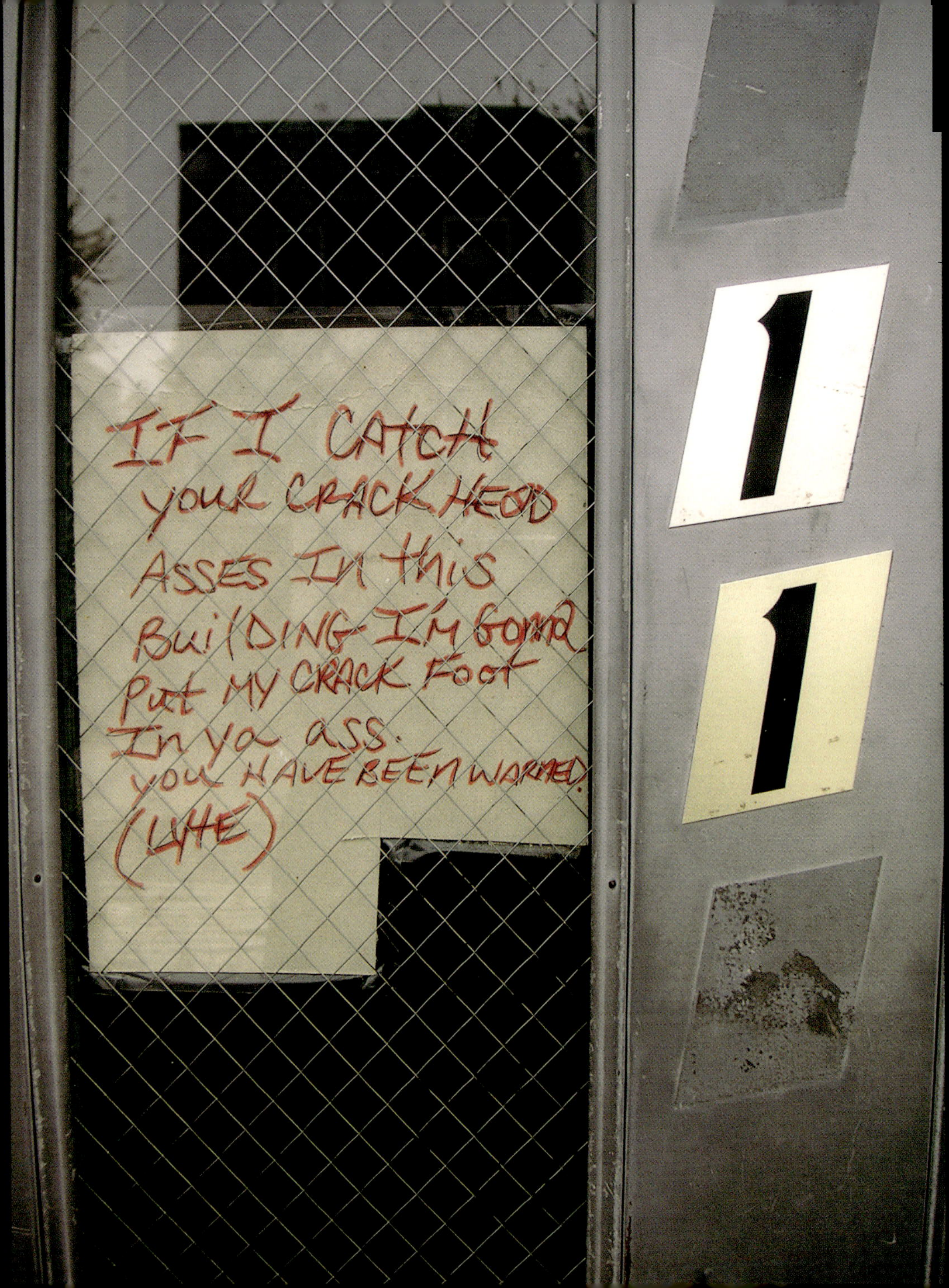

IF I CATCH
your CRACK HEAD
ASSES IN this
BuilDING I'M Gonna
Put MY CRACK Foot
In ya ass.
you HAVE BEEN warned.
(LYHE)

1

1

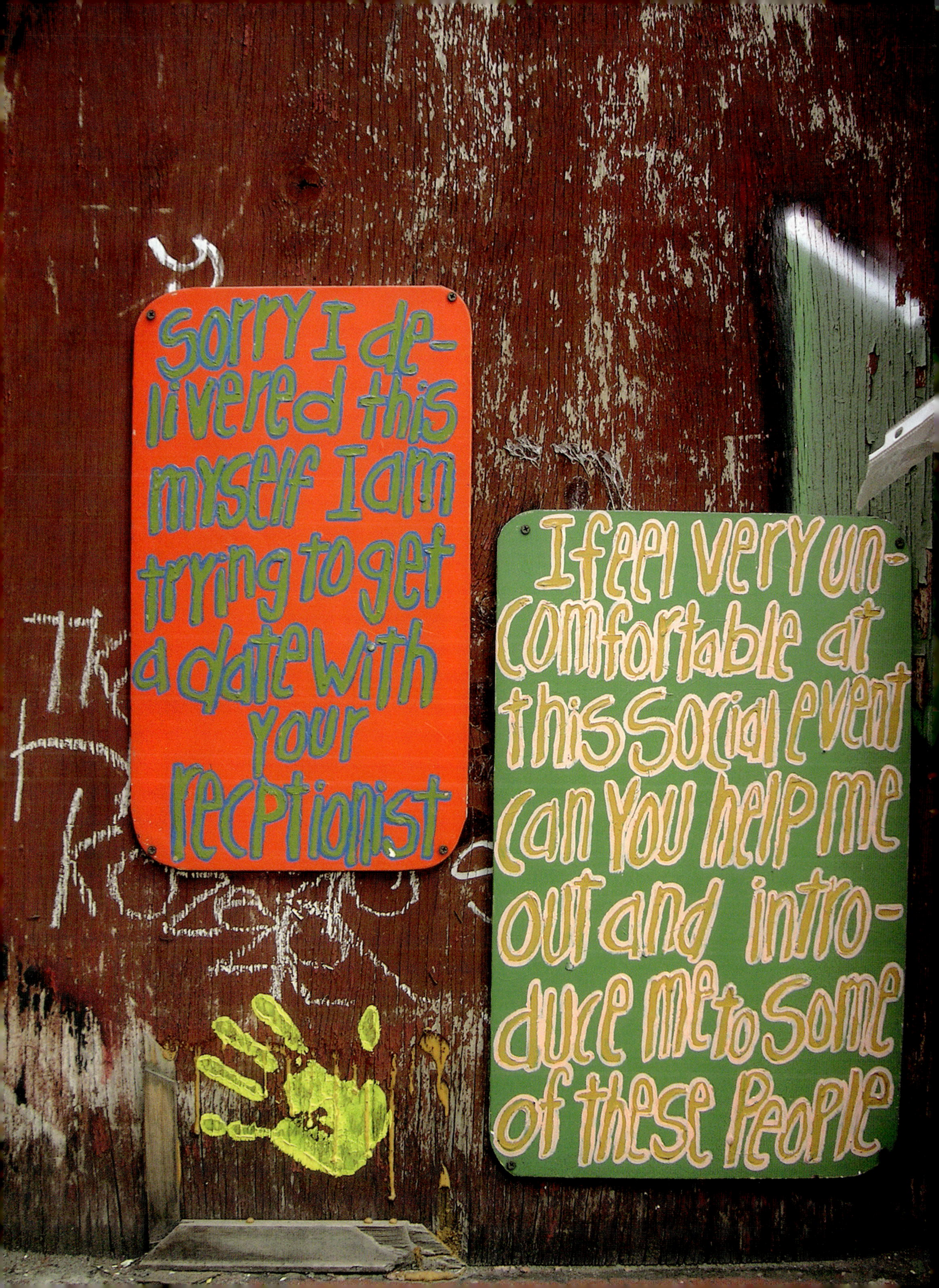
sorry I de-
livered this
myself I am
trying to get
a date with
your
recptionist
I feel very un-
comfortable at
this social event
can you help me
out and intro-
duce me to some
of these people

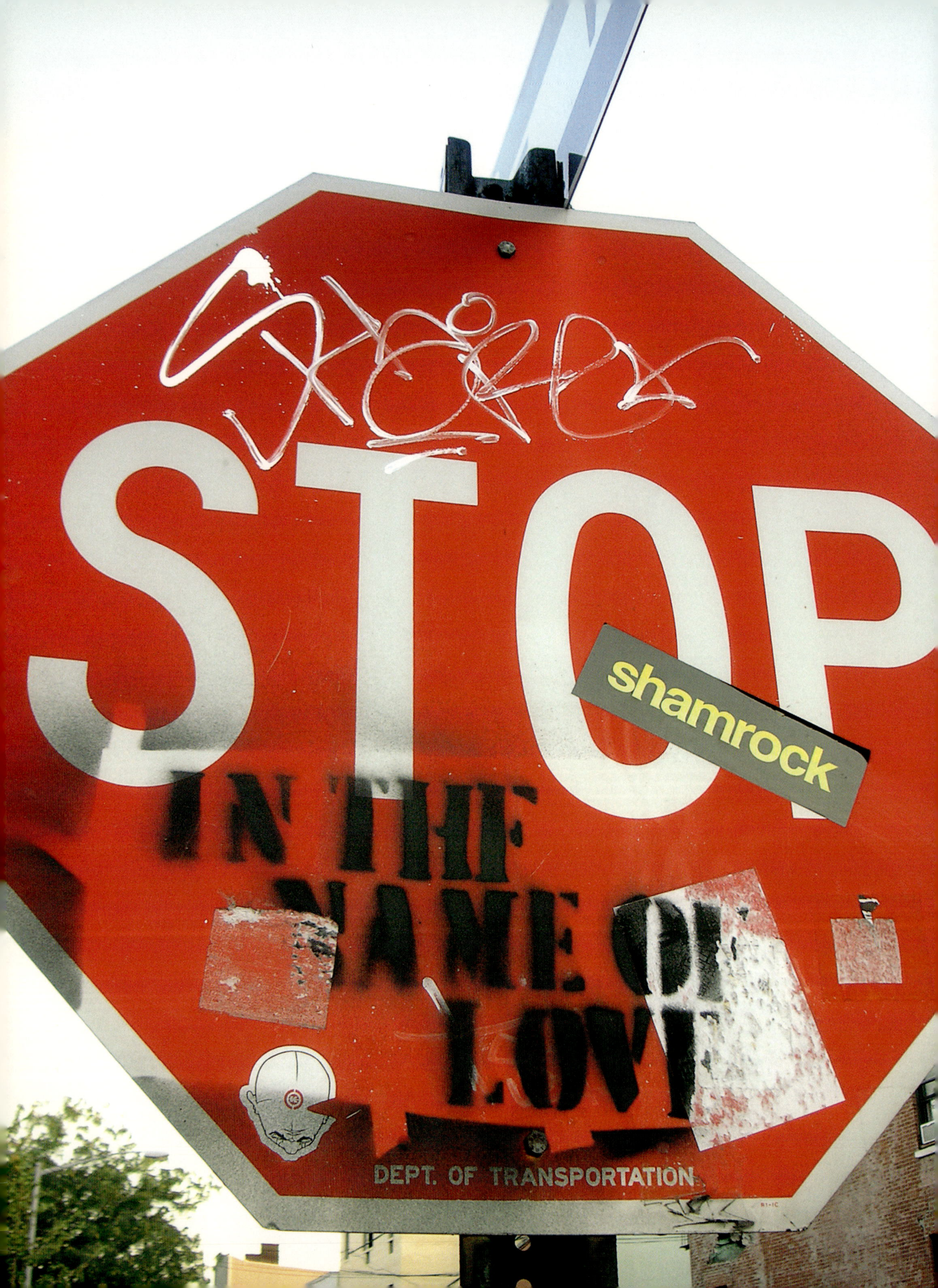
STOP
shamrock
IN THE
DEPT. OF TRANSPORTATION

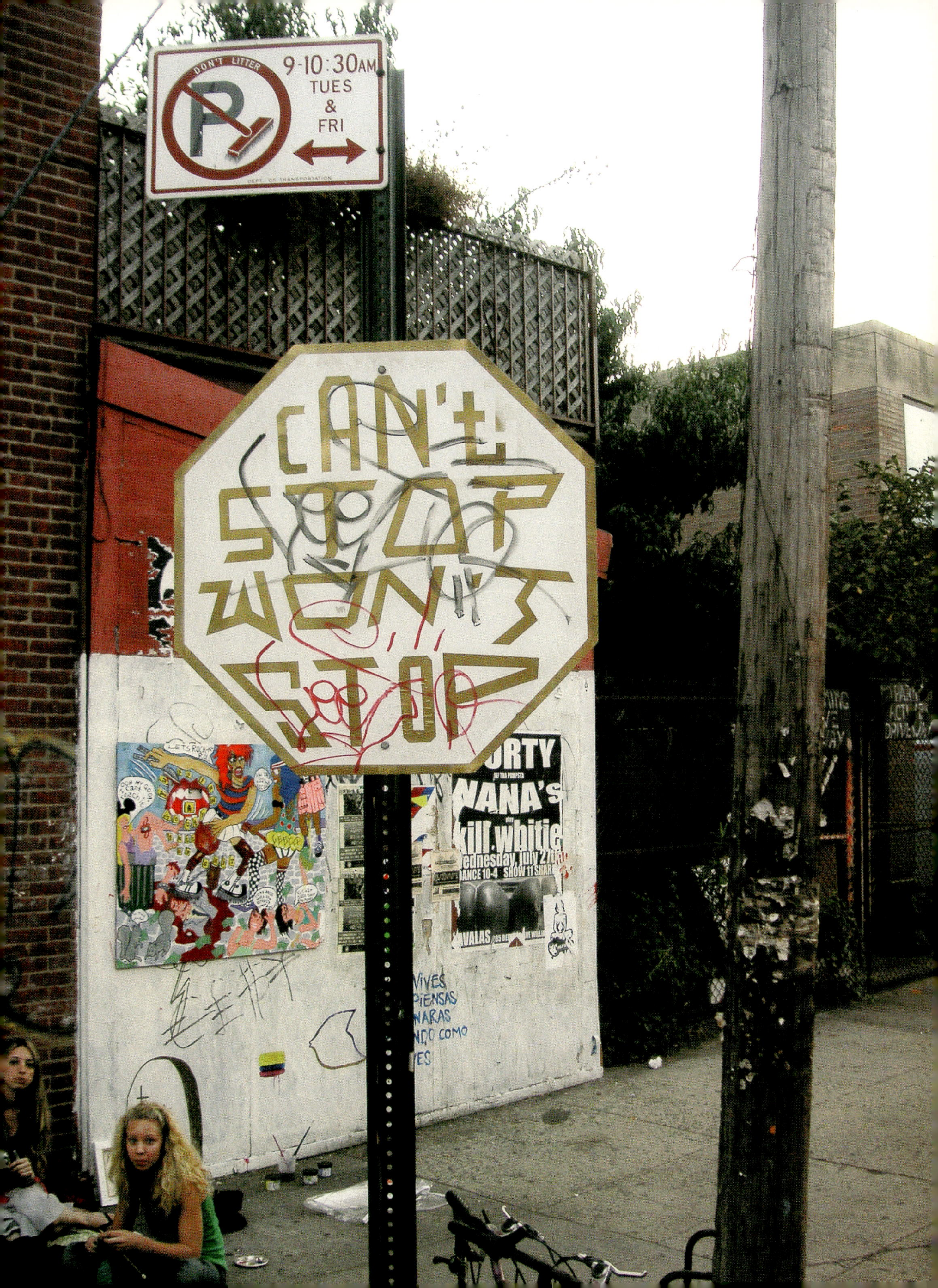
DON'T LITTER
9-10:30AM
TUES
&
FRI
CAN'T STOP WON'T STOP
kill whitie

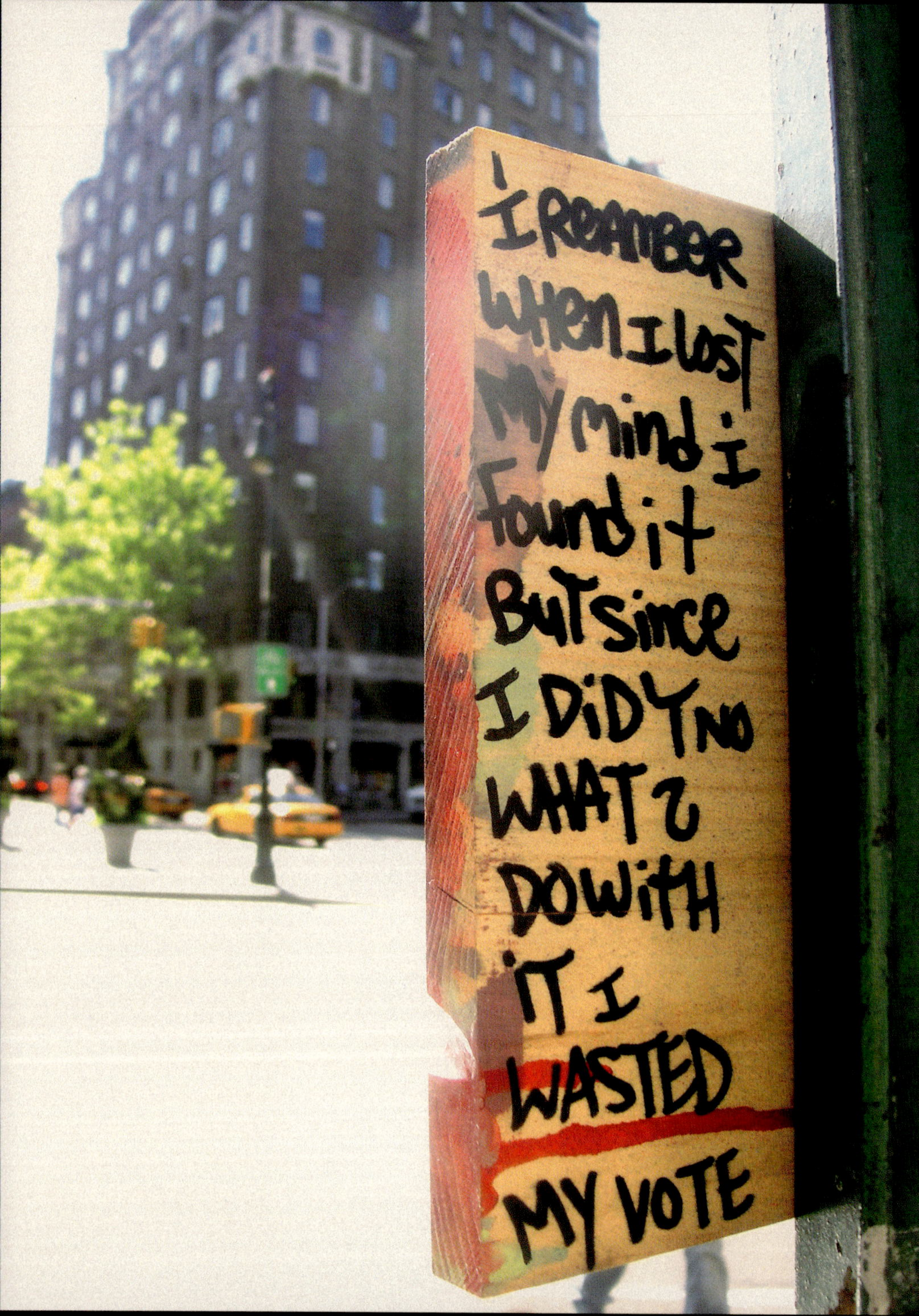

I Reamber
When I lost
My mind I
found it
But since
I DiD Y NO
WHAT 2
DO with
IT I
WASTED
MY VOTE

what's more frightening than 9-11?
The Puerto Rican Day Parade

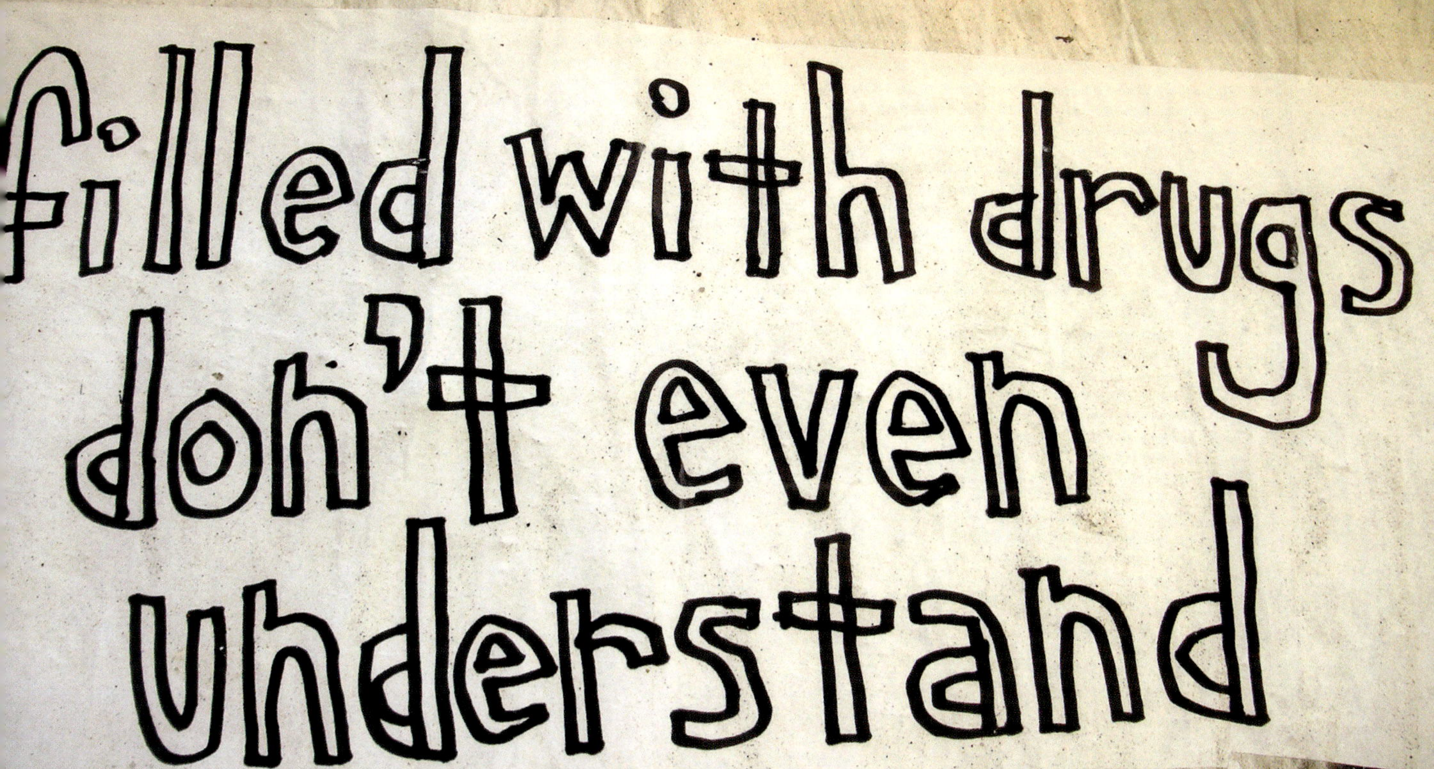

THIS
MEANS
NOTHING

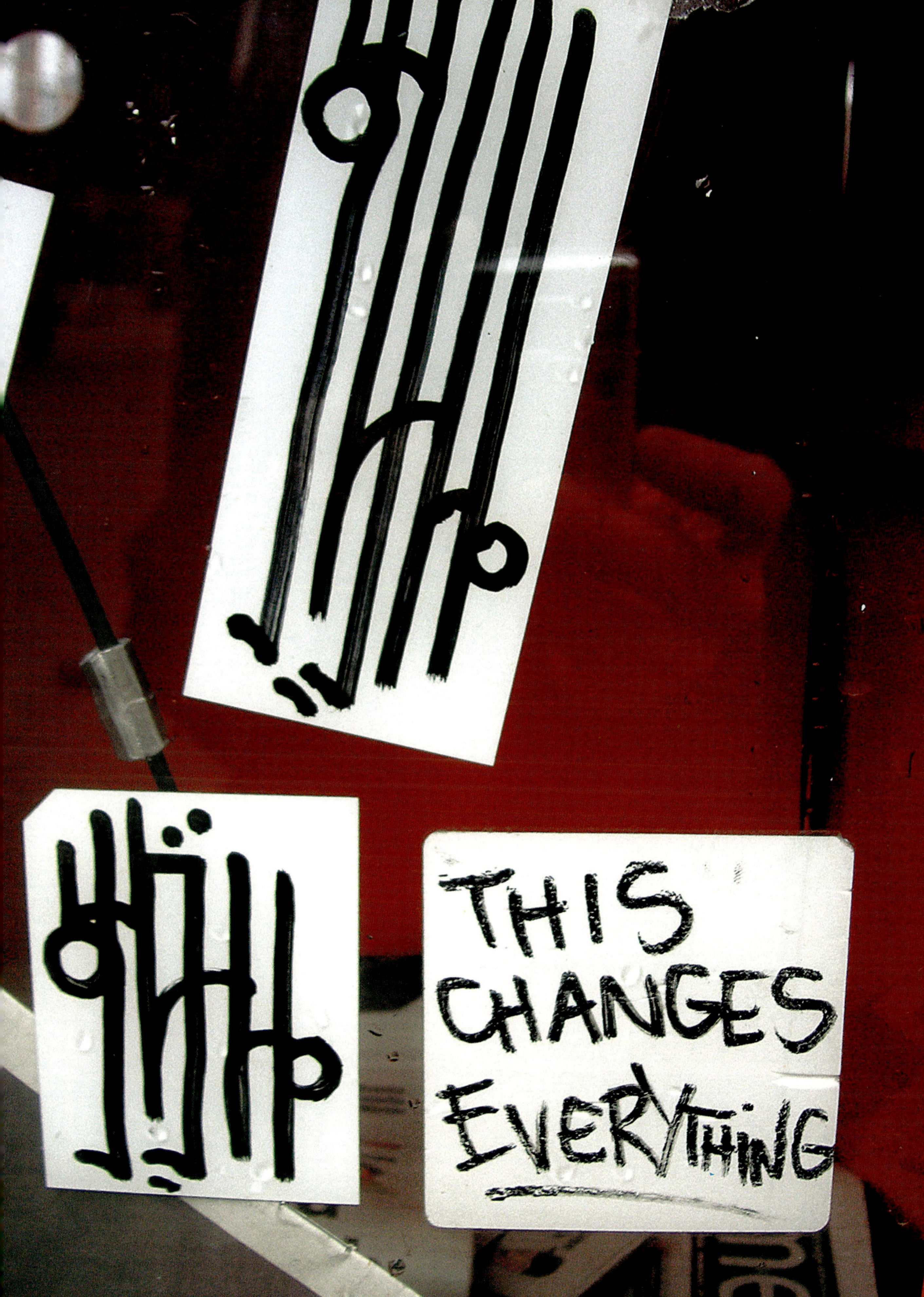
THIS
CHANGES
EVERYTHING

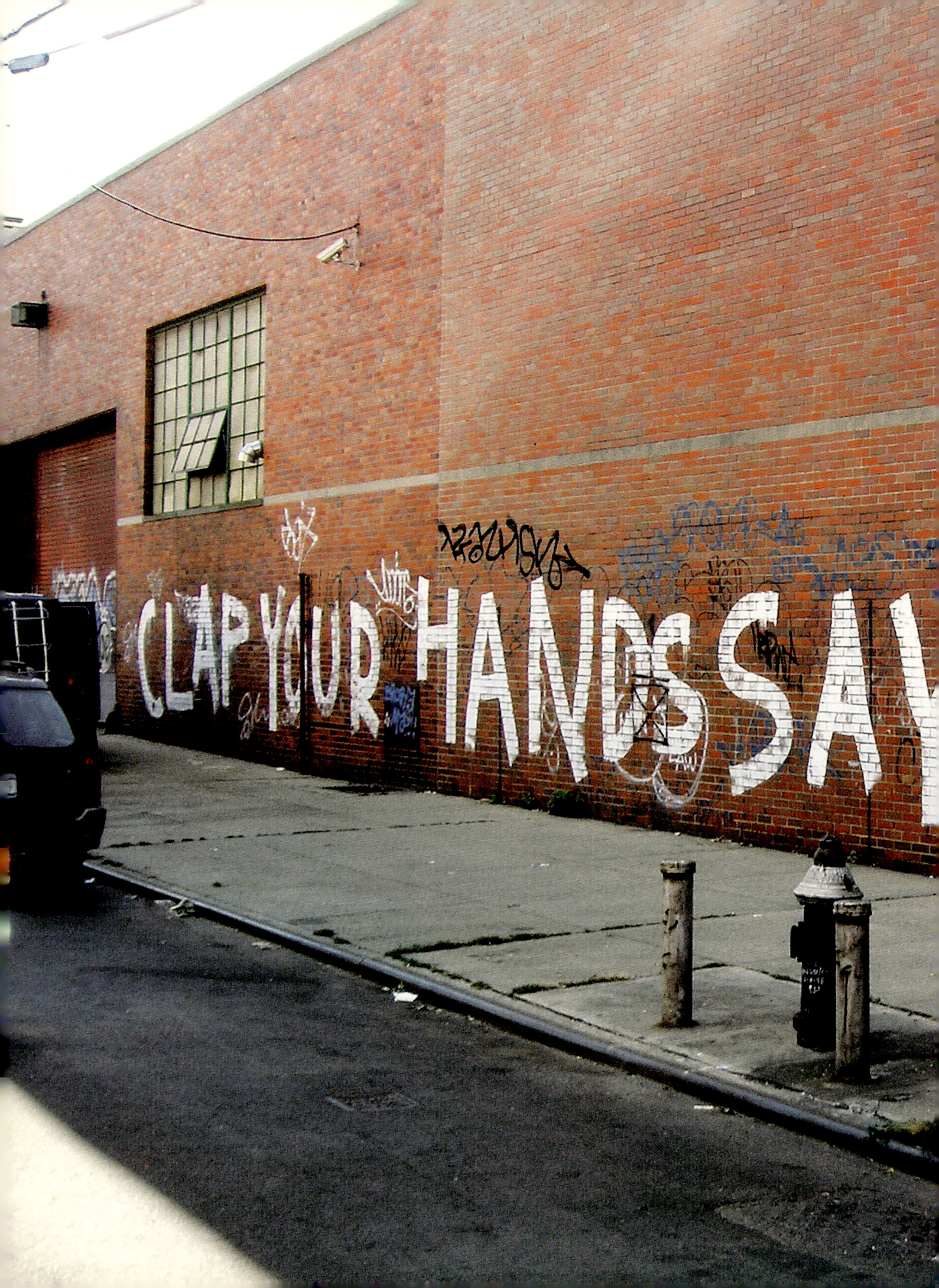
CLAP YOUR HANDS SA

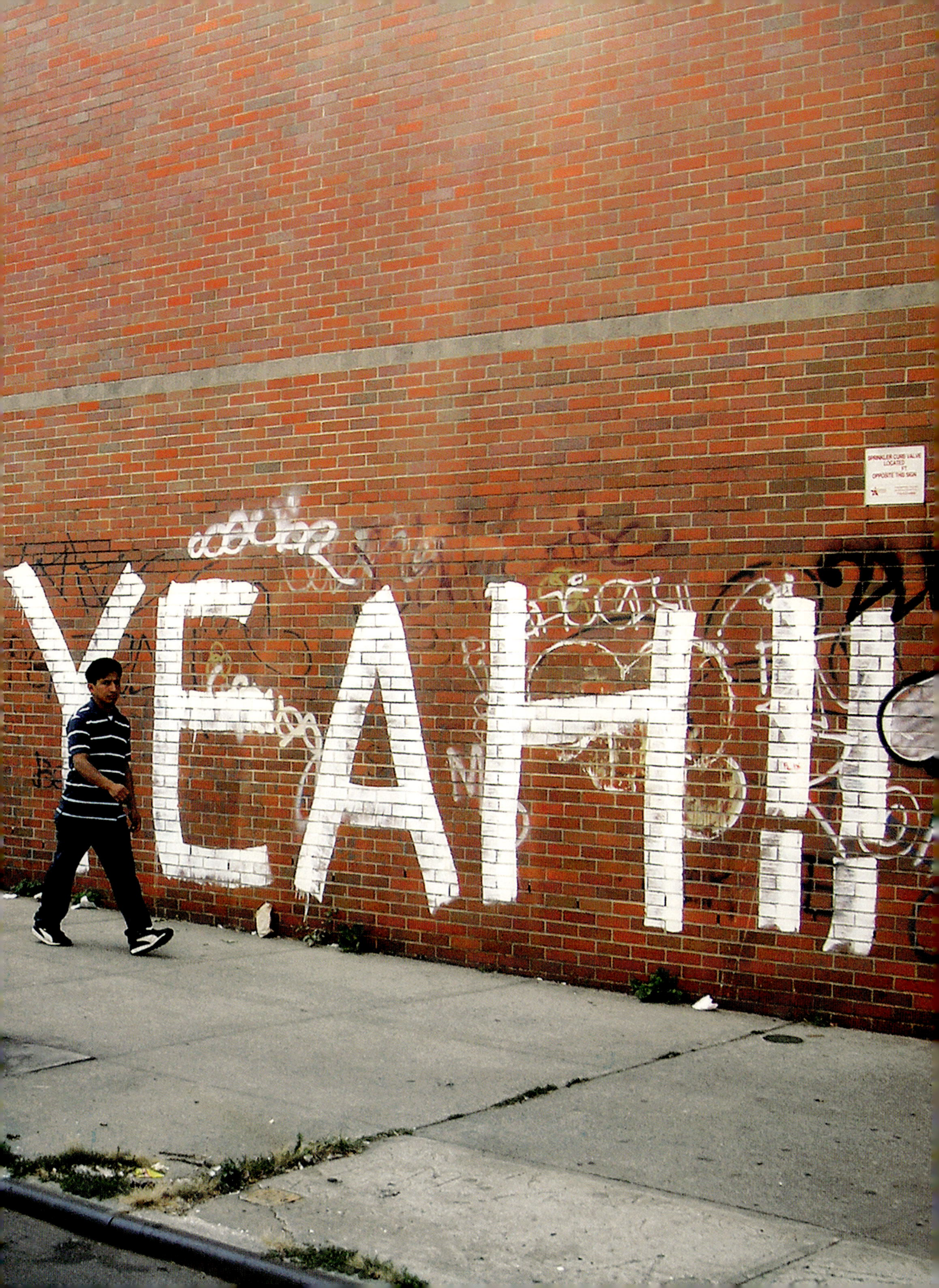
YEAH!

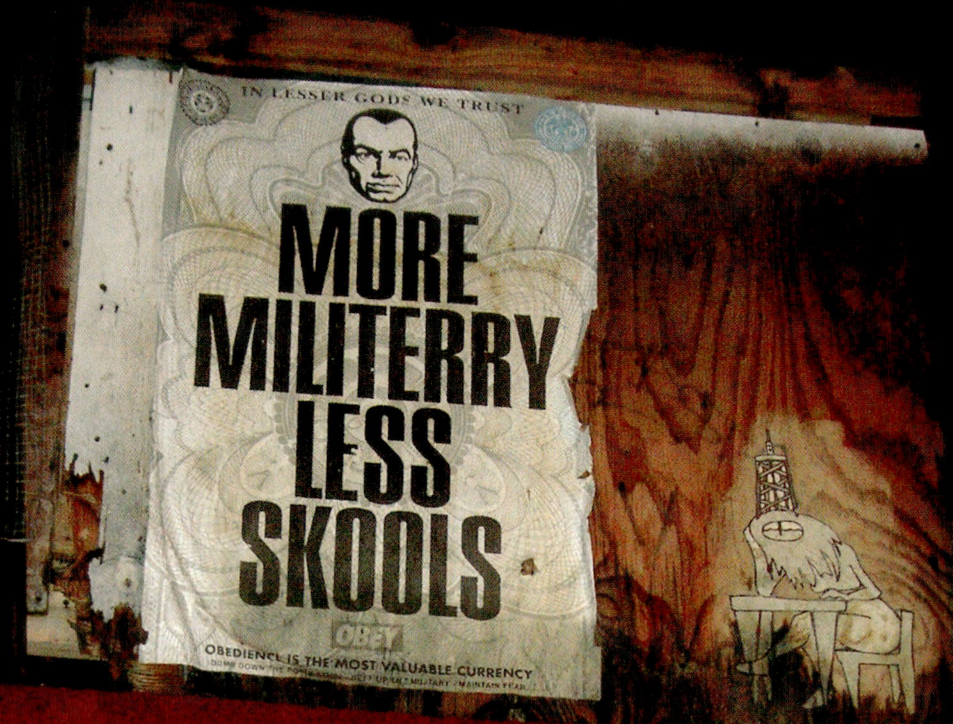
IN LESSER GODS WE TRUST
MORE
MILITERRY
LESS
SKOOLS
OBEY
OBEDIENCE IS THE MOST VALUABLE CURRENCY

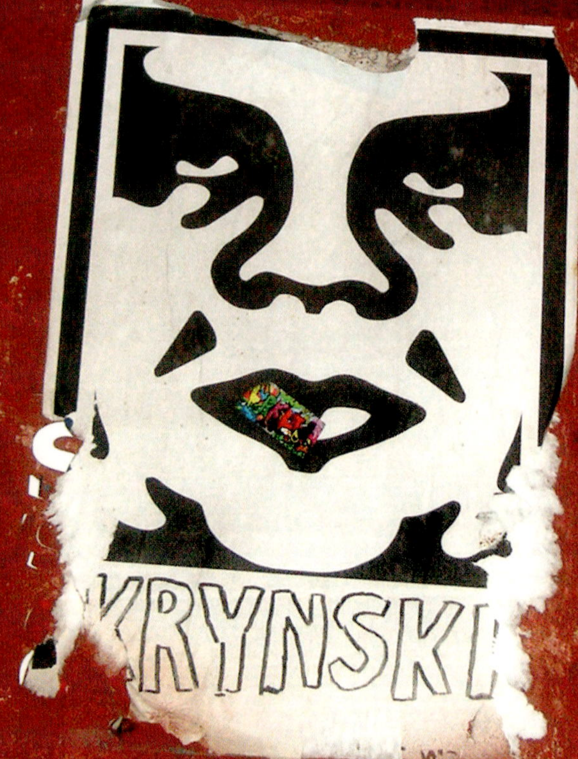
KRYNSK

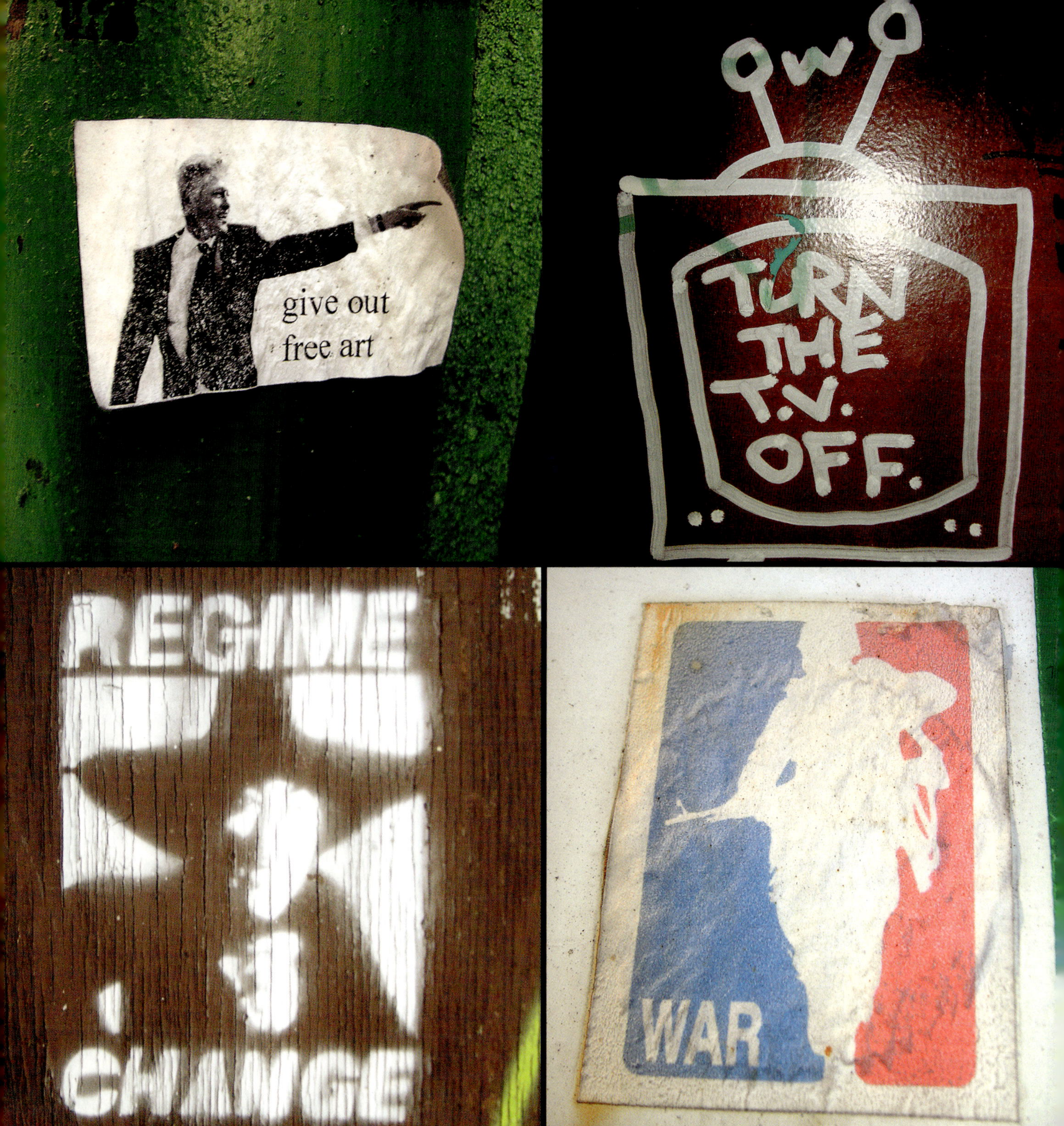
give out
free art
TURN
THE
T.V.
OFF.
REGIME
CHANGE
WAR

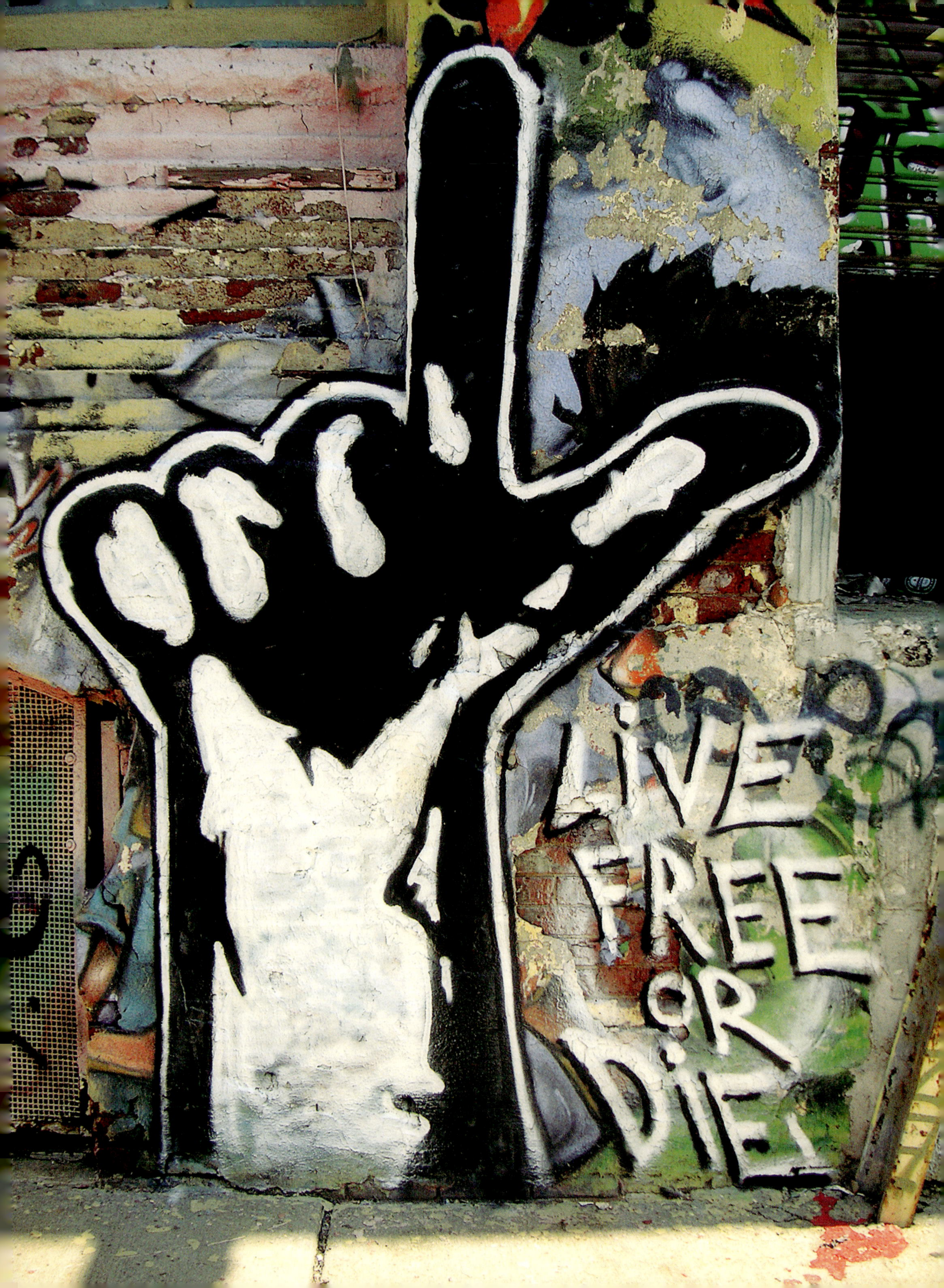
LIVE
FREE
OR
DIE

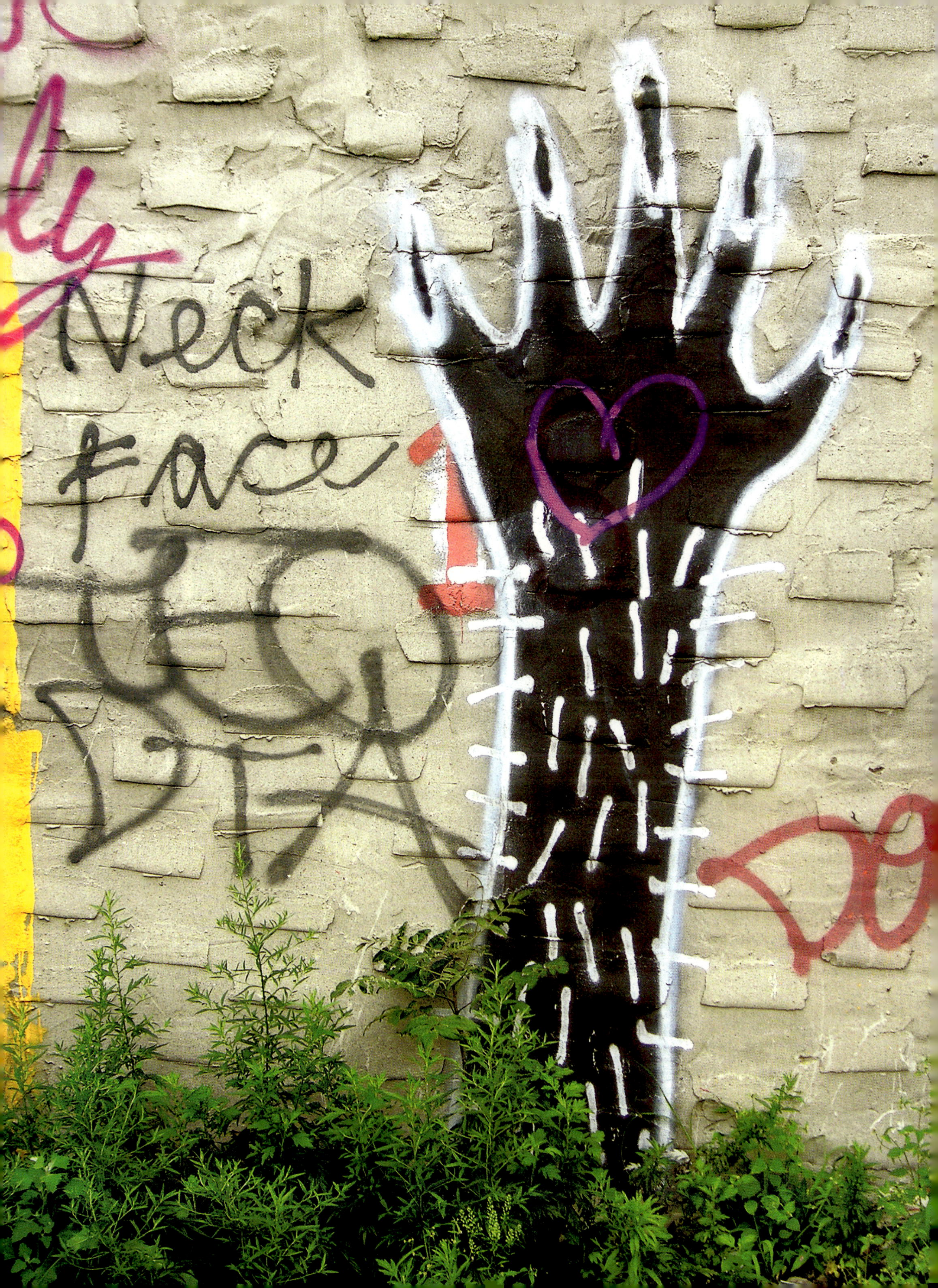
Neck
Face

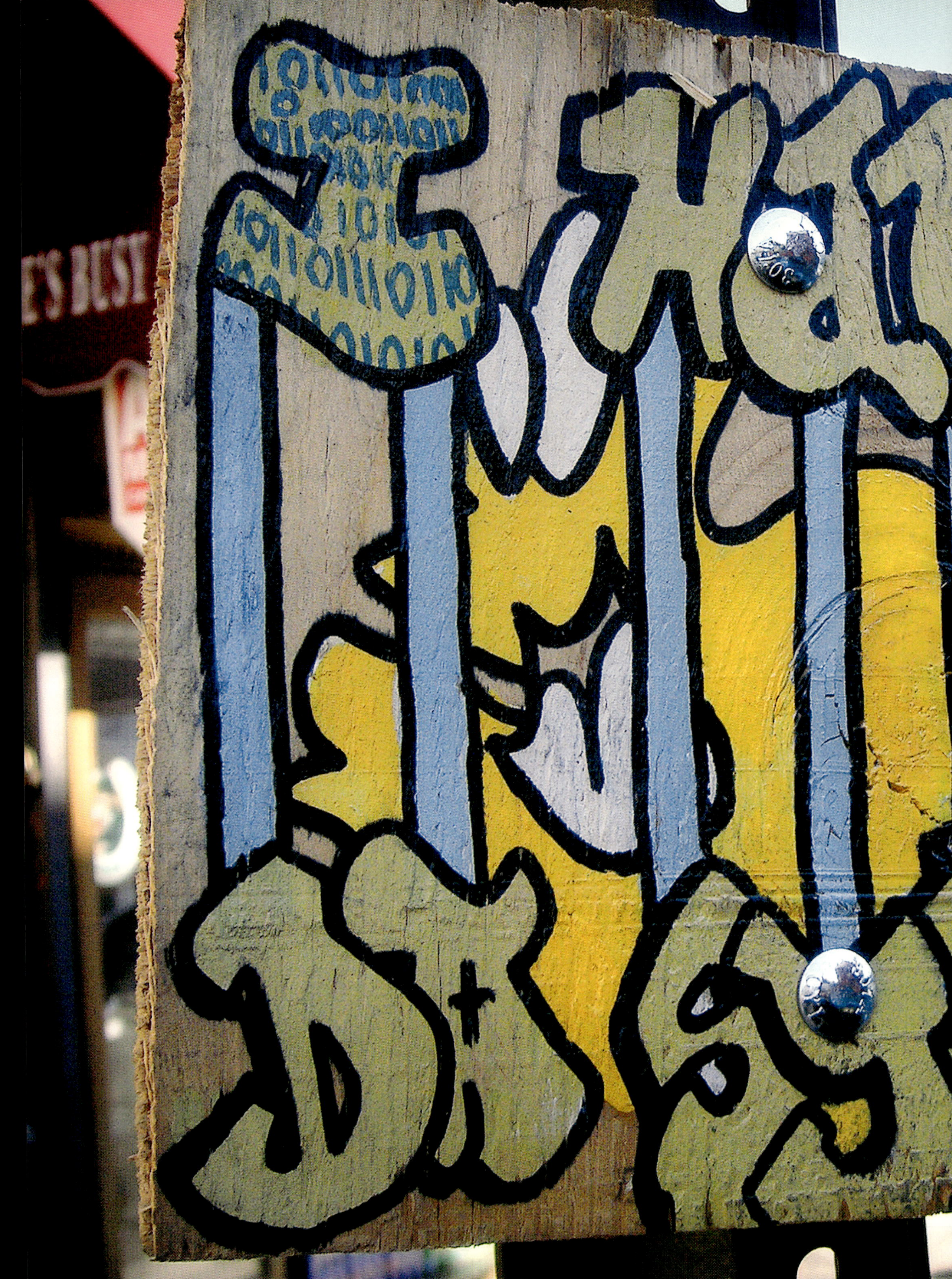
E'S BUST

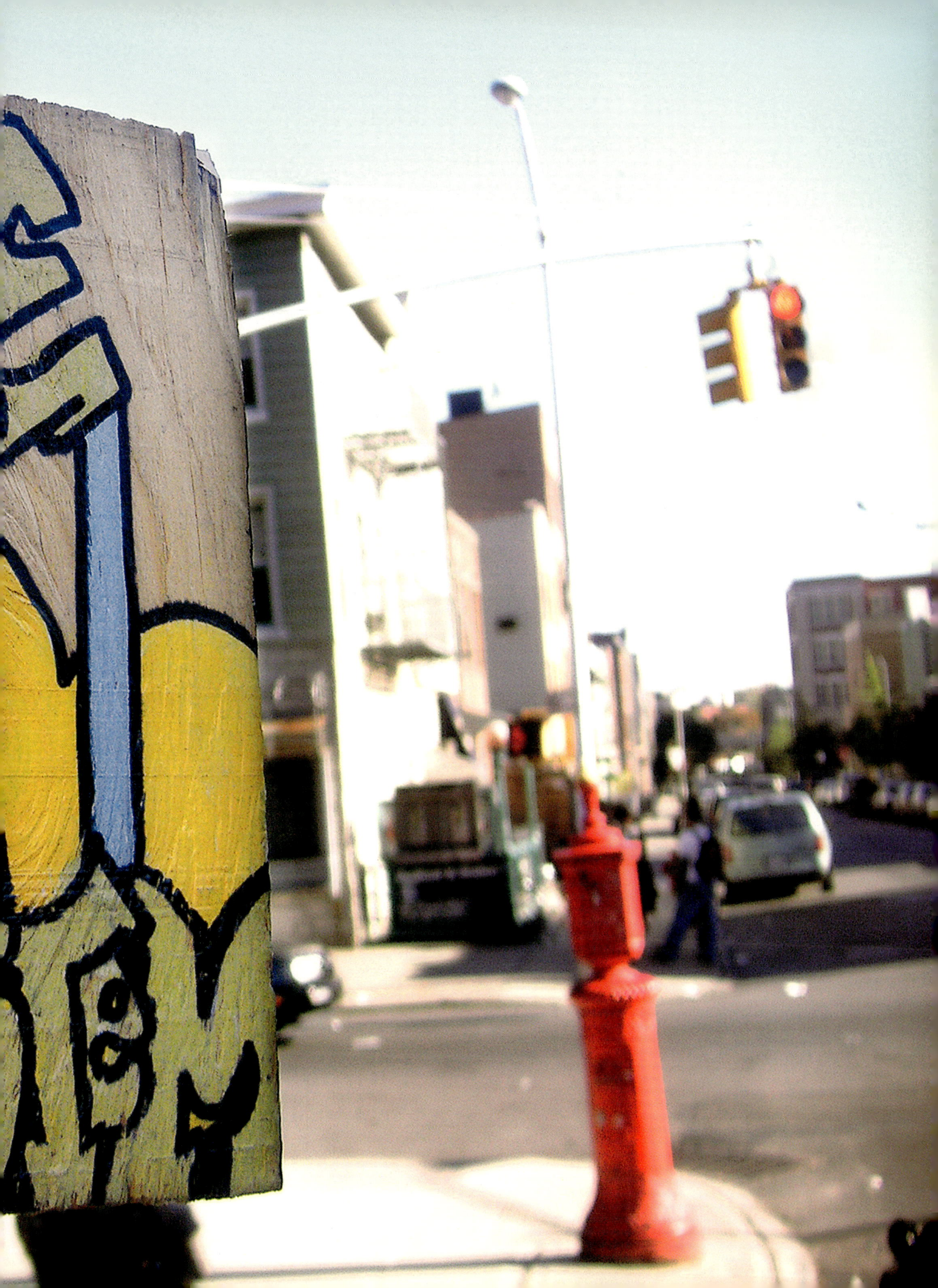

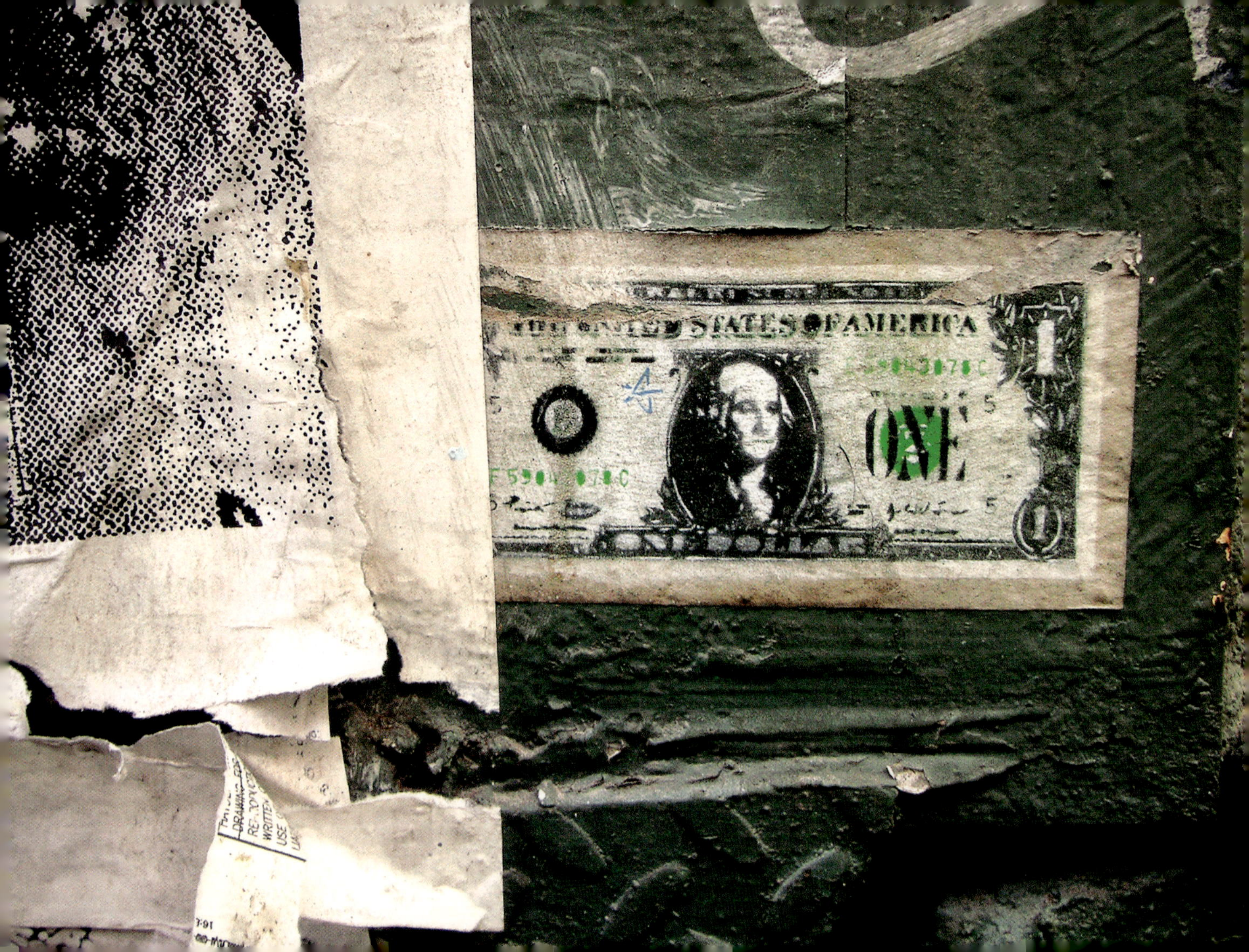
STATES OF AMERICA
ONE

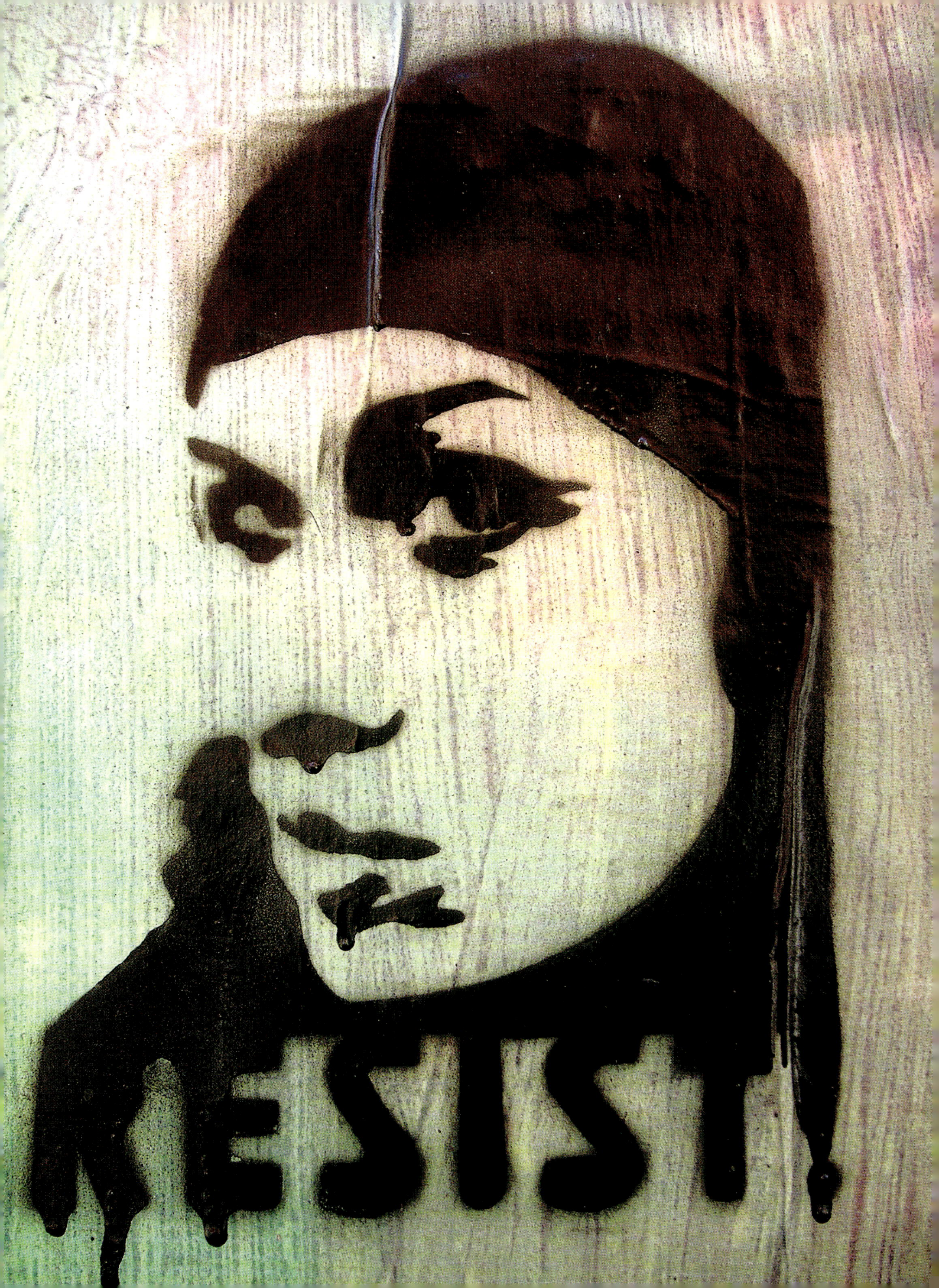
RESIST!

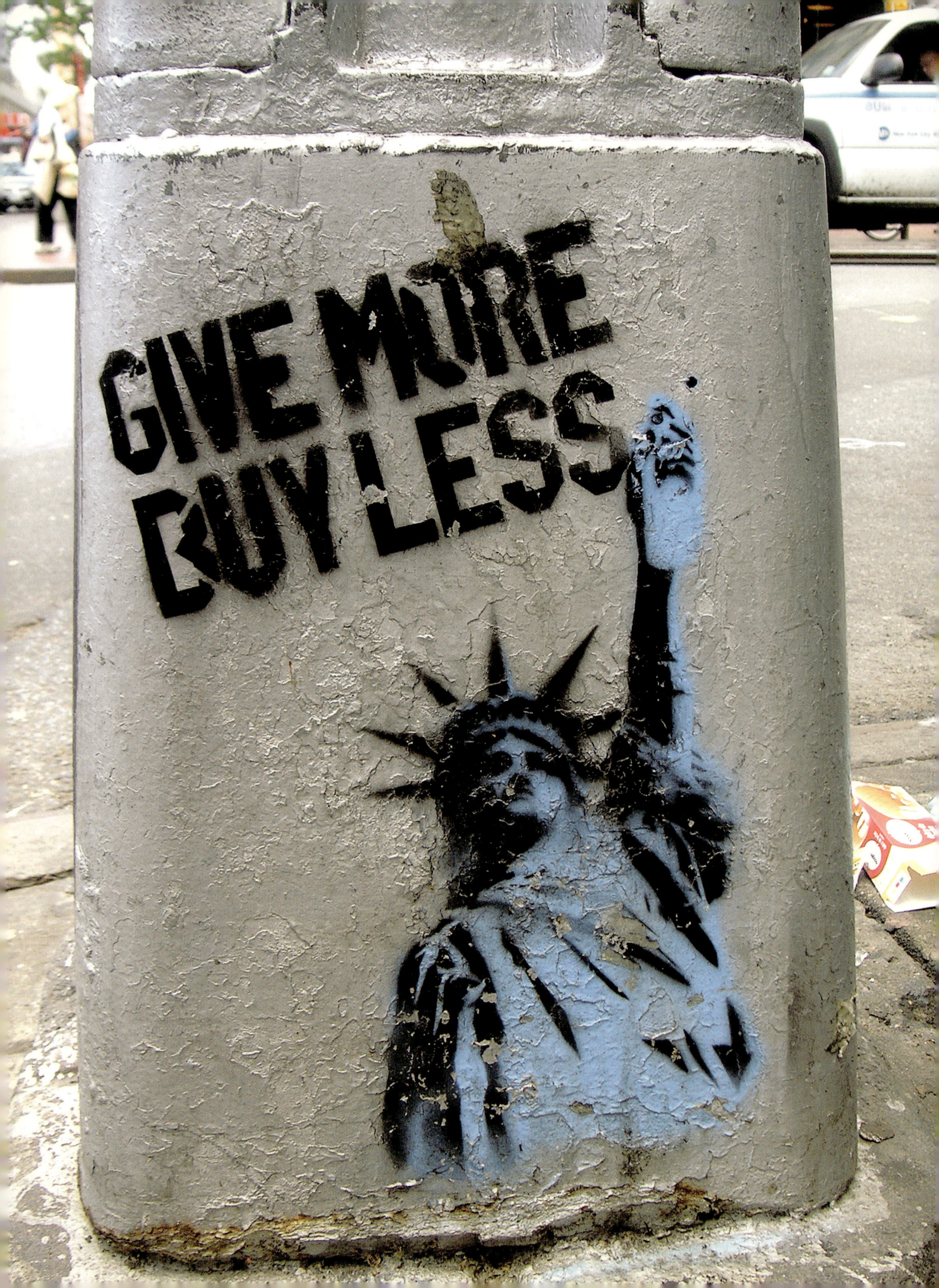
GIVE MORE
BUY LESS

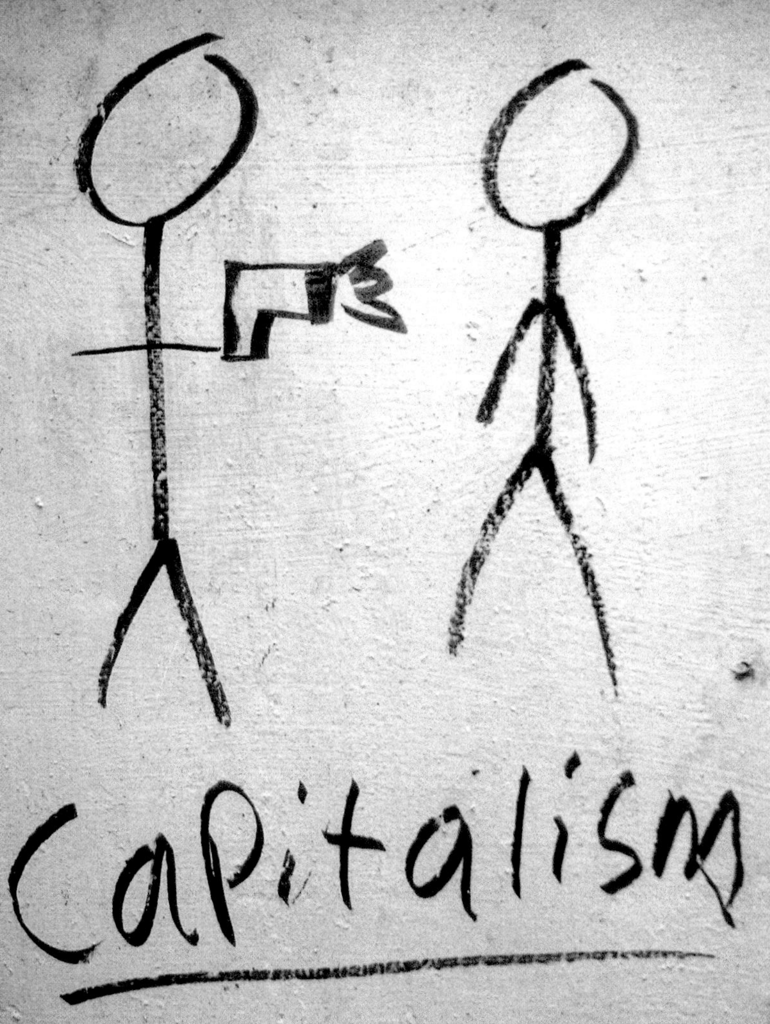
Capitalism

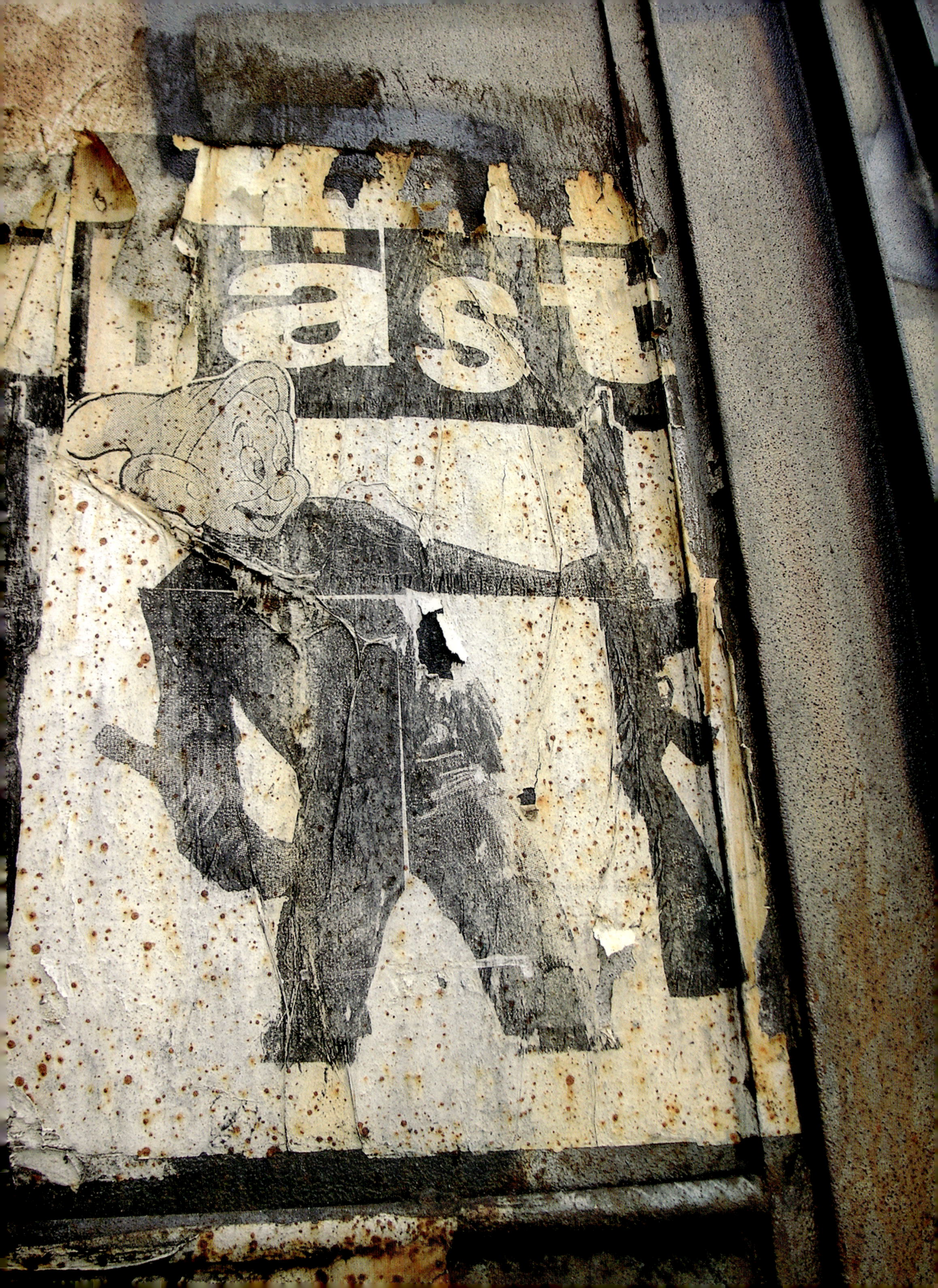
äst

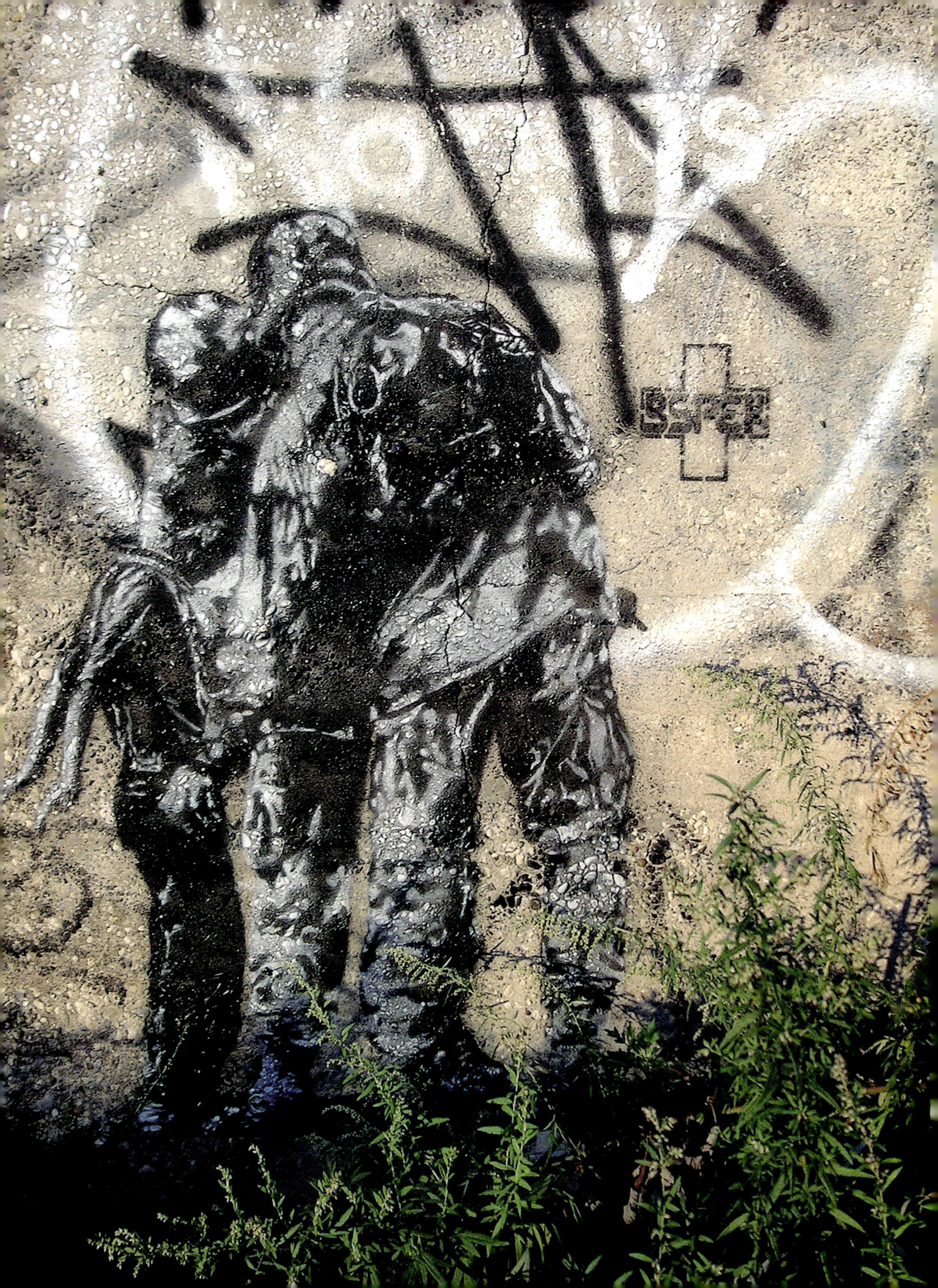

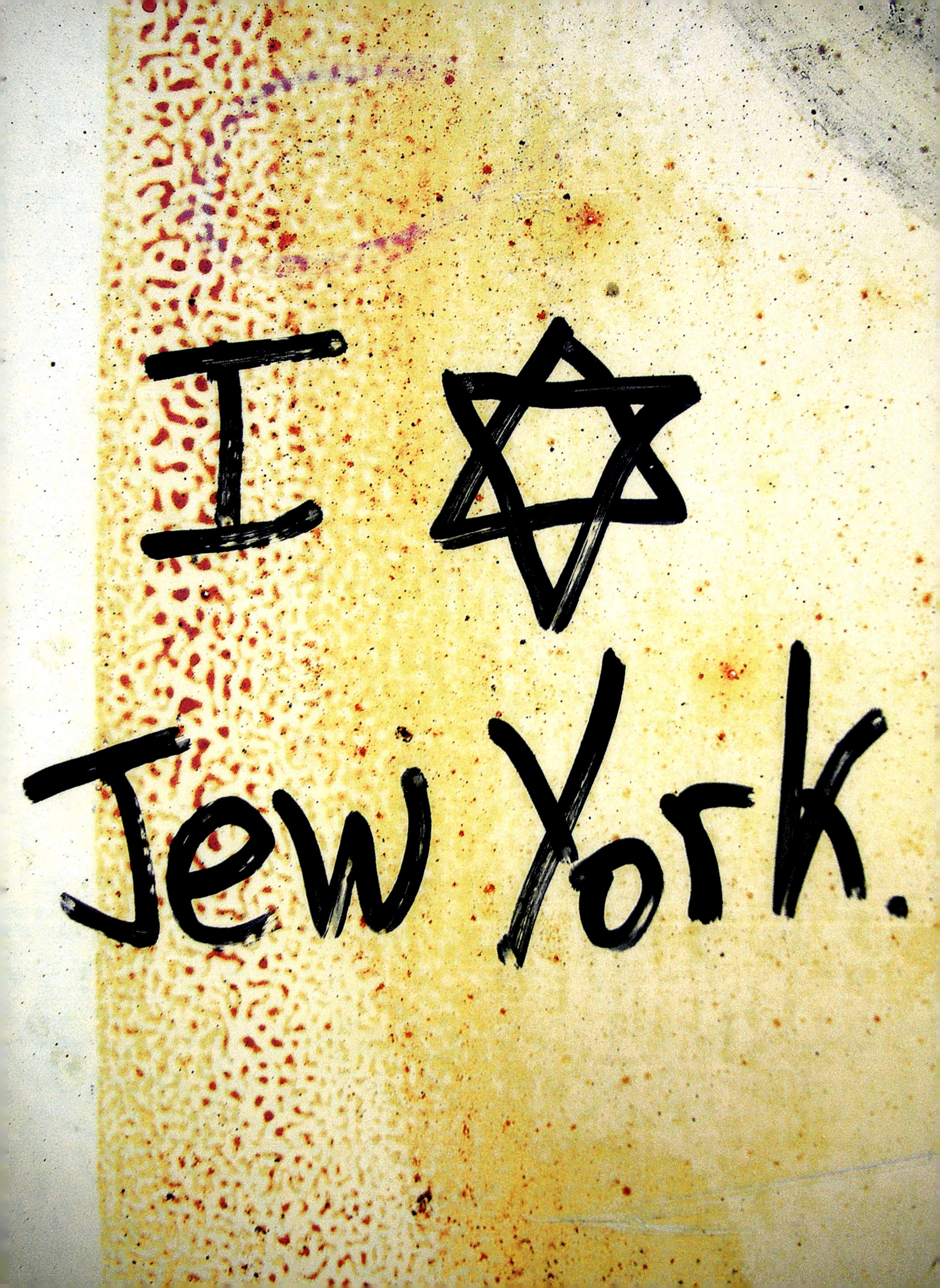

I ✡
Jew York.

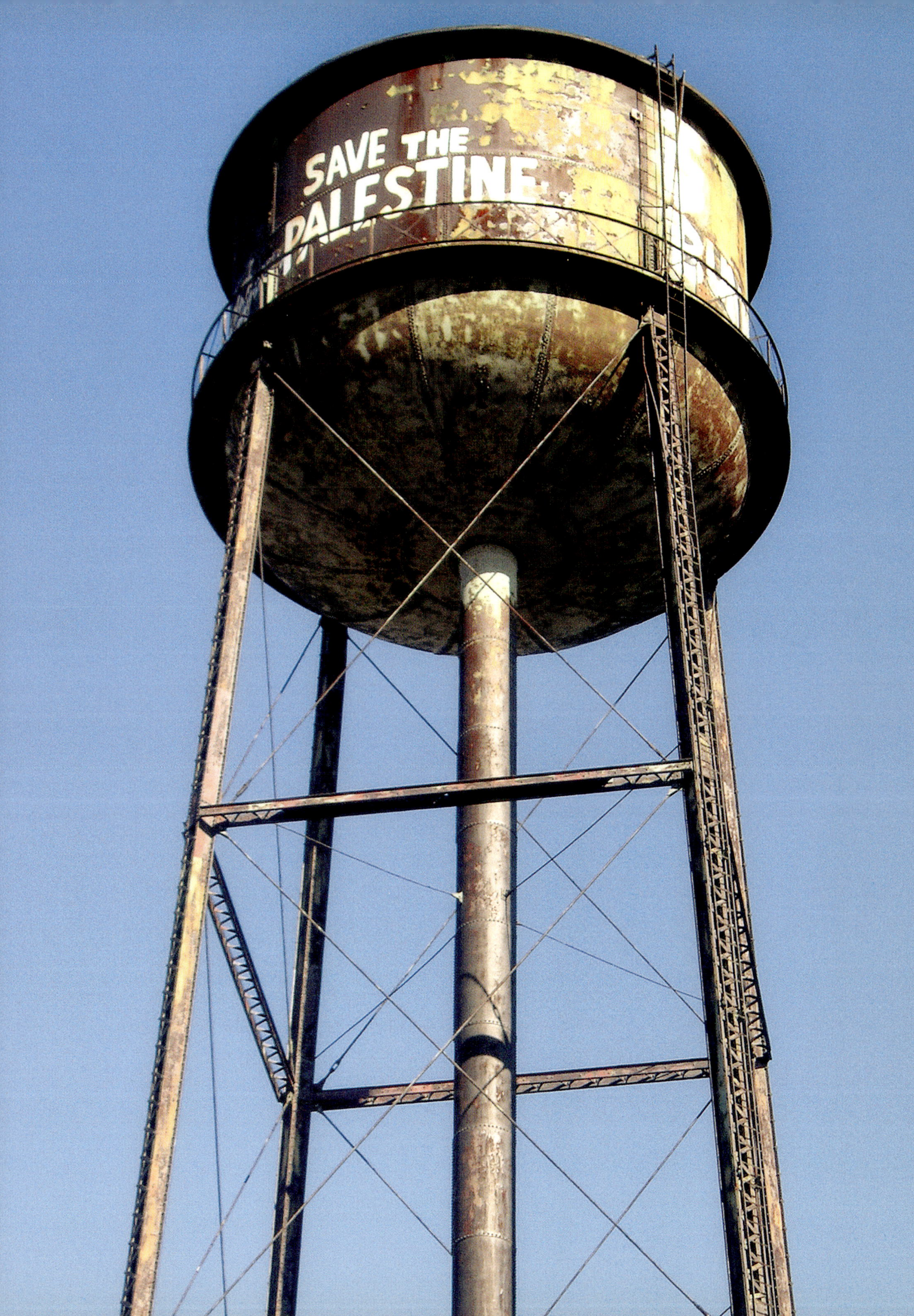
SAVE THE
PALESTINE

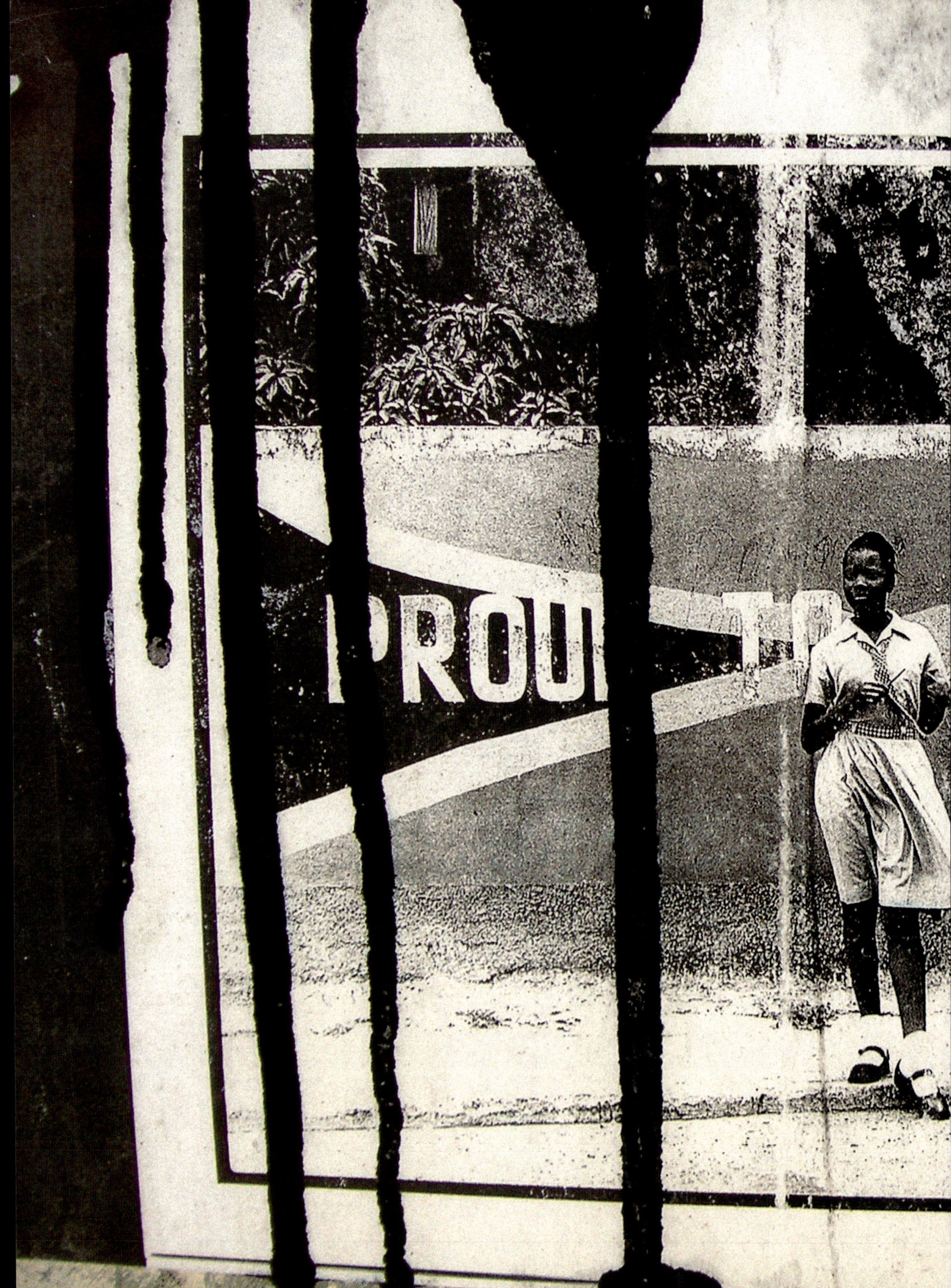
PROU

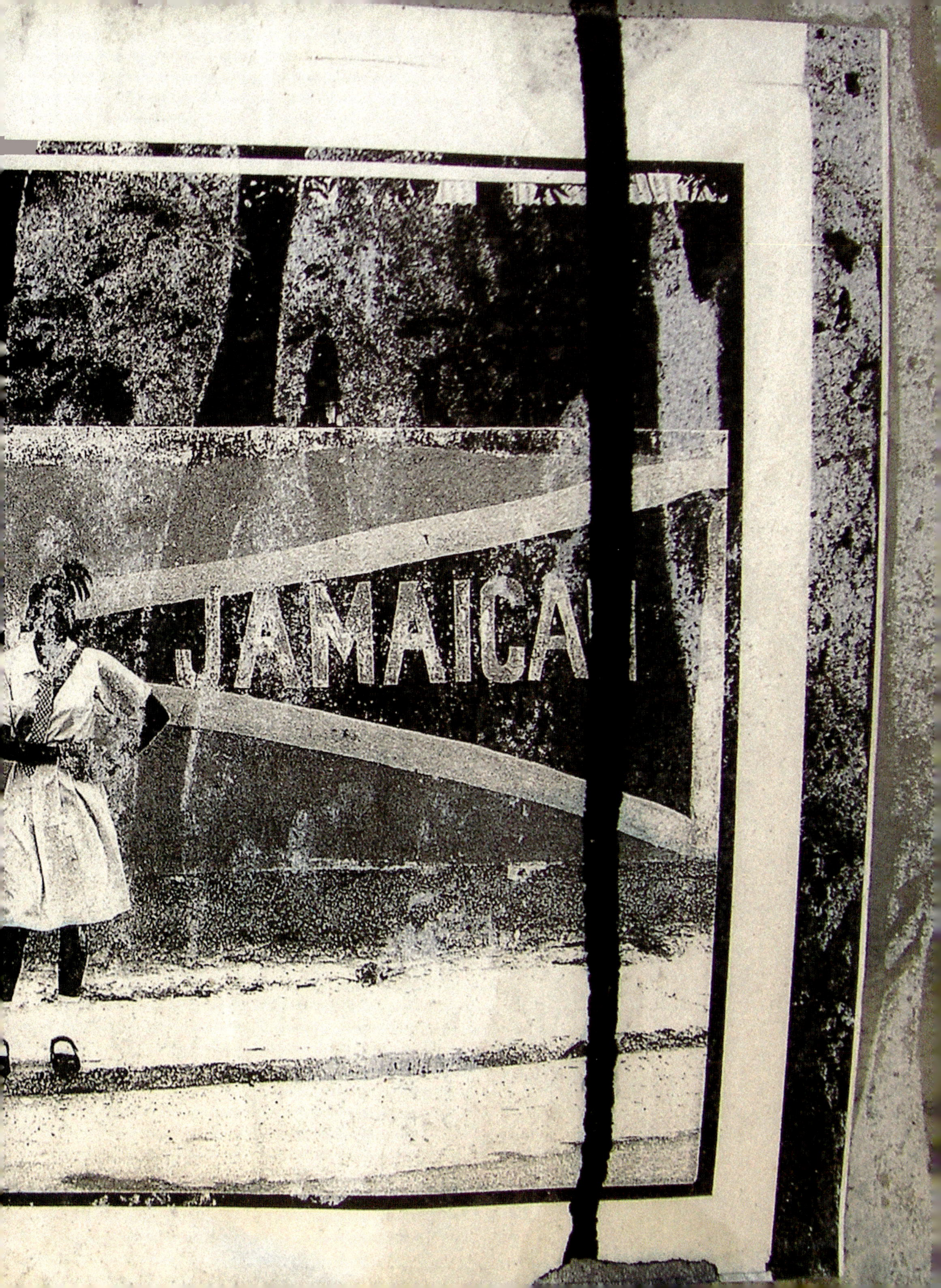
JAMAICA

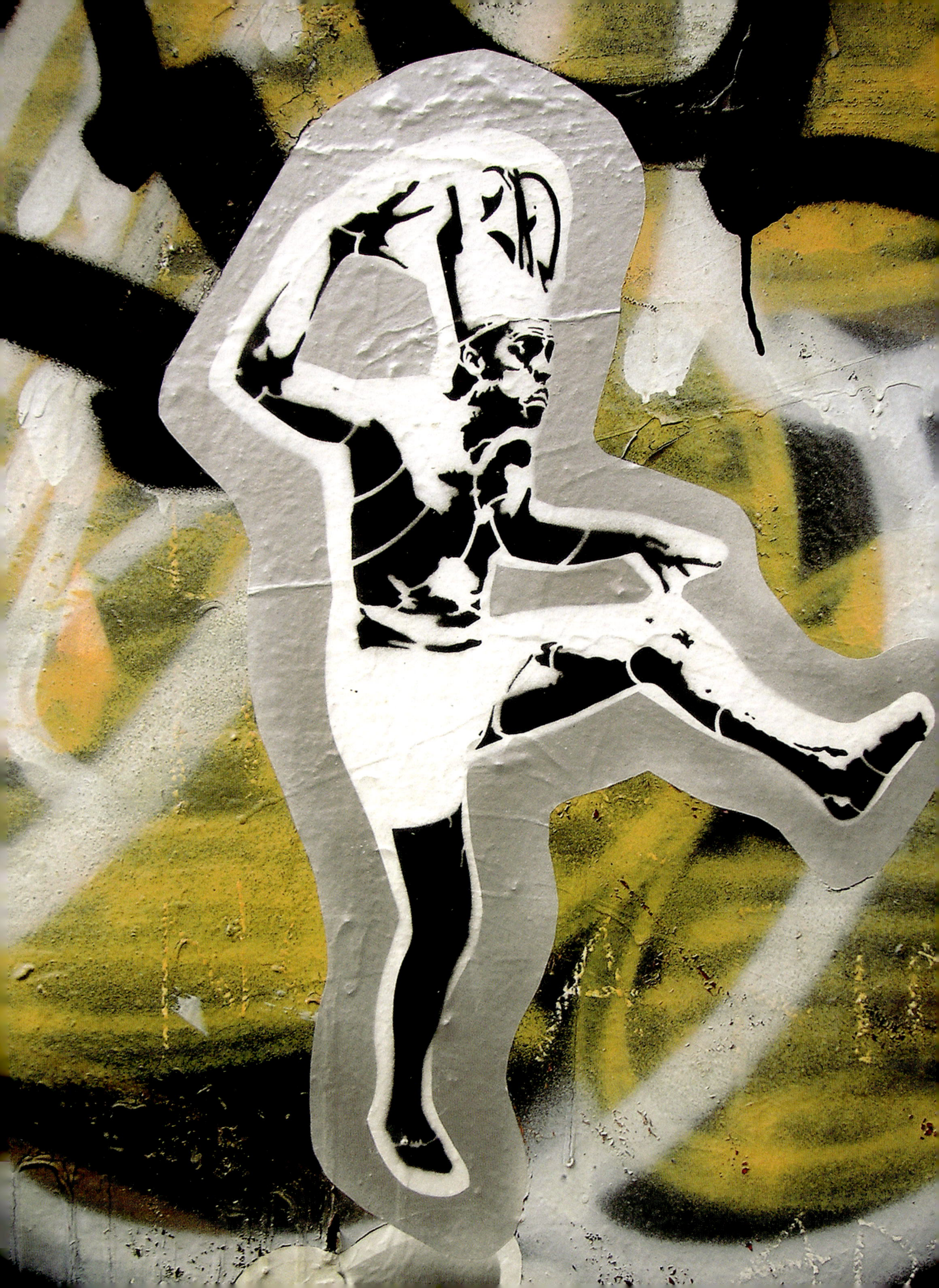

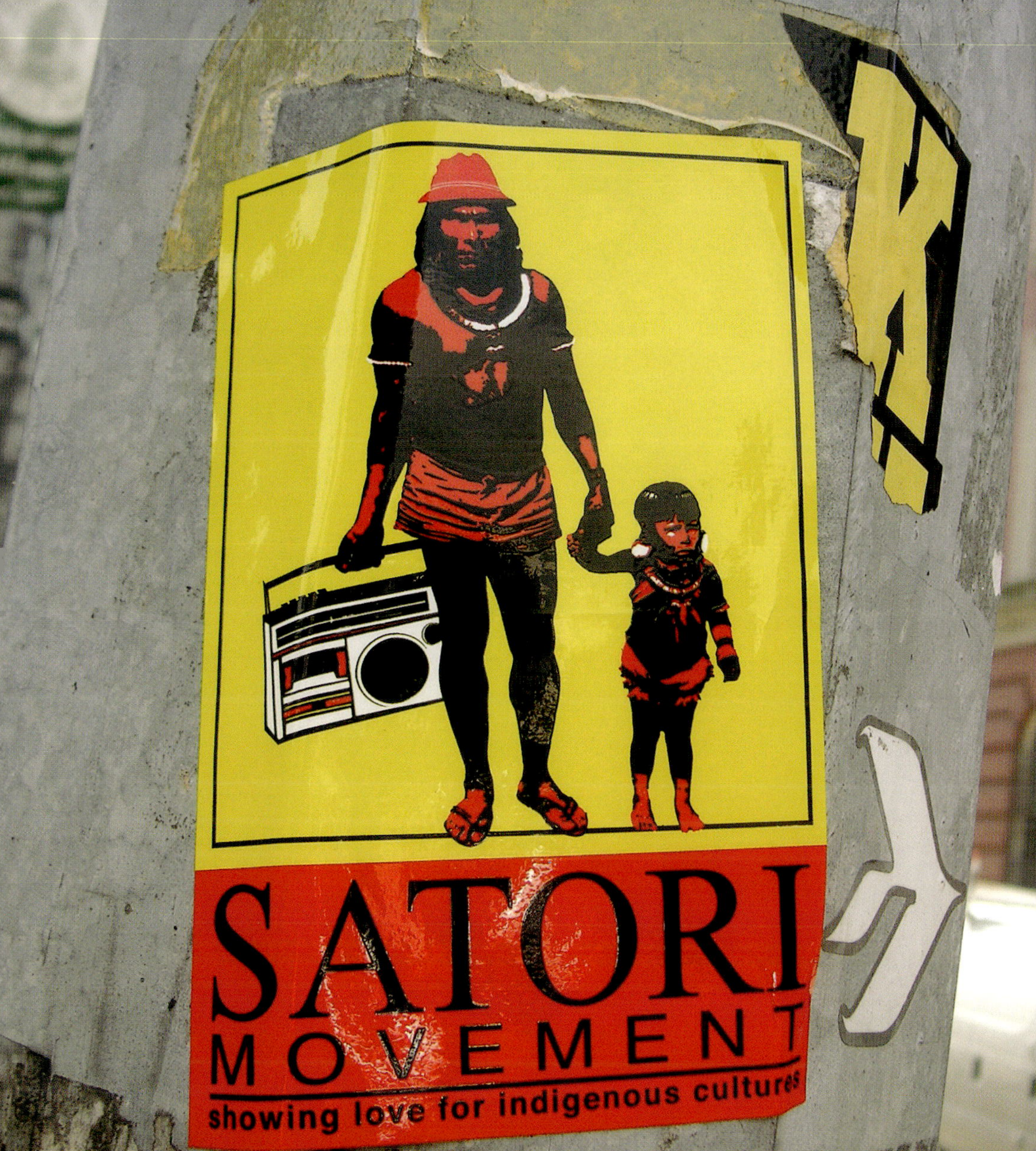
SATORI
MOVEMENT
showing love for indigenous cultures

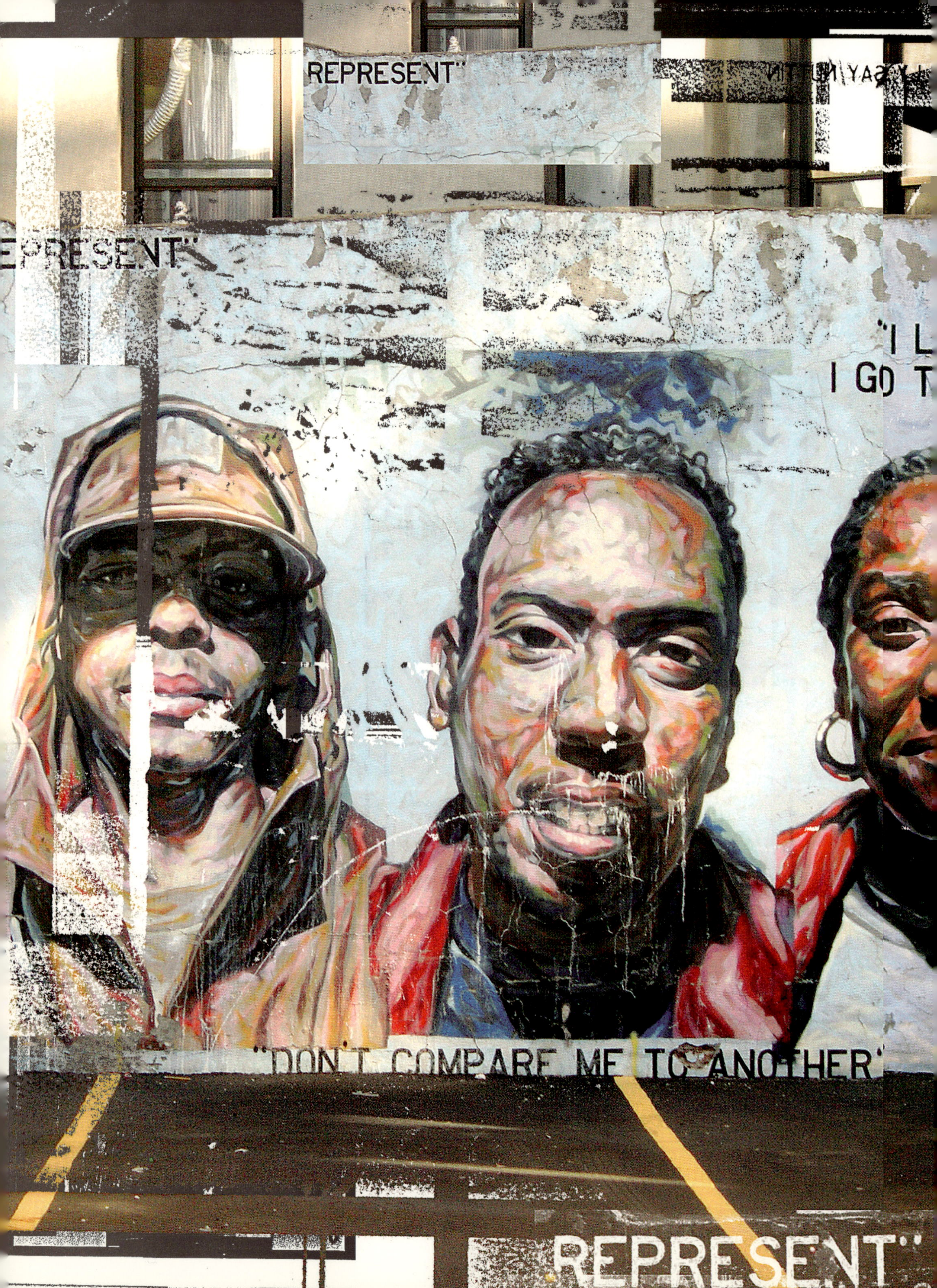
REPRESENT"
"DON'T COMPARE ME TO ANOTHER"
REPRESENT"

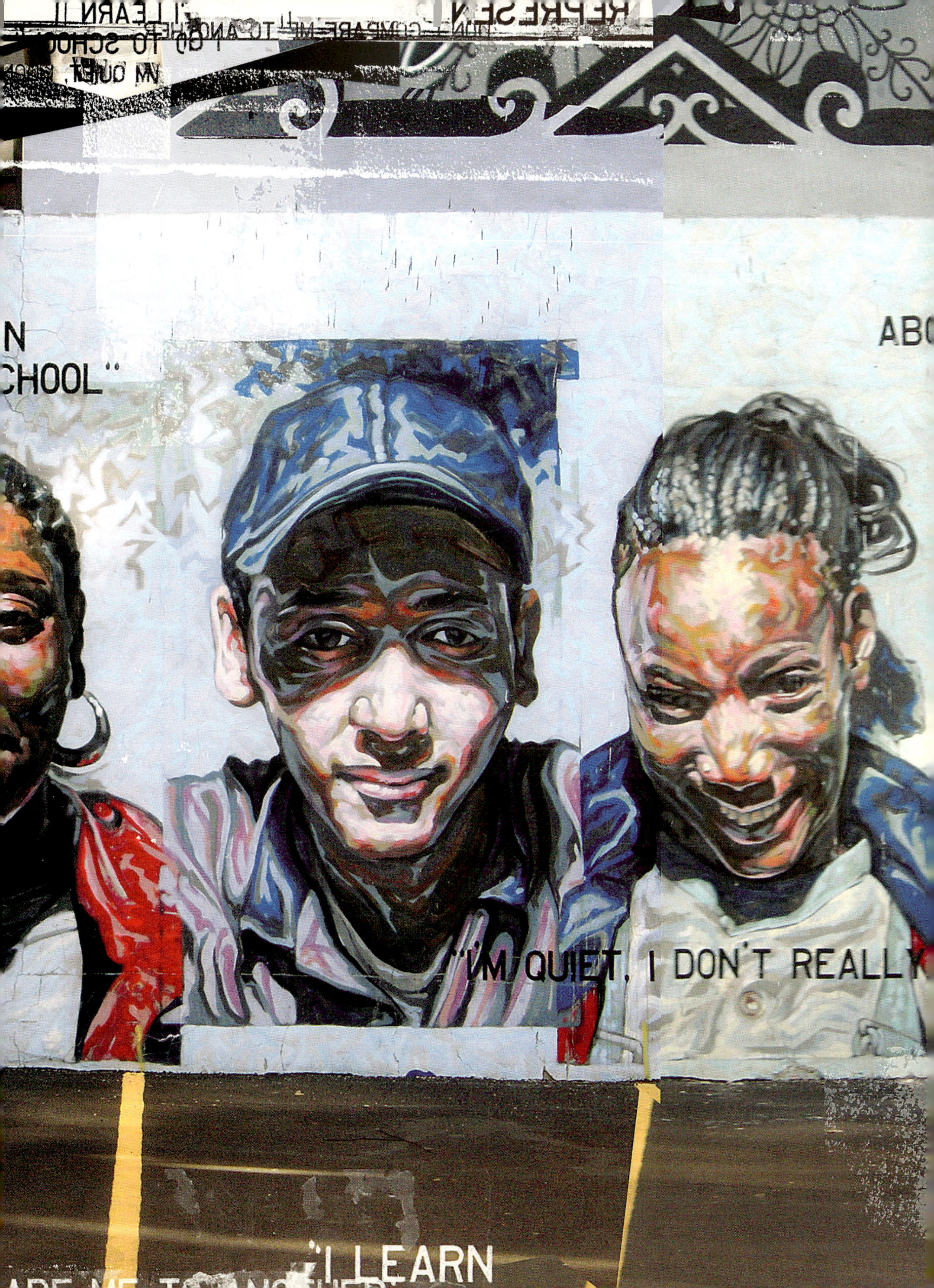

"I'M QUIET. I DON'T REALLY
CHOOL"
ABO
"I LEARN

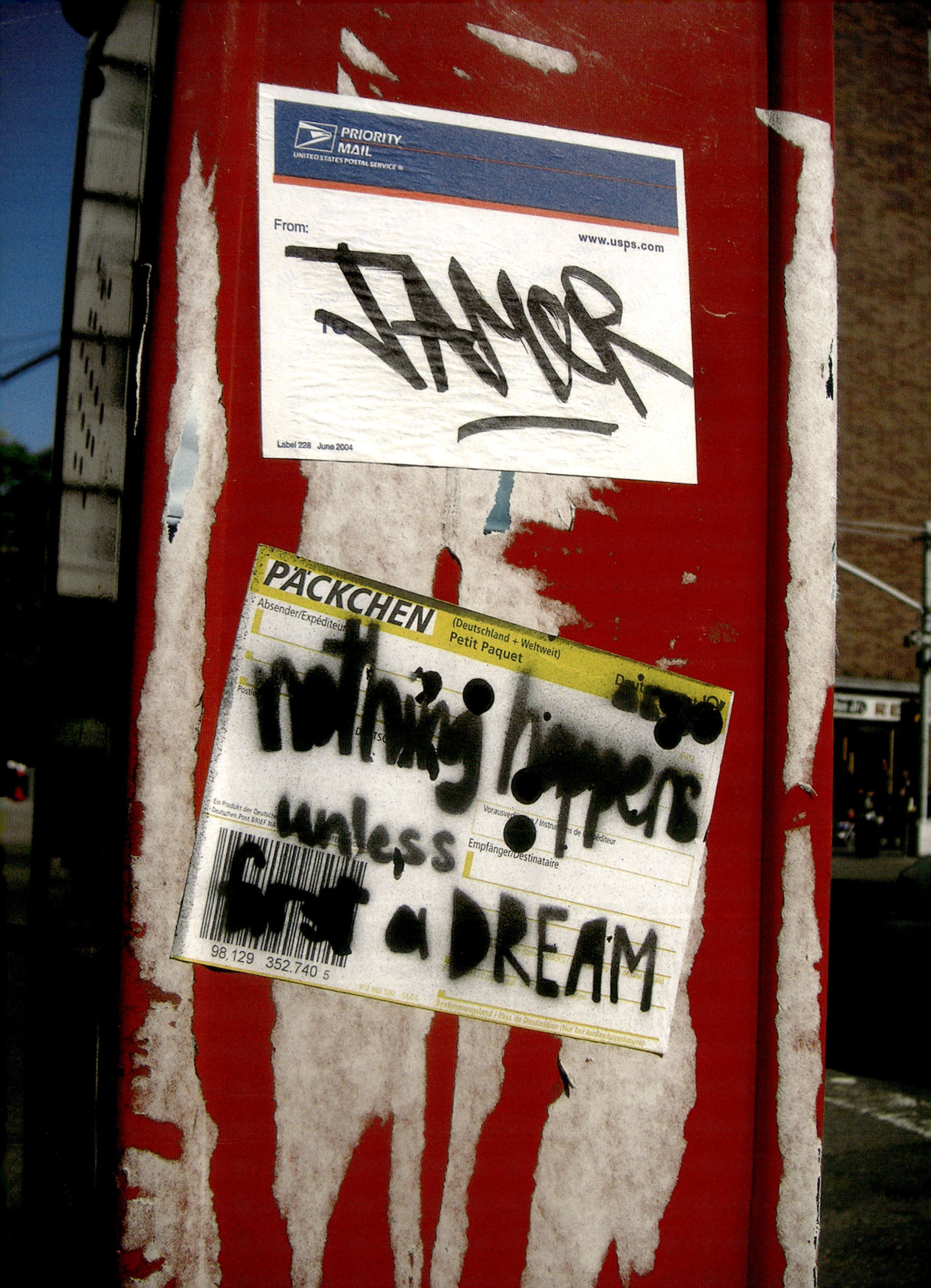
PRIORITY MAIL
UNITED STATES POSTAL SERVICE
From:
www.usps.com
Label 228 June 2004
PÄCKCHEN
Absender/Expéditeur
(Deutschland + Weltweit)
Petit Paquet
nothing happens unless first a DREAM
Empfänger/Destinataire
98,129 352.740 5

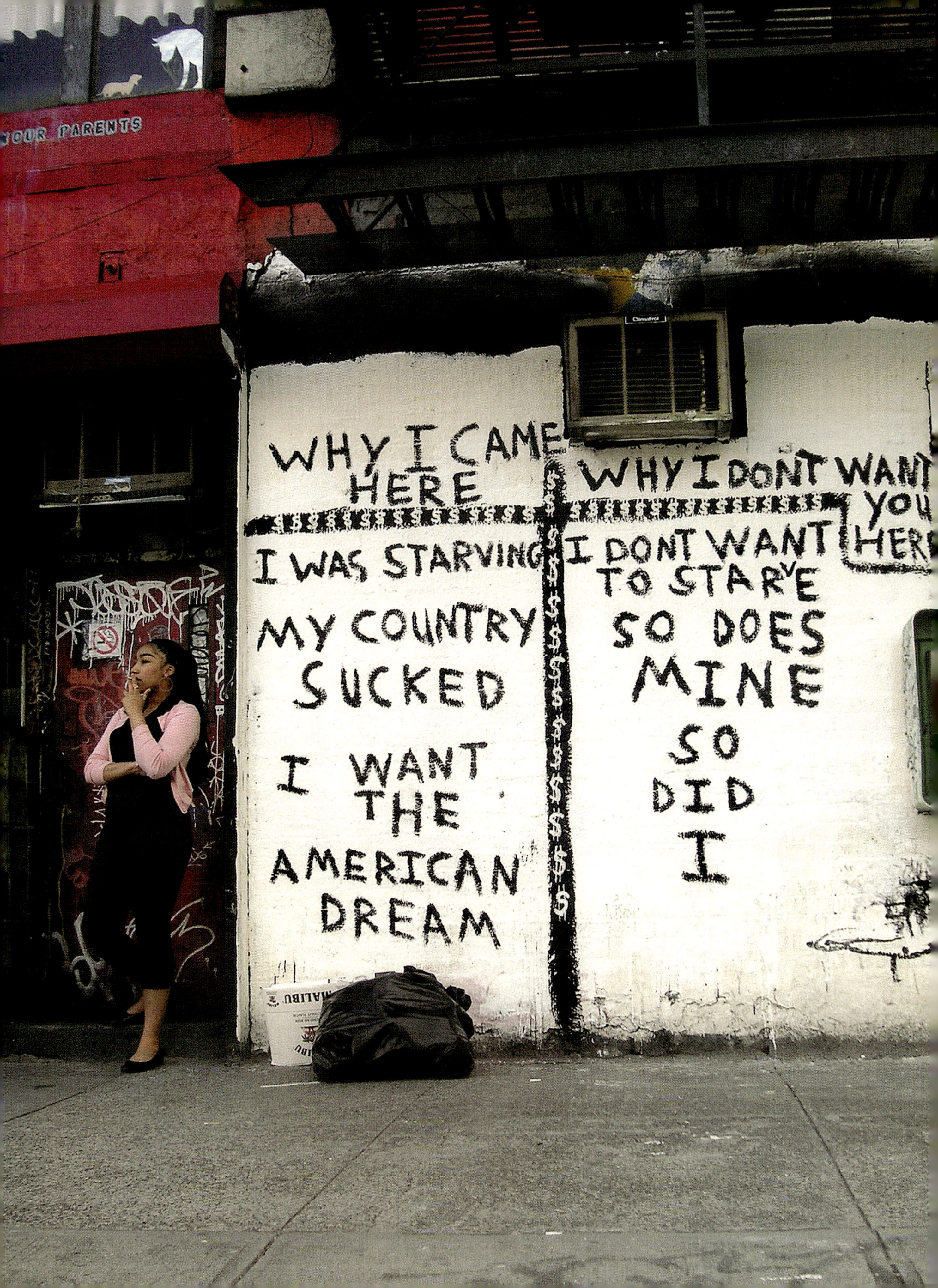

OUR PARENTS
WHY I CAME HERE
I WAS STARVING
MY COUNTRY SUCKED
I WANT THE AMERICAN DREAM
WHY I DONT WANT YOU HERE
I DONT WANT TO STARVE
SO DOES MINE
SO DID I
MALIBU

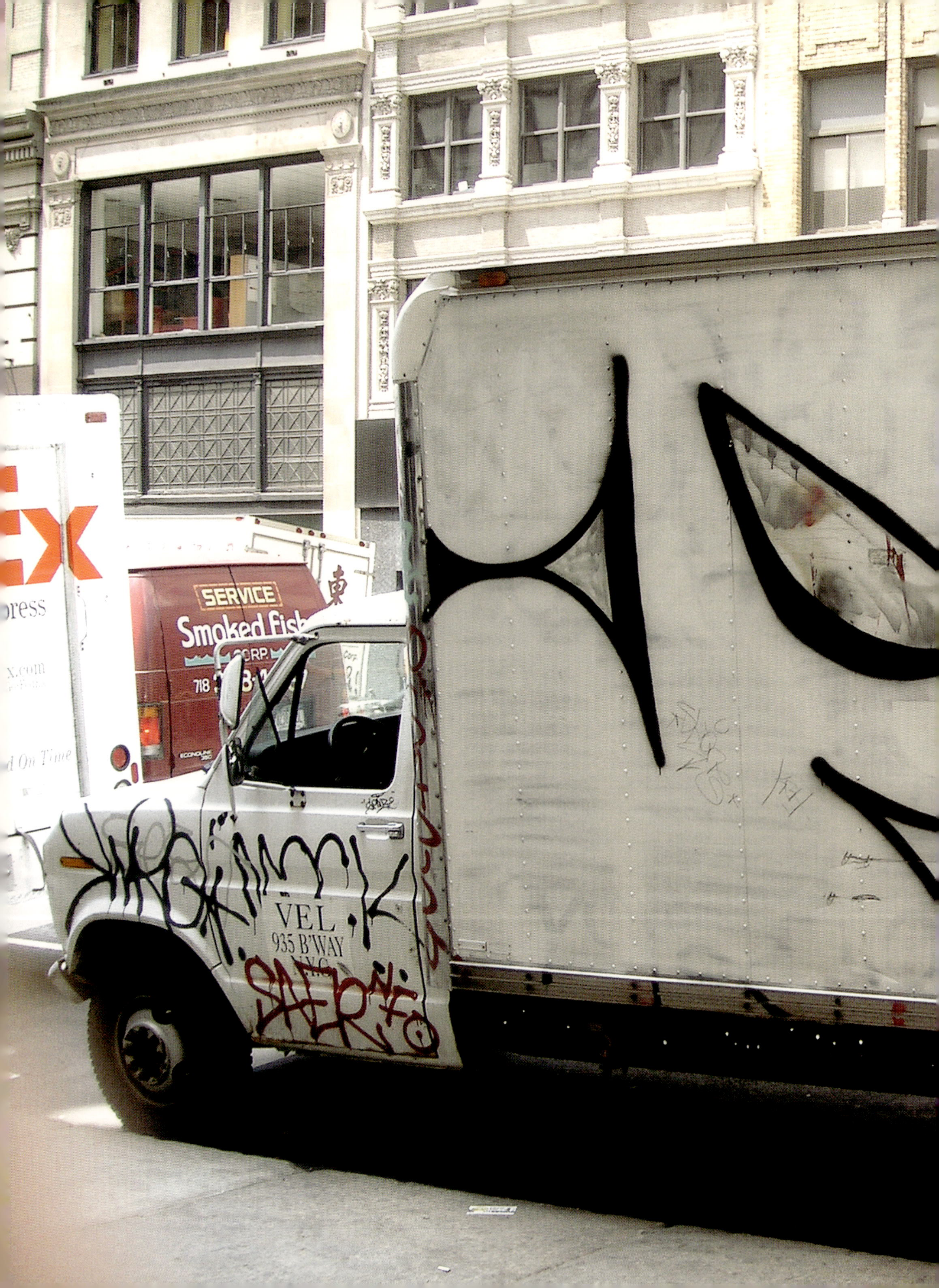
SERVICE
Smoked Fish
CORP.
VEL
935 B'WAY

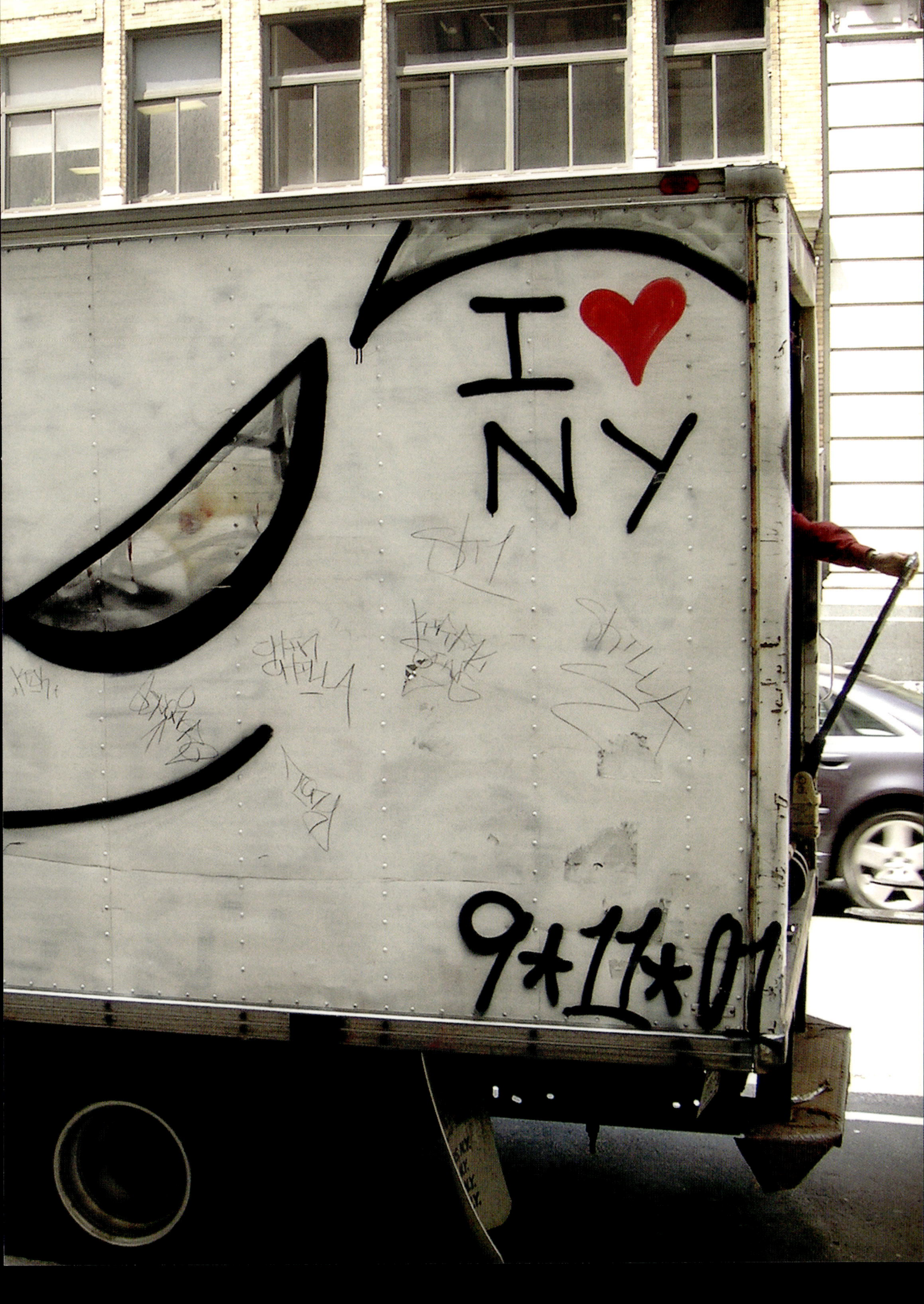
I ♥
NY
9*11*01

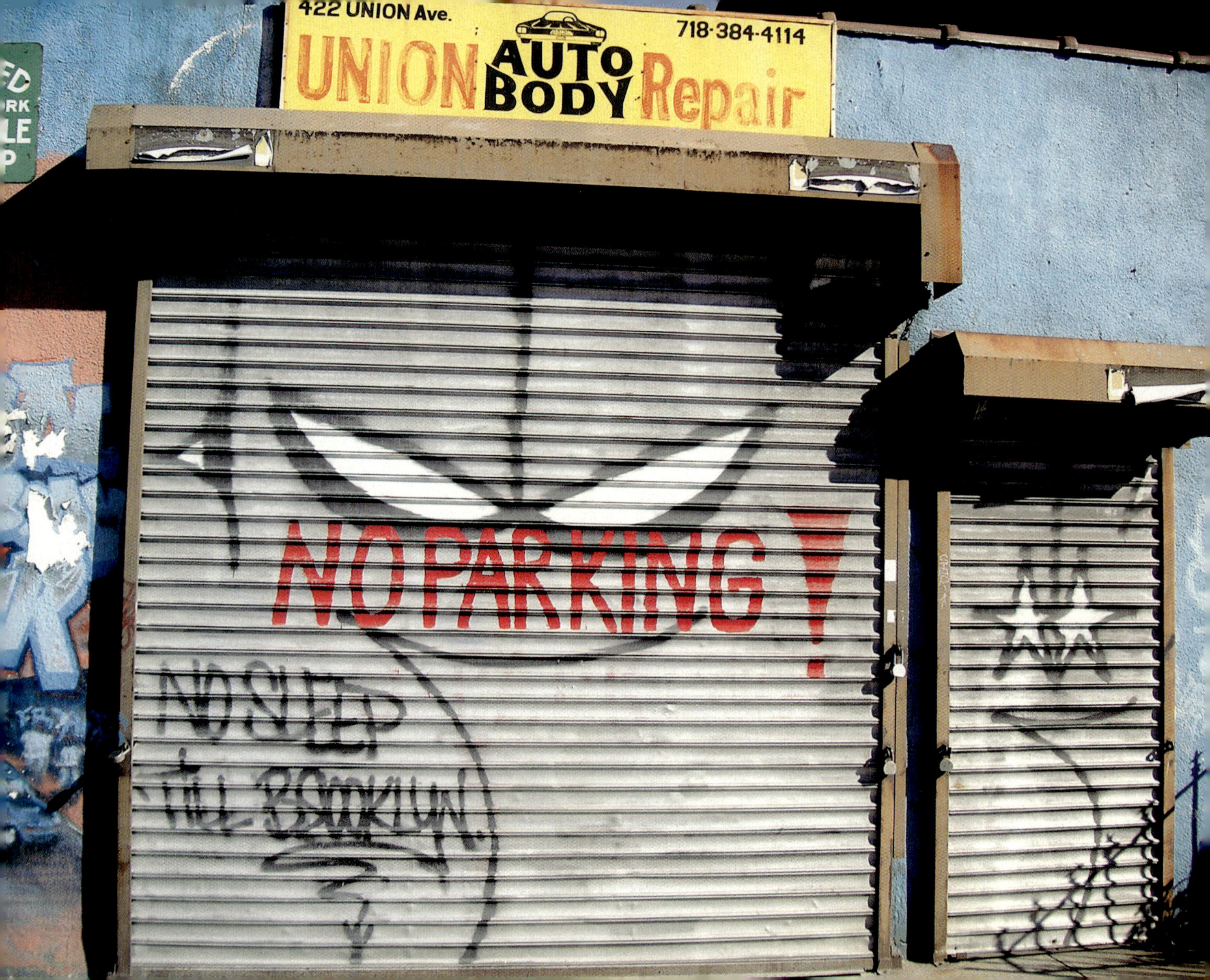
422 UNION Ave.
718-384-4114
UNION AUTO BODY Repair
NO PARKING!
NO SLEEP TILL BROOKLYN

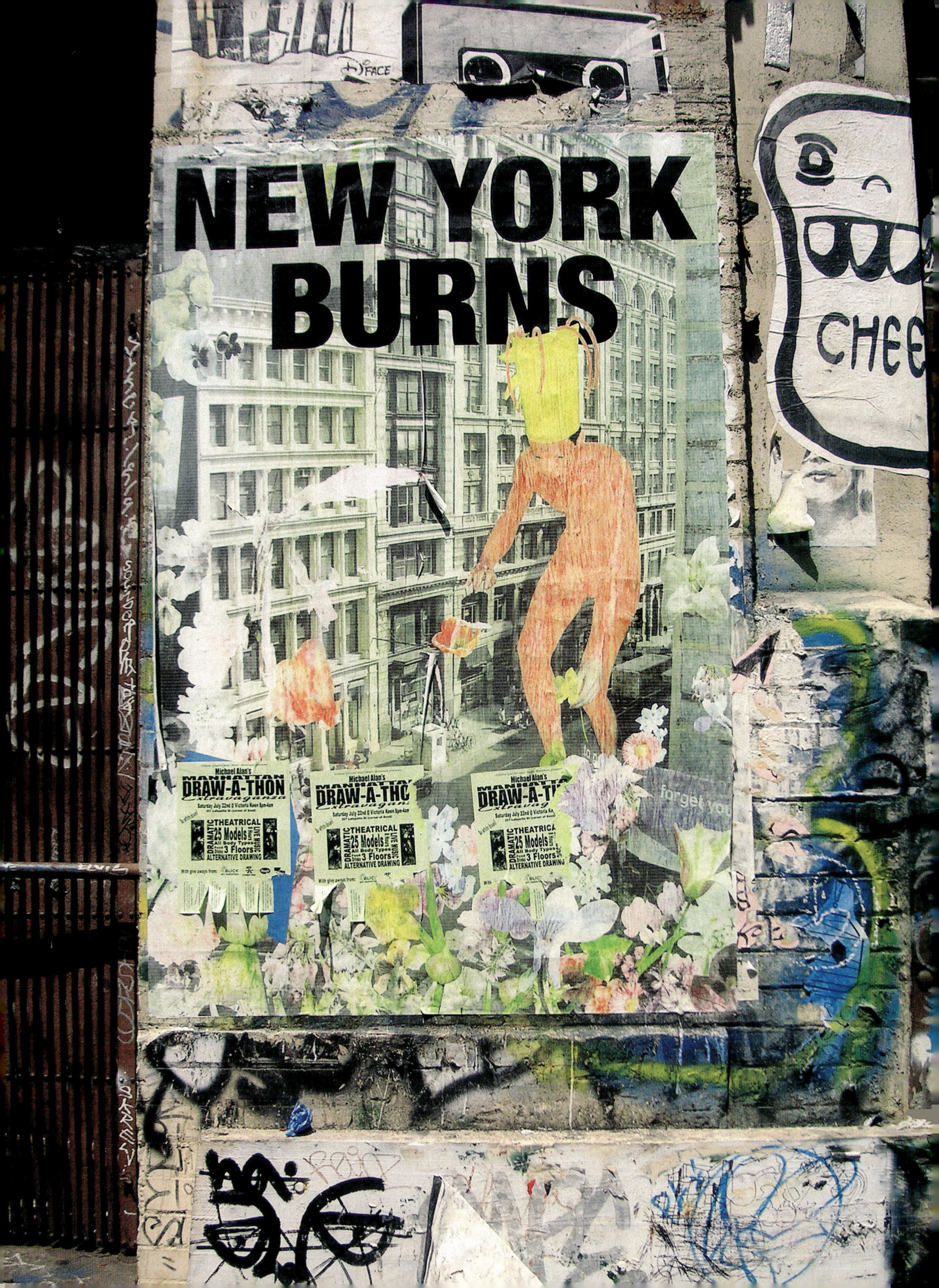
NEW YORK
BURNS
CHEE
Michael Alan's
DRAW-A-THON
THEATRICAL
25 Models
3 Floors
ALTERNATIVE DRAWING

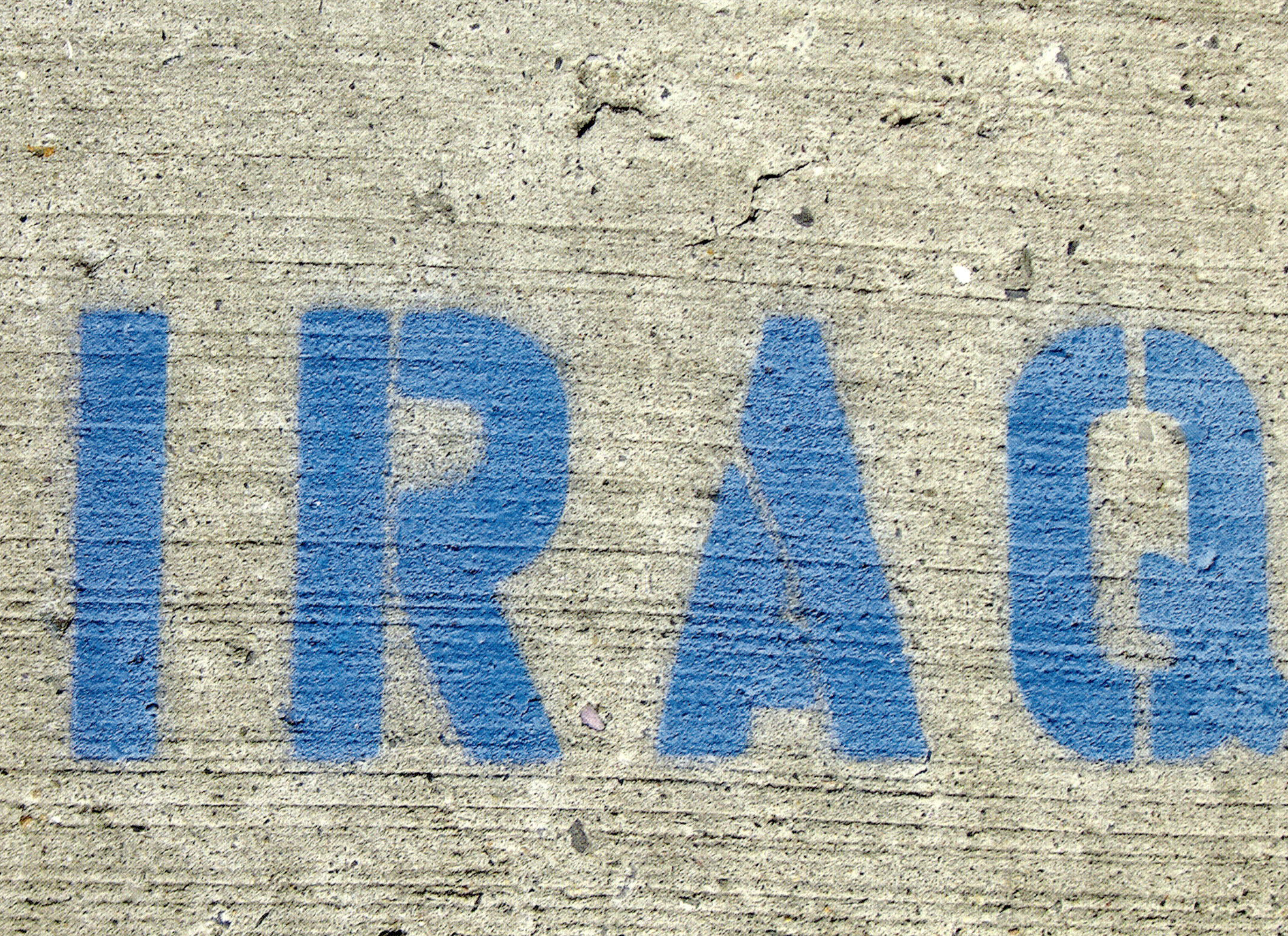
IRAQ

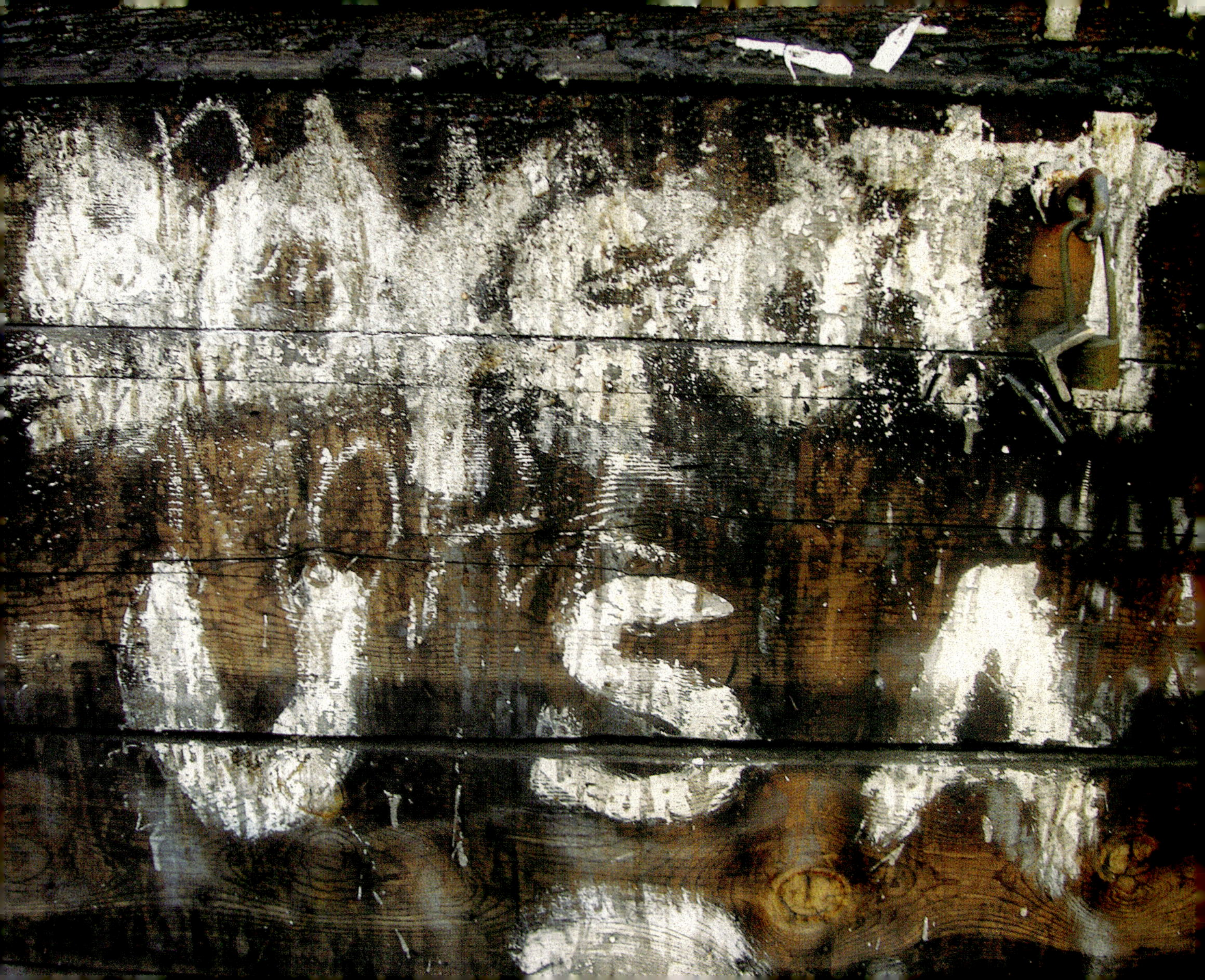

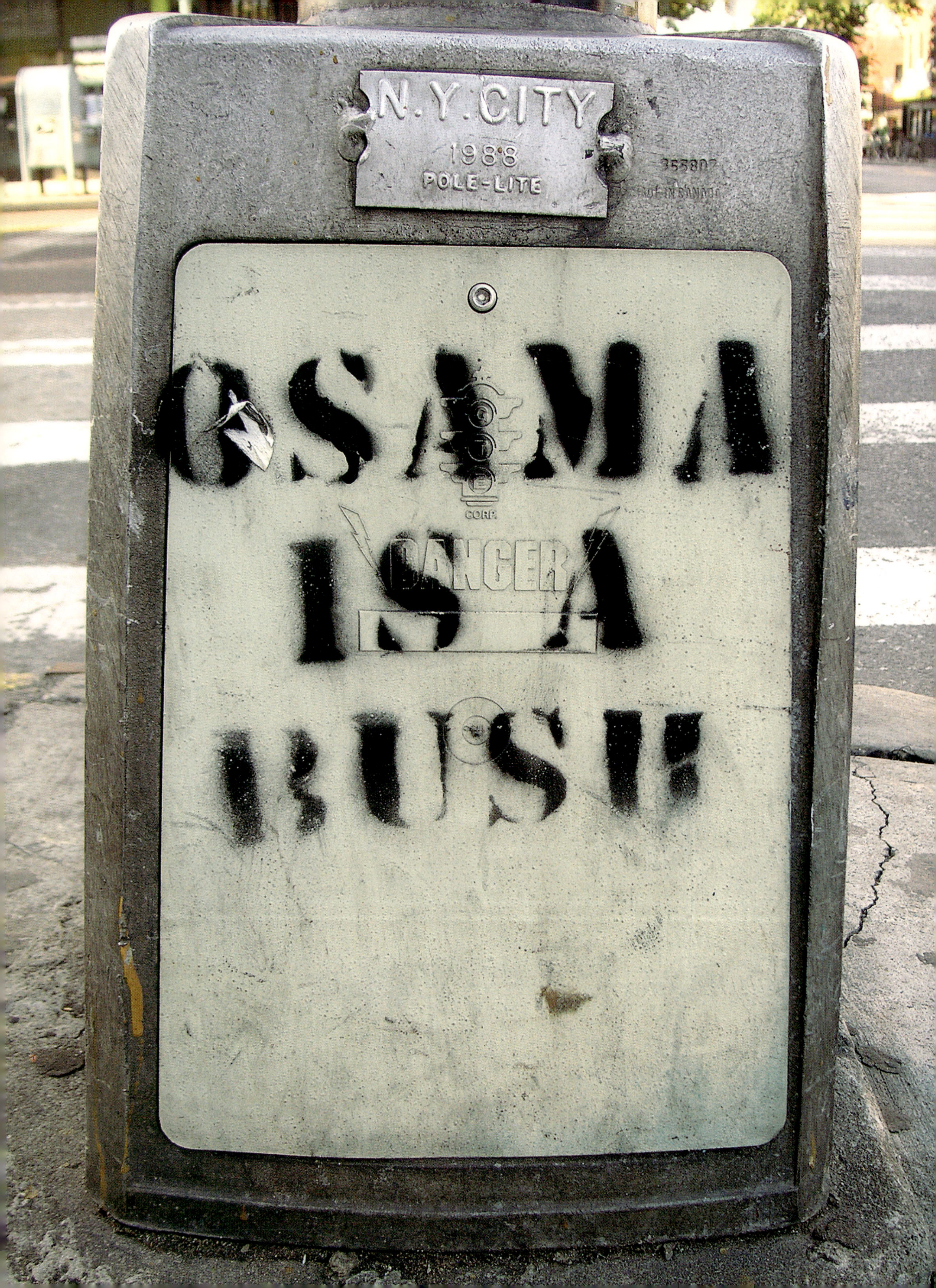
N.Y. CITY
1988
POLE-LITE
OSAMA
IS A
BUSH
DANGER

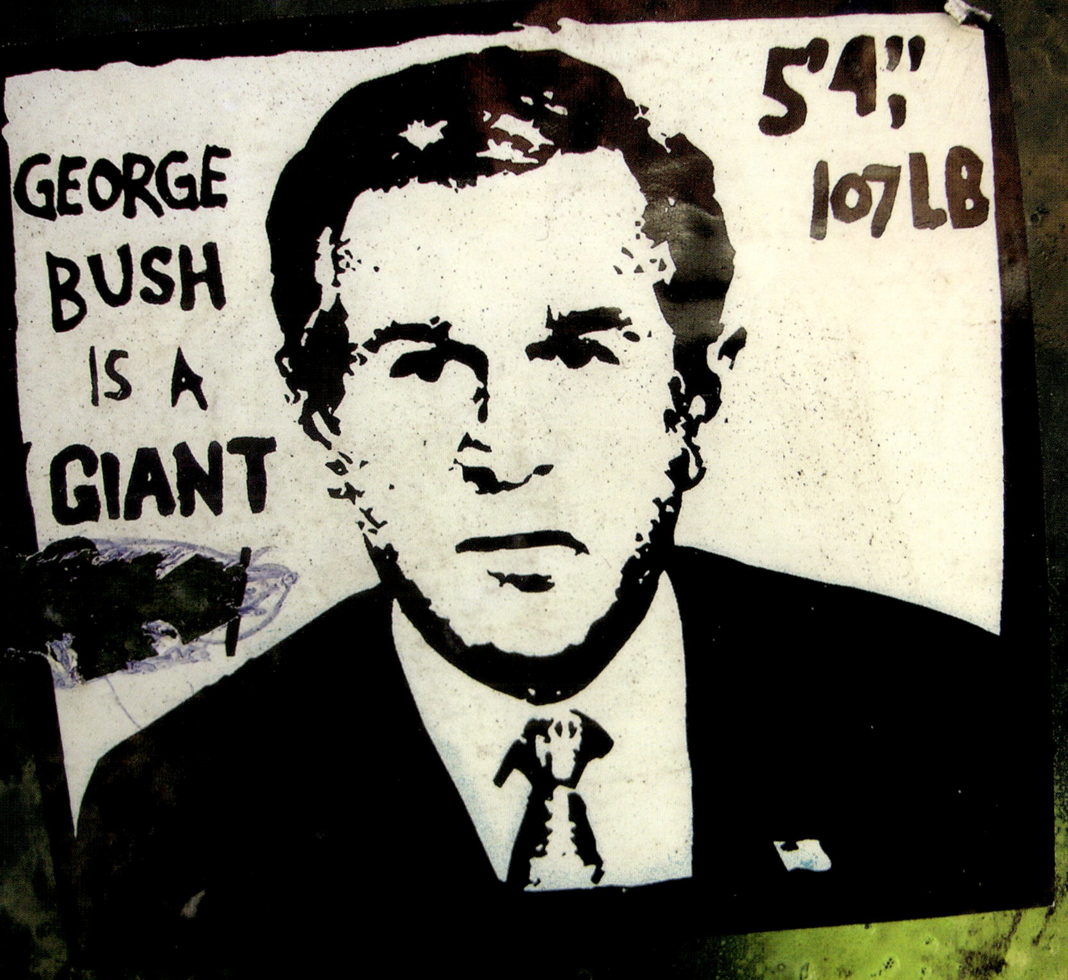
GEORGE BUSH IS A GIANT
5'4"
107 LB

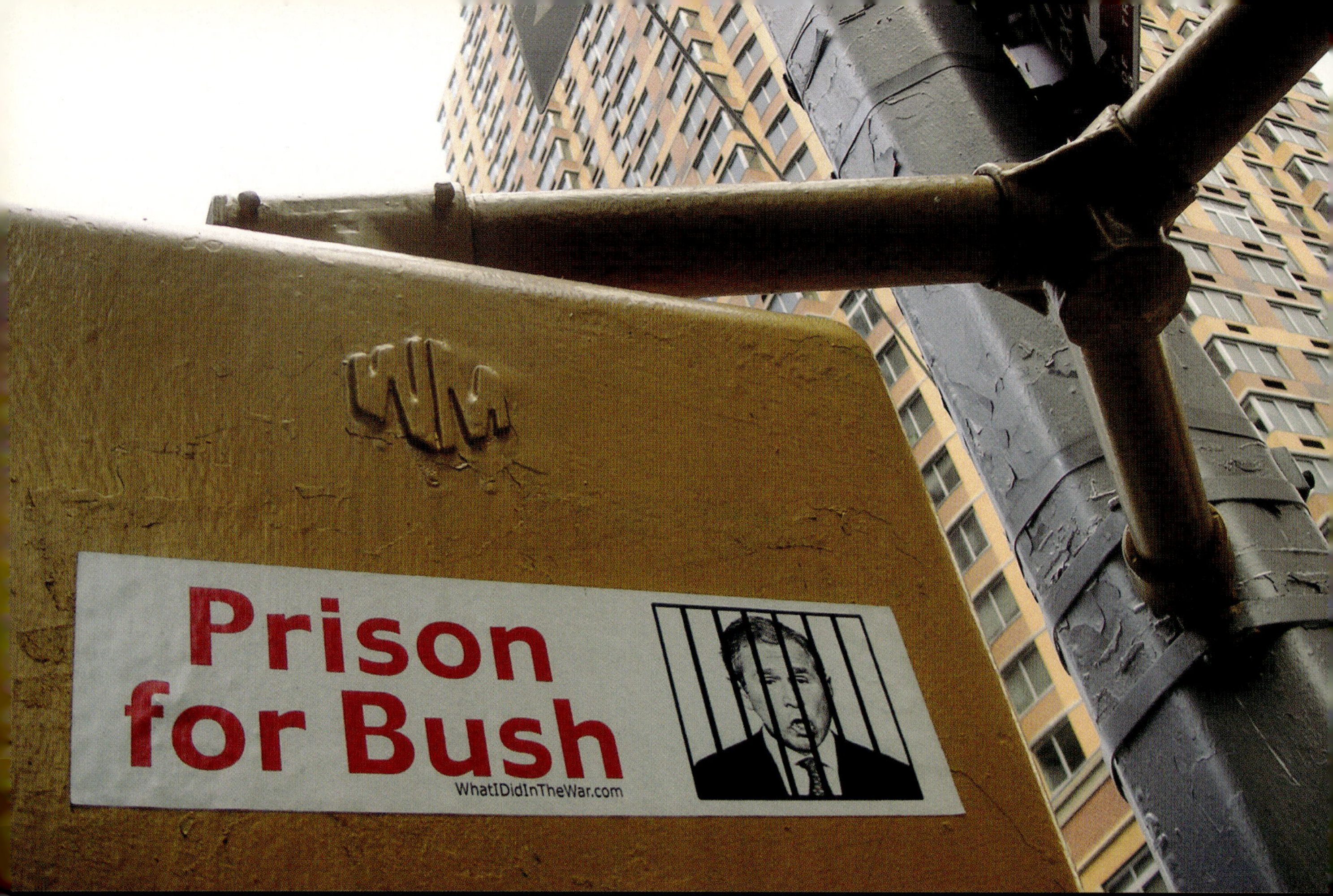

Prison
for Bush
WhatIDidInTheWar.com

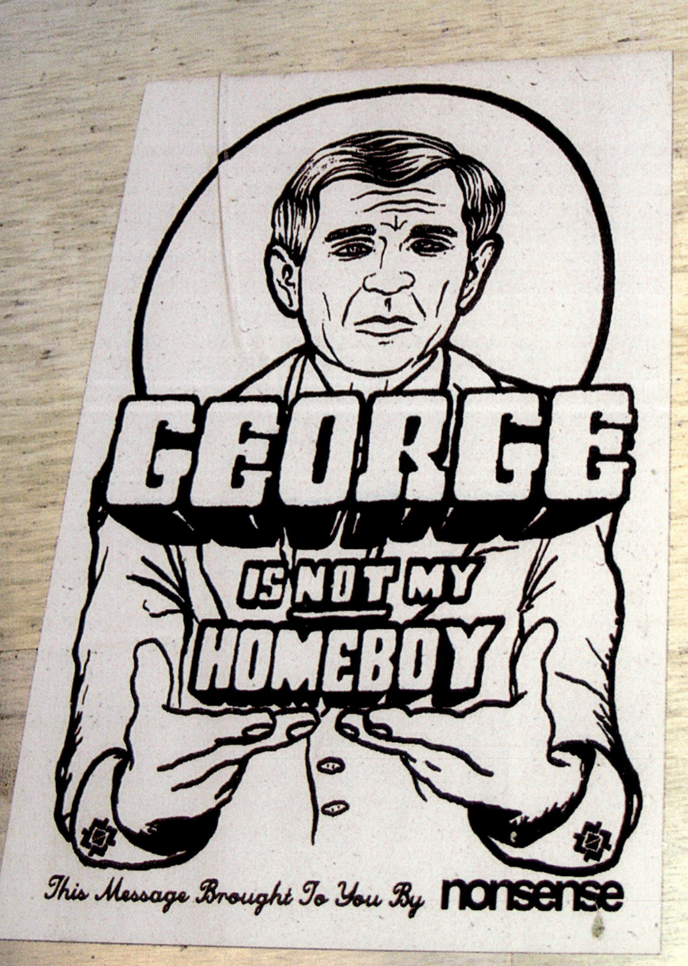

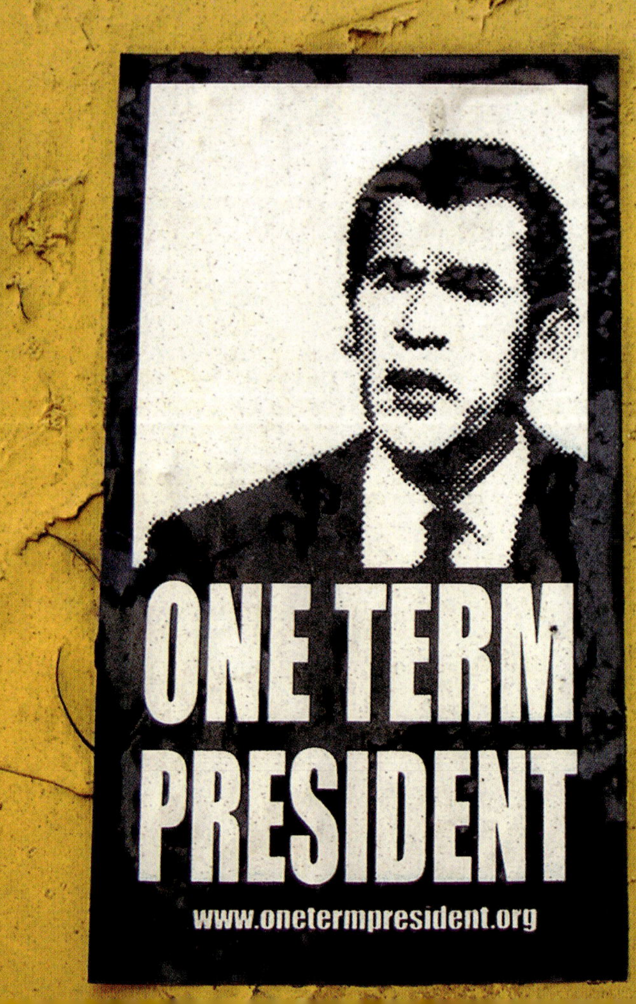

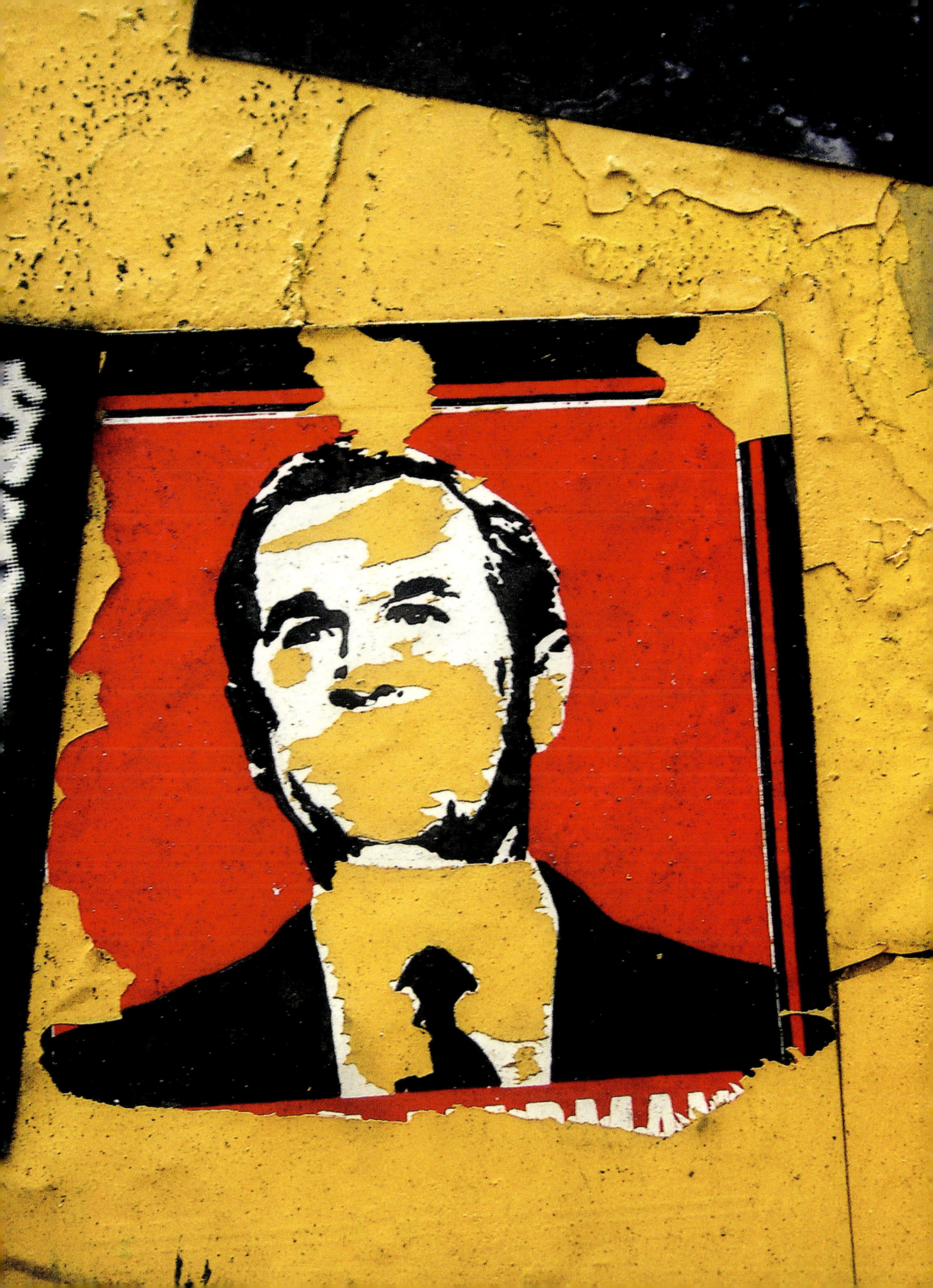

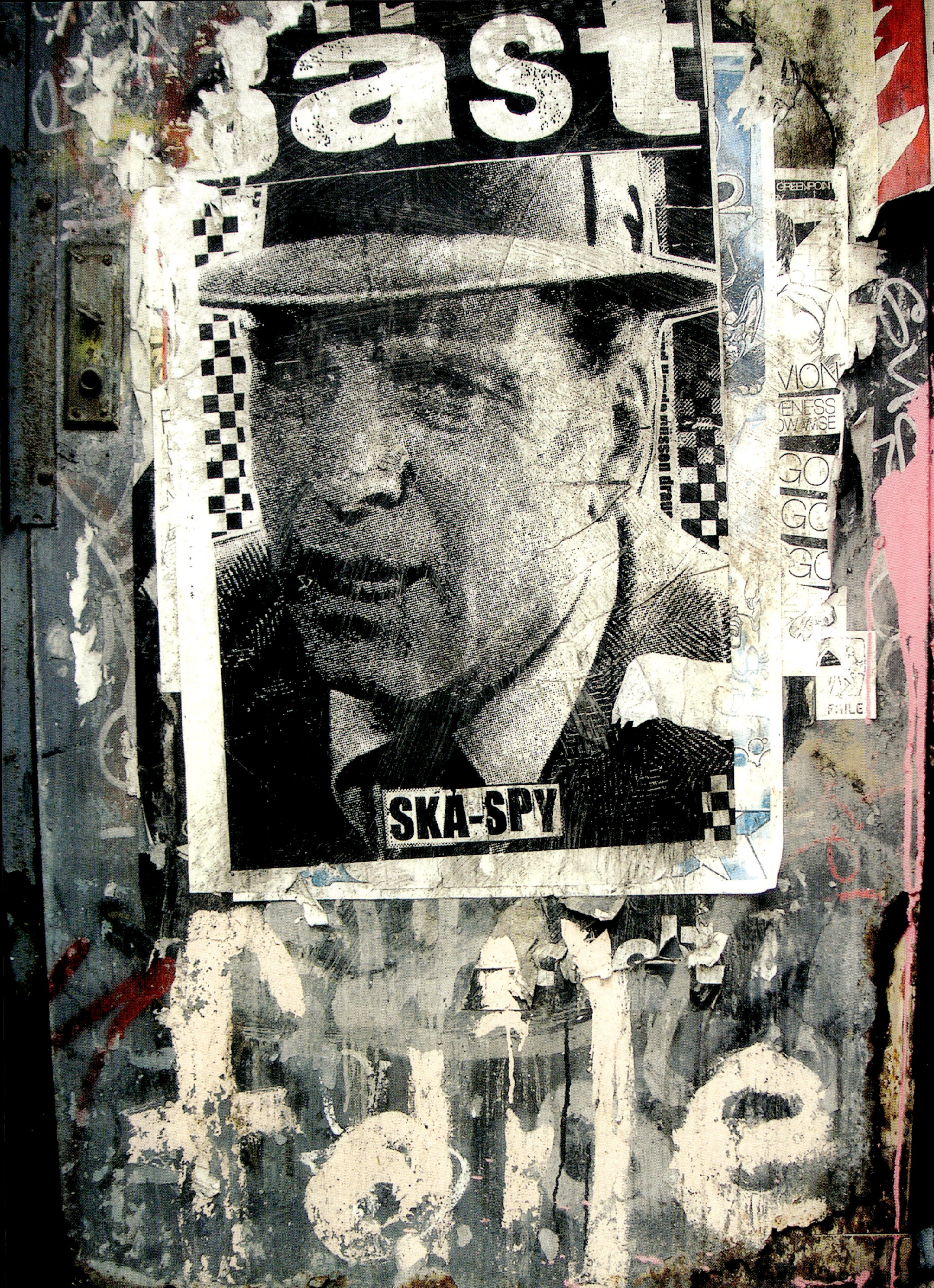
ast
SKA-SPY

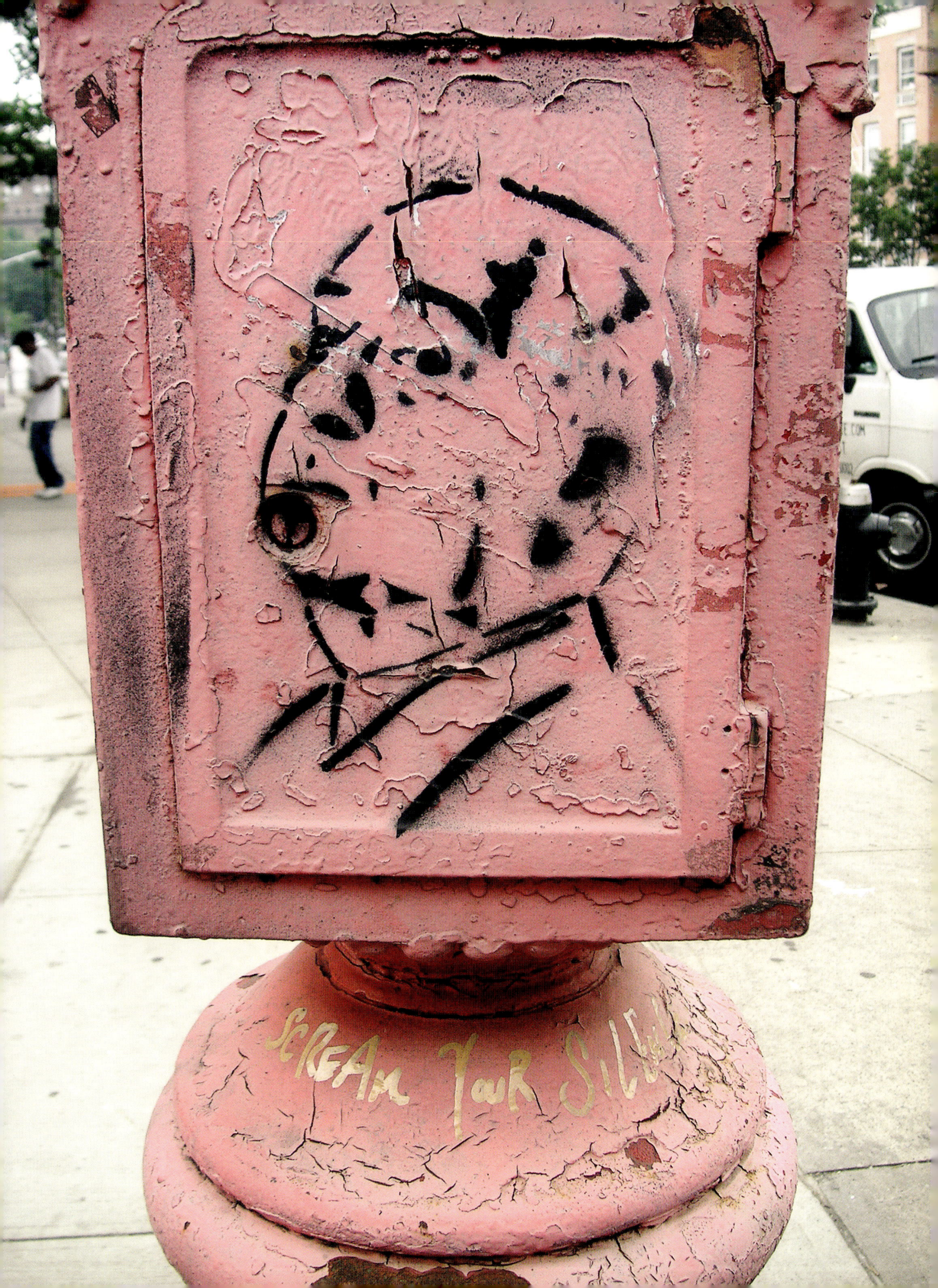
SCREAM YOUR

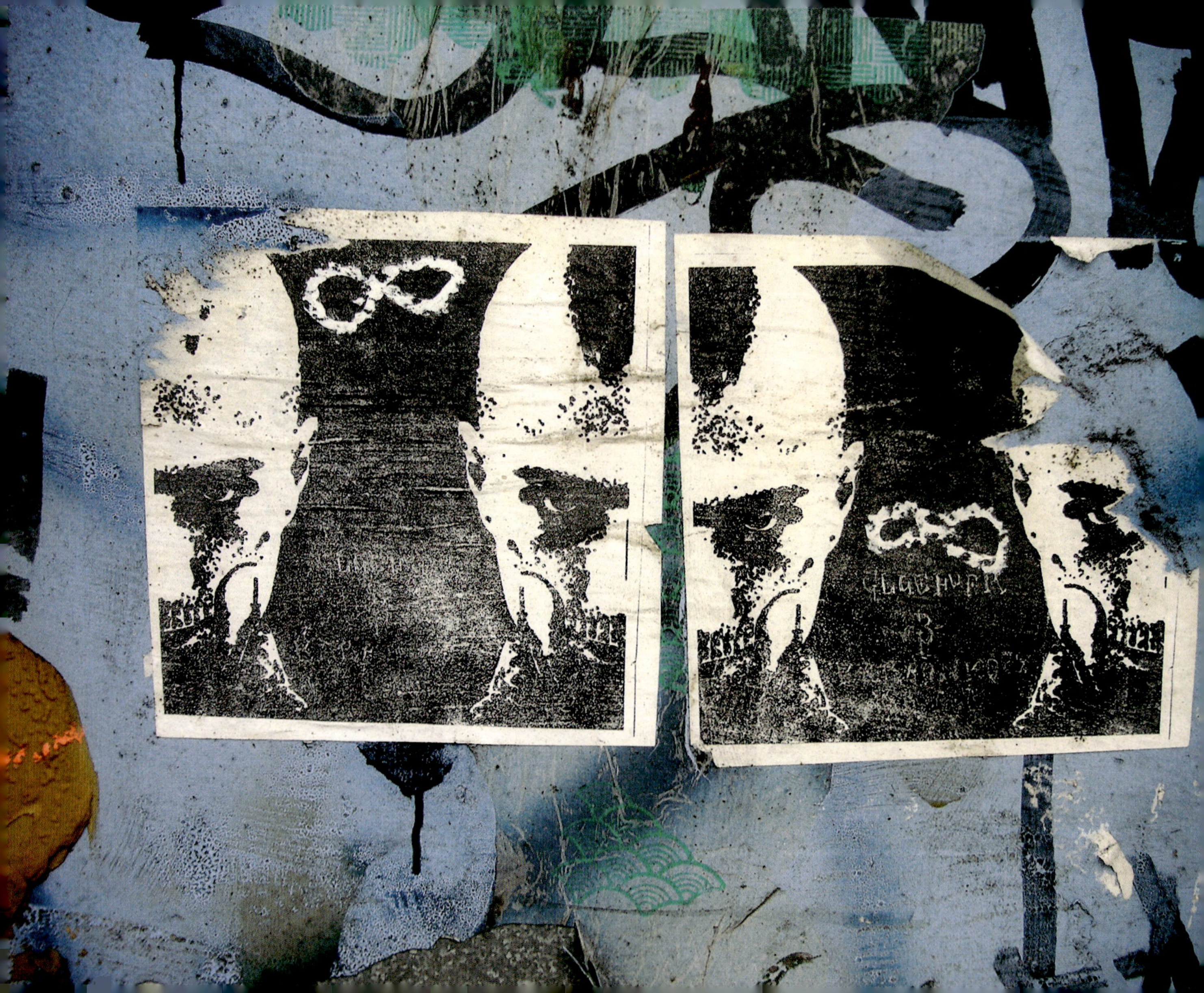

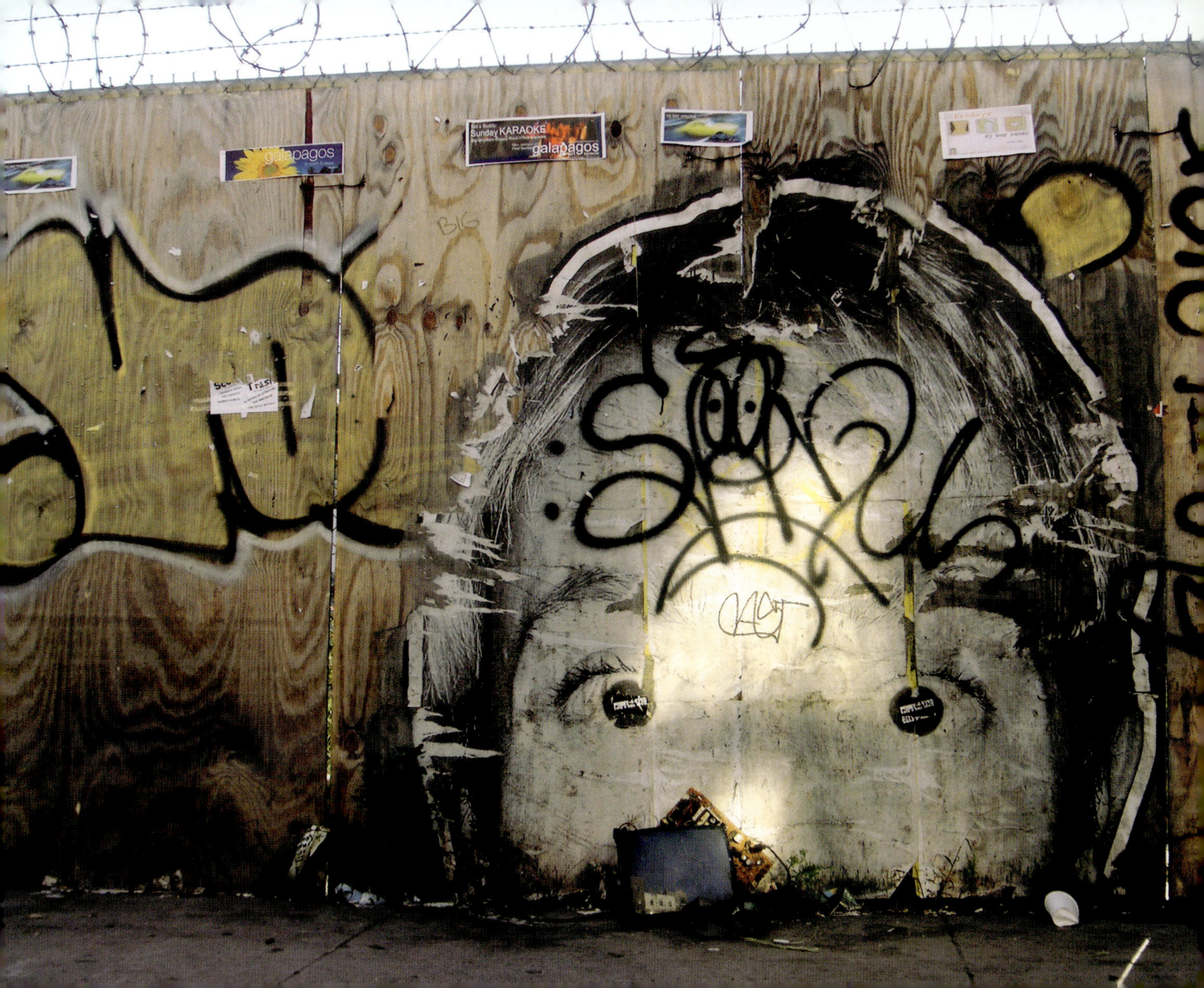
galapagos
Sunday KARAOKE
galapagos
BIG

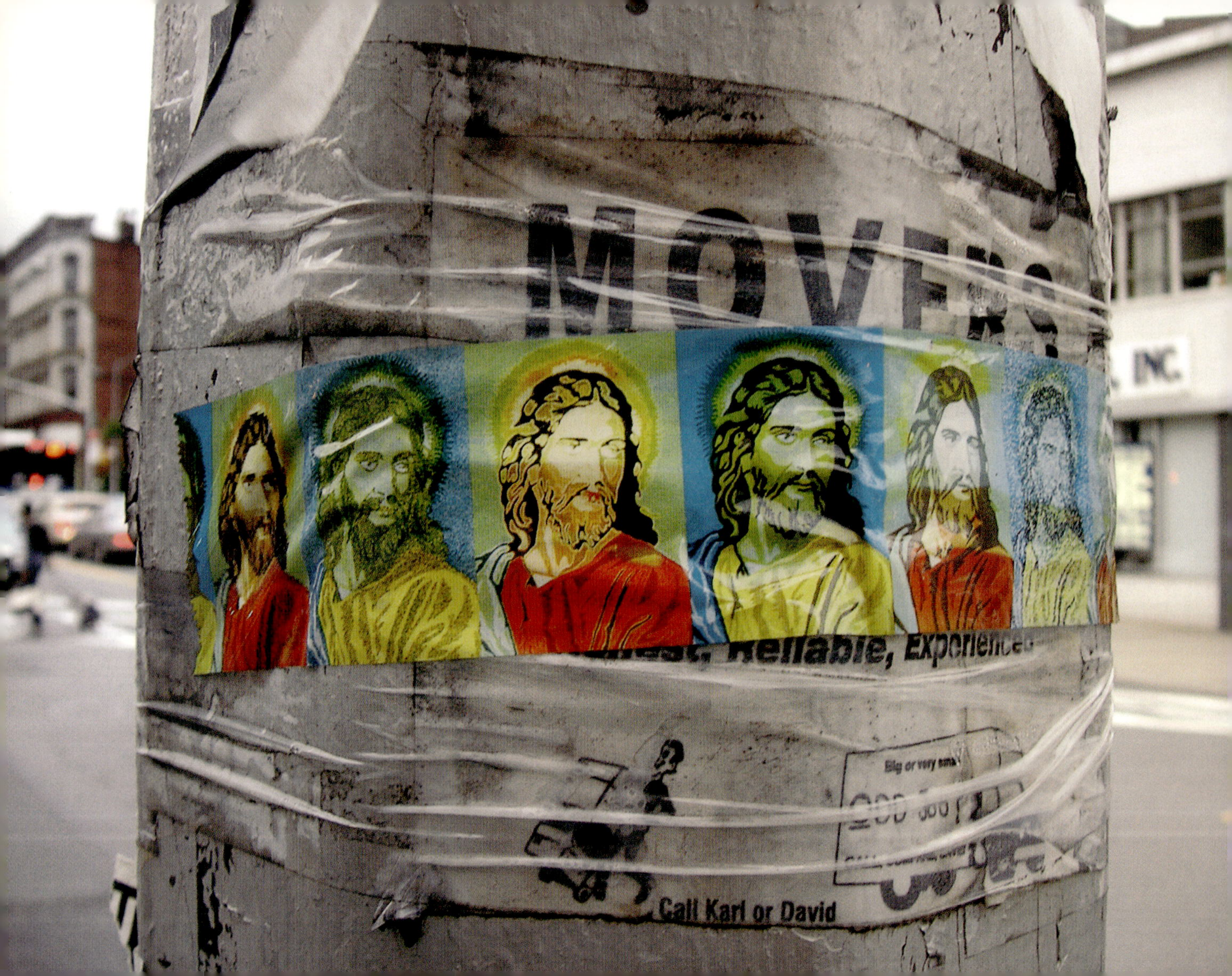
MOVERS
Reliable, Experienced
Call Karl or David
INC.

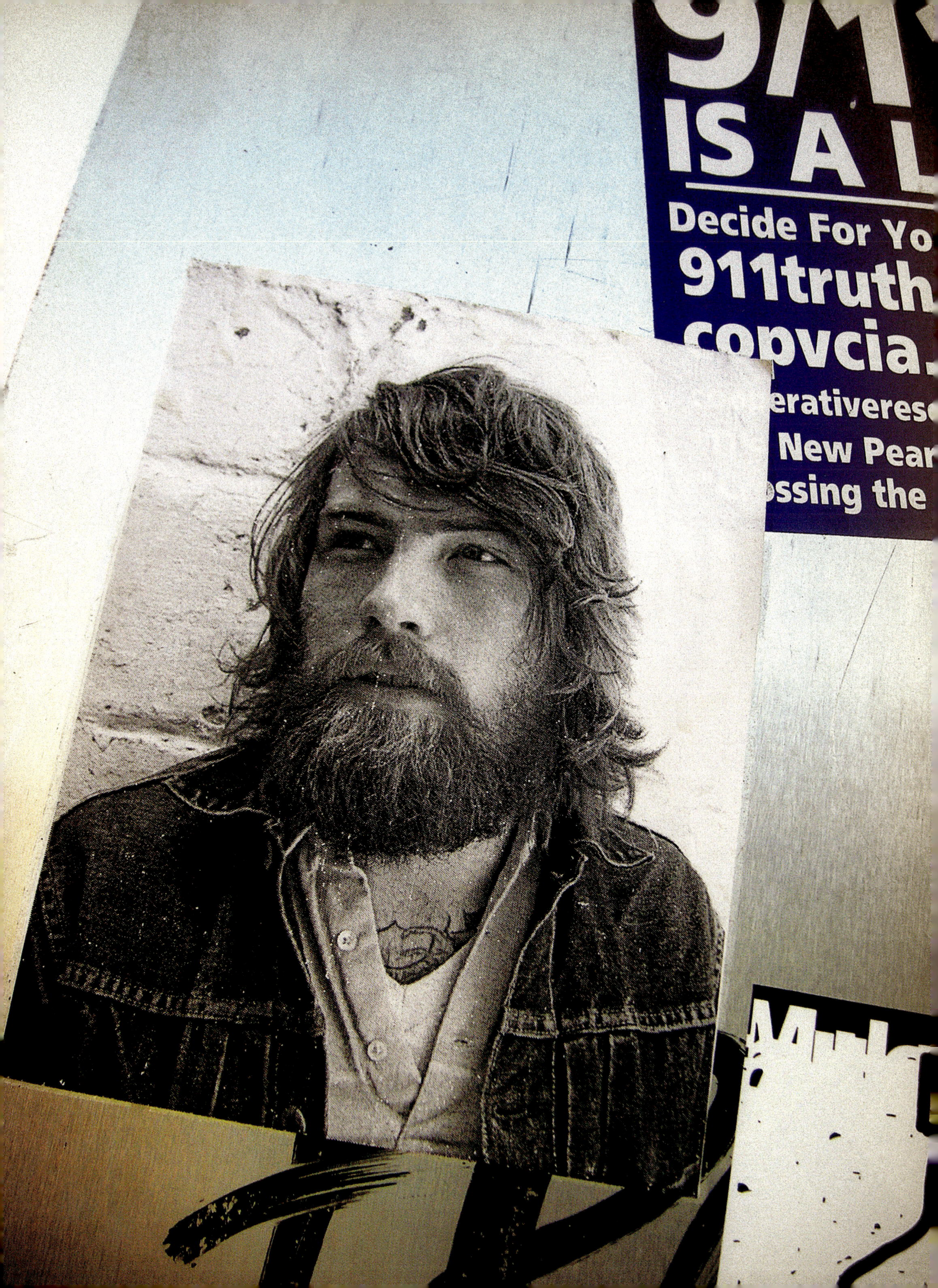
IS A
Decide For Yo
911truth
copvcia.
erativeres
New Pear
ssing the

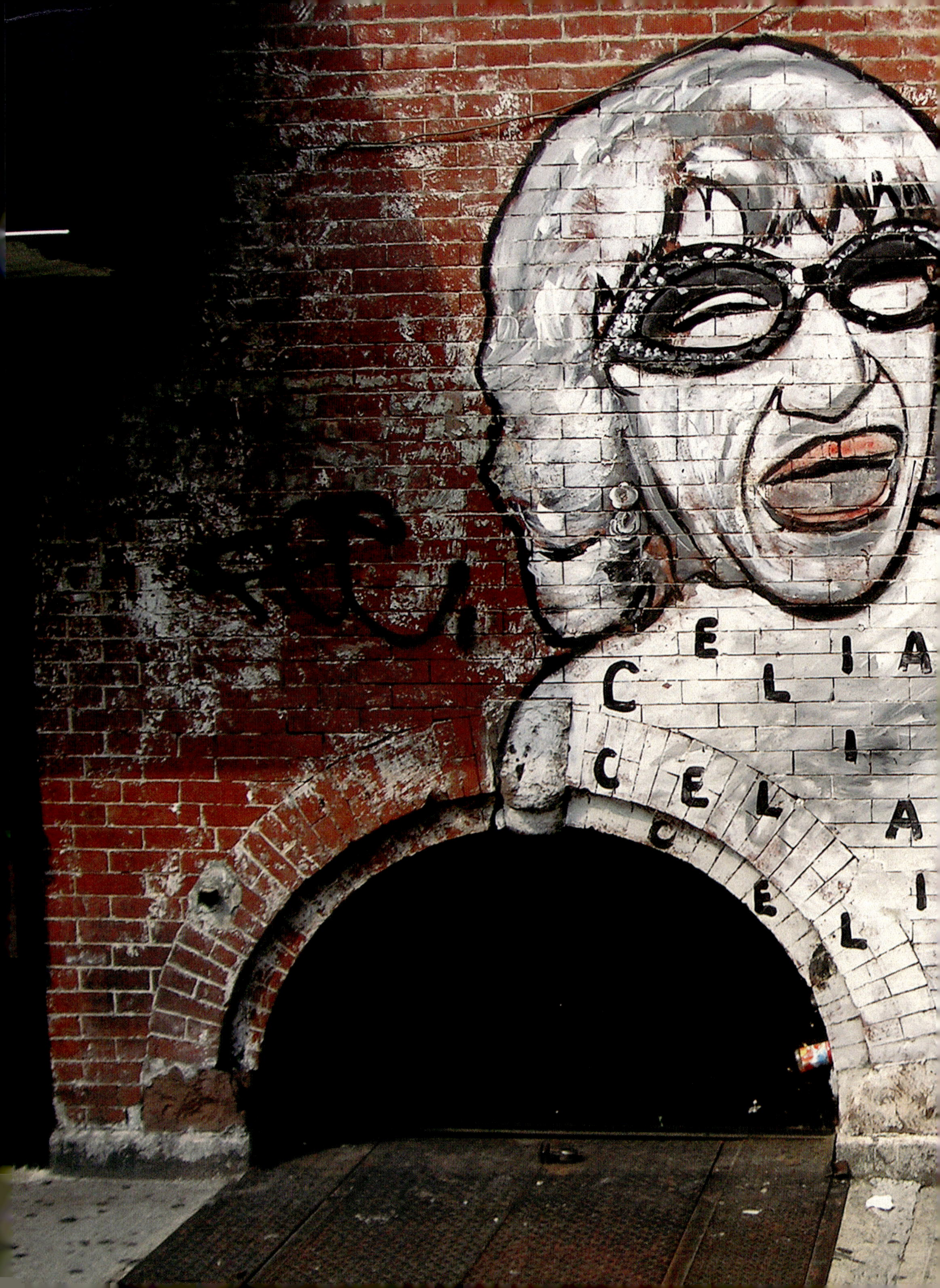
CELIA
CELIA
CELIA

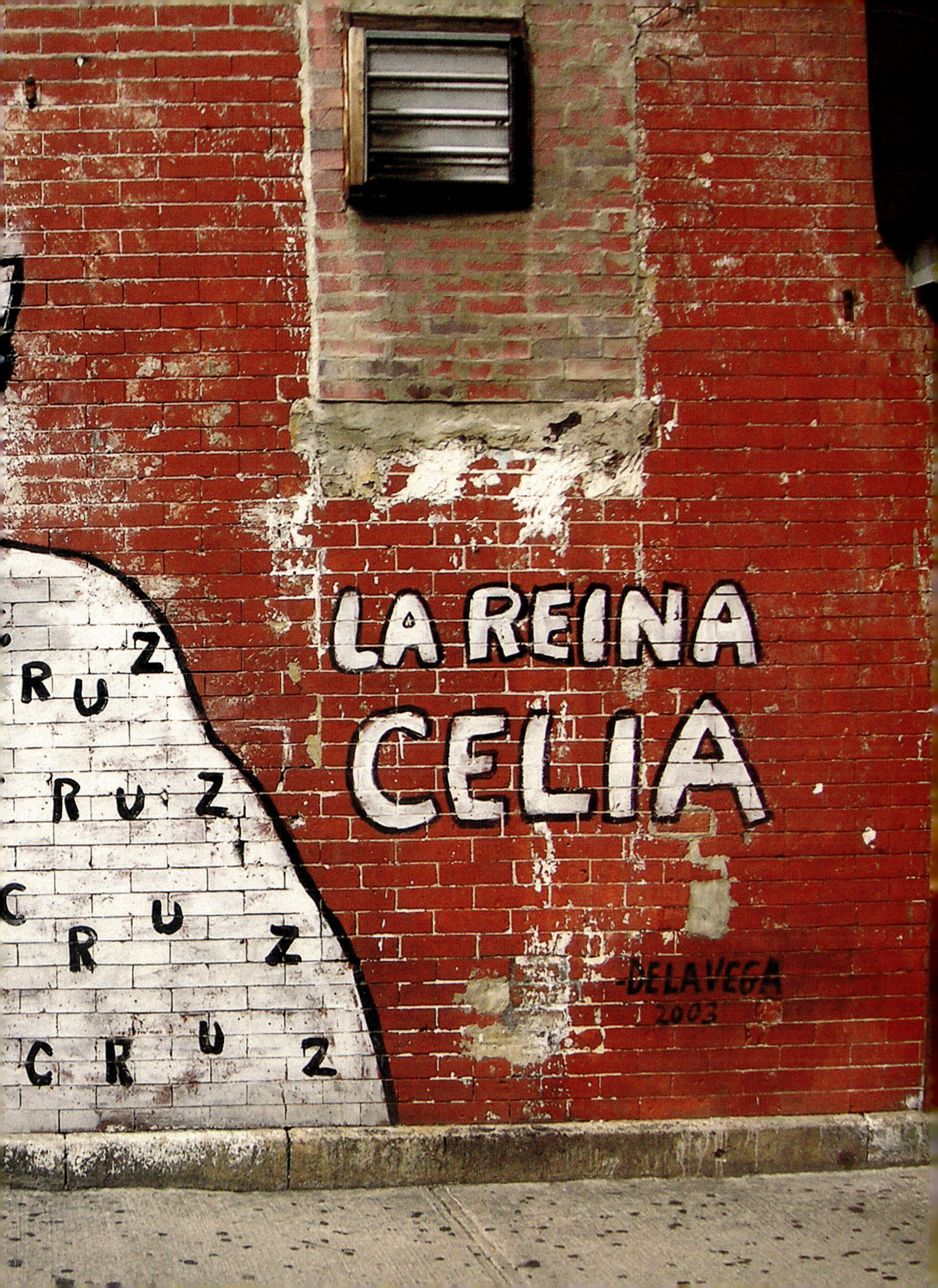
LA REINA
CELIA
-DELAVEGA
2003
RUZ
RUZ
CRUZ
CRUZ

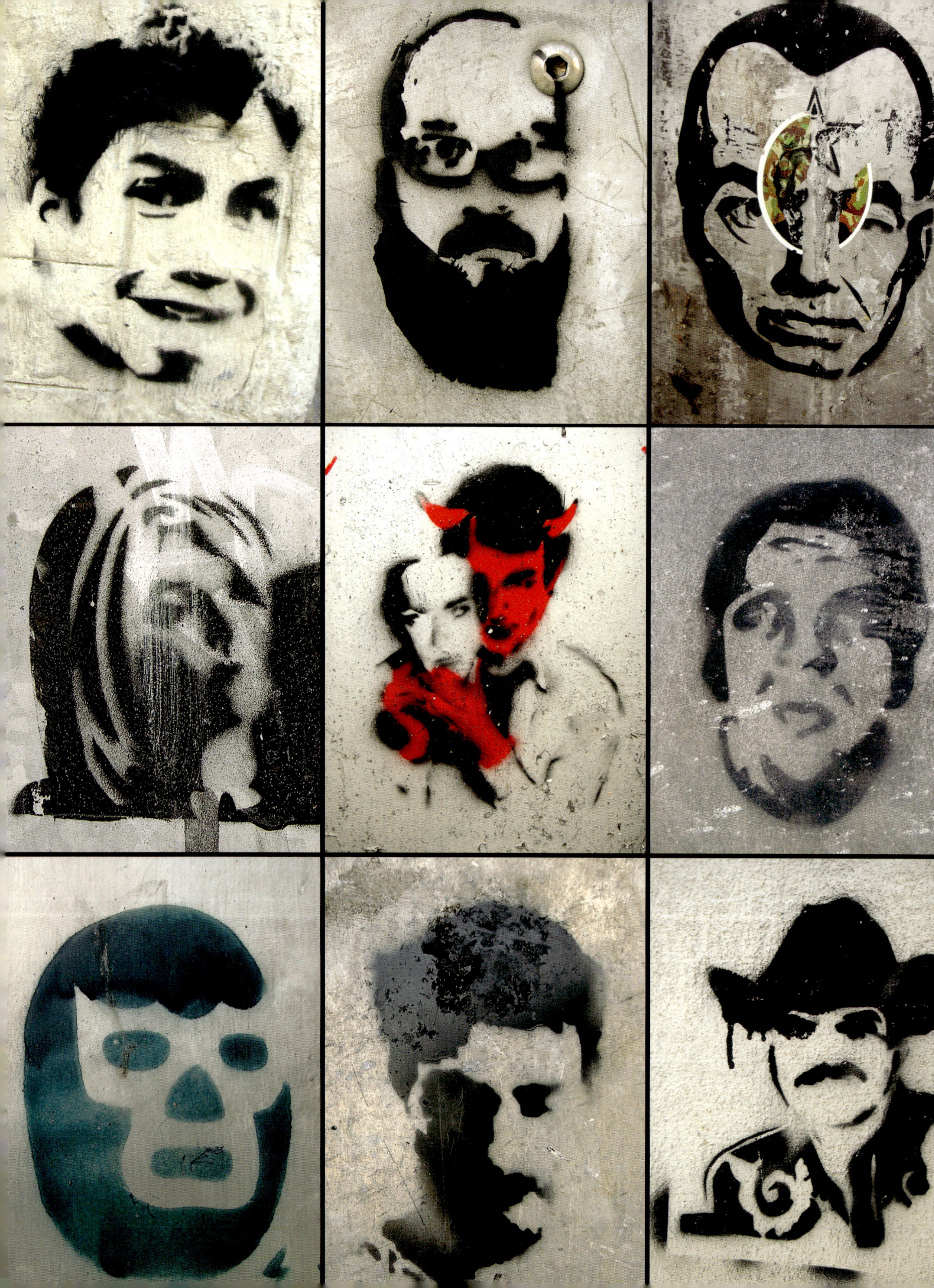

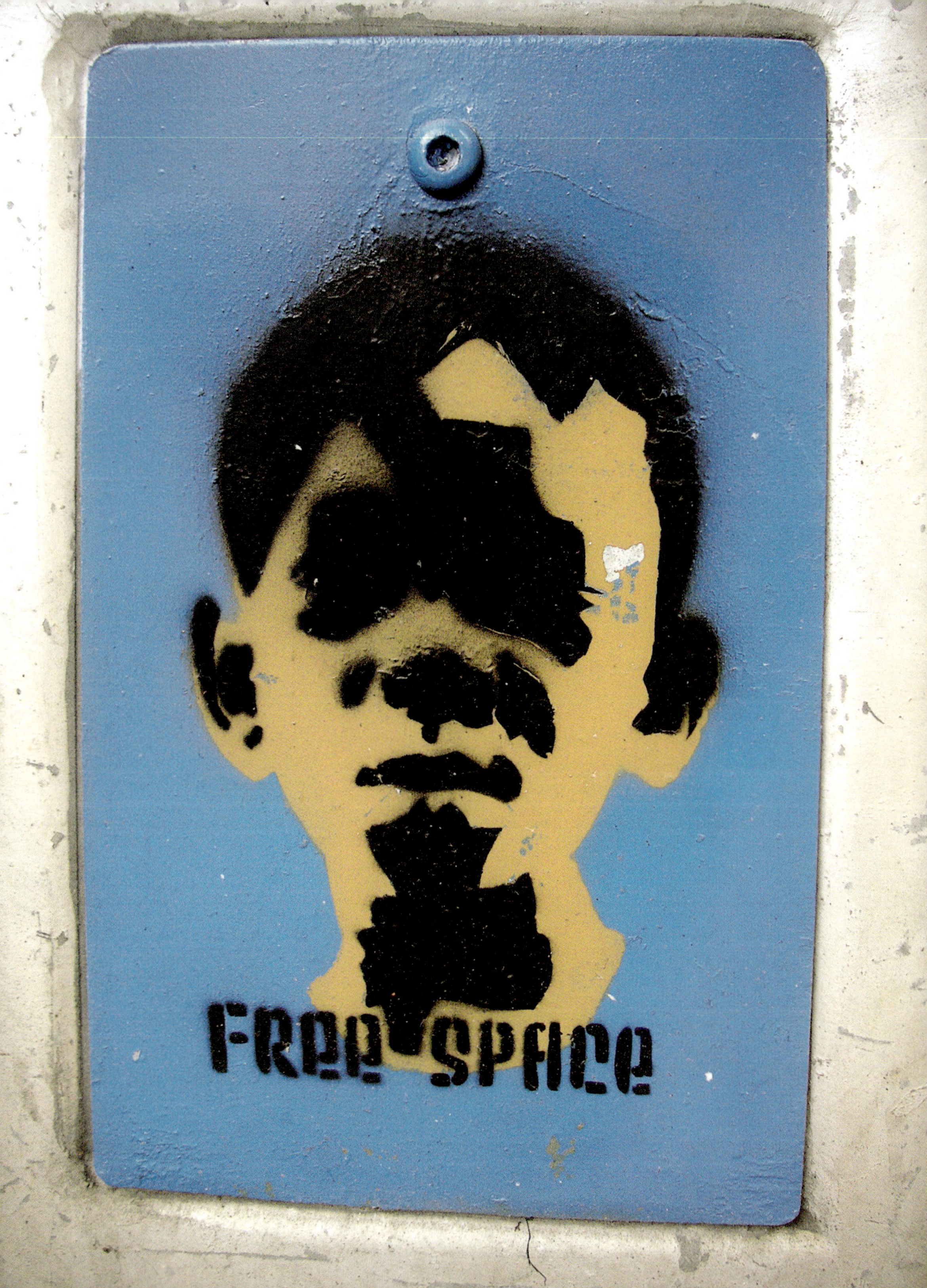
FREE SPACE

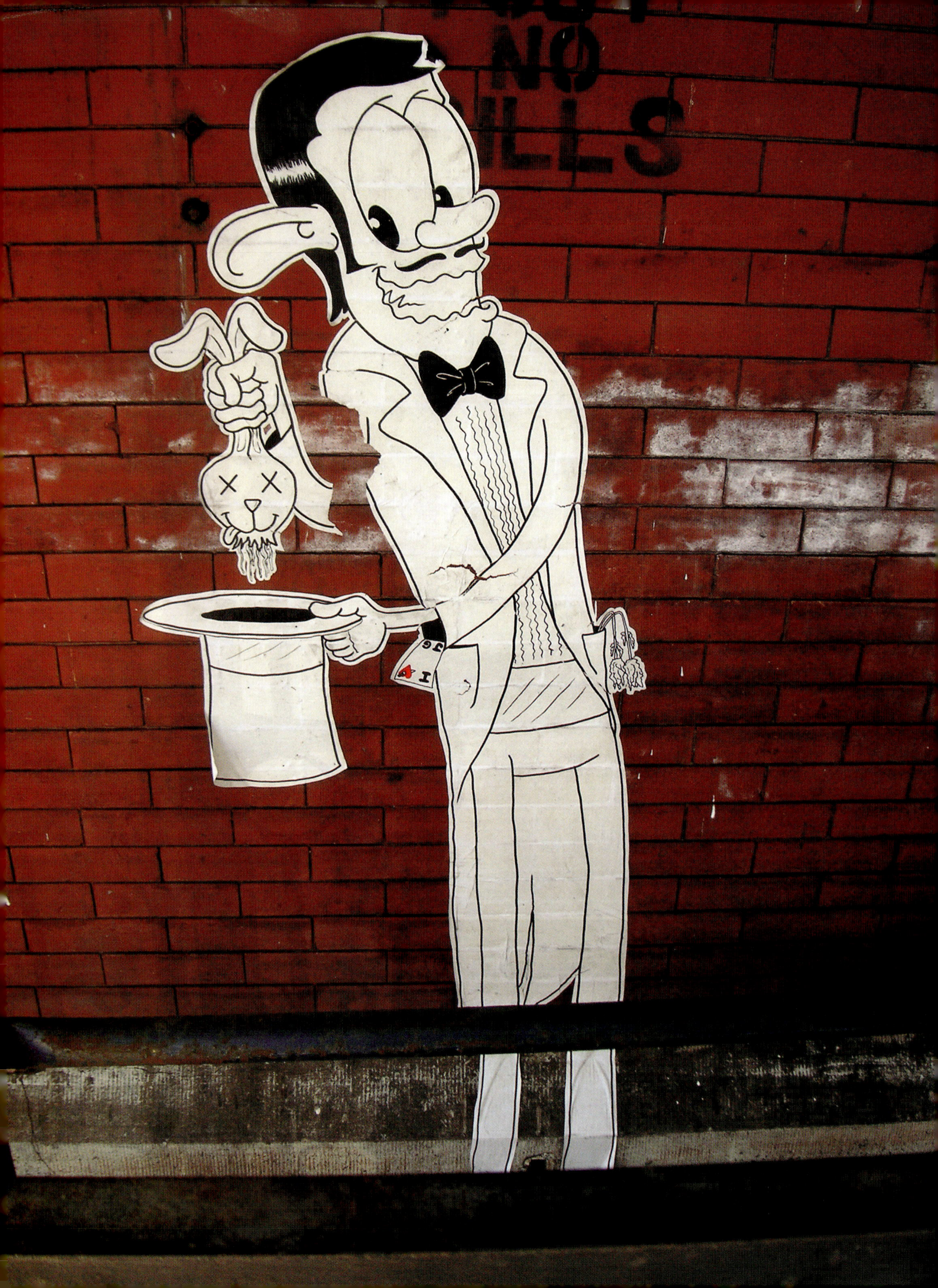
NO

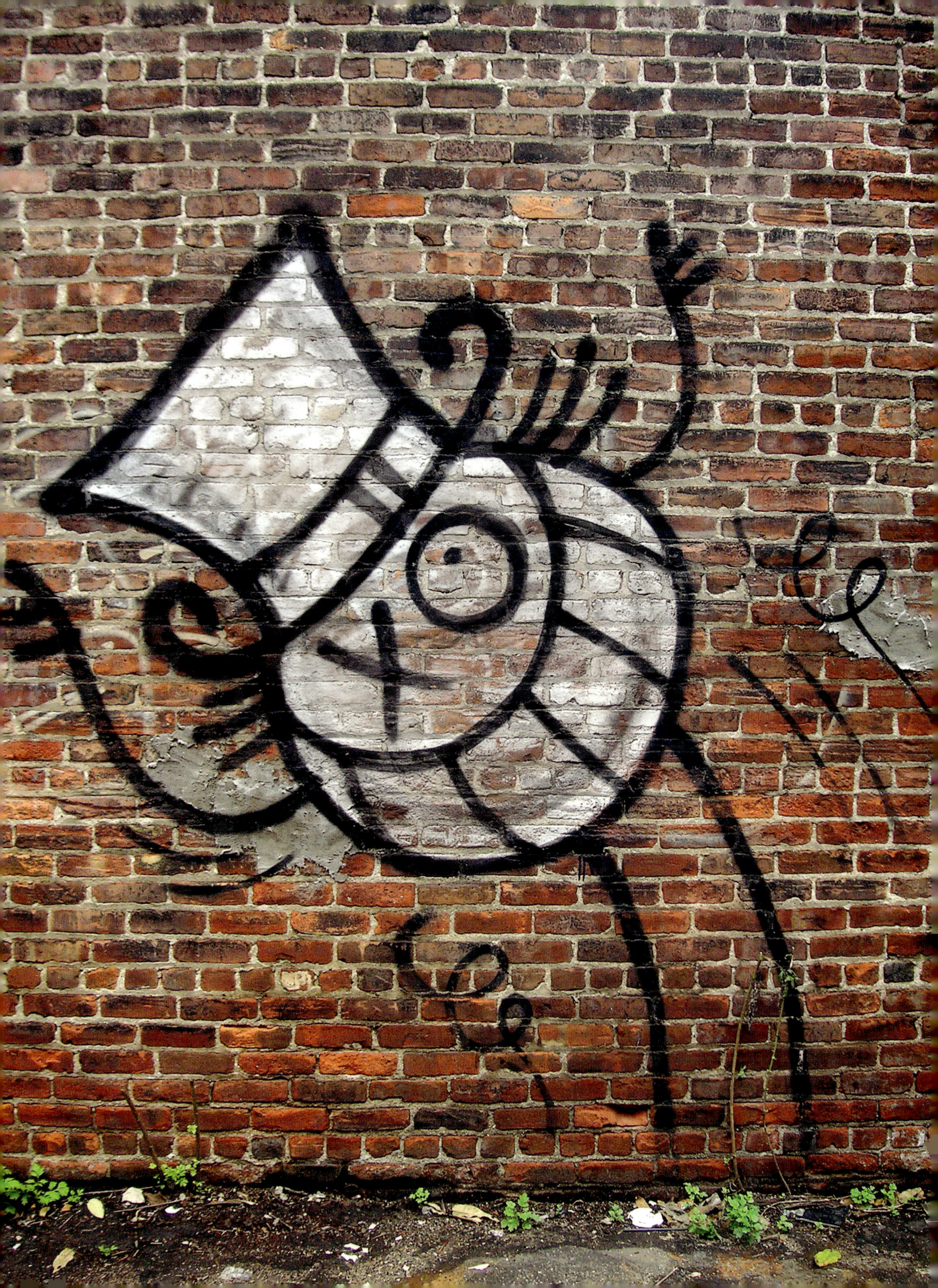

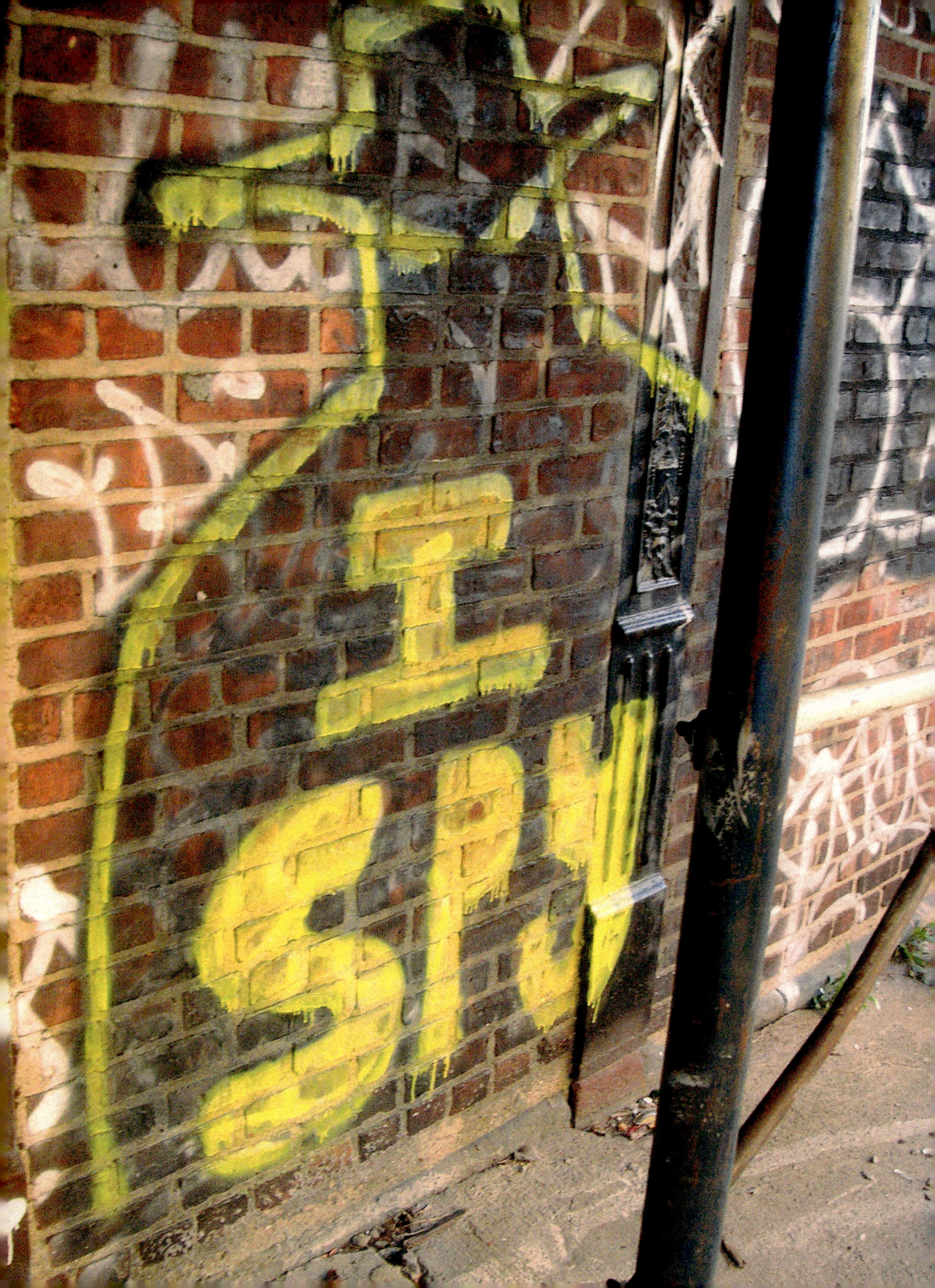
I SPY

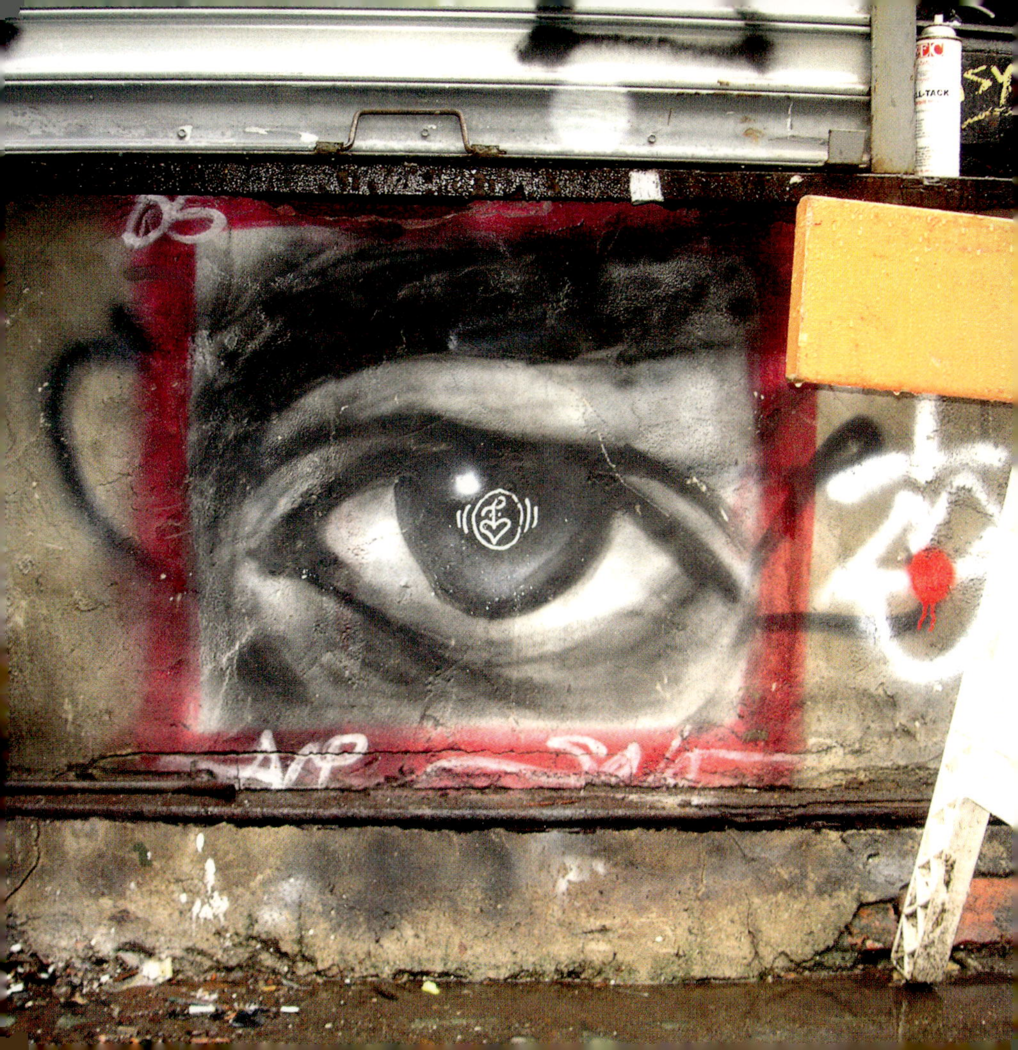

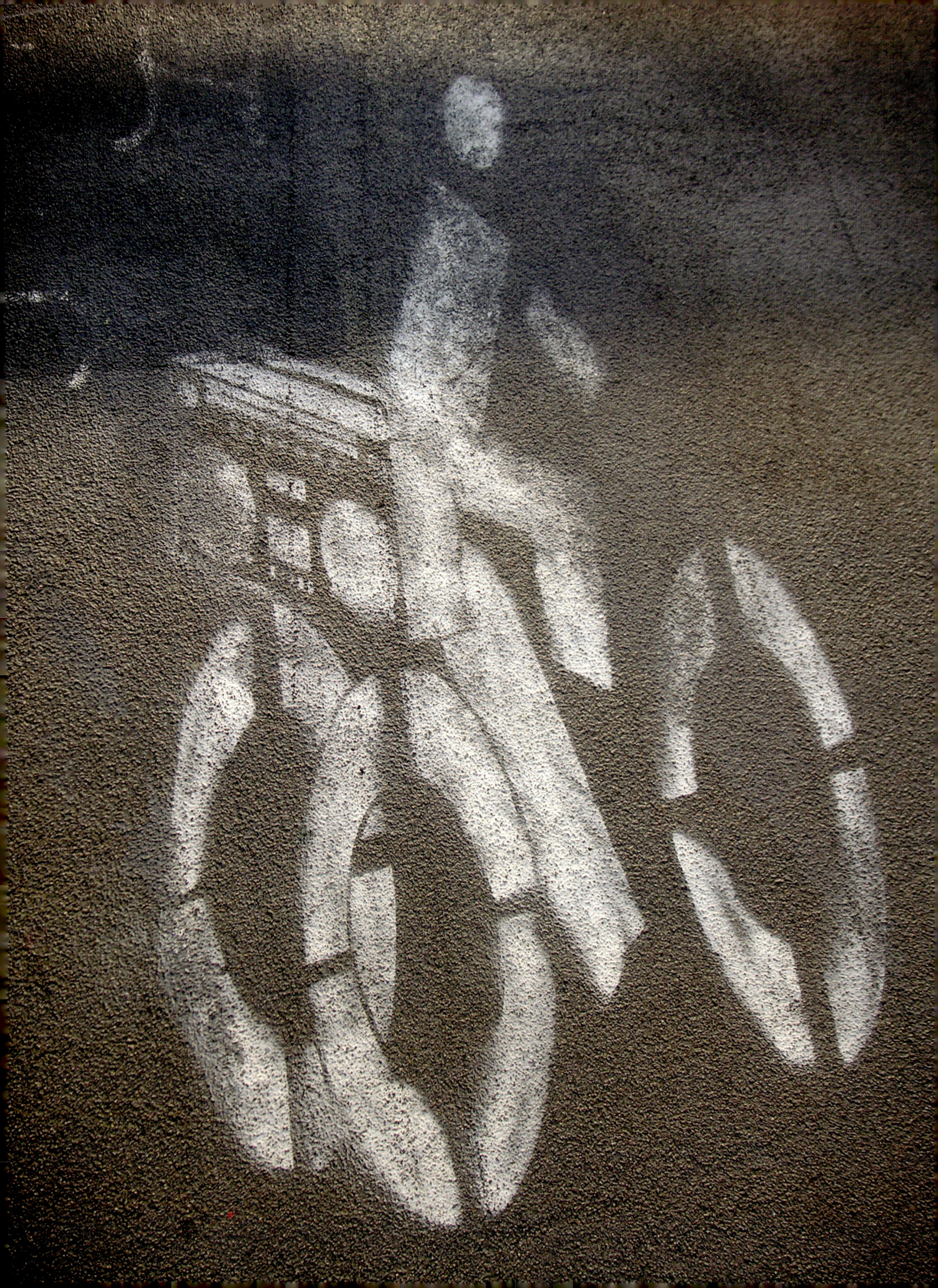

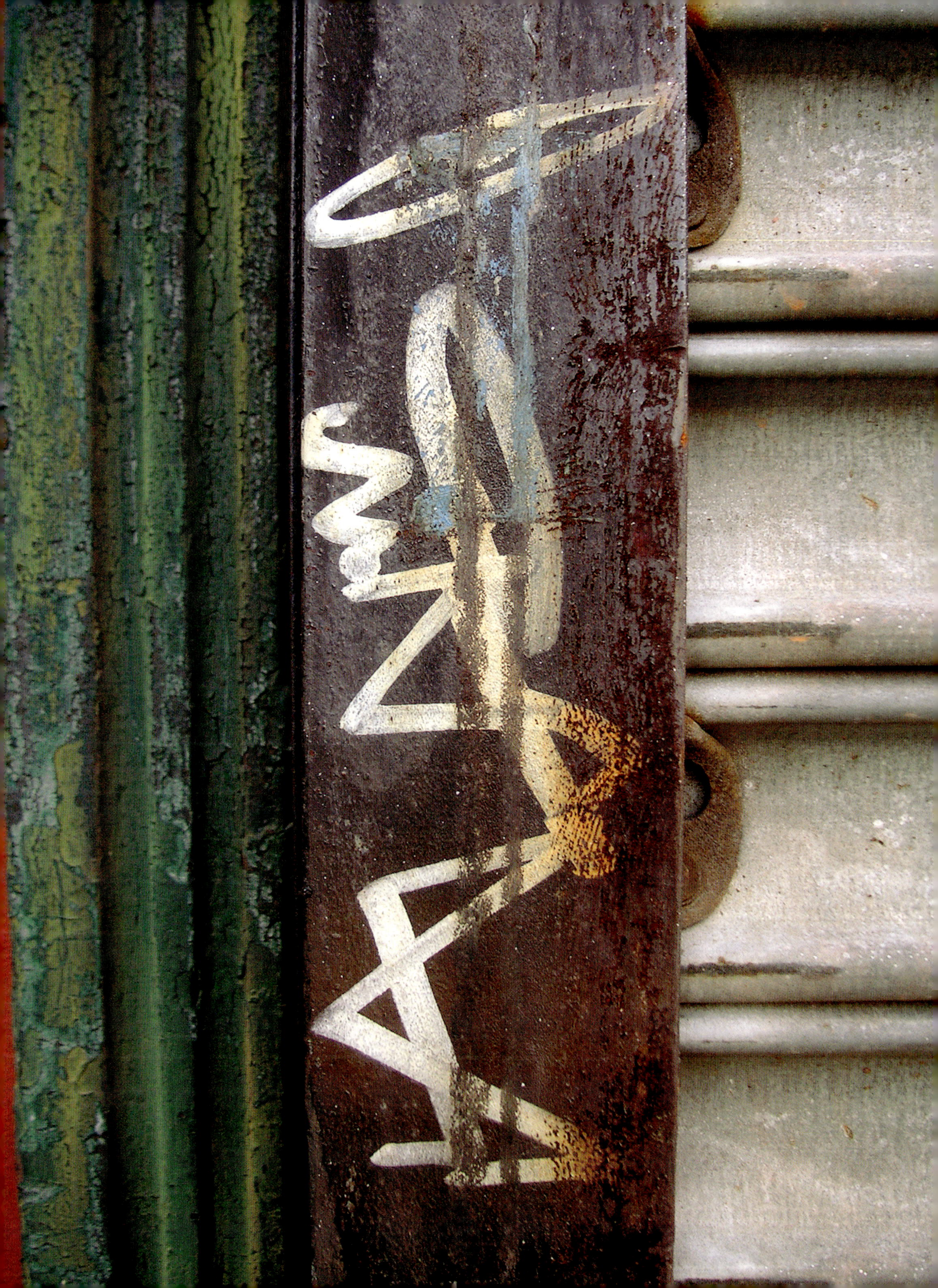

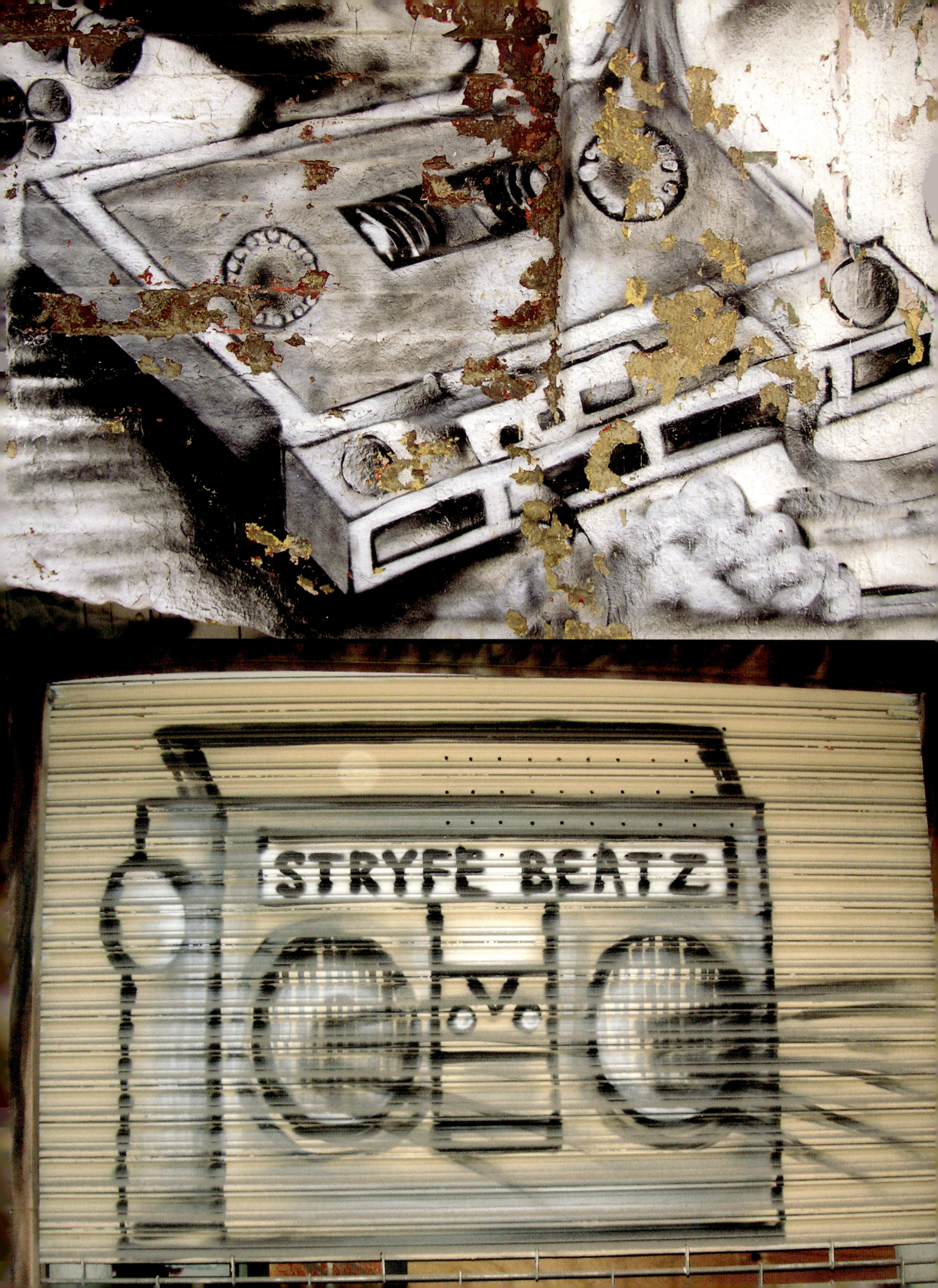
STRYFE BEATZ

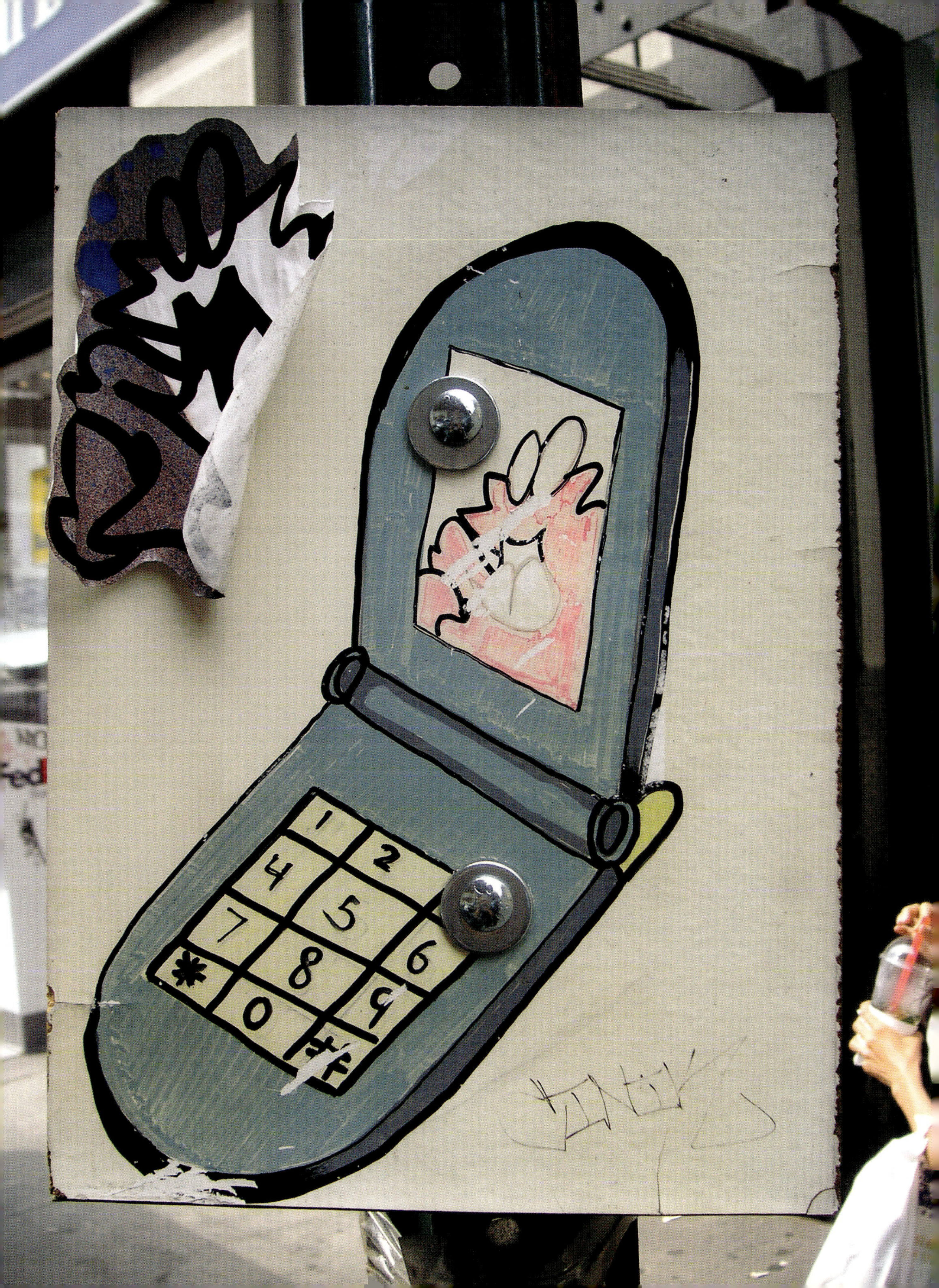

1 2
4 5 6
7 8 9
* 0 #

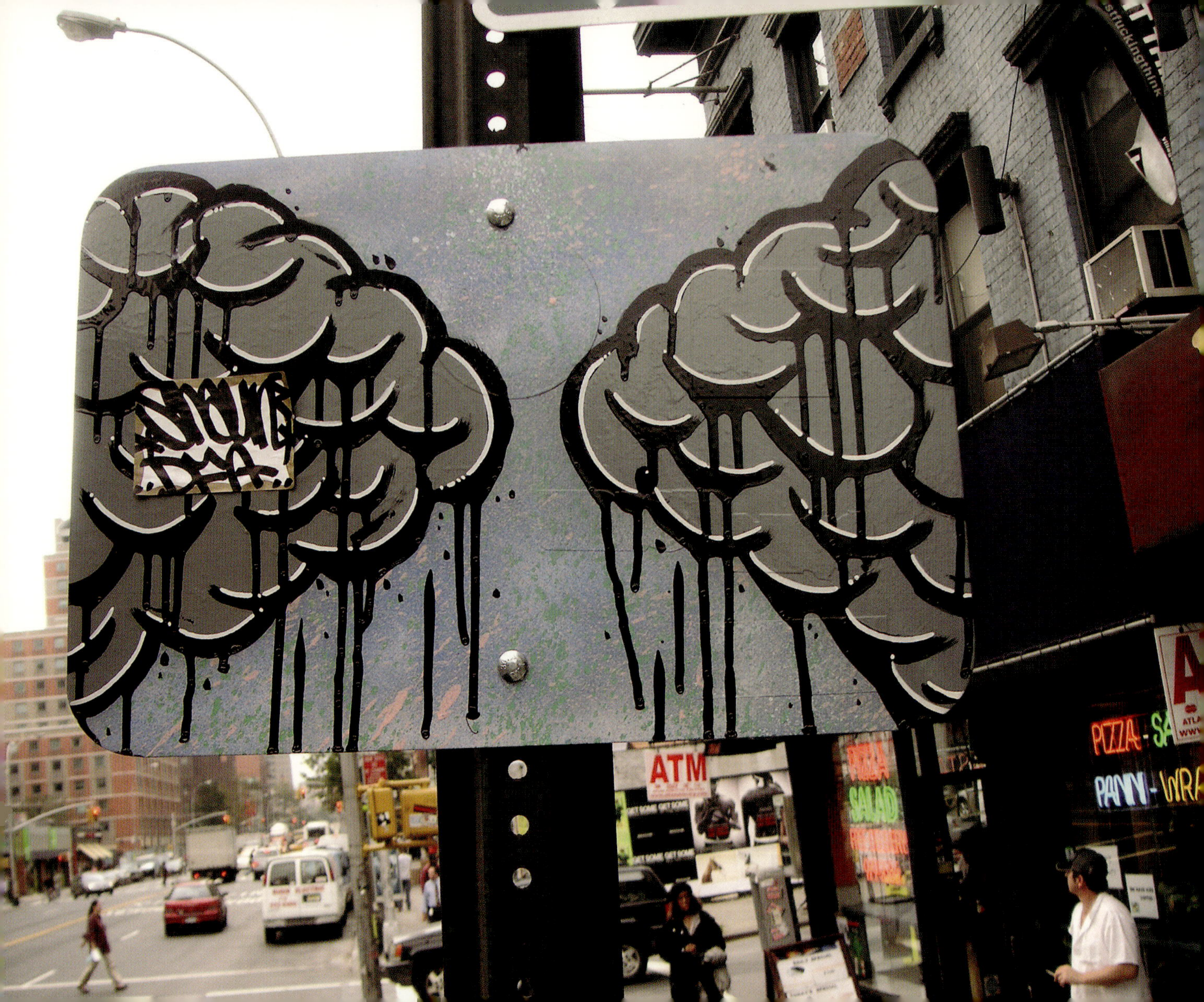
ATM
PIZZA
SALAD

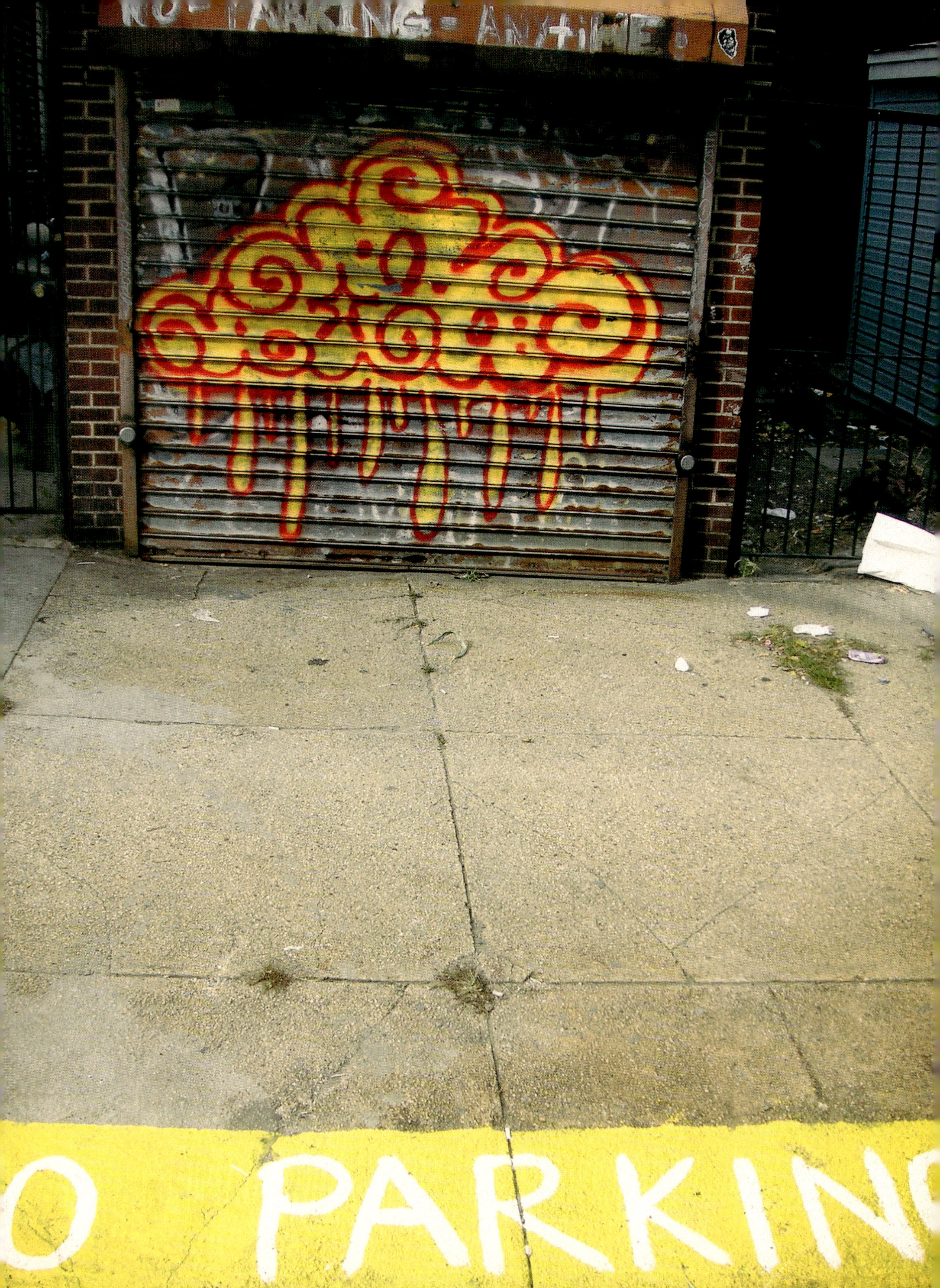
O PARKIN

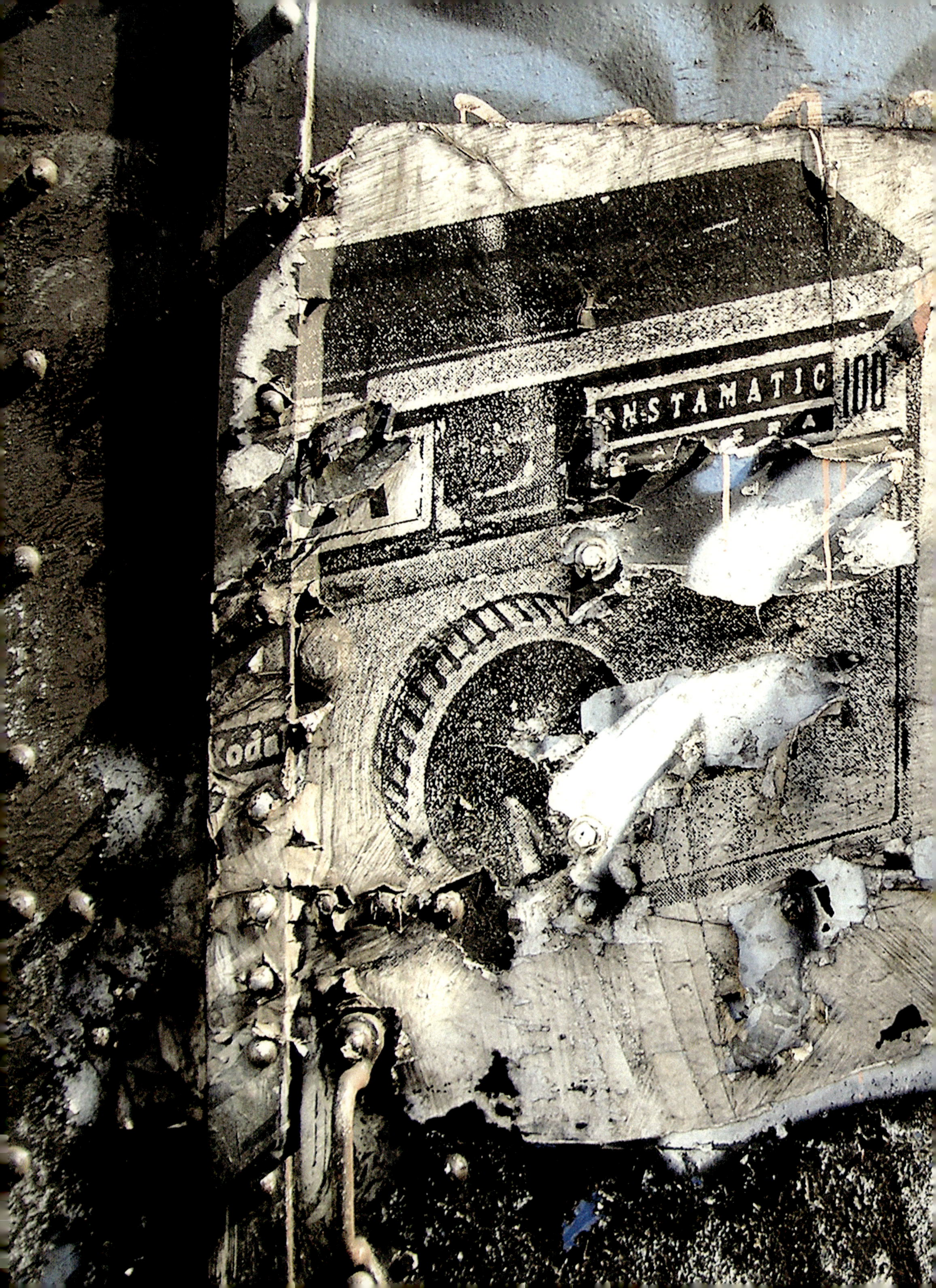
NSTAMATIC
100

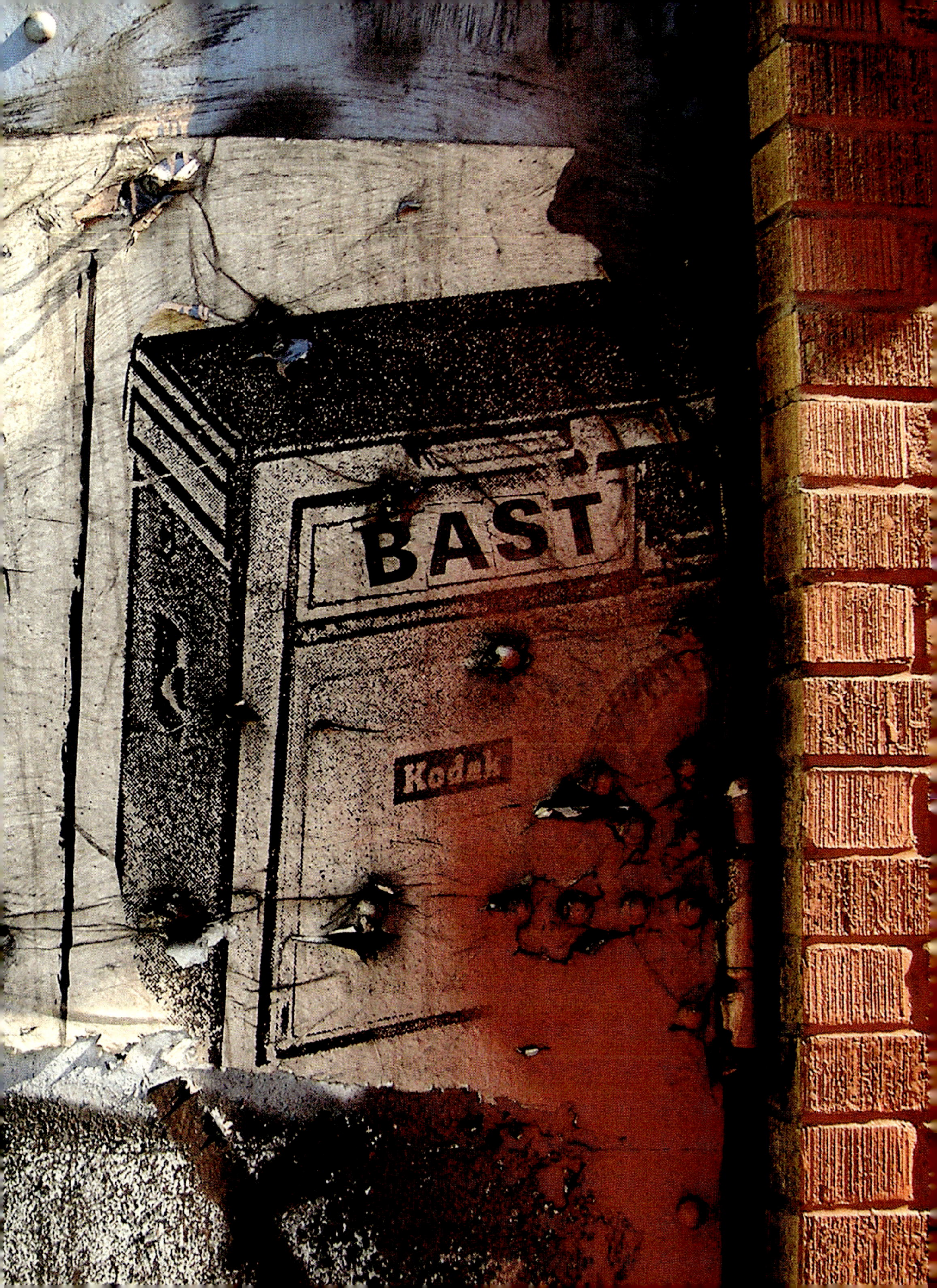
BAST
Kodak

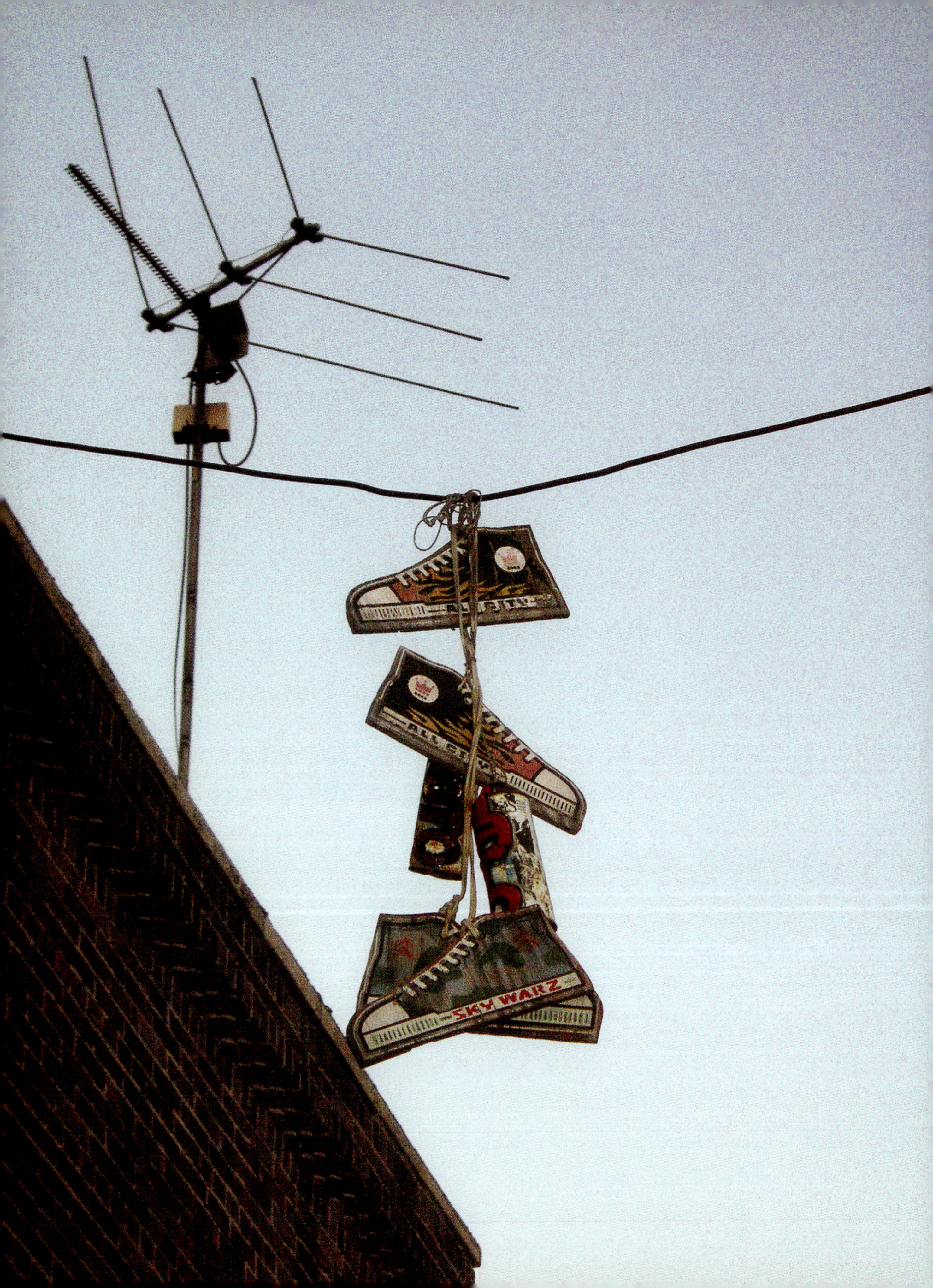
SKY WARZ

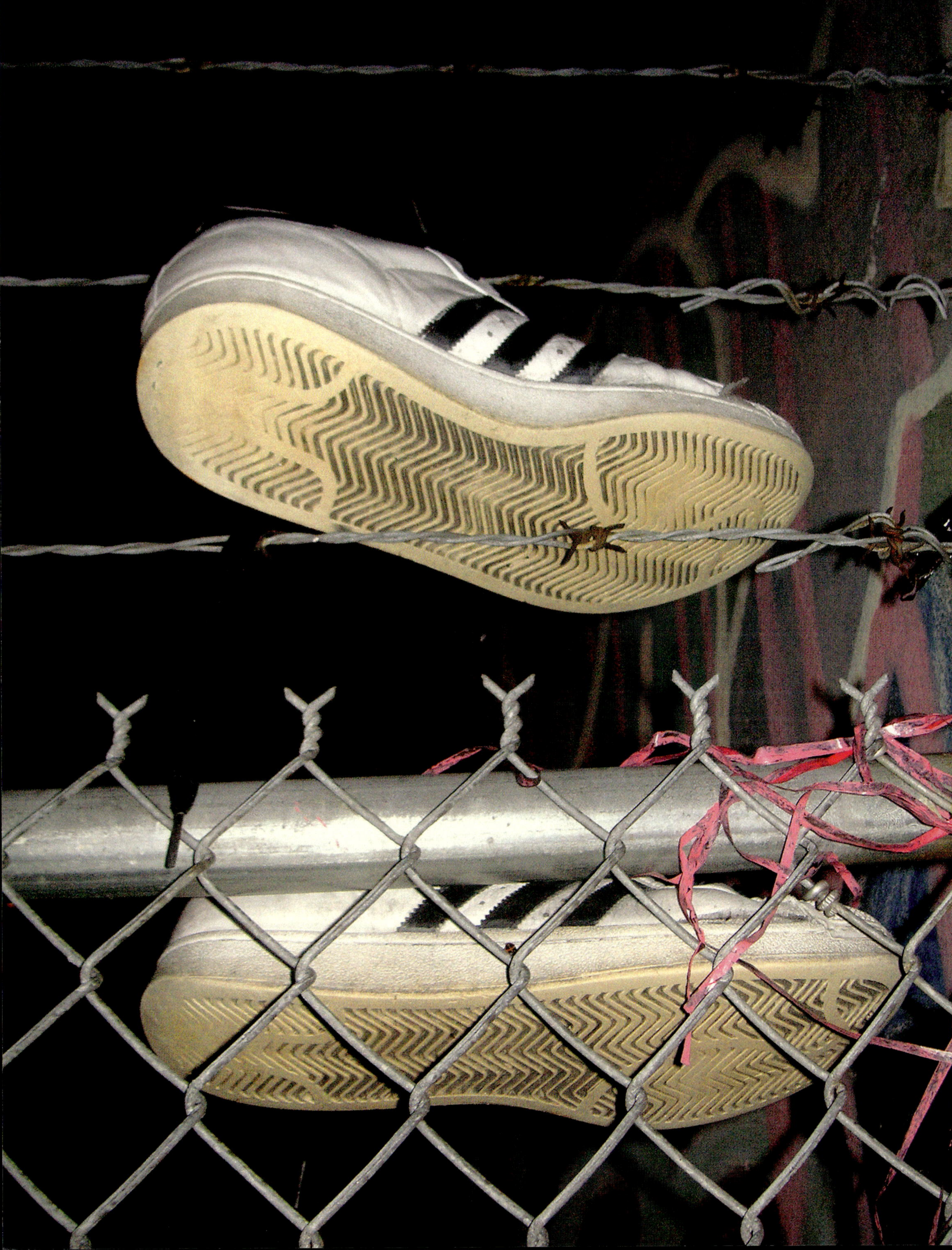

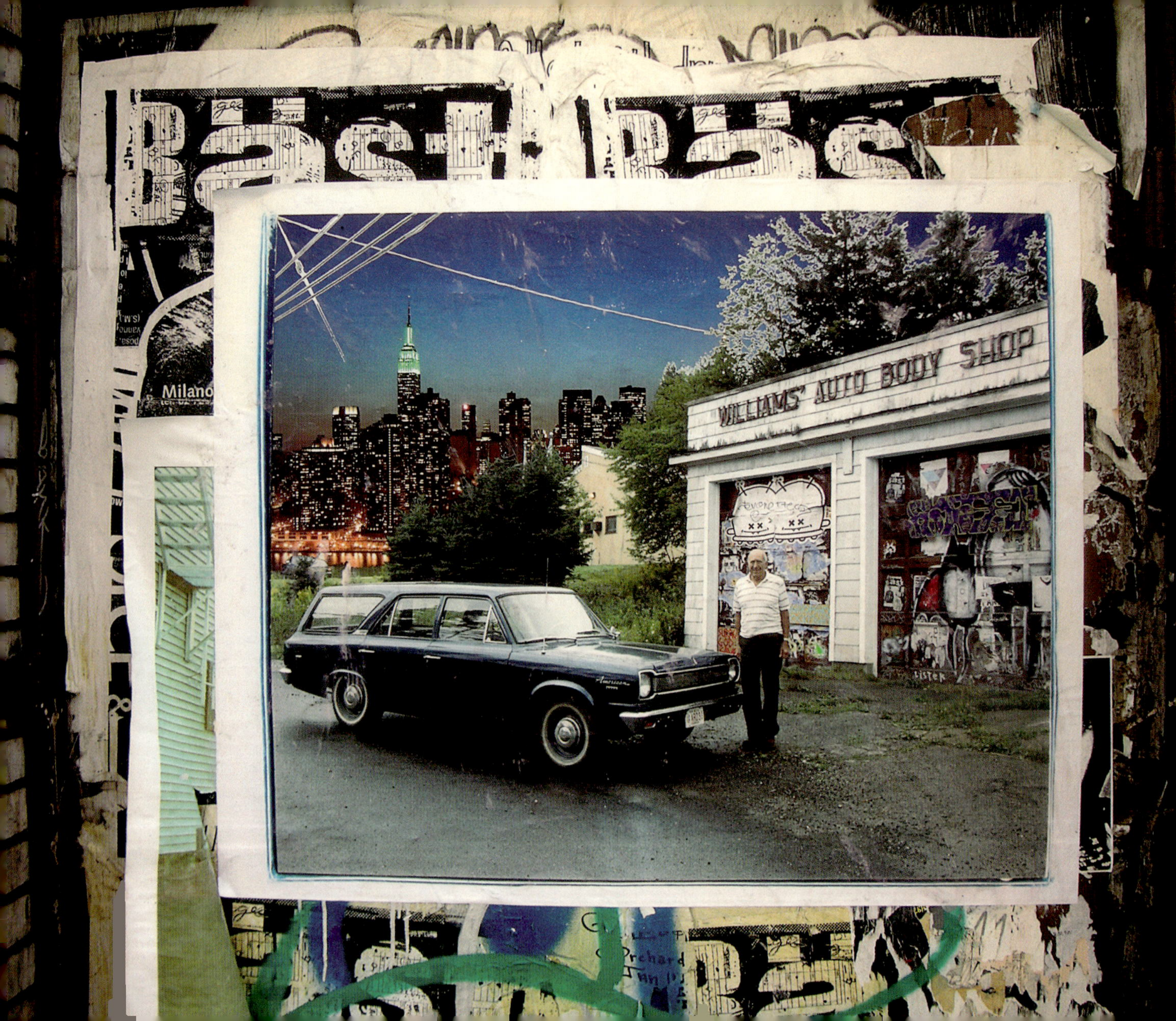
WILLIAMS' AUTO BODY SHOP
Milano

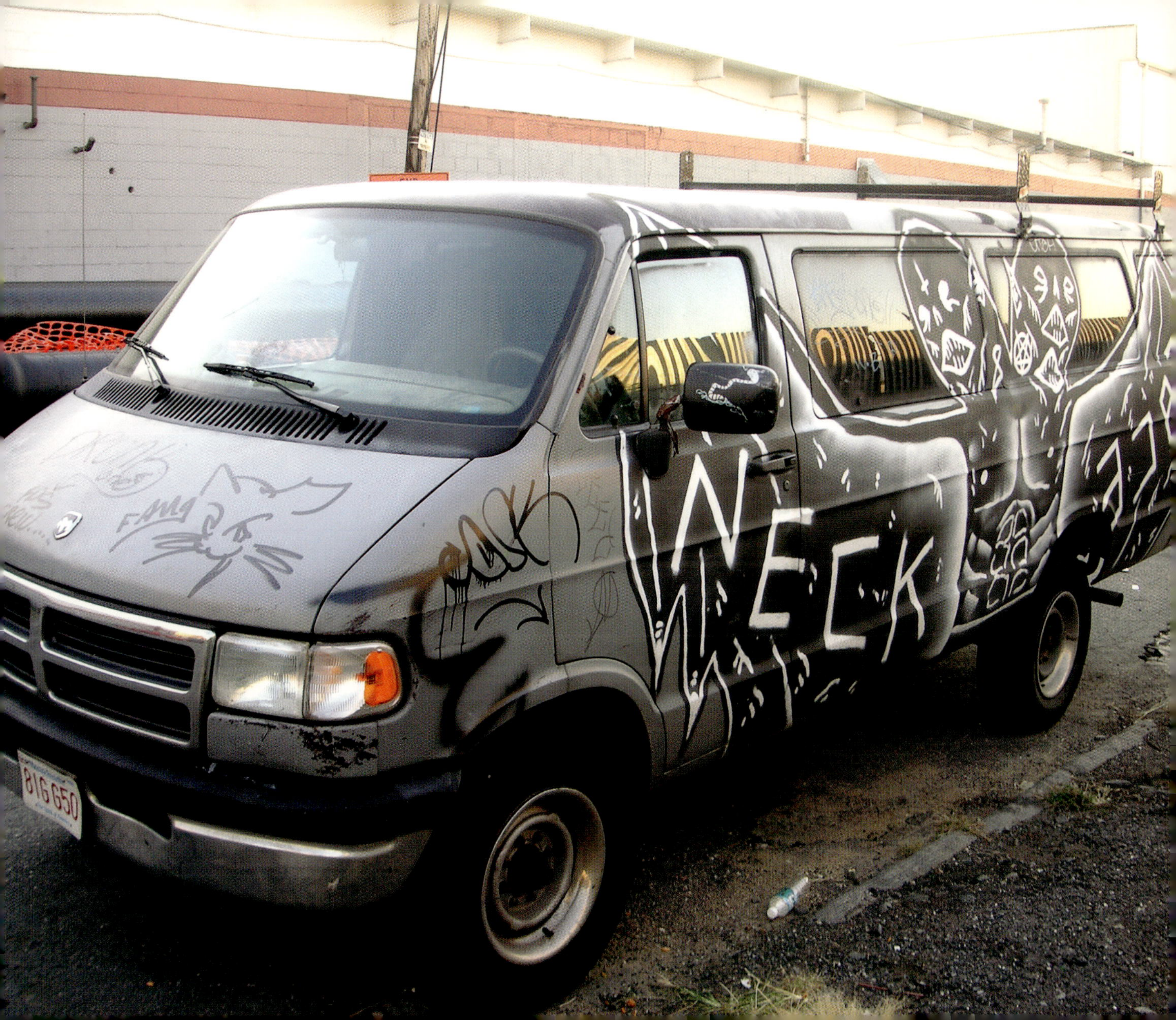
WECK
816 G50

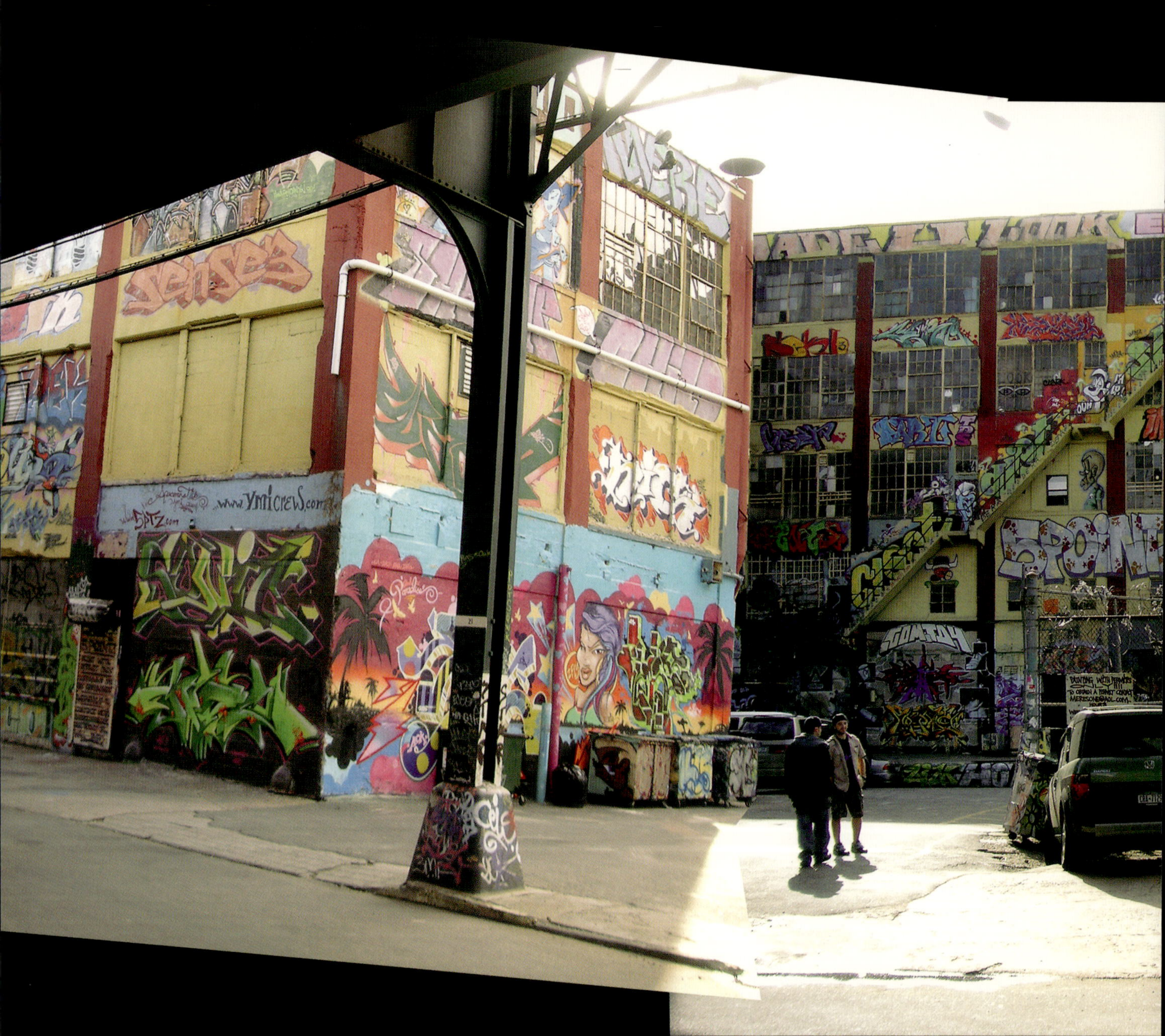
www.ymicrew.com
5PTZ.com
MERESONE@AOL.COM

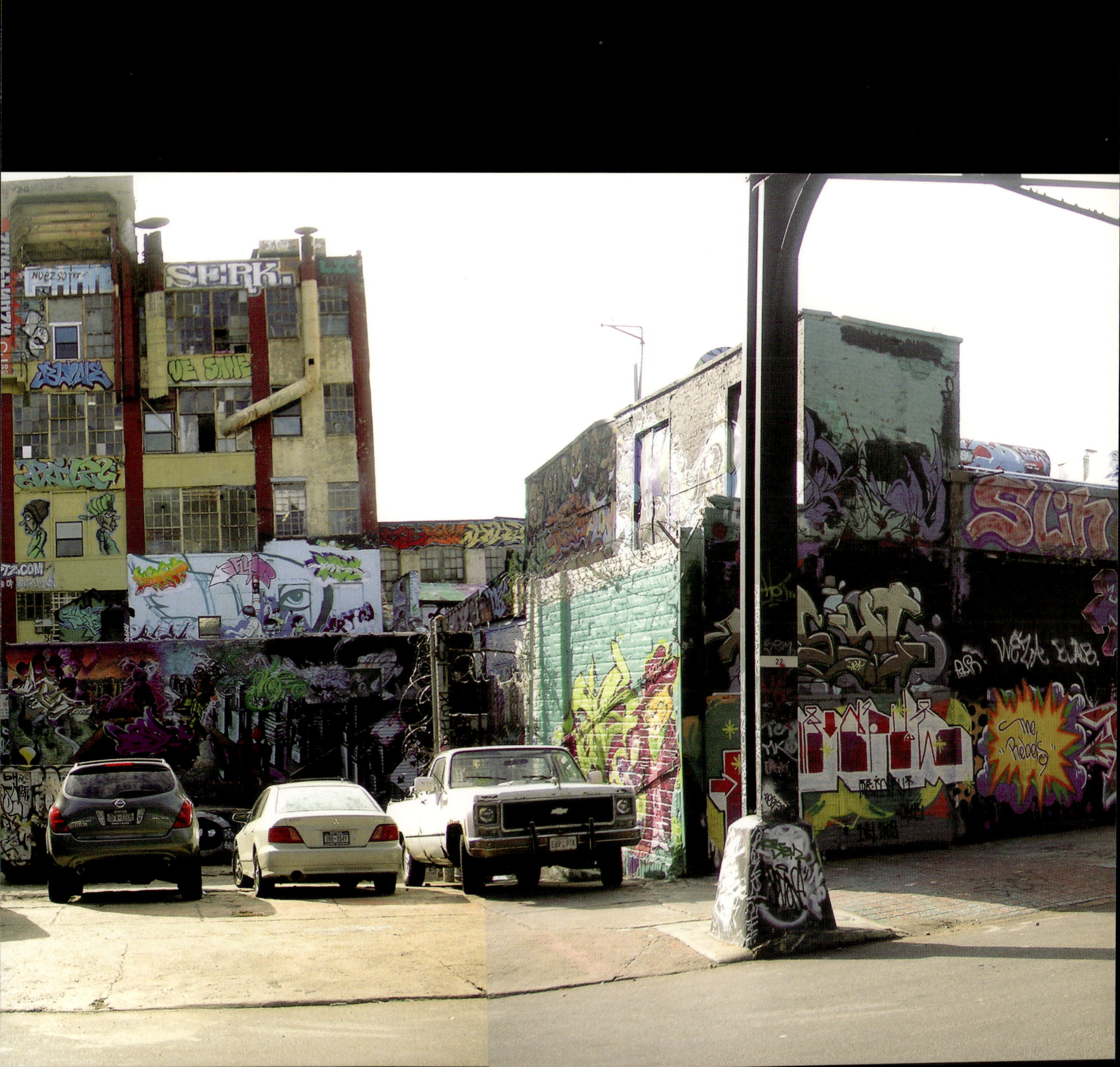
SERK.

Here is what New York City has given me to see...

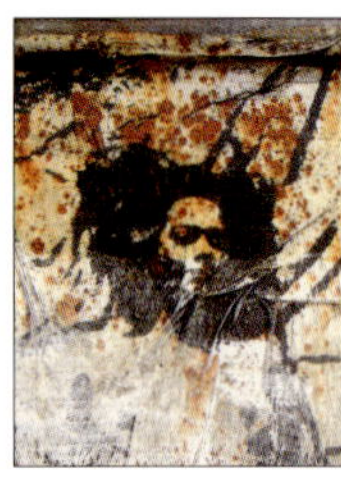

Shot in Manhattan: Rasta Head. This is a perfect illustration of the "time on street" art form, with organic elements playing tricks like magicians. Corrosion is one of my favorite transformations.

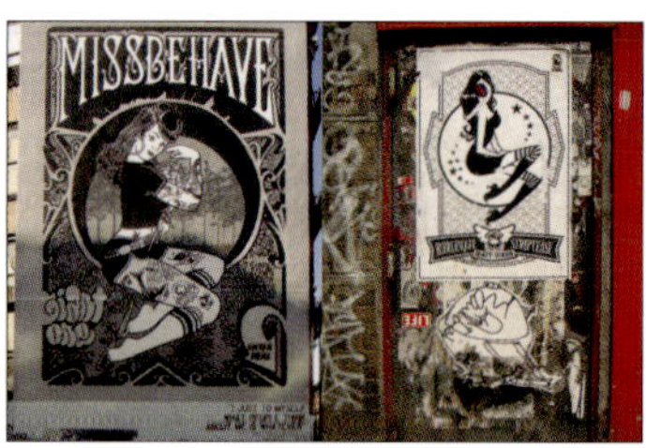

Both shot in Manhattan: West Coast artist Giant One paints a graff four stories high on a building section. The Matt Siren poster appears to be a copycat.

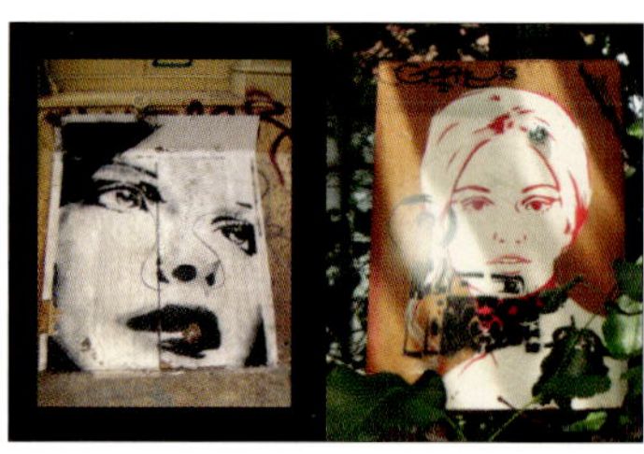

Both shot in Manhattan: from the sidewalks or hidden between tree branches, city ladies watch you pass by. By Gore B.

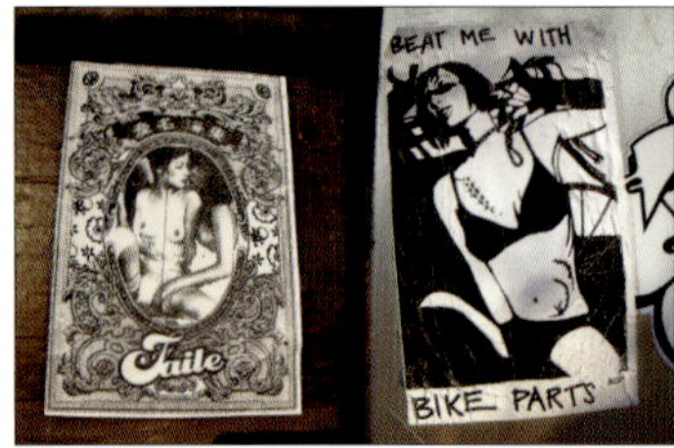

Both shot in Brooklyn: these sticker-sized sex practices were found in Bedford. Free your mind, do as you please. By Faile and GDP.

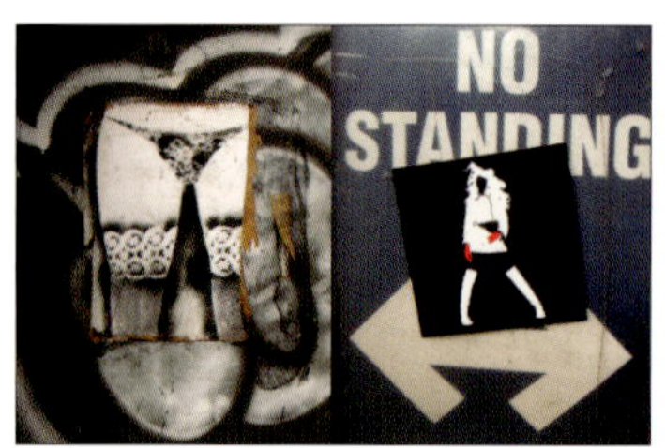

Both shot in Manhattan: two great illustrations of the prostitution lie of our day. These sexy ladies are outlaws. No standing.

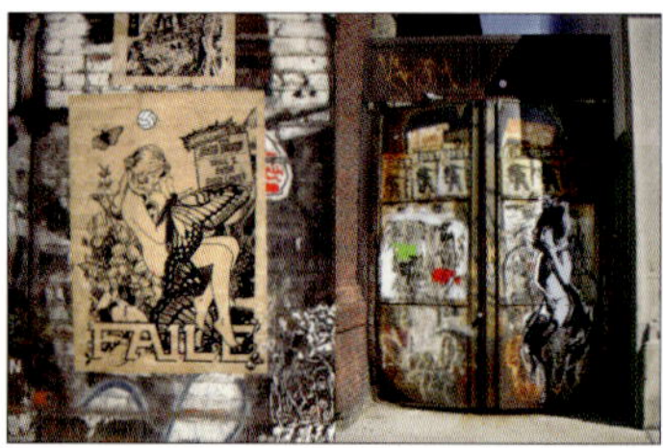

Both shot in Manhattan: A remarkably detailed silkscreen poster by Faile, and an accumulation on a rusted gate of work by Bast and WK Interakt, among others.

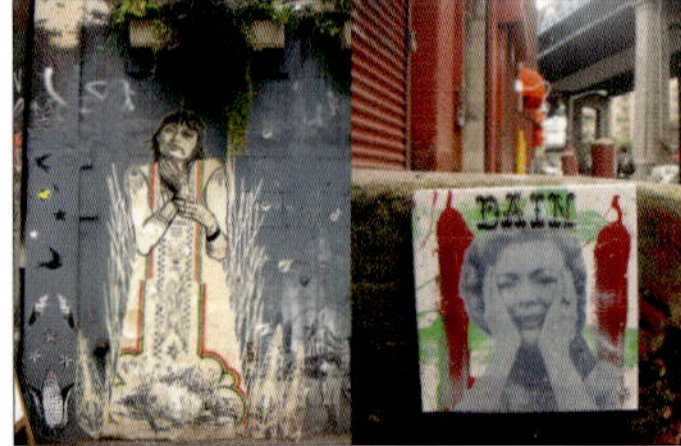

Left shot in Manhattan: paper cut by Swoon. Right shot in Brooklyn: tile affixed with scotch tape by Dain. Both of these reflect beautiful artistry and amazing technique.

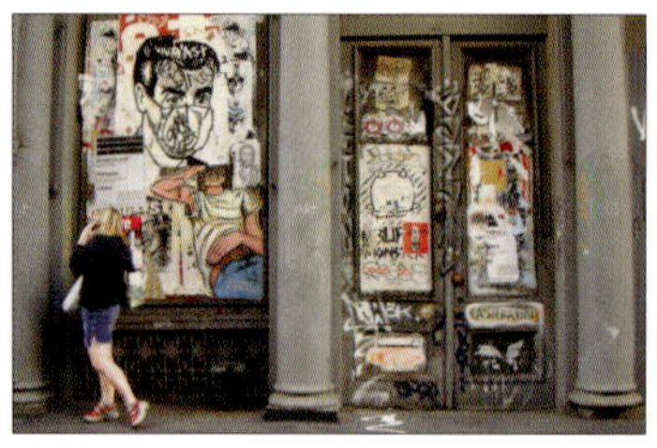

Shot in Manhattan: an abandoned storefront (but for how long?). In any case, these storefronts turned out to be instant walls of fame for combo spots.

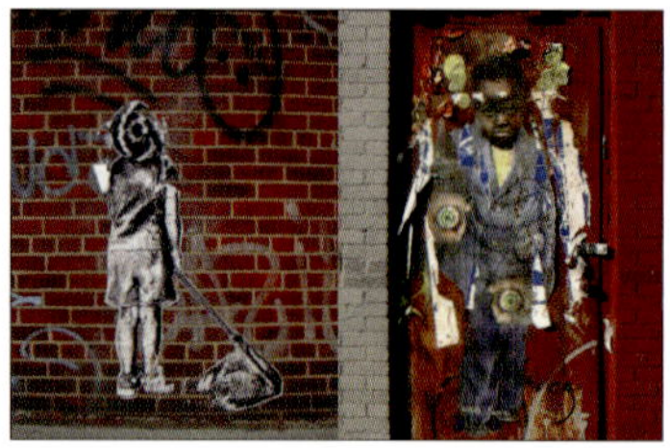

Left: white girl from Manhattan. Right: black boy from Brooklyn. Kids are everywhere—playgrounds, school buses, running around, *everywhere*—and that's a good thing. By Judith Supine.

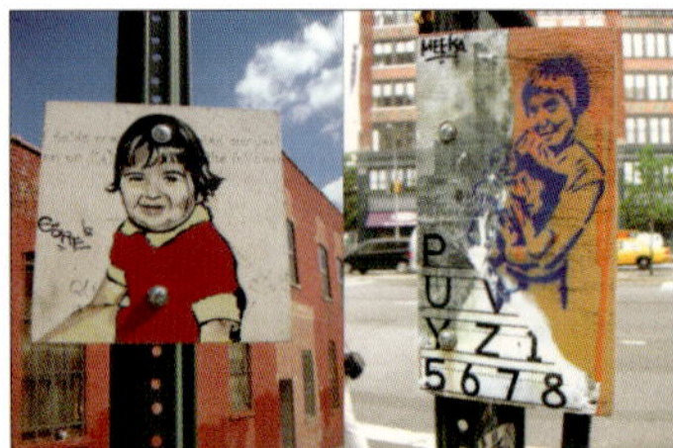

Left shot in Brooklyn: art by Gore B. Right shot in Manhattan: art by Meeka. In front of semi-abandoned industrial sites and in sections of downtown, these boards are filling up the landscape.

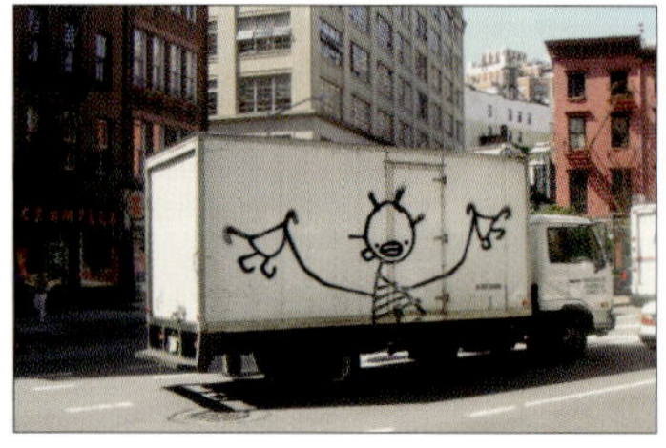

Shot in Manhattan: fat-cap tag on truck. I love this terror girlie and her natty dreads, riding wild across town.

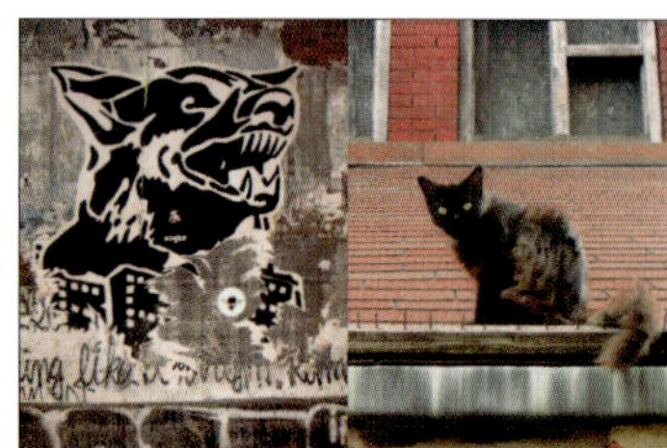

Left shot in Manhattan: art by Faile. Right shot in Brooklyn: this cat—creepier than any wild, barking dog—is at the house where *Dave Chappelle's Block Party* was filmed.

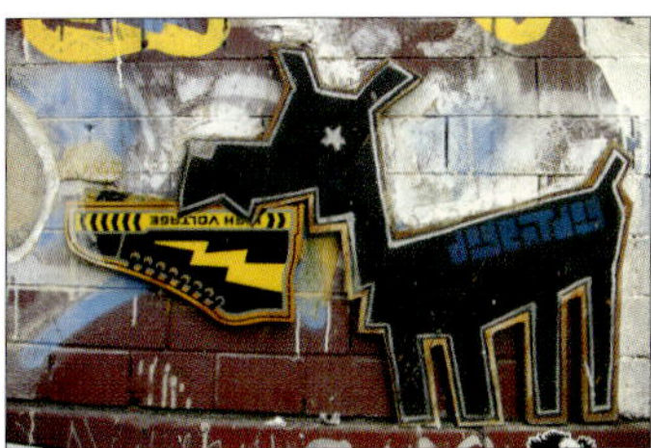

Shot in Manhattan: painting on plywood glued to the wall by Skewville.

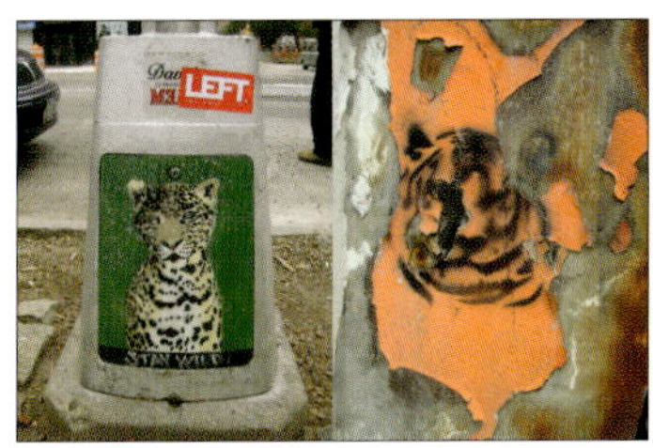

Both shot in Manhattan: the lifespan of a stencil. I like to see time applying itself to textures and giving a second meaning to the artist's initial message.

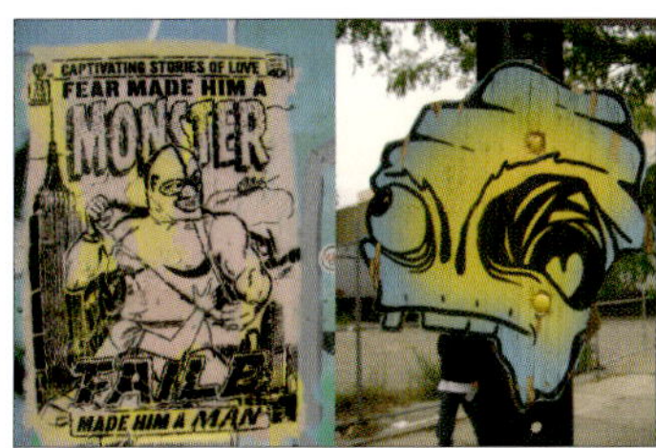

Both shot in Brooklyn: a poster-sized stencil by Faile, and a board monster by an unknown artist.

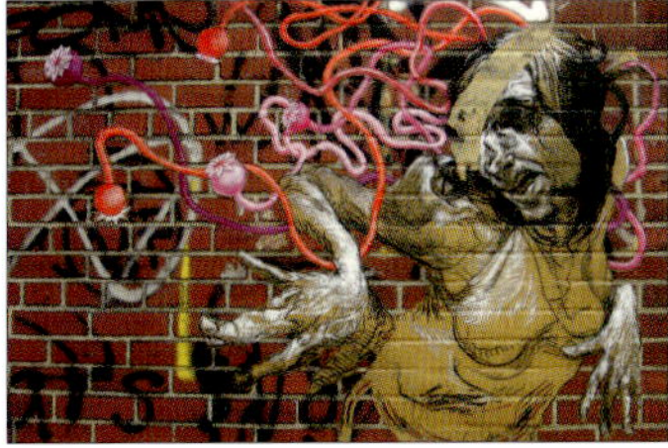

Shot in Brooklyn: this is such a disturbing wall, you wish she wasn't there—though the artwork is wonderful. By Elbow Toe.

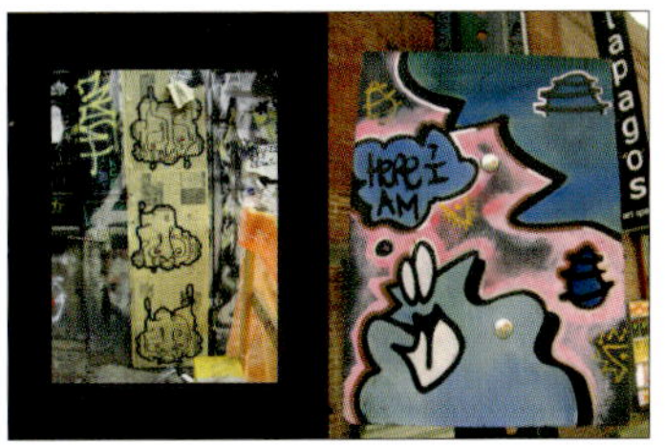

Both shot in Manhattan: a drawing on newspaper spreads and a board by Plasma Slug exemplify the variety of media used by street artists.

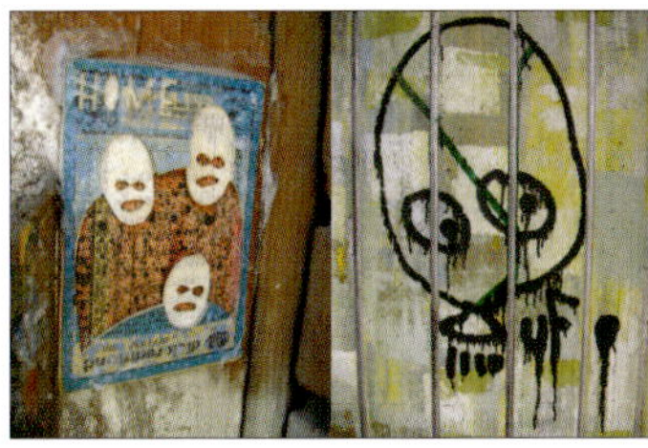

Left shot in Manhattan, right shot in Brooklyn: NYC is a town of aliens, illegal and otherwise.

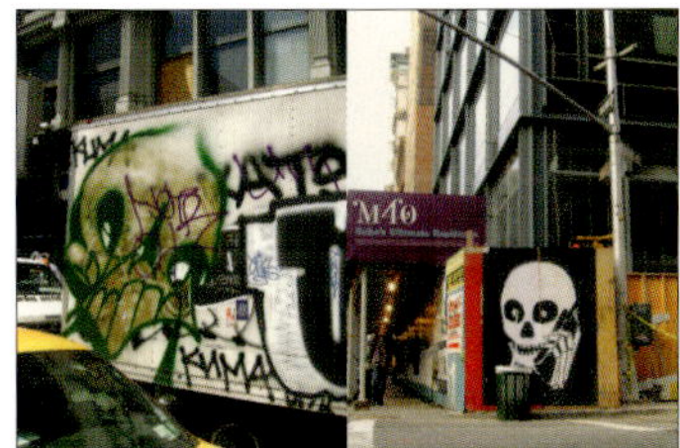

Left shot in Manhattan: NYC is crazy. So am I. I literally jumped into traffic to get this shot, and the cab driver nearly killed me. Right shot in Manhattan.

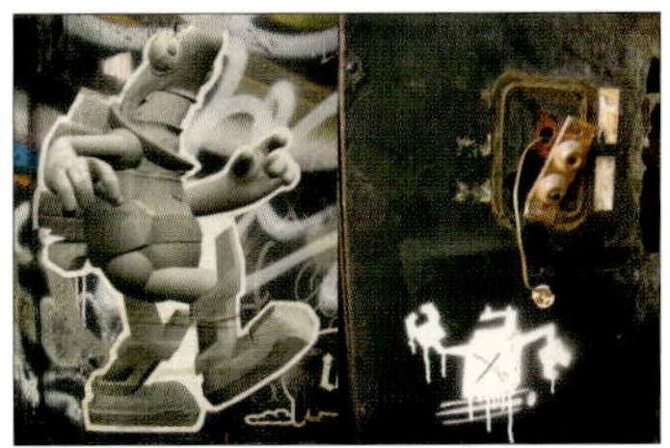

Left shot in Manhattan: LePos is originally from Toronto, Canada. Right shot in Brooklyn.

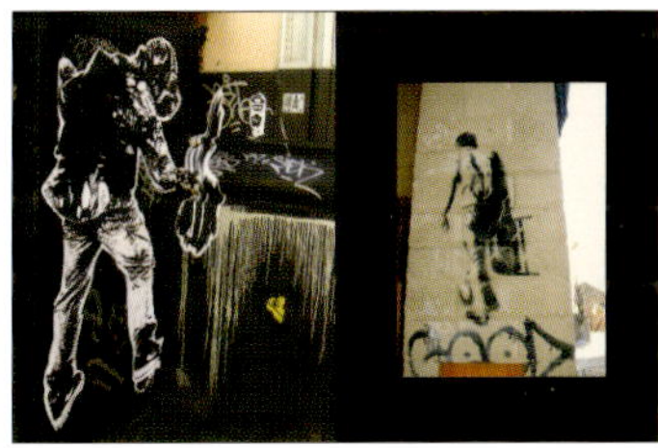

Both shot in Manhattan: graffiti soldier by WK Interakt, and a stencil by an unknown artist.

Left shot in Brooklyn, right shot in Queens: there are messages surrounding us everywhere, messages about everything. But what is the meaning of it all?

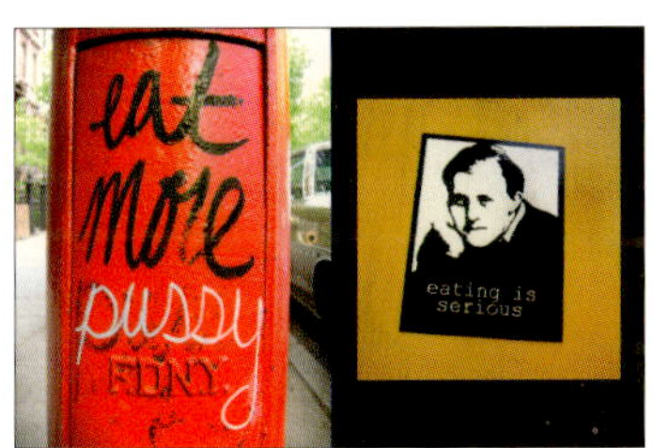

Left shot in Brooklyn, right shot in Manhattan: eat more shrimp, more salad, more soup, more pussy, or more sausage. But no matter what it is you eat, think about it.

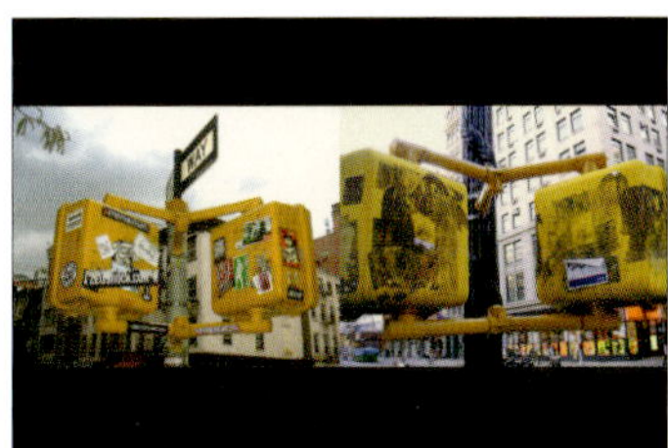

Both shot in Manhattan, on the backs of crossing signals: one looks good, the other one is trashed. Which one is which?

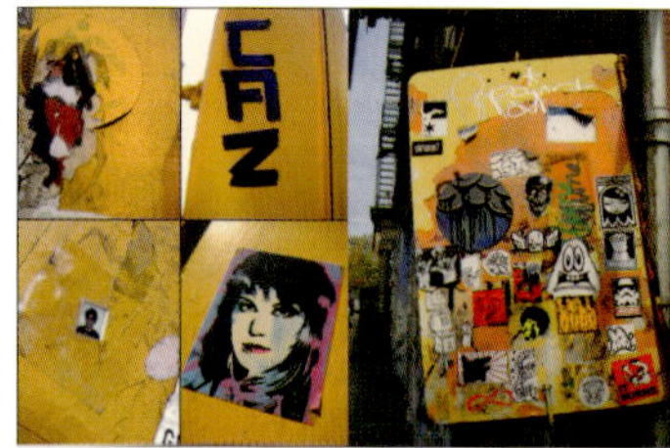

All shot in Manhattan: isolated or in combos, sticker mania in NYC—the place to represent and be seen. Word.

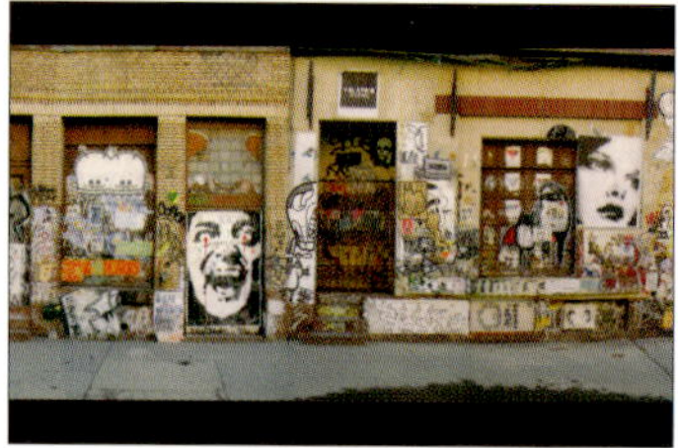

Shot in Manhattan: Wooster Street Wall of Fame, October 2006. You have to know the date because it changes every day. (A must-see if you visit downtown.)

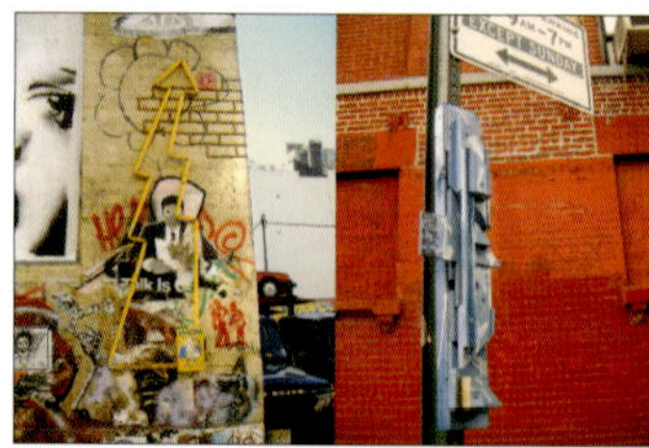

Both shot in Manhattan: the right end of the Wooster Street Wall of Fame. The yellow arrow is made out of plumbing pipes, while the blue Gore B arrow is made of assembled woodcuts.

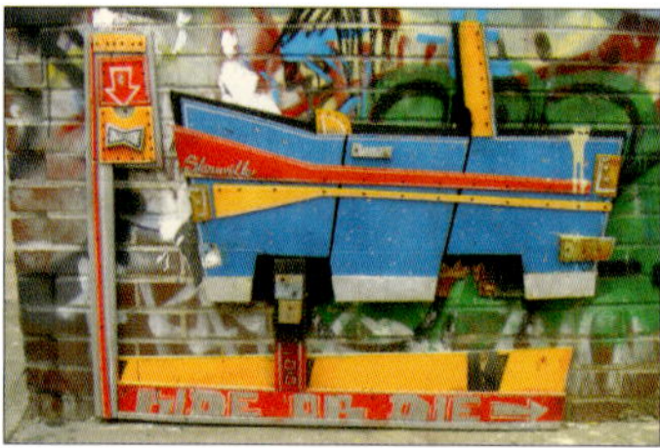

Shot in Manhattan: the Skewville convertible parked here got looted. Ride or die.

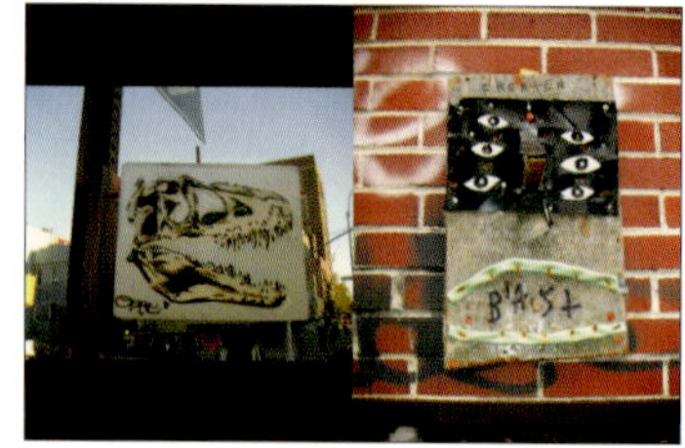

Left shot in Brooklyn: Gore B's T-Rex was the first 3-D sculpture I saw, but there are many more, like this Bast piece from Manhattan (right).

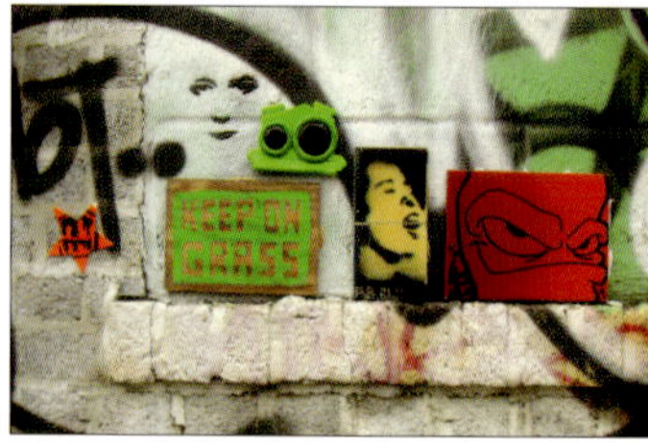

Shot in Manhattan: this collection is in perfect condition. Most of the time they end up looted, destroyed, or covered by other artwork. Enjoy.

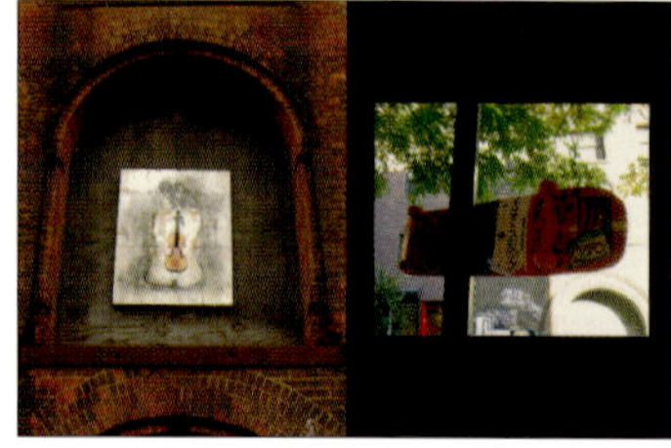

Both shot in Manhattan: the most unusual items can be found on the streets, like a violin or a skateboard. Choose your weapon.

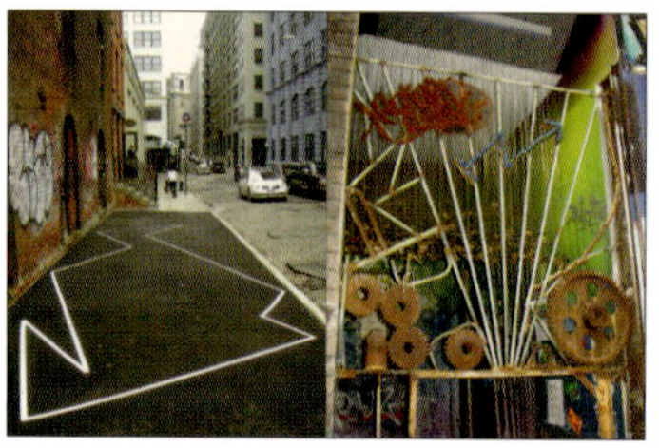

Left shot in Brooklyn: tape on the sidewalk, left over from a street festival in DUMBO. Right shot in Manhattan: gate with welded letters by Revs.

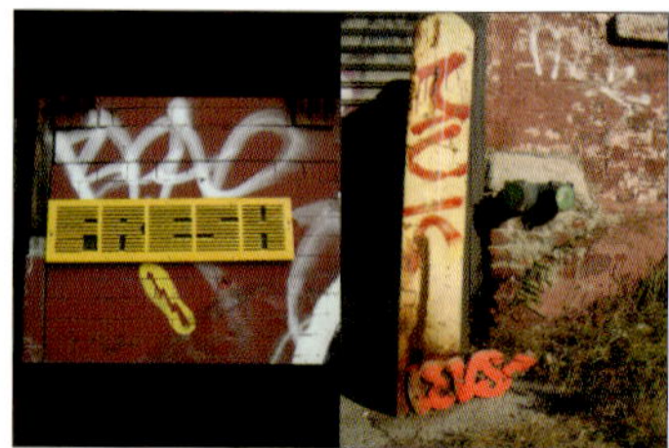

Left shot in Manhattan: this "FRESH" sign has since been covered by a huge billboard. Right shot in Brooklyn: Revs welded his tag, as an anti-theft or longevity measure.

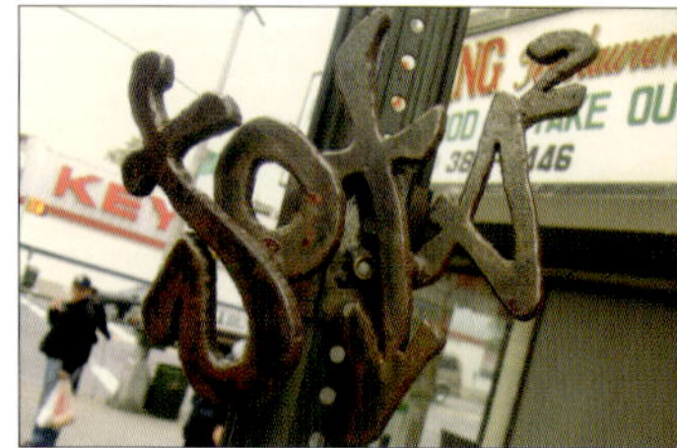

Shot in Brooklyn: this Jota 2 metal tag is one of my favorite pieces. I came across it while grocery shopping in the Montrose Avenue neighborhood.

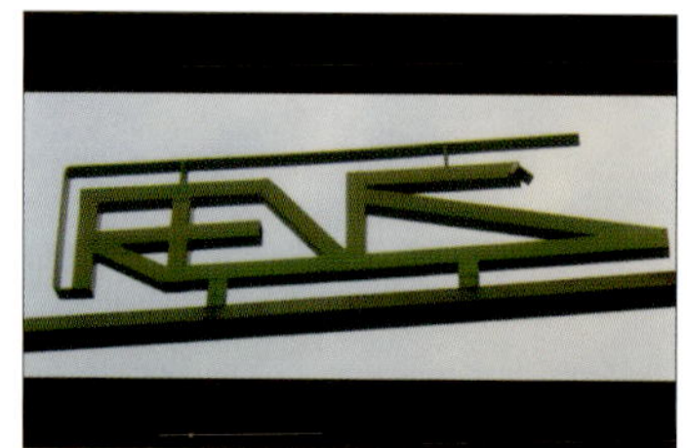

Shot in Brooklyn, under the Williamsburg Bridge: I walked by this huge Revs construction dozens of times, never reading what looked to me like an ordinary sign.

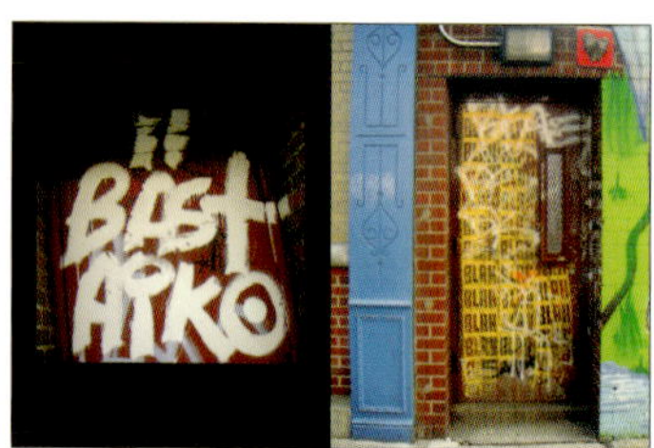

Both shot in Manhattan: brush or paint roller tags.

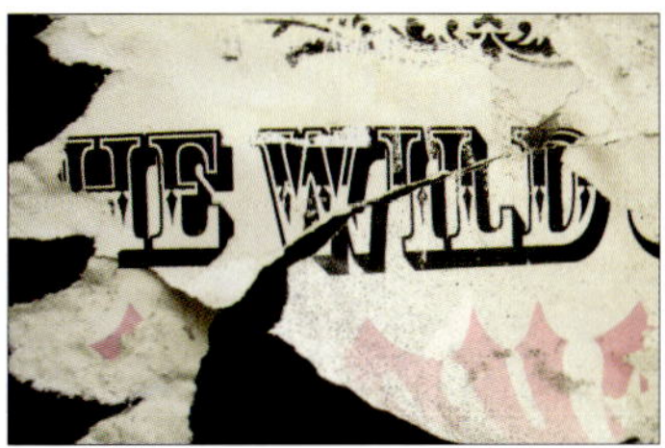

Shot in Manhattan: detail of ripped poster.

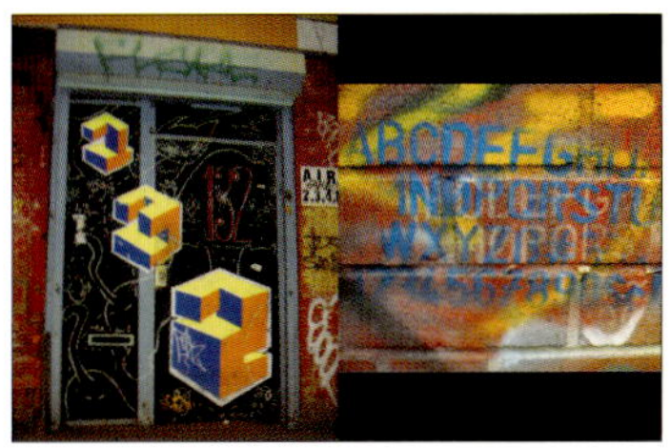

Left shot in Brooklyn: superb 132 collage. Right shot in Manhattan: color alphabet.

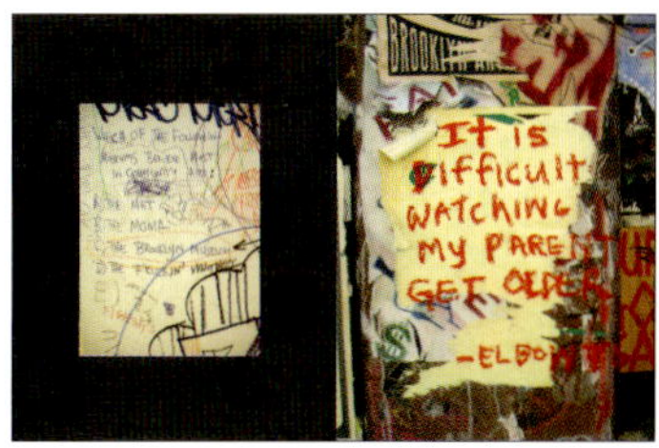

Left shot in Manhattan. Right shot in Brooklyn, at the Brooklyn Museum: detail from the tag wall. I love these thoughts on life and social issues.

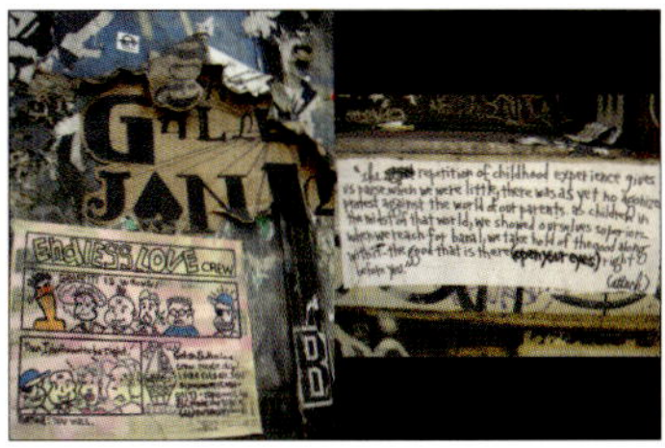

Both shot in Manhattan: like pages from a book of rhymes.

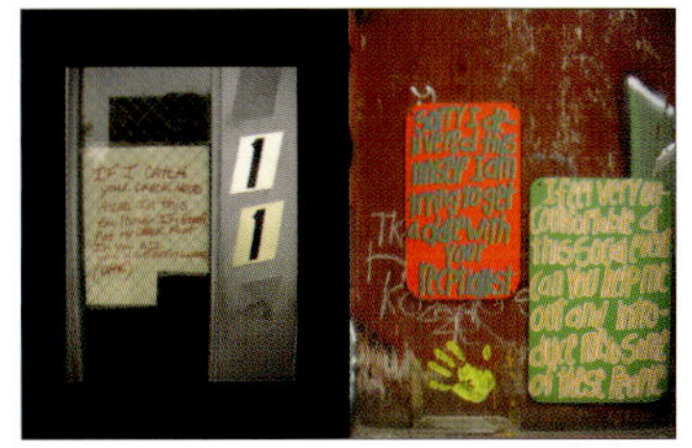

Both shot in Brooklyn: off of Gates Avenue, this guy has had enough of crackheads. In DUMBO, this guy wants some more.

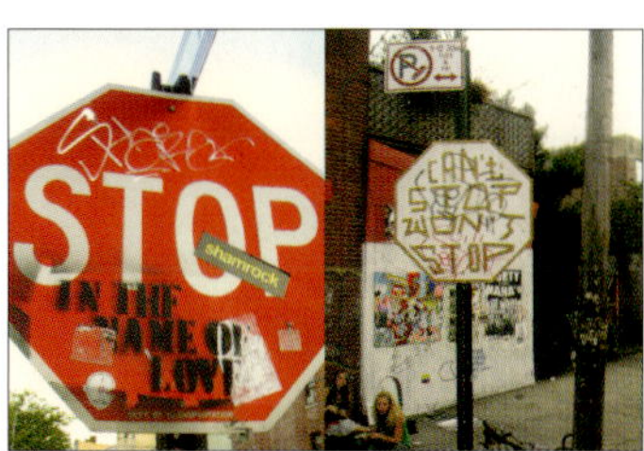

Both shot in Brooklyn, on Bedford Avenue.

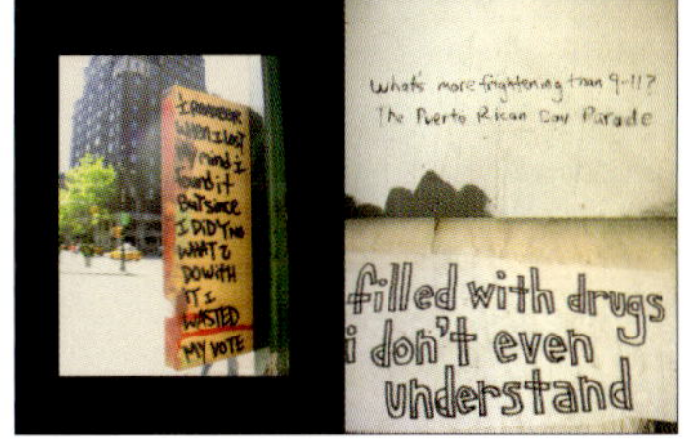

Left and bottom right shot in Manhattan. Top right shot in Brooklyn, in an abandoned factory building in Greenpoint just outside the Polish section of town.

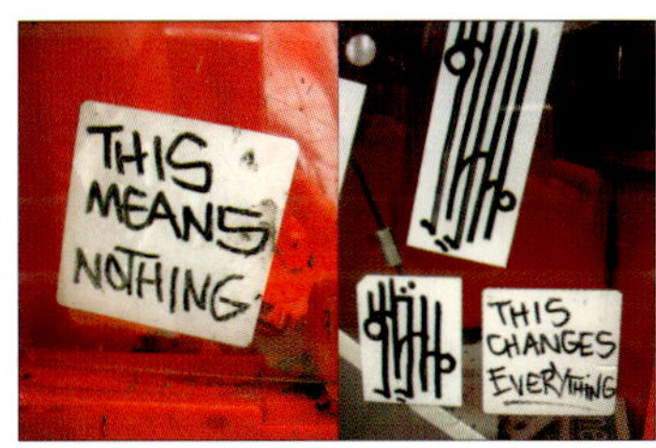

Left shot in Manhattan, right shot in Brooklyn: these are key shots for me, a huge part of the personal experience I had making the book.

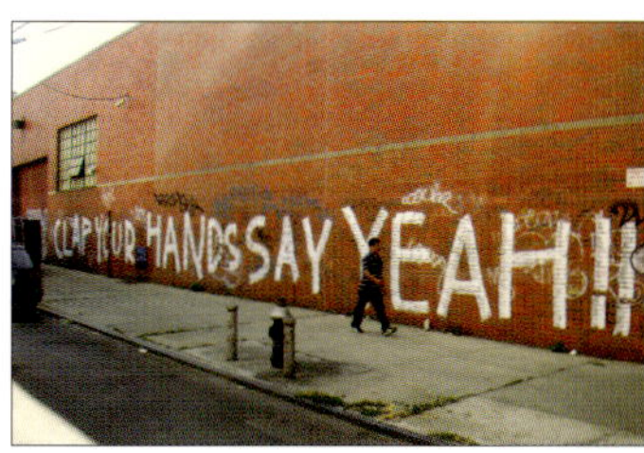

Shot in Brooklyn: I snapped a clear shot. Then I heard, "What the hell do you think you're doing?" The mechanic from the shop next door thought I was from an insurance company, trying to snitch shit. "That ain't me, sir," I said. "If it's for graffiti, that's cool," he replied. "There's plenty around."

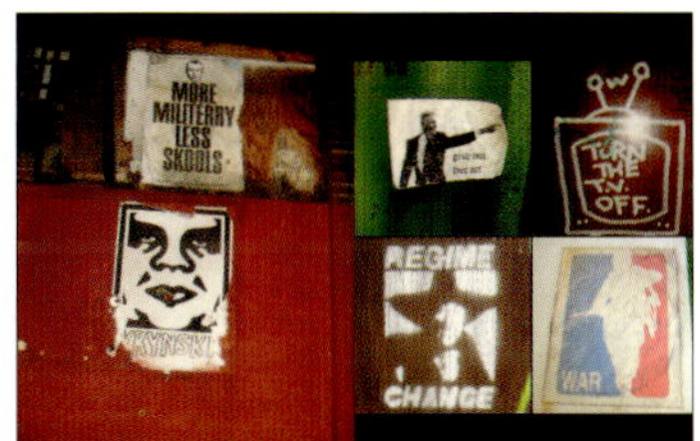

Left shot in Brooklyn: Obey posters. Right shot in Manhattan and Queens: various pieces.

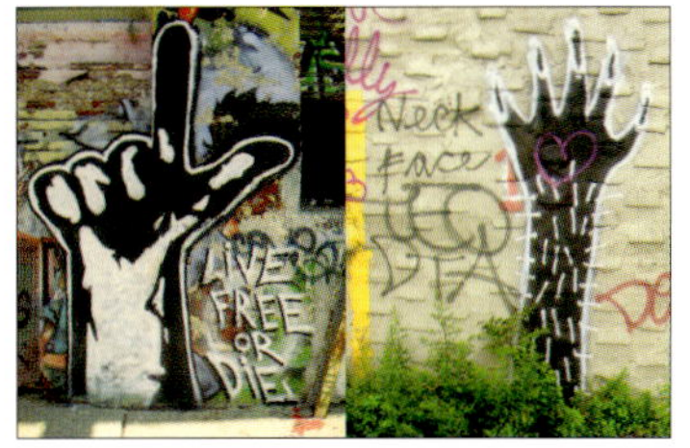

Left shot in Queens at 5 Pointz. Right shot in Brooklyn: artwork by Neck Face.

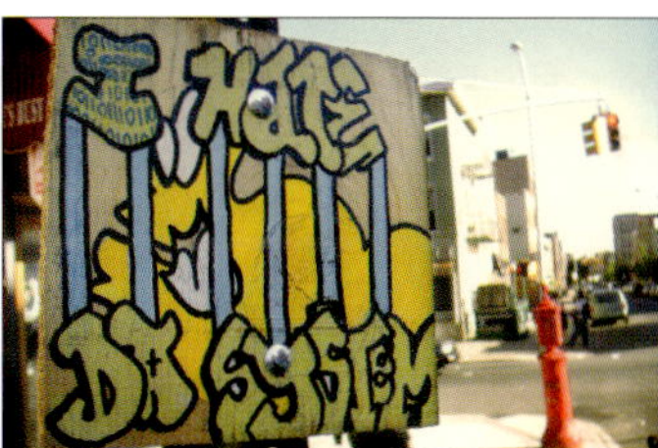

Shot in Brooklyn: this Plasma Slug plywood piece is one of my favorites. Probably 'cause I hate the system too.

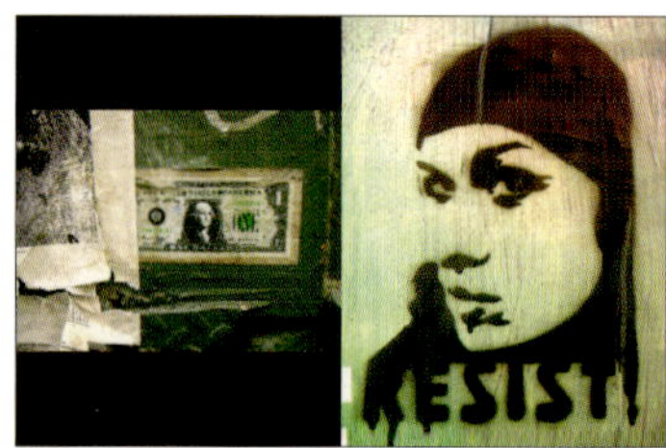

Both shot in Manhattan: these stencils are completely different, but they both have strong political messages.

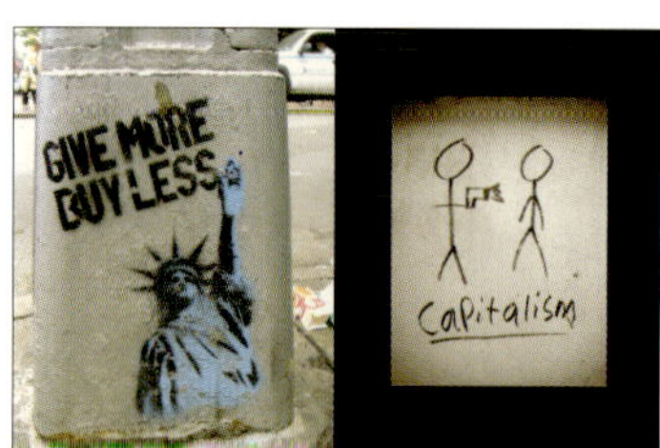

Both shot in Manhattan: some might disagree, but to me, Manhattan has become an open-air mall for people to over-consume in.

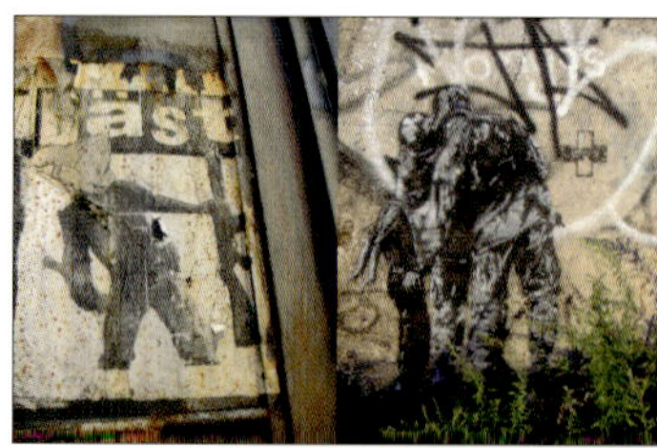

Left shot in Manhattan, right shot in Brooklyn by the riverfront: Graffiti and street art are a war on urban spaces. It's no wonder some of the images are violent.

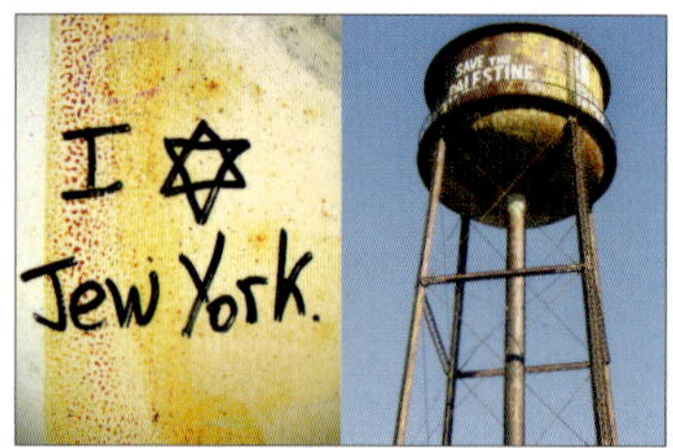

Both shot in Brooklyn: I love it when street messages hit you in the face from both sides.

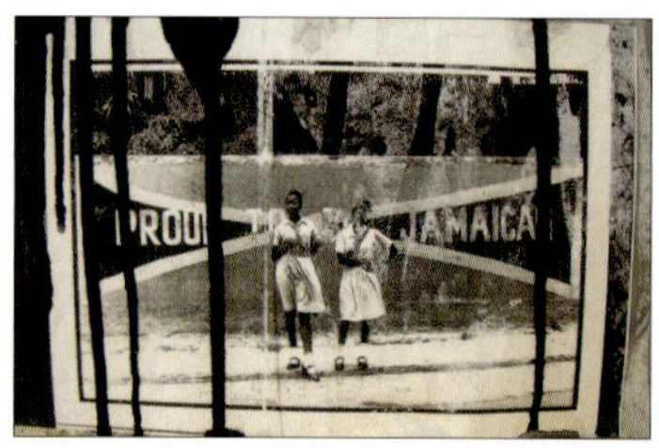

Shot in Brooklyn: this one's dedicated to all Yardies massive. Remember your roots, remember your culture, and remember where you came from.

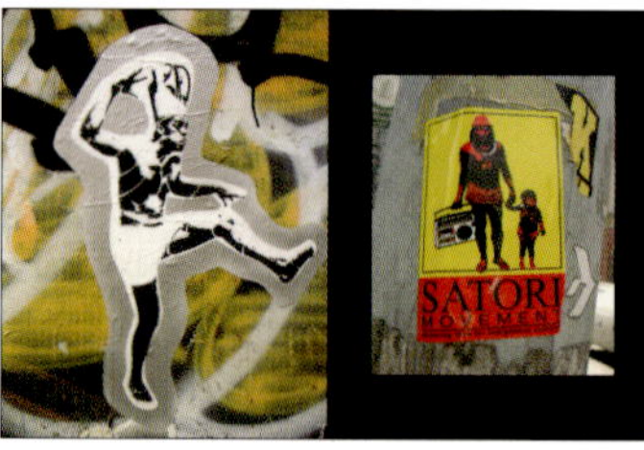

Both shot in Manhattan: a shout-out from the streets of New York City, all of its communities, from African Kings to indigenous tribes.

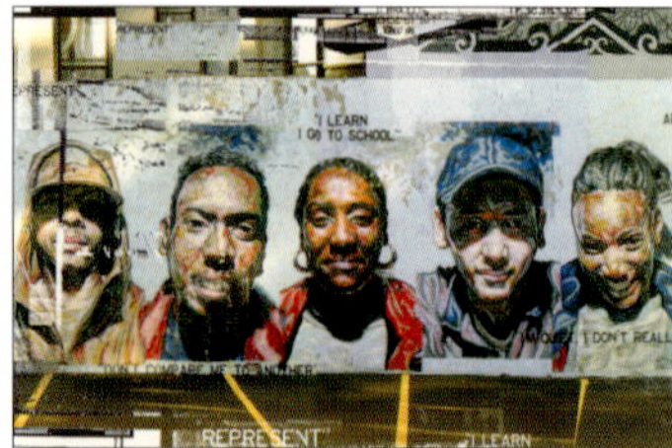

Shot in Manhattan: education is the key. This is an old downtown mural. The parking lot was unusually empty.

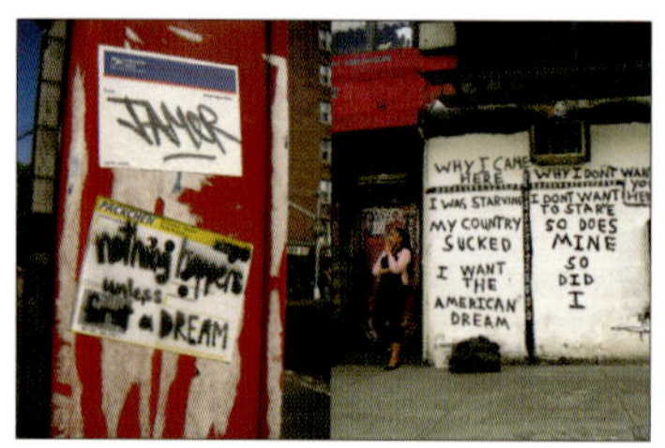

Both shot in Manhattan. Left: international exchange with a US postal label by Jamer (France), and a German postal label by an unknown artist. Right: the complexity of issues surrounding immigration today.

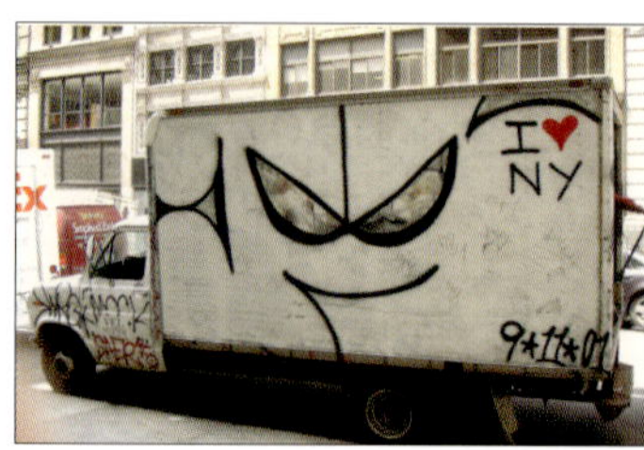

Shot in Manhattan: just one of thousands of graffs dedicated to the city of New York.

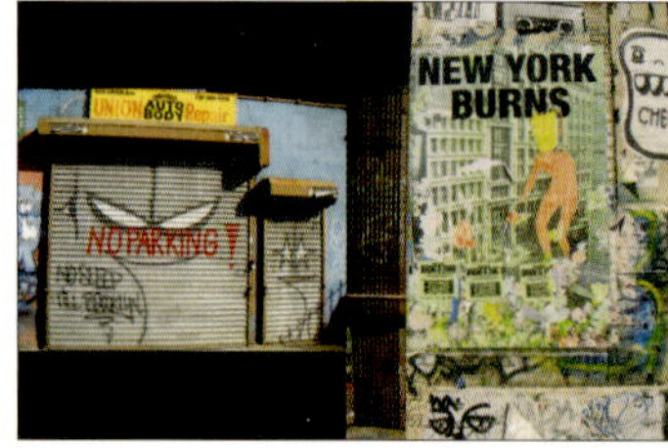

Left shot in Brooklyn (where else?), right shot in Manhattan.

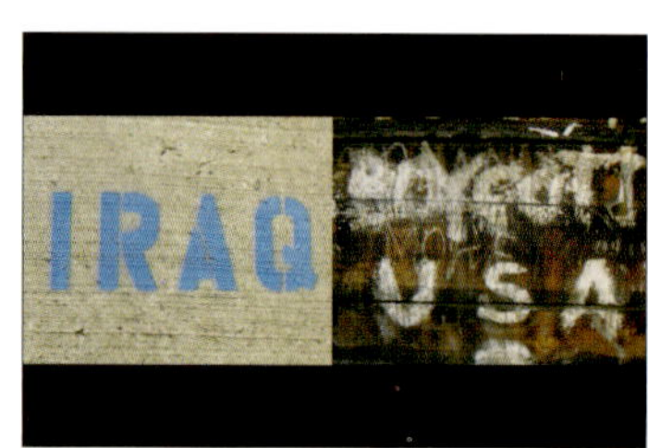

Left shot in Brooklyn: stencil on sidewalk. Right shot in Manhattan: chalk on a burned wall. Urban surfaces mirror political concern.

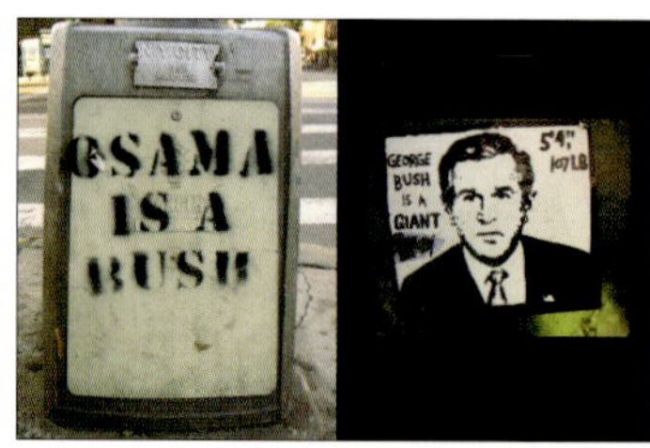

Left shot in Manhattan. Right shot in Brooklyn: this G. W. Bush shot was one of 300 in an exhibit. A month later as I was flipping through the prints, my jaw dropped. Some girl had kissed the picture, leaving her lipstick print on it forever.

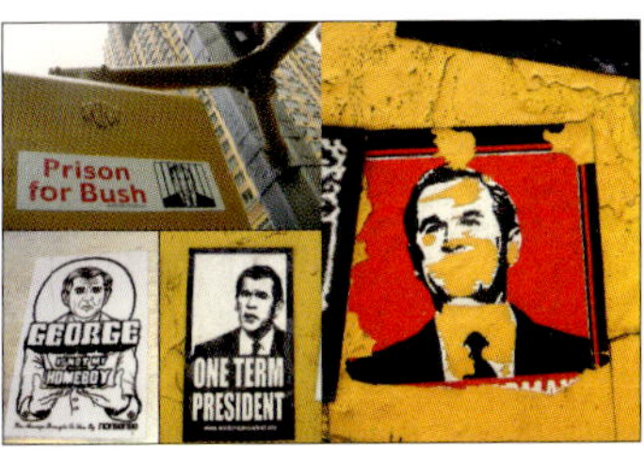

Left shot in Manhattan, but can be found all over town. Right shot in Manhattan: this sticker was repainted by NYC cleaners. The paint didn't stay, except on his mouth.

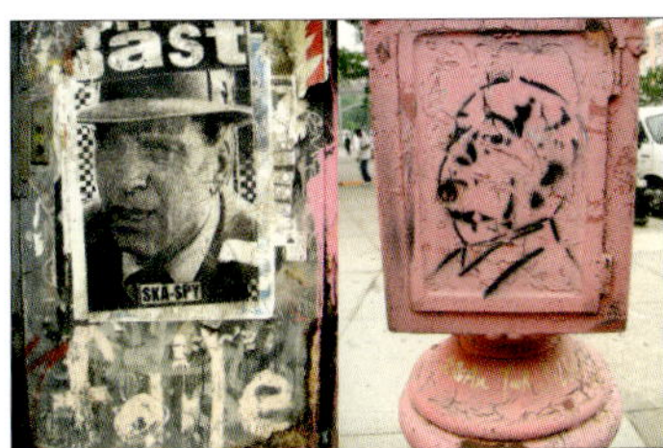

Both shot in Manhattan: I love it when the street reappropriates popular culture. Check out the "Scream Your Silence" subtitle to the Hitchcock stencil. Perfect.

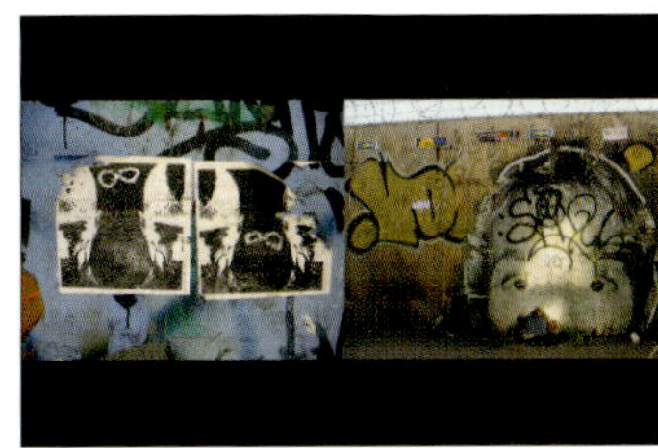

Left shot in Manhattan, right shot in Brooklyn: all the classics are out on the street, to be seen by the masses and the youth, straight to your face, suckaz.

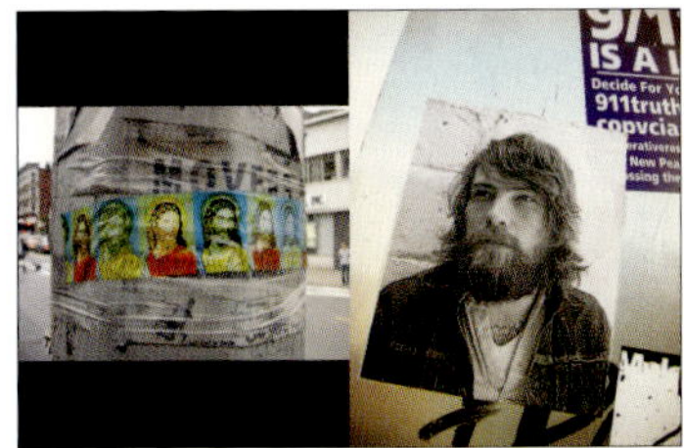

Both shot in Brooklyn: Dollar store scotch tape and hippie-faced Jesus. Divine.

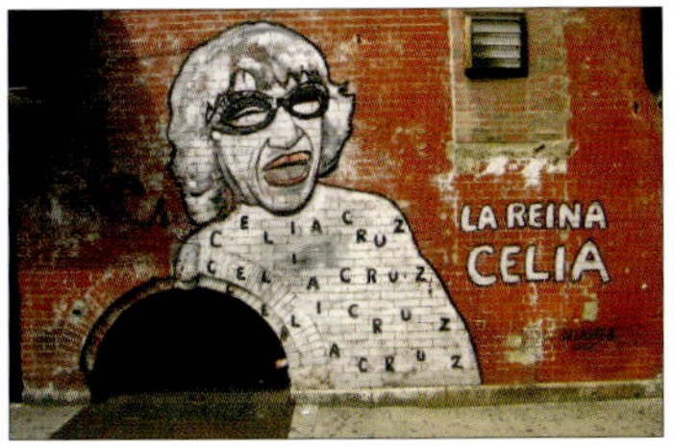

Shot in Manhattan: this tribute to La Reina Celia Cruz is one of De La Vega's contributions to Spanish Harlem, where he creates colorful cultural murals for the Latino community.

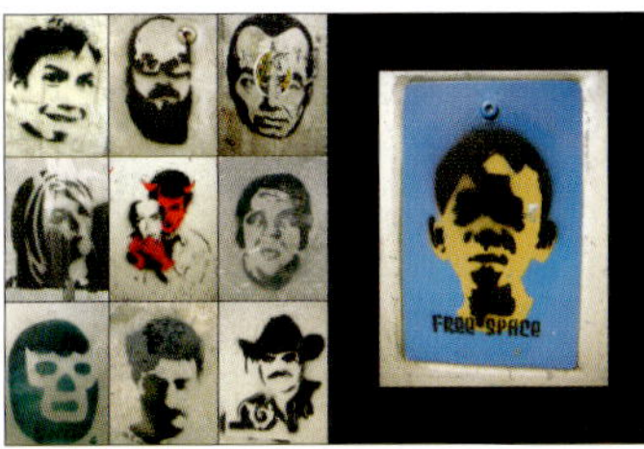

Shot all over town: these stencils can be found on the pedestals of lampposts, cool four-sided spots.

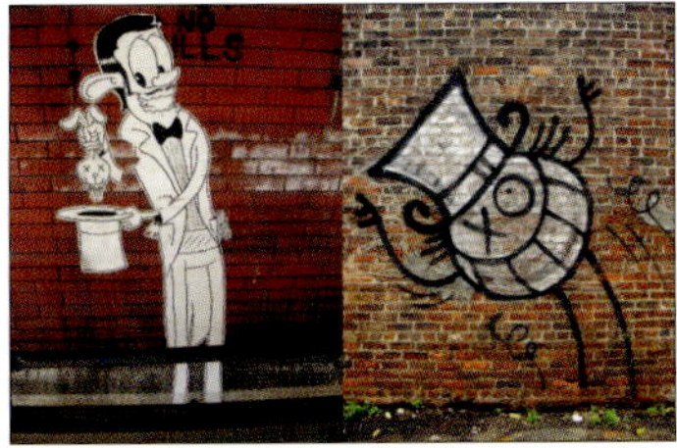

Left shot in Manhattan: straight out of the hat. Right shot in Brooklyn, DUMBO area: Mr. André with his "shadock" jack-in-the-box.

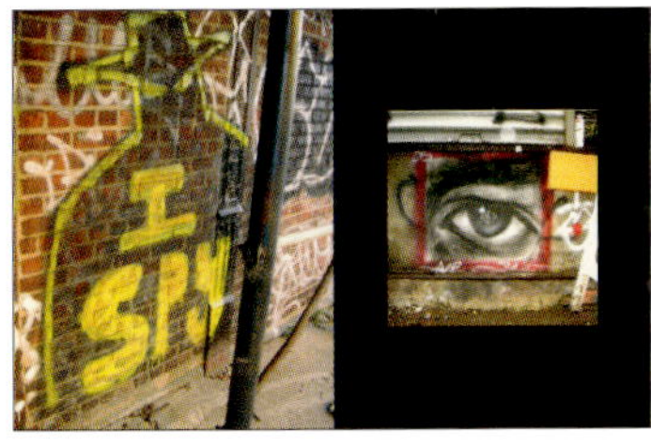

Left shot in Brooklyn, right shot in Manhattan: spying…spying…spied. There are cameras everywhere—smile! Big Brother is here to stay, unfortunately.

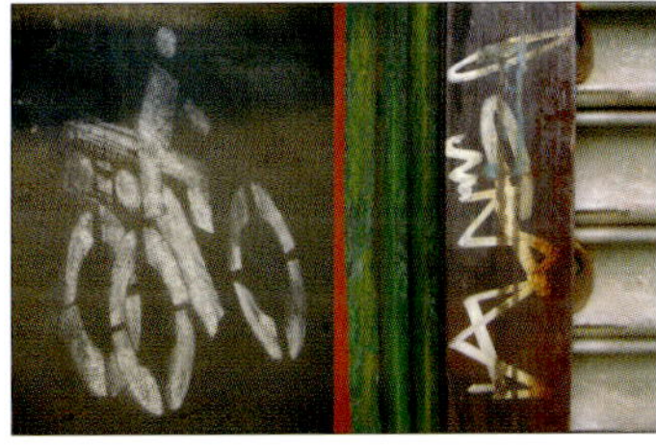

Left shot on the Williamsburg Bridge. Right shot in Brooklyn: the old-timer "Voice of the Ghetto" tag, down from the man's house, where we used to stay high, play music, and and ride bikes like in the old teenager days.

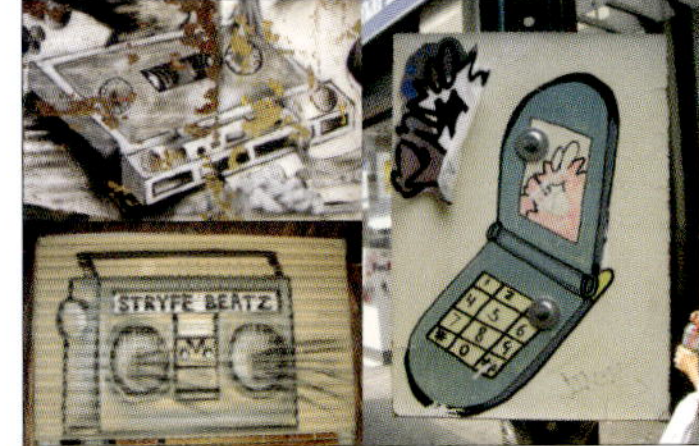

Top left shot in Queens, bottom left shot in the Bronx, right shot in Manhattan: when I was little, we used to play our shit on tape with a Sony Walkman. Now, you gotta be down with digital. We traded in the ghetto blaster for a phone.

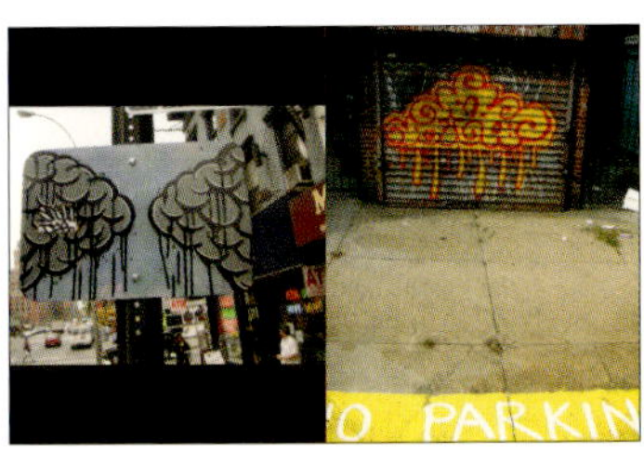

Left shot in Manhattan: this sign is a good example of street art camouflage. Right shot in Brooklyn.

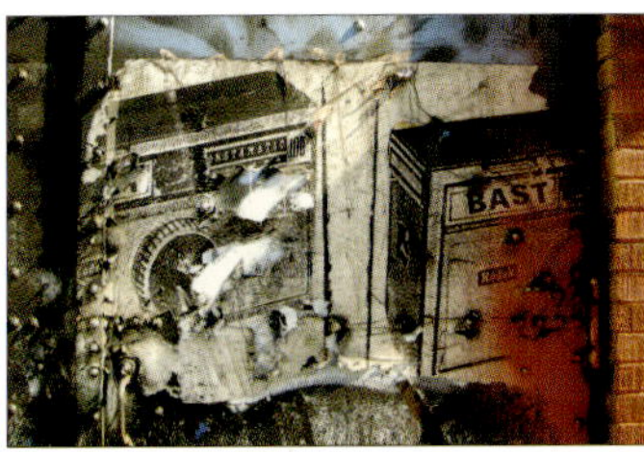

Shot in Brooklyn on the Red Hook docks, far away from everything: this is what it means to me to shoot in New York City. Sometimes you have to go far to find the gems.

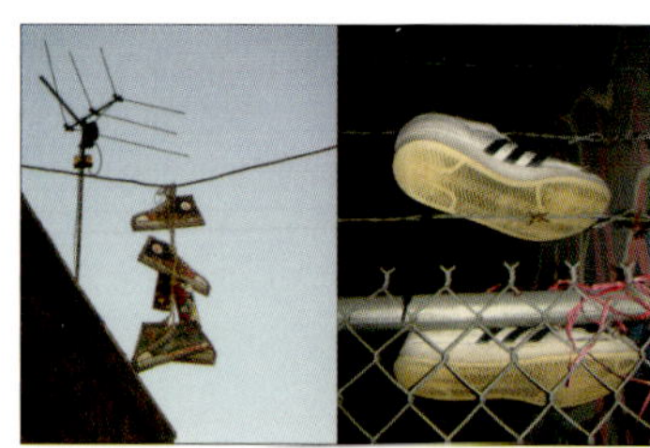

Left shot in Brooklyn, right shot in Manhattan: hanging shoes are a New York City classic. Nowadays, some are real and others not. Welcome to kicks town. That's street art, son.

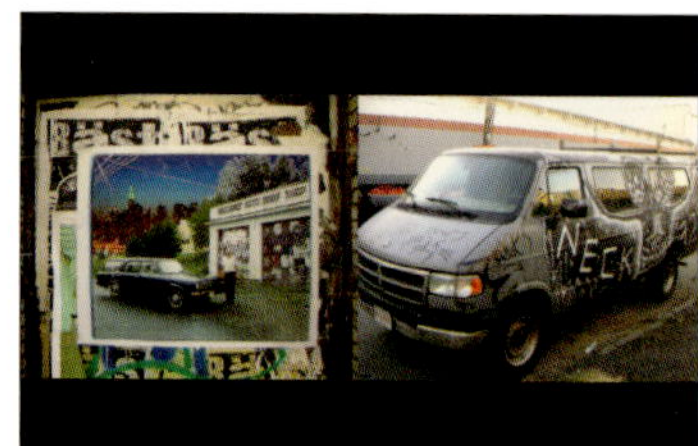

Left shot in Manhattan, right shot in Brooklyn: cars, vans, and trucks are the city's new trains, bearing tags and graff from A to B. But no more lines; it's a random route.

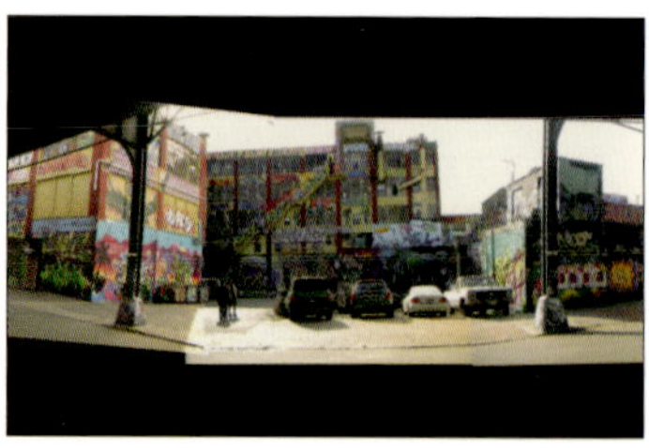

Shot in Queens in October 2005: graffiti's still alive in NYC, right where it was born. And judging by the 5 Pointz building, cared for by Meres and Nic One, it's not going to give up soon.

Acknowledgments

To all street artists, the ones featured in this book and all the others whose work I've seen but could not show here: this book was inspired by the work you've made, both together and as rivals, out in the streets of New York. Thanks for giving me food for my eyes and questions for my mind.

I would like to thank all of the people who participated in the making of this book:

My parents, who brought me to NYC when I was 12. Nicola, Isabelle, Anna… Mamie.

All of the people who helped me through my New York adventures.

The entire Somma Family: the loving, adopted family of my heart. Thank you for your never-ending love, support, and trust.

The powerHouse Books and powerHouse Arena team, thanks for working with me side by side. Plenty more to come, right, Sara? Thank you for your trust in me, Miss Rosen.

My worldwide crew: PG, 132, Dissident Sound Movement, DJ Cab, Jamalski—remember trust or get organized, Sista Natalia, Linda Bouriche, DJ C-real, DJ Rebel, DJ Oil, Le Syndicat (but who's the prez???), Troublemakers, Shogun, G-zep, Krussia, Vincent "Mafioso" Vega, 88.8 fm Marseilles Posse, Inspekta Madjou, Robex, CEP, DJ Jeho, Félipé Oza, DJ Kafra, Olivier aka Dr. Zoomy, Martin, El Cheo, MI-one, Sleepy Gaby, Anis, Marie, J-Loïs, Acuz, Ruze, Bonar, Nice, Mozes, Dire, Phes, Yass and Sgerim, El Furioso ("rrrhhhhhhr!"), Wendy, Lawet (RIP), Dane, Ripley, Ruedi One, DJ Beb, the Ruffian, Seb Carayol, AAA, Rebel, Ozor, Liz (been a long time), Cuik, Don Fruschetutto, DJ Lord, Chuck D and Public Enemy (still #1), Yogi (man the Chibidots are next), Chocoboss, Acet 1, PM, Rish, Meres One, Nic One, Fume, the 5 Ptz activists, Madhavi, Camellia with Luv, Lexo le Manouche, Amy, Mantra Posse, Mirko, Jaime, Jennifer, Intensity, Joe, Barbès D, Zin, Simon, Victor from Ballas, Fred Berthet, Bruno Bessadi, Stef le relou, Emma & DJ Post, DJ R, DJ Richard, Patrice, Eric, Sista Fatou, Dr No, Mannix, Matt Le Suisse, Félix & Soleil, PHM, Mr. Lips, Flow, Jay Be, Alex, Izmo, Cedric Claquin, Kano from Koogah Sound, Tholonet Crew, Pierre, Laurence, Alex, Sophie, Jacques, Chimène, Catine, Tawalp, Ludo, Marimars, Osmoze, Losing Control, Did & Ren-C, Pal Joey, DJ Ph, Torsion Crew, DJ Youz, Prince Freedom, Bad Drick-C, Sylvain, Yann, Ulan Bator Crew, Matthias, Derrick, Robert, Patate Records, Feu Rouge Gang, Daddy Polo, Name Code// Records, Step Ahead Prod, Jacques 2 Chabannes, Arnaud Taillefer, Karim, Jonone, Bower mob. With loads of love, Miss Mu.

The next generation: Hicham, Idriss, Yasmine, Bowie B, Meyli, Oscar, Maya, Matthias, Amen…and all those babies to come. (Remember, kidz: Education and Knowledge is Power.)

Last but not least, my full-time work partner, who's been helping me out since day one. Never-ending thanks, love, and respect to Monsieur Qui. Friends and partners, that's how we roll.

In memory of:
Antonio Cavaliere: My grandfather, who died during the making of this book. Never-ending respect for teaching me the love of paper.
Mud: You'll skate up in the clouds, bro.
Yann Quelennec: You'll do it all up there.
And all of the friends we lost in their struggle for a cause, rest in peace.

Published in the United States by powerHouse Books,
a division of powerHouse Cultural Entertainment, Inc.
37 Main Street, New York, NY 11201-1021
telephone 212 604 9074, fax 212 366 5247
e-mail: thismeansnothing@powerHouseBooks.com
website: www.powerHouseBooks.com

First edition, 2008

Library of Congress Cataloging-in-Publication Data:

Le Bijoutier.
This means nothing / by Le Bijoutier.
p. cm.
ISBN 978-1-57687-417-2
1. Photography of art. 2. Graffiti--New York (State)--New York--Pictorial works.
3. Photography, Artistic. 4. Documentary photography. I. Title.
TR657.L42 2008
779'.975173097471--dc22
2007060119

Hardcover ISBN 978-1-57687-417-2

Separations, printing, and binding by Pimlico Book International, Hong Kong
Art direction: Monsieur Qui (http://mrqui.free.fr)
Translator and writing assistant: Gabrielle M. M. Brock (sleepygaby@gmail.com)

A complete catalog of powerHouse Books and Limited Editions is available upon request; please call, write, or change everything on our website.

10 9 8 7 6 5 4 3 2 1

Printed and bound in China